CARRIER
GLORIOUS
The Life and Death
of an Aircraft Carrier

John Winton

SAPERE
BOOKS

CARRIER
GLORIOUS

Published by Sapere Books.

20 Windermere Drive, Leeds, England, LS17 7UZ,
United Kingdom

saperebooks.com

ISBN: 978-1-80055-417-7.

TABLE OF CONTENTS

ACKNOWLEDGEMENTS

A great many people have contributed their memories, letters, journals and diaries to this book. I wish particularly to thank the late Mrs Hope Slessor, Mrs Michael Riviere (Bridget D'Oyly-Hughes), and Captain J.B. Heath, OBE, RN. I also wish to thank:

The late Vice-Admiral Sir Conolly Abel-Smith, GCVO, CB; Mrs Josephine Ash. Mr Ron Birch; Air Vice-Marshal Nigel Blair-Oliphant, CB, OBE; Rear-Admiral A.S. Bolt, CB, DSO, DSC; the late Captain Jack Broome, DSC; Mr David Brown, MEng, CEng, FRINA, RCNC; Mr Joe Brown; the late Captain David Buchanan-Dunlop, DSC.

Commander J.K. Cannon; Mr. Alf Carpenter; Lieutenant-Commander John Casson, OBE; Captain Nigel Clogstoun-Willmott, DSO, DSC*; Mr Michael Cobb; Mr Bill Collier; Mr Sebastian Cox; Mr T.P. Cox; Air Vice-Marshal Peter Cracroft, CB, AFC; Air Chief Marshal Sir Kenneth Cross, KCB, CBE, DSO, DFC.

Admiral Sir William Davis, GCB, DSO, DL; Mr Martin Dawes; Mr Jim Dixon; Rear-Admiral V.D'A. Donaldson; Mrs Patricia Donnan; Lieutenant S. Donovan, MBE; Mr Walter Drax; Mr Graham Roy Drucker; Lieutenant-Commander George Duncan, OBE; Mr Trevor Dunhill.

Mr George Elliott; Mr David Ellison; Lieutenant-Commander John Ellyatt, DSC, VRD, RNVR; Air Vice-Marshal Geoffrey Eveleigh, CB, OBE; Commander Robert Everett, OBE.

Air Commodore T.P.P.F. Fagan, CBE; Squadron Leader Tony Fairbairn; Captain H.L. St. J. Fancourt, DSO; Fleet Air Arm Officers' Association; Captain Godfrey French, CBE.

Wing Commander R.P. Garnons-Williams, AFC; Commander G.R.M. Going, DSO, OBE; Mrs Betty Goodman; Captain J.R. Gower, DSC; Captain The Rev. Geoffrey Gowlland; Mr Eric J. Grove, MA.

Commander Hugh Haggard, DSO, DSC; the late Commander J. W. Hale, DSO; Commander R.C. Hay, DSO, DSC; Mrs Nora Healiss; Mrs Betty Heycock; Vice-Admiral Sir Arthur Hezlet, KBE, CB, DSO, DSC; Mr Roy Hinton; Mr Cyril Hobbs; Mr Charles Hodgson; Mrs Lilian Hooke; the late Admiral Sir Charles Hughes Hallett, KCB, CBE; Mr John Hull.

Air Commodore Patrick Jameson, CB, DSO, DFC; Commander C.A. Jenkins, OBE; Mr David Jolliff.

Lieutenant-Commander Arthur Keep; Captain C.L. Keighley-Peach, DSO; Mr Ludovic Kennedy; Lord Keyes.

Commander A.F.C. Layard, DSO, DSC; Commander W. Sitwell Lea OBE; Lieutenant H.W. Le Breton; Captain E.G. Le Geyt, DSC; Lieutenant-Commander R.T. Leggott, MBE; Air Commodore L. Levis OBE; Mr David Lidstone; Mr Stafford Lidstone; Captain J.S.S. Litchfield, OBE; Captain Peter G. Loasby, DSC.

Commander H.P. Madden; Major A.E. Marsh, Royal Marines; Lieutenant-Commander Derek Martin; Lieutenant-Commander Robert McBride; Mr Colin McFadyean; Major-General J.L. Moulton, CB, DSO, Royal Marines. Mr James O'Neill.

Mr William Hugh Parkin; Captain Jasper Parrott, CBE; Major R.T. Partridge, DSO, Royal Marines; Mr James Pickering, AFC, AE, FGS, FSA; Mr John Pinkerton.

Rev Jim Radcliffe; Mr Tom Rivers; Mr Michael Riviere; Commander R.H.S. Rodger, OBE; Mr Nicholas Roskill; Captain G.A. Rotherham, DSO, OBE; Wing Commander Peter Rusher, DSO.

Commander N.J. Scarlett-Streatfeild, DSC; Air Commodore G.P. Seymour-Price, CBE, AFC; Group Captain John Shepherd; Mr Tim Slessor; Commander John Seymour Stead; Mrs Mollie Steel; Miss Marion Stewart; Captain A.W.F. Sutton, CBE, DSC.

Dr Geoffrey Till; Rear-Admiral A.D. Torlesse, CB, DSO.

Commander A.O. Watson; Captain T.A. Wells; the late Captain A.S. Whitworth, DSC; Rear-Admiral Guy Willoughby, CB; Mrs M. Wollacott; Mr David Woodcock; Lieutenant-Commander Gerard A. Woods; Mr David Wright.

CHAPTER 1: FROM BATTLE CRUISER TO AIRCRAFT CARRIER

GLORIOUS HAD HER beginnings in an old man's dream. In October, 1914, Winston Churchill, who was then First Lord of the Admiralty, brought back — not without misgivings — Lord Fisher to be First Sea Lord. Since 1908, and very probably earlier, Fisher had a dream of mounting an expedition to the Baltic, to land an army on the Pomeranian coast, ninety miles from Berlin, and thus achieve one smashing, decisive *coup* which, he believed, would bring Germany to her knees.

No sooner had he returned to the Admiralty than Lord Fisher, with what Churchill called 'explosive energy', summoned to London all the naval constructors and ship-building firms in the country and, as Churchill said, 'in four or five *Glorious* days, every minute of which was pure delight to him', put in hand a huge construction programme for ships ranging from battle cruisers to small barges. The total number in this 'unparalleled Armada' was 612, including no less than five light-draught thirty-three knot battle cruisers. According to Fisher's *Memories*, this colossal building programme was authorized at a meeting held on 3 November, 1914, only four days after Fisher became First Sea Lord. In fact, not quite all those vessels were actually ordered on that day, the chief emphasis of that meeting being the ordering of submarines, and some of the vessels ordered, particularly the destroyers, were intended for use in the North Sea by the Grand Fleet. Nevertheless it was that meeting which provided the main impetus for the 'Baltic Project' ships, of which *Glorious* was one.

In the event, the 'Baltic Project' was never carried out, but many of the ships for it were built, including three 'light cruisers' (so called because Treasury approval had already been obtained for 'light cruisers'). Fisher himself called them 'large light cruisers'. To Churchill they were 'an old man's children' and 'their parent loved them dearly'.

Their names were *Furious*, *Courageous* and *Glorious*. They certainly were large, at more than 18,000 tons, and heavily armed: *Furious* eventually had two 18" guns, and the other two ships had four 15". As Fisher explained, 'The *Furious* and all her breed were not built for salvoes. They were built for Berlin, and that's why they drew so little water and were built so fragile... Their guns with their enormous shells were built to make it impossible for the Germans to prevent the Russians from landing on the Pomeranian coast.'

Furious' design took an independent path from an early stage, but *Courageous* and *Glorious* remained sister-ships. A minute by Fisher on 29 January, 1915, stated that it was intended to build these light cruisers 'within the year'. Matters did not move quite as fast as that, but still astonishingly quickly by today's standards. The designs were begun on 21 January and the ships officially ordered on 29 January. The first drawings and the body plan were sent out to the building firms — Armstrong's Naval Yard, at Walker on the Tyne, for *Courageous*, Harland & Wolff at Belfast for *Glorious* — on 6 February, 1915. Two days later Fisher was writing to Beatty: 'I forget if I told you, we have started the new "light cruisers" [Fisher's inverted commas] which will join your flag next December.' Once again, Fisher was being optimistic, but the keel plates were laid very quickly — *Courageous'* on 28 March, 1915, *Glorious'* on 1 May — and the ships were launched — *Courageous* on 5 February, 1916, *Glorious* on 20 April.

Besides the main armament, the ships had eighteen 4-inch BLIX guns in six Mark I triple mountings, arranged in the open on the shelter deck, twelve firing on either broadside; two 3-inch high-angle guns; four 3-pounder Hotchkiss saluting guns; five Maxim guns; and two submerged torpedo tubes in a torpedo room forward. Six pairs of 21-inch torpedo tubes were fitted later.

The main machinery was of the type fitted in the light cruiser *Champion* and consisted of four geared turbines, each driving one propeller shaft, and each with an estimated 22,500 shaft horsepower, to give a total of 90,000 SHP at about 340 shaft rpm. There were four engine-rooms, one to each shaft. Steam was provided at 235 lbs/sq in pressure by eighteen Yarrow small-tube boilers, in three boiler-rooms, six to a boiler-room. The engines were made by Messrs Parsons (*Courageous*) and Harland & Wolff (*Glorious*).

Glorious was completed at a cost of £2,119,000. She was the second ship of the name in the Royal Navy, the first being the French 74-gun *Glorieux*, captured at the Battle of the Saintes in the West Indies in 1782; she foundered five months later. Her badge was a golden five-petalled rose on a background of a silver-rayed sunburst. Her motto was *Explicit Nomen*. Her first commanding officer, Captain Charles B. Miller, CB, RN, was appointed on 27 August 1916, and she commissioned with 787 officers and men on 14 October, 1916. She left Belfast for her trials at 8 pm on 23 October, 1916, and at once suffered her first mishap, hitting a buoy on her port side on her way to Carrickfergus. At the same time a knocking was heard inside the starboard centre Low Power turbine casing. The 'Astern' turbine blading in the LP casing was found to be stripped. The ship was docked for examination of the port outer propeller, which was found to be scuffed and scraped, but not badly damaged.

Glorious suffered another mishap on 19 November when the steamer *Corib*, trying to manoeuvre past her to get out into Belfast Lough, struck *Glorious* forward of 'Y' turret and damaged her upper deck. *Glorious* at last sailed for the Tail of the Bank on the Clyde on 30 December, 1916, and anchored overnight, before starting full power trials over the measured mile off the island of Arran the next day. Her highest speed was a mean 31.25 knots, achieved at a mean 327½ rpm, and a mean SHP of 88,550 at a displacement of 21,270 tons.

Glorious joined the fleet at Rosyth on 6 January, 1917. She and *Courageous* were handsome, even graceful ships, with their turrets and superstructures symmetrically arranged around their single large funnels. With no side armour and only light deck and turret armour, they were much more vulnerable than they looked. They were, in Churchill's phrase, light in the bone. They had been built and launched in secrecy and were actually known as 'Mystery ships'. Tennyson-d'Eyncourt, the Director of Naval Construction, himself called them 'Hush-Hush ships'.

The sailors of the Grand Fleet were much less polite. They called *Courageous* and *Glorious* the *Outrageous* and the *Uproarious*. The two sister ships and *Furious* were known as *Helpless*, *Hopeless* and *Useless*. Nobody was disposed to make allowances for the fact that these ships had been specifically designed for action against shore targets in the shallow waters of the Baltic, not to stand in the line of battle in the North Sea. But now, like Othello, their occupation was gone.

Courageous commissioned on 28 October, 1916, and began her trials on 14 November. On the night of 8 January, 1917, when she was working up to full power off May Island in the Firth of Forth, she was steaming at thirty knots into a head sea when she broke her back abreast the forward 15" turret. Her fo'c'sle, between the breakwater and 'A' barbette, was severely buckled. Side plates between the upper deck and the forecastle deck were also buckled. There were leakages from an oil fuel tank and a reserve boiler feed water tank. The ship's stem had lifted by about three feet.

At the inquiry, ships' officers stated that the sea that night was 'State Four', with a wave height of about seven feet, and board members were inclined to agree that the damage was due to weakness of design. However, as a result of doubts expressed by the junior member, Constructor Lieutenant V.C. Shepheard (later Sir Victor and a future Director of Naval Construction) further reports were called for which showed that the state of the sea that night was not Four but between Six and Seven, with wave heights of sixteen-eighteen feet.

The board still decided that the damage was a design weakness but Shepheard refused to sign the report and added a minority view, stating that in his opinion damage was caused by an error of judgment on the part of the ship's officers and the ship's speed should have been reduced. The Admiralty eventually accepted Shepheard's opinion. Extra stiffening plates, weighing another 130 tons, were added to *Courageous* that spring of 1917, and to *Glorious* a year later.

In October, 1917, *Furious*, *Courageous* and *Glorious* were part of a large force (twenty-seven light cruisers and fifty-four destroyers) which sailed from Rosyth, Scapa or Harwich to look for the German ships which carried out the raid on what became known as the '*Mary Rose* Convoy'. Two 3,800 ton, 34-knot German cruisers, *Bremse* and *Brummer*, both armed with four 5.9" guns, steamed at high speed through all the patrol lines and, early on the morning of 17 October, surprised a convoy of twelve merchant ships, sailing from Marsten in

Norway to Lerwick in the Shetlands, escorted by the destroyers *Mary Rose* and *Strongbow*. Both destroyers and nine of the merchant ships were sunk. With some luck, and a little more foresight, the German ships could have been intercepted as they made their retreat. But both escaped.

A month later there was another chance of action. By November, 1917, minesweeping in the Heligoland Bight to keep submarine base approaches free of mines had become the German Navy's most important task. The minesweepers had been forced to sweep further and further until eventually they were operating some 150 miles from their bases, covered by destroyers and cruisers who themselves on occasion needed battleship cover.

The Admiralty had accurate and timely intelligence on much of this activity. For 17 November an ambitious sortie was planned involving a considerable force: the 1st Cruiser Squadron, of *Courageous* (flag of Vice-Admiral T.D.W. Napier) and *Glorious*, with four escorting destroyers; the 6th Light Cruiser Squadron, of *Cardiff* (flag of Rear-Admiral E.S. Alexander-Sinclair), *Ceres*, *Calypso* and *Caradoc*, with four destroyers; the 1st Light Cruiser Squadron, of *Caledon* (broad pennant of Commodore W.H. Cowan), *Galatea*, *Royalist* and *Inconstant*, with two destroyers; and the 1st Battle Cruiser Squadron, of *Lion* (flag of Vice-Admiral Sir W. Pakenham), *Princess Royal*, *Tiger*, *Repulse* and *New Zealand*, with nine screening destroyers.

This force was to steam across the North Sea to a position about halfway along the western edge of a large British minefield in the Heligoland Bight and, having reached a rendezvous point, turn north-west and sweep before them any German forces they found, either destroying them themselves or driving them towards the 1st Battle Squadron, of six battleships and eleven destroyers, lying in wait in cleared water between the eastern edge of a German minefield and the top north-western limit of the British field.

It was an admirable scheme and it should have worked, but by that stage of the war the North Sea and the Heligoland Bight were strewn with minefields laid by both sides. Full knowledge, even of the British minefields, was not available to all the British commanders on 17 November. In fact only Beatty, the C-in-C, and Pakenham had detailed and up-to-date charts. The others, especially Napier, knew only of some fields. The seeds of uncertainty were thus sown.

All the ships involved in the operation had sailed by half past four on 16 November and just before dawn the next day, at about 6.15am, the leading cruisers were steaming east-north-east at 24 knots towards the mine barrier. *Courageous* was leading, three cables (600 yards) ahead of *Glorious*, with the 6th LCS on the port beam, though not in sight. The 1st LCS was supposed to be on the starboard beam but was in fact about three miles astern of station. *Lion* and the other battle cruisers were some ten miles away on *Glorious'* port quarter. Visibility was only about two miles in fog when the sun rose, like a great red ball in the fog-bank, at 7.17am. But hopes of action ran high.

There could not have been a better day. The German Navy was indeed just about to carry, out a major sweeping operation in the very area where the British cruisers were to rendezvous. The ships would inevitably be strung out over a considerable distance and would require a powerful covering force. Admiral von Reuter, commanding the 2nd Scouting Group, had ordered the 6th Minesweeping Half Flotilla, the 2nd and 6th Minesweeping Support Half Flotillas, the 12th and 14th Destroyer Half Flotillas, and his own squadron of light cruisers, *Nurnberg* (flag), *Königsberg*, *Frankfurt* and *Pillau*, to assemble in the central part of the mine barrier early on 17 November. Two battleships, *Kaiser* and *Kaiserin*, were ready near Heligoland to give support.

Visibility improved as the sun climbed higher and it was *Courageous'* lookouts who first sighted the enemy at 7.30. *Glorious* was able to make the thrilling signal 'Enemy in sight bearing due east' four minutes later.

In the prevailing haze it was difficult to make out the enemy ships clearly from *Glorious'* bridge. There seemed to be three groups: minesweepers and/or destroyers to port; some eight or ten shapes, possibly submarines on the surface, ahead; and three light cruisers to starboard. *Courageous* opened fire with her forward 15" guns on a light cruiser fine on the starboard bow at 7.40. *Glorious* fired her main armament for the first time in anger two minutes later, on another cruiser on the starboard bow. *Glorious'* target was judged to be steering south but ranging was difficult in the mist and *Glorious'* first range set, 10,000 yards, was hopelessly short. *Glorious* also opened fire with her 4" secondary armament at maximum range of 13,200 yards, but they too were well short.

There never was a naval action for which the phrase 'the fog of war' was more apt than that in the Heligoland Bight in November, 1917. For Napier's ships there were bafflingly brief glimpses of the enemy, appearing and disappearing in the mist. Target silhouettes showed up faintly in the murk, only to fade before they could be properly identified. The whole action was remarkable for the number of mysterious floating objects, periscopes, smoke clouds and other puzzling sightings. It seems that at no time was Napier really certain of his enemy's strength, course or speed. At various times he took his ships to the south-east, to the north and back to the south again. He appeared to forget (certainly he did not use) the great speed possessed by *Courageous* and *Glorious*, and actually reduced speed at a critical point.

Yet at the outset Napier held a clear advantage. The light to the east, where the sun was rising, was very much better than to the west. Napier's ships had caught their enemy totally unaware. The first fall of shot was the first inkling the Germans had that they were in danger. But once von Reuter realized that he had run his ships into considerable opposition, he ordered them to turn through 180 degrees and steer southeast towards the battleships and to make smoke.

Napier, meanwhile, seemed always at a loss for a solution. Bearing in mind the danger areas of those minefields he had been told about, and the 'safety line' which he had already decided it would be imprudent to cross, he shuttled up and down the enemy's dense smokescreen while his ships, the light cruisers, Pakenham's battle cruisers and especially Rear-Admiral Phillimore's flagship *Repulse* fired when they could at what they could.

Glorious' gunnery was in general undistinguished. At one point she opened fire with her 15" guns at enemy light cruisers, range 7,200 yards, and the salvo was well short. At the same time fire was opened with secondary armament, range 10,000 yards, and these salvoes fell over. Thus *Glorious* was short with her main 15" and over with her secondary 4". At 8.33am, when the 15" guns were firing at a range of 18,000 yards, there was a premature burst in the left gun of the forward turret. For a few minutes the situation was confused. The 4" opened fire on a 'periscope', but checked almost at once when it was seen to be a buoy. 'Anti-aircraft shrapnel' was observed in the sky, although no aircraft were seen.

Glorious' 15" guns opened fire for the third and last time at 9.07am, at a maximum range of 23,000 yards. The splashes were all 'a long way short'. The enemy range appeared to be well over 30,000 yards. At 9.50 *Glorious'* log recorded 'nothing in sight'. By ten o'clock all ships were retiring, and forty minutes later a thick fog descended to end the day's proceedings. *Glorious* and the rest of the Rosyth ships arrived in the forenoon of 19 November.

The post-mortem then began. It was found that everybody, but especially *Courageous* and *Glorious*, had expended prodigious amounts of ammunition. *Courageous* had fired ninety-two 15" shells, *Glorious* fifty-seven, for one hit, shared between them, on one of the light cruiser *Pillau's* gunshields. The two ships had also fired 180 4" High Explosive and two hundred and thirteen 4" common shell, for no result whatever. The light cruisers had done no better: they fired 2,519 6" shells to achieve a total of three hits. *Repulse*, who had fired the last shots in the battle, had one hit on *Königsberg*, penetrating the upper deck and starting a serious fire in a coal bunker. These five hits, one by *Repulse*, one by *Courageous* or *Glorious* and three by the light cruisers, caused German casualties of twenty-one killed and forty wounded.

The Germans claimed five hits on the battle cruisers, six on the light cruisers and seven on the destroyers. They actually achieved seven: the light cruisers hit *Cardiff three* times, causing serious fires, and *Calypso* once, mortally wounding her Captain, while *Kaiser* and *Kaiserin* scored hits on *Caledon* on her water-line and her forward turret. There were a hundred British casualties.

Inevitably there were complaints about the efficiency of the British ammunition. The British ships had fired 3,170 6" and 4" shells, of which 82% were Lyddite Common, which, as Napier complained to Beatty, 'do not seem to have injured the enemy's vitals'. There were other mitigating factors, it was claimed: the readiness of the Germans to make large turns away at the slightest sign of attack, the vigourous zigzagging by the Germans, the general haze and fog and smoke, the difficulty of ranging and firing at targets which were only seen as gun-flashes on the distant, hazy horizon.

But the most criticism of all was directed at Napier himself. While Pakenham, Alexander-Sinclair and Cowan were all commended, Napier had execrations poured upon his hapless head from all directions. Jellicoe, the First Sea Lord, found his behaviour in not closing the German light cruisers at the start 'inexplicable'. Everybody said they could not understand why Napier had steered north at one point to clear the northern end of the smoke screen, or why he at no time used the full speed of the ships he had. Napier replied that from what he could see in the earlier stages the enemy was steering north-westwards (as indeed they were, in the earlier stages) and he had headed to cut them off. The question of why he had not used full speed was never answered.

Napier, who had flown his flag briefly in *Glorious* for a couple of months of spring and summer earlier in the year, returned on 29 December to fly his flag in the ship over the New Year. At midnight on New Year's Eve the youngest boy seaman on board, dressed in his best Number Ones, brought the year in according to ancient tradition by striking sixteen bells on the ship's bell. In the wardroom the officers toasted 1918 and hoped for better things. It was by now clear to everybody that on that day in the Heligoland Bight the enemy had presented *Glorious* and *Courageous* with the perfect opportunity to employ their two best talents, their speed and their 15" guns. Everybody looked forward, though with more hope than conviction, to trying conclusions with the enemy a second time. But many staff officers were saying, at least privately, that 'They'll never come out again'.

Glorious went to refit in Devonport, the ship's home port, in February and March, 1918. The strengthening of the sides, made necessary by *Courageous'* mishap, was carried out. It had been decided in August, 1917, to fit both ships with flying-off decks. Ramps were constructed on top of 'A' turret for a Sopwith 1½ Strutter spotting aircraft, and on 'Y' Turret for a Sopwith Camel fighter.

After refit *Glorious* sailed for Scapa and then returned to the Firth of Forth on 12 April. Operating from Burntisland, she continued her training programme of exercises and drills, days at sea, gunnery firings, launching and recovery of her aircraft. A German seaplane dropped two bombs on *Glorious* at 9.45 on 1 June when she was at sea, but both missed.

The very last excitement of the First World War for *Glorious* began at 3.45am on 5 November, 1918. She and *Courageous* were among ships anchored off Burntisland when, in strong winds, the seaplane carrier *Campania* dragged her anchor and collided with the battleship *Royal Oak*. Both ships then dragged down on to *Glorious*, astern of *Royal Oak*, causing damage to *Glorious'* upper deck fittings and gangways. *Campania* was cleared from her entanglement with *Glorious* by 5am, *Royal Oak* half an hour later. But *Campania* was badly damaged and at 8.35 that morning she sank in position, according to *Glorious'* log, '1490, 187 yards from Red Light on Burntisland'.

When the Armistice was declared, *Glorious'* siren joined in the joyful bedlam of hooting and whistling from every ship, large and small, in the Forth. 'Splice the mainbrace' was piped and an extra tot of rum to all hands served at 7pm. Foghorns and sirens boomed and resounded for some three hours that evening while sailors danced and cheered on the upper deck. It had been a long and a dangerous war. They had survived. Many had not.

There was one last sortie: Operation ZZ. Very early on 21 November, 1918 the whole Grand Fleet, of 370 ships and 90,000 men, with the 6th U.S. Battle Squadron and a French cruiser and two French destroyers, put to sea for a rendezvous some forty miles east of May Island in the Firth of Forth. In open water the huge line of ships split into two columns, six miles apart, each column with more than thirty battleships, battle cruisers and cruisers, with a destroyer stationed abreast each squadron flagship. *Glorious'* log recorded: '9.12am, sighted five German battle cruisers. 9.15 sighted nine German battleships and seven light cruisers'. There were also forty-nine German destroyers.

Von Reuter, flying his flag in *Friedrich der Grosse*, led the German ships between the two lines of British ships which had their guns loaded, although still trained fore and aft, and their ship's companies at action stations, in case of last minute resistance. But there was none and, as the German ships passed by, the British turned through 180°, by squadrons, to escort them.

It was a bright sunny day, with a little early mist, but the surrender was an unexpectedly quiet, almost funereal occasion, although the fleet cheered Beatty as he passed in his flagship *Queen Elizabeth*. At 11am Beatty signalled: 'The German flag is to be hauled down at sunset today, Thursday, and will not be hoisted again without permission.' *Glorious*, like many ships, held a service of thanksgiving, and in the afternoon lower deck was cleared and all hands piped to muster aft on the quarterdeck. At 3.57pm, when the Royal Marine bugler sounded 'Sunset', all hands turned aft and saluted. Meanwhile the German ensigns were hauled down for the last time. Beatty sent a general signal, congratulating all ships on the victory. King George V had also sent a message of congratulation to his fleet. And, that, after four years, was that.

In 1919 *Courageous* and *Glorious* were both laid up in reserve. *Jane's Fighting Ships* that year pronounced their professional *nunc dimittis*: 'Their cost of maintenance is high. It does not appear that they will have a long life.'

In the Reserve Fleet *Glorious* was demoted to a Commander's command, but in January, 1921, under Captain Rowland H. Bather CBE, she became the Turret Drill Ship at Devonport, with a reduced complement of 203 officers and men. In April she flew the flag of Rear-Admiral Charles D. Johnson, CB, DSO, MVO, Rear-Admiral Reserve Fleet Devonport. But by November, 1922, under Captain John E. Cameron, CB, MVO, the appointment had been again downgraded to Senior Officer, Reserve Fleet Devonport.

Moored between two buoys in the Hamoaze, *Glorious* still attracted the admiring glances of schoolboys and newly joined young sailors, as the very model of what a handsome fighting ship should be. She might have remained there, while the wind and tide murmured of what might have been, until the day she was towed away to be broken up. Instead, she was to have a future which nobody could have foreseen. Her sister ship *Furious* had begun the first of her many metamorphoses while still building; in March, 1917, it was decided to remove her forward 18" gun and replace the mounting with a seaplane hangar surmounted by a flying-off deck, (on which, on 2 August, 1917, off Scapa Flow, Squadron Leader Dunning achieved the historic first landing). After several more chances, *Furious* finally emerged as a flush-deck aircraft carrier in 1925.

By then it had been decided to convert *Courageous* and *Glorious*, too, into aircraft carriers.

It could be said that the Royal Navy achieved its air arm in spite of itself and pioneered the first aircraft carrier in a series of inspired experimental lurches. The unfortunate *Campania*, which had once been a Cunard liner regularly running between Liverpool and New York, was only one of many conversions. *Empress* and *Engadine* were converted cross-Channel ferries and, with a third, *Riviera*, carried out the first naval air strike in history, against the Zeppelin base at Cuxhaven on Christmas Day, 1914. *Ark Royal* was a collier, bought off the stocks at Blyth in Northumberland and completed as a seaplane carrier. *Manxman* was a converted packet, *Nairana* an Australian mail steamer, *Vindex* an Isle of Man packet, *Pegasus* the Great Eastern steamer *Stockholm*. Pre-war, the kite balloon ship *Manica* carried manure along the Manchester Ship Canal. *Argus*, the world's first true aircraft carrier, with a flush flight deck 567 feet long from stem to stern, was converted from the ex-Italian liner *Conte Rosso*; from *Argus*' deck in October, 1918, in the Firth of Forth, Commander Richard Bell Davies, VC, DSO, flying a Sopwith 1½ Strutter, made the first historic flight-deck take-offs and landings.

When in 1917 the case for a 'unified air service' was examined the Admiralty, either through ignorance, indifference or lingering doubts about the real value of air power at sea, did not fight its own corner with any force or conviction. When the Air Force Bill became law on 1 April, 1918, the Royal Naval Air Service was abolished at a stroke, and all its resources — more than 100 air stations, some 55,000 officers and men, more than 2,500 aircraft — were transferred to the newly-created Royal Air Force. Squadron Commanders RN became Majors RAF, Flight Commanders became Captains,

Petty Officers became Sergeants. Many of the best air-minded naval officers transferred to the RAF and for most of the inter-war period the Navy had no senior officers with much knowledge of, nor sympathy with, the world of the air. 'Air' officers who did stay in the Navy with dual RN-RAF ranks suffered perennially from an occupational unease, constantly aware that their career prospects were in jeopardy because they were aircrew.

Having, almost by default, let control of their air arm go to the RAF, the Navy spent the best part of the next twenty years trying to wrest it back. Both sides, the Admiralty and the Air Ministry, with occasional interventions by the War Office, fought a grim, bitter paper battle, bombarding each other with minutes and memoranda, which sometimes descended to personal abuse. The Air Ministry believed in the 'unity of the air': all who flew, over land or sea, should belong to a common service. The Admiralty believed that all those who served in the Navy should have a 'sea-sense' and should be properly trained and led in the 'naval way', whether they served on, under or over the sea. Both arguments had merit, but they were mutually irreconcilable.

In 1920, to the immense disapproval of the Air Ministry, the Admiralty formed a Naval Air Section, with just one officer, Bell Davies. But it was the seed from which the future Naval Air Division grew. In 1921, against opposition from the Air Ministry, the Admiralty formed a naval observer branch, contending that naval observers were naval officers first, foremost and all the time; special air skills were certainly needed, but these could be taught by the Navy in the same way that it taught its gunnery and other specialists.

In 1923 the Balfour Committee rejected the Admiralty's claim to have their own naval air service, deciding that the

Fleet Air Arm (an early use of the term) was to form part of the Air Service. Naval officers in the Fleet Air Arm were therefore 'attached' to the Air Service, would be posted to naval units by the Air Service and would 'serve under the immediate command of Air Service Officers, yet afloat they will be under the ultimate command of the Naval Officers of the Fleet'.

Although the Balfour Report did make concessions, such as that the Navy would have a great say in demanding the aircraft types it wanted, it caused extreme gloom at the Admiralty. Bell Davies found Captain Dudley Pound, Director of Plans, 'sitting at his desk studying the report with a scowl on his face; Tom Calvert [Commander, also in Plans, who later took over the Naval Air Section] was walking about swearing; evidently it was bad news. I was given the substance of it by Calvert: the air units in the fleet were to remain RAF.'

In March, 1923, after yet another furore over a plan that the FAA should absorb the RAF's Coastal Area (in years to come, Coastal Command), Lord Haldane was appointed arbitrator. He 'knocked together' the heads of Trenchard and Admiral Keyes, Deputy Chief of Naval Staff, (who were also, in fact, brothers-in-law) and gave them three months to reach an agreement. The Trenchard-Keyes Agreement, as it was known, did not change the central decision of the Balfour Report but it did carry out some fine tuning which suited the Admiralty. The Balfour statement that 'not less than 30% of pilots on carriers to be RAF' was transmuted into 70% of pilots, and all observers of course, in the FAA should be naval or marine officers. Naval officers should continue to wear naval uniform, wear wings on their left sleeves, and would only be employed on naval air work.

This removed a good deal of previous uncertainty about career prospects, and doubts among many young naval officers, who would have liked to fly, but did not volunteer on the grounds that they might thereby be disloyal to the Navy.

The attitudes of senior naval officers, when told that a junior wished to volunteer to become a pilot, remained mixed. Some were very glad to be able to tear up an application, saying 'Another soul saved!' Pound told one volunteer that flying was 'poppycock' and would 'ruin his career'.

On the other hand, St John Fancourt, who went on to a distinguished FAA career, had the idea put to him by his Captain, when he himself was quite happy with his lot in a destroyer in Malta. 'My Captain, Ambrose Abby, encouraged me. He said, if you stay in destroyers all you'll get is a brass hat and a bald head, *if* you're lucky!' Likewise, Lieutenant Owen Cathcart-Jones, Royal Marines, was told by his then superior officers, Group Captain Forbes and Admiral Larken, that flying had 'enormous possibilities for the future' and (a very pertinent point in those days) was a good way of avoiding the Axe.

An earlier Admiralty appeal for volunteers in 1920 was worded in such a lukewarm, unenthusiastic way that it attracted only nine respondents, of whom two were unfit and three were retired under the 'Geddes Axe'. The Air Ministry, understandably and with a certain degree of truth, accused the Admiralty of not *wanting* volunteers. The 1924 appeal, possibly because it was more sincere, attracted many more volunteers. Fifty officers joined the first training course at No 1 Flying Training School, Netheravon, in June, 1924. The course was to last ten months, consisting of six months elementary flying training at Netheravon, followed by a period at coastal stations for training on naval aircraft, and for instruction in naval air work, after which the successful were appointed to relieve RAF officers as pilots in the Fleet Air Arm. The second course, of thirty officers, joined in January, 1925, and there were four courses a year.

Pilots had a knack of attracting attention, which was not always welcome. The same Cathcart-Jones, flying a Fairey Flycatcher in the Mediterranean on 21 August, 1929, decided to bombard a friend of his, serving in one of the battleships. The only suitable missiles he could find, snatched up from the wardroom heads on his way up to the flight deck, were several packets of sheet lavatory paper, brown.

Unfortunately for Cathcart-Jones, his ship identification was not infallible. Unknown to him, the battle squadron had reversed order, so that the flagship *Queen Elizabeth* was the rear ship and the startled head over which Cathcart-Jones released his lavatory paper belonged, not to his friend, but to the Commander-in-Chief, Admiral Field. At the subsequent investigation, Cathcart-Jones thought hard and told his Captain and his Wing Commander that he needed the brown paper as a marker to show when he would have released his bombs, had he been carrying any. Neither of his superiors believed it, but both decided to believe it.

On the other hand, nobody who saw it would ever forget the brilliant musical show 'Suffering Wildcats', with a male cast entirely drawn from the Fleet Air Arm, staged at Malta in 1926. The producer was Lieutenant Anthony Kimmins RN, who had been one of the first fifty on No 1 Course and was then a pilot in 422 Flight in *Eagle*. (To cap it all, in 1928, Kimmins married the show's soubrette, Miss Betty Hodge, daughter of Admiral Sir Michael Hodge, the C-in-C, Atlantic Fleet.)

By 1924, when work began to convert *Courageous* and *Glorious*, the Royal Navy had two more carriers, *Eagle* and

Hermes. Eagle had been laid down as a dreadnought for the Chilean Navy, the *Almirante Cochrane*. Work stopped on her from August, 1914, until 1917, when she was bought off the slip and converted as an aircraft carrier to a design by Tennyson-d'Eyncourt. She commissioned for trials in April, 1920, and finally completed, to carry twenty-one aircraft, in 1924. *Hermes*, begun in January, 1918, was the first ship of the Royal Navy to be purpose-built as a carrier, and would have been the first in the world had not a post-Armistice lack of urgency allowed the Japanese to commission *Hosho* first. She was completed to carry fifteen aircraft in February, 1924.

Glorious arrived at Rosyth on 1 February, 1924. She was to be rebuilt completely, from the hull upwards. All superstructure above the fo'c'sle and shelter deck, all bulkheads, the conning tower, director tower, masts, derricks, the bridge, funnel and uptakes were removed. The boiler uptakes were to be led to a single funnel on the starboard side, which rose from a narrow 'island' superstructure which also housed the bridge, flag deck, searchlights, gun control position and flight deck control position.

The main weights had been removed by May, 1924, and her four 15" guns, with the four 15" guns from *Courageous* (undergoing similar conversion at Devonport) were added to the reserve maintained for ships of the *Royal Sovereign* and *Queen Elizabeth* Class, and for *Hood*. Eventually, all eight guns were mounted in the battleship *Vanguard* in 1945, the forward four from *Courageous*, the after four from *Glorious*.

Much thought was given to the gun armament for *Courageous* and *Glorious* as carriers. *Eagle* had nine 6" 50 calibre and four 4" anti-aircraft guns, *Hermes* six 5.5" and three 4" anti-aircraft guns. The US Navy was reported to be fitting eight 8" and twelve 5" anti-aircraft guns to the new carriers *Lexington* and

Saratoga (as indeed they did), while the Japanese were fitting ten 8" and twelve 4.7" anti-aircraft guns in *Kaga* and *Akagi*. For a time ten 8" guns were considered for *Courageous* and *Glorious*, but here *Eagle* provided some useful practical experience. She had exercised with light cruisers in a series of exercises EJ 1,2,3 and 4 with the Atlantic Fleet in February and March, 1922. In three exercises out of four it was deemed the light cruisers would have sunk *Eagle*, although the light cruisers themselves would have been sunk twice or damaged by torpedo-carrying aircraft. Thus it was decided that no aircraft carrier could reasonably be expected to carry out a gun duel. The two ships were equipped with sixteen single 4.7" High Angle/Low Angle guns, mounted eight on each side on the original fo'c'sle deck level. This was a very light armament, designed for anti-aircraft use and for defence against nothing larger than a destroyer.

The flight deck was 25 lbs 'D' quality steel plate, designed to withstand an impact and detonation of a 20lb bomb, with two hangars, each with a headroom of sixteen feet, below it. The flight deck itself was planned on a spacious scale. Its total length was 465 feet and there was a second lower flying-off deck, 156 feet long, forward. It was 310 feet from the after end of the island to the forward end of the after lift; the distance between the two lifts was 342 feet. The flight deck breadth was 100 feet, with a clear breadth inside the island of 84½ feet. The island itself was 73½ feet long. The original legend said that there was a ramp abreast the funnel 'for the run-up of the flight deck forming the ramp for the Arresting Gear'. Athwartships arrester wires were not fitted until later, and the fore-and-aft wires tried in *Furious* had not been successful; so it seems that the ramp itself (which remained throughout the ship's life) was intended by its gradient to arrest aircraft.

Aircraft required special fuelling arrangements and here again *Eagle* provided some useful practical data: off Malta, on 1 May, 1925, she used 1,525 gallons of petrol in one day's flying. *Glorious* was designed to carry 30,000 gallons of petrol, displaced from specially constructed tanks and forced up to the hangar, where fuelling normally took place, by pressure of sea water. The ship also carried 3,750 gallons of lubricating oil and 1,000 gallons of paraffin.

The official legend and drawings for the reconstruction of the ship were approved on 12 February, 1925, but by then a move to Devonport had been under consideration for some time. By December, 1927, *Glorious* was at Devonport (having been towed there when Rosyth closed) for the final fitting-out.

The hangars had fireproof curtains, made by Milne's Works, Liverpool, with special brailing-up arrangements. The two aircraft lifts, made by the Express Lift Co., of Westminster, had a total travel of 40 feet 9 inches (that is to say, the travel from the lower hangar deck up to the flight deck) for the forward lift and 38 feet 6 inches for the after lift. The lifts were designed to carry loads of five tons at 50 feet/second and were supposed to rise through their limits in not more than sixty seconds and descend in not more than sixty-four seconds. The forward lift was tested with a Fairey 111F spotter reconnaissance plane with nine men on it, the after lift with a Blackburn Dart and eleven men. Both lifts were hydraulically operated, with emergency stop-valves.

As the completion date came nearer, the pace of the trials accelerated. The date had already been delayed considerably and the ships' reconstruction generally had taken much longer than planned, because of shortage of money. There was a gun inspection in August, 1929, and bomb-lift trials, and trials on the new direction-finding equipment. Flight deck flood-lighting was installed and tested. There were trials on all kinds of new equipment, from the oil-fired cooking ranges in the galleys to the F.8 camera installation (which photographed every deck landing) in the island, and from the fire curtain rollers in the hangars to a new shutter-type 'Affirmative' lamp (giving a pilot permission to land) mounted abaft the island and wire-operated by the Wingco. The decision to fit a catapult had been taken in September, 1928, and a catapult was available, subject to trials, early in 1929. It was fitted at the forward end of the flight deck on the starboard side.

At last *Glorious* recommissioned at Devonport on 7 January, 1930, and completed to full complement of 725 officers and men (with the Fleet Air Arm to join later) on 24 February. Her commanding officer, appointed to her on 7 August, 1929, was Captain Dashwood Moir, DSO. Moir was nearly fifty years old and was coming to the top of the Captain's seniority list. *Glorious* was, in fact, his last appointment before retirement. He was a 'salt-horse', i.e. nonspecialist officer, and had won his DSO for good service in torpedo boat destroyers in 1917. He had served in the South African war in 1901 and had been mentioned in dispatches for his part in the Aro Expedition in 1902. He was a dour Scot whom nobody got to know very well. St John Fancourt said Moir 'never came out of his cabin except to point the ship up into the wind'. One of the RAF officers on board, Flight Lieutenant T.P.P.F. ('Paddy') Fagan, the signals officer, said Moir 'never smiled much'.

In the opinion of everybody who served in the ship at that time, it was the Commander and Executive Officer, Kenneth Edwards, who carried the wardroom and the ship. 'A great man, a great character,' they say of him still, 'and greatly loved by everybody, though he did hit the bottle a bit.'

For the first four months after recommissioning *Glorious* carried out an intensive programme of trials and training. There was an inclining experiment on 15 February (to check the ship's stability figures) followed by handling, steering and circling trials, a four-hour full-power trial, trials on streaming paravanes (for cutting mine wires), with final gunnery trials on 6 March. On 18 March, steaming off Portsmouth, *Glorious* landed on the first of her aircraft, Nos 406 and 408 Flights, each of six Fairey Flycatchers, and sailed for the Clyde for aircraft handling and flying trials, with measured mile runs off Arran on 23 and 24 March. *Courageous* had completed and recommissioned on 5 May, 1928, but on 26 January, 1930, her plates had buckled yet again while in dock in Malta. In April *Glorious* was docked at Devonport for further stiffening of her ship's side, but on 29 April, 1930, she was at Spithead, ready to go.

Her conversion had increased *Glorious*' displacement to 22,500 tons and her complement to 1,216 officers and men, including 468 FAA personnel (with RAF). She was designed to carry forty-eight aircraft, but very rarely had as many embarked. The more usual complement was thirty-six and even that was too many to operate comfortably without a nearby diversion airfield ashore.

Glorious' third Flycatcher Flight, No. 405, embarked on 26 May. The Fairey Flycatcher was a single-seat fighter which could be converted as a seaplane or amphibian. It was powered by a 400 hp Armstrong Siddeley Jaguar IV engine and could do 133 mph at 5,000 feet, reducing to 110 mph at 17,000, with a normal service ceiling of 19,000 feet, and rate of climb of about 100 feet/minute. It was armed with twin synchronized Vickers guns, firing forward through the propeller arc, and could also carry four 20lb bombs below the wings. The

Flycatcher weighed less than a ton unloaded, and it had hydraulically operated wheel brakes which could bring it to rest in fifty yards.

The first operational Flycatcher Flight, No. 402, formed in 1923 and embarked in *Eagle*. The Flycatcher remained the standard fleet fighter until the introduction of the Nimrod in 1934. It was one of the most popular and successful fleet aircraft of all time. It was easy and safe to fly, easy to deck-land and superb for aerobatics, with a heart-warming, full-blooded engine roar. The Flycatcher was always in demand for displays at air shows. It could be dived vertically at full throttle until terminal velocity was reached and if the engine were then suddenly throttled back, a curious sound, the famous 'Blue Note', could be heard for miles. *Glorious'* 'Flycatcher Flights delighted to practise such manoeuvres as climbing up and away from the ship fanning out in a 'Prince of Wales' feathers motif'. The Flycatcher had an endurance of less than two hours, however, and a perpetual complaint of its pilots was that they did not get enough flying time. Of *Glorious'* three Flights, 406 was commanded by Flight Lieutenant G.R.M. Clifford RAF, 408 by Lieutenant E.M.C. Abel-Smith RN (who in 192,7 had become the first naval officer to command his own Flight) and 405 by Flight Lieutenant C.R. Smythe RAF.

On 19 May, when the ship was off the Isle of Wight, the ship's two Flights of Blackburn Ripons flew on. They were No 461, commanded by Lieutenant-Commander A.G. Elliot, and 462, commanded by Flight Lieutenant H.E. King RAF. The Ripon had succeeded the Dart as the standard FAA torpedo-bomber, entering service with 462 Flight in *Furious* in 1929. It was a two-seater, powered by a 570 hp Napier Lion X1A, which gave it a top speed of 126 mph at sea level and an endurance of three hours, although its performance dropped off markedly when carrying a torpedo or bombs. It had a fixed Vickers gun forward, and a free-mounted swivelling Lewis gun aft. It could carry a Mark V111 or Mark X torpedo, or one 1,100lb smoke container, or three 520/550lb bombs.

The last aircraft to fly on, actually on 24 June, were two flights No. 441 (Flight Lieutenant N. Young RAF) and 447 (Flight Lieutenant L.B. Duggan RAF) of Fairey 111Fs. The 111F was another classic aircraft of the FAA and was the most widely used aircraft of all between the wars. It was a spotter/reconnaissance, with a crew of three: pilot, observer and telegraphist-air-gunner (TAG). It had one 570 hp Napier Lion X1A, giving it a maximum speed of 120 mph at 10,000 feet, and service ceiling of 20,000 feet, with an endurance of between three to four hours. The Fairey 111F was armed with one fixed Vickers forward and a manually-operated Lewis gun on a Scarff ring or Fairey high-speed mounting in the rear cockpit and fired by the TAG. It could also carry up to 500lbs of bombs under the wings and had a role as a high-level bomber. But its principal use with the fleet was spotter-reconnaissance. It was still a comparatively new aircraft in the fleet, having first gone to sea in 1928, when it replaced the earlier 111Ds of No 440 Flight in *Hermes* and equipped Nos 445 and 446 in *Courageous* when she recommissioned the same year.

With everyone embarked, *Glorious* had forty-two aircraft: eighteen Flycatchers, twelve Ripons and twelve 111Fs. Her air branch totalled some seventy officers and nearly 300 men. Of the officers, about twenty were naval observers, thirty were naval officers borne for flying duties (with additional RAF rank), and the remaining twenty were RAF officers seconded to the ship for carrier duties. Some RAF officers thoroughly enjoyed the life and served for some time in carriers: Flight

Lieutenant Fagan served for four and a half years and Flying Officer P.D. Cracroft RAF, a Flycatcher pilot in 408 Flight, for even longer, in three carriers, *Furious*, *Glorious* and *Courageous*. Of the 280 men nearly all were RAF personnel with their own warrant officers and regulating staff, (although they were ultimately under the authority of the Captain) and the RAF provided nearly all the skilled technical repair staff on board.

The senior air branch officer was a Wing Commander RAF, in *Glorious* Anthony Rex Arnold, a distinguished officer with the DSC and DFC who later rose to Air Commodore. According to Fagan, Arnold was 'a man of Army background, and a little intolerant of naval customs'. Arnold had Squadron Leader W.H. Dunn, DSC, as his assistant, and four Flight Lieutenants to handle stores, signals, and operations.

A typical Flight of that era, not just of Fairey 111Fs but of all aircraft, was 447, which was first formed on 26 April, 1929 (by renumbering 421 Flight) for 111F service in *Furious*, and was now embarked in *Glorious*. There were six pilots: Duggan the Flight Commander, two Flying Officers RAF, A. le R.S. Upton and J.C.T. Marshall, and three Lieutenants (P) RN, A.O. Watson, E.J.E. Burt and H.P. Madden, who also had the additional rank of Flying Officer RAF. The observers were RN officers from the ship, all qualified (or Acting) observers, who were detailed to or withdrawn from that particular Flight by the ship's senior observer; generally, but by no means invariably, they would fly with the same Flight and the same pilot. The RAF provided a Flight Sergeant, an Airframe Sergeant, an Engine Fitter Sergeant, corporal airframe riggers and engine fitters, leading aircraftsmen and AC is. The Flight would also include naval telegraphists/air gunners, able seamen for aircraft handling, a storeman, three Royal Marine orderlies, one RAF 'batman', and very probably a naval cook, attached to the flight. The total number of officers and men in a typical Flight would therefore be about thirty.

Glorious sailed after the 111Fs had landed on to join the Mediterranean Fleet at Malta. On passage east of Gibraltar she suffered a series of those mishaps which occasionally embarrassed her. Some days, after evening quarters, the ship stopped while hands were piped to bathe over the ship's side. The main turbines were still hot, with a reduced vacuum being maintained in the main condensers. In this condition the turbines had to be turned under steam periodically through several revolutions. This was to prevent heat-warping of the turbine rotor, and consequent reduction of the design clearances between rotor and casing blades while the rotor was stationary.

Evidently this precaution was not properly taken. On three evenings, when the ship got under way again, first the starboard outer main turbine, followed by the starboard inner, and then the port inner turbine, were badly damaged and the shafts had to be locked while the ship, somewhat shamefacedly, proceeded to Malta on the port outer shaft, arriving on 2 July, 1930. Luckily there was enough wind to fly off the aircraft to Hal Far at the speed provided by one shaft.

While the officers and ship's company stayed on board, the air crew lived in the new, spacious, high-ceilinged Officers' Mess designed by Lutyens for the RAF. The Flights amused themselves in various ways. Malta was an island of tiny fields bordered by stone walls. 408 Flight competed to see who could land their Flycatcher closest to the airfield perimeter wall. Abel-Smith won but he was subsequently disqualified on the grounds that his Flycatcher was upside down at the time.

Glorious had no air-conditioning, but air ventilation trunks ran the length of the ship under the deckhead beams, discharging air into offices, messes, and workshops via 'punkah louvres'. In the ventilation system, according to Lieutenant Humphrey Madden of 447 Flight, 'there were two huge colonies, one of white rats, the other of brown. So large were these colonies that neither could exterminate the other. They lived in the air trunks and their tails hung down outside through the louvres, mostly in the forepart of the ship, above the alleys and store-rooms, but they would also chase each other alongside the pipes anywhere in the ship. Sometimes, four of these creatures would be hanging by their claws on the outside of the wardroom pantry door when it was locked. Often, when one was having a bath in the wardroom bathroom, rats would congregate at the end of the trunking behind the metal grille and eye the bather silently.'

At last, early in December, 1930, the repairs were finished and the ship sailed on the 8th for a short pre-Christmas shakedown cruise to Suda Bay in Crete, exercising and carrying out flying training while on passage.

Preparations for a day's flying would begin on the previous evening, with a general briefing of aircrew. Lists of names of pilots and observers, the aircraft and the times to fly off would be posted on the wardroom and other noticeboards around the ship. Very early the next morning, well before dawn, the Flight Deck party, of some twenty to thirty seamen, under a petty officer and the Flight Deck Officer (an RAF officer), would begin to bring up aircraft on the lifts and range them on deck. Aircraft usually took off in the order of longest endurance, Fairey 111Fs first, for reconnaissance, followed by Ripons, if a likely target had been sighted, and then by Flycatchers, for the defence of the carrier herself against counter-attack, or possibly bombing or machine-gun strafing of the upper deck of a target.

For aircrew there would be cocoa laid out on the wardroom table, for those who wanted it, but not early breakfast, (nor, in the 1930s, any regulations against flying on an empty stomach). Pilots often wore a very gentlemanly flying rig, of Number Five uniform with superfine monkey jacket and trousers, white shirt, stiff collar and black tie, or possibly, for an early flight, a silk scarf, silk gloves under thick flying gauntlets, a leather flying helmet, and over all, a Kapok lifejacket.

The 111Fs were ranged on deck with an RAF engine fitter sitting in each pilot's cockpit. Starting up followed a familiarly frantic ritual. Aircrew of the times say, 'The only reason Henry I never laughed again after the White Ship went down was because he never saw a Fairey 111F being started.' The Napier Lion X1s, with permission given from the bridge, were started by inserting two long starting handles, one each side, which were wound by engine fitters, faster and faster, until the engine fired and settled down to run steadily. The handles were removed and quickly stowed in special racks one either side behind the pilot's seat.

With the engine running, the RAF corporal fitter would let it idle until the temperatures started to rise, when he would open the throttle a little. As he did so, the pilot mounted from the port side, while the corporal fitter climbed out and down the starboard side. When the pilot was in the front seat and strapped in, he would watch the oil and water temperature gauges climb to their correct readings and check that the oil pressure was normal. At a signal the wheel chocks were whipped away and the engine fitter flung himself across the tail of the aircraft while the pilot opened the throttle to full, holding the control column fully back. Ailerons, rudder, tail camber flaps were all tested through the full range of movement, the altimeter (which could vary by seventy feet with barometric pressure) was set, and then, while holding the control column still with his right shoulder, in a most awkward stance, the pilot had to bend down to his left and, with both hands, set what was universally called 'that pernicious P.4 compass' to the ship's course.

Meanwhile, the observers received their final briefing from the Senior Observer in the chart-house (there was no briefing room): details of search patterns, patrol heights to fly (not normally above 6,000 feet), wind speed estimates (found by balloon), W/T frequencies to keep, and the ship's probable movements while the aircraft were away. As the observer manned his aircraft he would carry with him a large sack containing a chart-board, range finder, navigating notebook, code book (weighted), watch, dividers, parallel ruler, pencils and binoculars. Communication in those days between pilot, observer and TAG was by 'Gosport' speaking tube, linking the cockpits.

When the steam jet forward showed the wind directly down the flight deck, and with the Affirmative signal from the Wingco above, the Flight Deck Officer would dispatch each aircraft individually. On taking departure from the ship, each aircraft would climb to patrol height independently. As soon as all aircraft were away, and it was clear that nobody needed to make an emergency return and landing, the flight deck parties would fall out, one watch remaining at immediate notice for flying operations. Then, depending upon reports from the 111Fs or upon the day's flying programme, Ripons and/or Flycatchers were ranged.

Although the ship's Flights came under the command of the RAF ashore when at Hal Far, their training and fleet duties were, by mutual consent, handled and controlled by the ship. It was the duty of the ship's Senior Observer to coordinate the weekly flying programme and agree the serials with the staff of the C-in-C Mediterranean. The weekly flying programme for fleet aircraft requirements was handled from Hal Far. The chain of command seemed vague and susceptible to misunderstandings and 'double bookings', but in practice it worked.

The numbers of aircraft which *Glorious* normally embarked was many more than could be operated without an airfield ashore, or a second carrier in company. The lack of airfields was a serious limitation on naval flying. Only Hal Far at Malta, and the RAF stations in Palestine and Egypt, at the extreme eastern end of the Mediterranean, were available for naval aircraft. Thus a great many days' flying had to be carried out in conjunction with Hal Far.

A typical day's flying programme for *Glorious* off Malta in the early 1930's was:

0800: Land on fighter squadron from Hal Far

0815-1115: Deck landing training for new pilots, ordered out from Hal Far as required

0900: Search and reconnaissance exercise for six Fairey 111Fs from Hal Far, briefed ashore, but working with the ship, and returning to Hal Far

1130: Fly off fighter patrol

1145: Ship acting as target for a 'light' torpedo attack by Ripons, mounted from Hal Far, and opposed by fighters

1215: Fighters attack splash target towed by the ship with practise bombs, before returning to Hal Far

1330-1530: High Angle firings by ship's guns at sleeve target towed by Fairey 111F from Hal Far, marked by other Fairey 111Fs observing the sleeve Ship anchors off Malta on completion

2000: Ship weighs anchor, to sea for night deck landing training

2400: Aircraft called up from Hal Far as required. Night shadowing exercise by one or more 111Fs from Hal Far. Ship anchors on completion.

Apart from the ramp level with the island, *Glorious'* flight deck was innocent of any impediment which could be called arresting gear. For landing, the ship steamed so as to provide some 30-35 knots wind speed directly down the flight deck. The aircraft would approach from astern at landing speed (some 50-55 knots for a 111F) and touch down on the flight deck. The Flycatcher had brakes but the other aircraft relied upon the pilot's judgment.

As soon as an aircraft touched down, seamen handlers who had been waiting and taking shelter at the edge of the flight deck ran out and grabbed the aircraft's wings, to bring it under control. Sometimes, when a pilot misjudged his approach or his landing speed, an aircraft might run forward as far as the semicircular forward edge of the flight deck, thus 'finding the D' in shove-ha'penny parlance, and the handlers had a long way to go. Sometimes, indeed, the aircraft ran right over the forward edge and landed on the lower flying-off deck below.

There was no crash barrier and therefore there could be no deck park of aircraft. One aircraft had to be struck down below and the lift returned to flight deck level before the next aircraft could land. If the after lift was used, a tail trolley would be placed under the tail skid and the aircraft wheeled backwards down the flight deck until it reached the lift, while the pilot opened his throttle as necessary to check the aircraft's progress.

Meanwhile the waiting aircraft flew round the ship 'in the groove' and when the Affirmative signal showed that the flight deck was clear and ready, the nearest aircraft turned out of the groove and approached to land on. The rate of landing on therefore depended upon the pilots' skill, the energy of the aircraft handlers, the speed of the lifts and, of course, on the Wingco's nerve. Beyond a certain point there was little scope for improvement. But a good rate between touch-downs for those days would be about two and a half minutes.

Amidships and on either side of the flight deck were the 'palisades', formidably constructed barriers of wire and steel set out at an angle of 45 degrees from the deck edges. These were designed to catch an aircraft and prevent it sliding or falling over the side into the sea. They were intended as safety measures, but they could themselves be dangerous if an aircraft touched them after the pilot had decided to 'go round again' for another landing.

An aircraft in the 'palisades' had to be lifted out by sheer legs. These were rigged by a 'Seamen's Sheer Legs Party', who were freed from all other duties and had their work in their part of ships arranged so that they could reach the flight deck when piped with a minimum of delay. For night flying the Sheer Legs Party were closed up on the flight deck at all times while flying was taking place.

Aircrew, and especially Flycatcher pilots, were always seeking ways to lighten the tedium of their days. There was an alternative method of flying off Flycatchers: six of them started their engines in the small forward hangar. When their engines were at full revolutions and the hangar air was blue with smoke, the forward door would be opened and the Flycatchers would take off, one by one, from the lower flying-off deck. Even this was too dull for some, who would indulge themselves in a quick, and totally illicit, roll as soon as they left the deck, replying on the forward edge of the flight deck above to hide them from the gaze of the Wingco on the bridge.

CHAPTER 2: BLUE AND GOLD — FLYING DAYS IN THE MEDITERRANEAN

THE MEDITERRANEAN FLEET which *Glorious* joined in 1930 was just emerging, under the new C-in-C, Admiral Sir Ernie Chatfield, from a long period in which 'staff control' had been taken to ludicrous lengths. Under Field and Keyes, Chatfield's predecessors, every movement, every activity, of every man in every ship for every minute, hour and day was planned beforehand and had to be reported afterwards. There were daily, weekly, monthly and annual reports on a multitude of subjects, from the frequency of ships' boiler cleanings to the number of school hours worked by midshipmen. Ships had to signal on everything from fuel remaining at 8am to the composition of football, cricket or hockey teams and the numbers of spectators. If it came on to rain in Grand Harbour, neither officer of the watch nor even his captain dare order awnings to be sloped or guns covered until the flagship had signalled so to do. When it stopped raining, no ship dare dry up decks or uncover guns until the flagship had spoken.

When Chatfield first took his fleet to sea he looked at the detailed orders left by his predecessor 'in amazement. I read that the fleet would leave harbour at 10am on the... Outside it would form into divisions in line ahead disposed to port... Sunset would be at... All this in the minutest detail.' This, as Chatfield said, was 'staff work run mad' 'I said: "Who can tell me at 5pm tomorrow if the fleet will be able to do what is here laid down? There may be thick weather or a steamer crossing our track or a hundred and one events that may make it not the best thing to do". I told James [the Chief of Staff] to tear it up. I would not train the Fleet in this way.'

Chatfield was particularly interested in the potential of air power at sea. (He was himself to be the chief instrument through which the Navy was eventually to regain its air arm.) For naval aviation the 1920s and 1930s were times of innovation, for exploring and discussing a new weapon's possibilities and limits. 'We were the generation, with experience of the First World War, who were determined to put right the errors and omissions we had met,' wrote Geoffrey Gowlland, a young observer who joined *Glorious* as a Lieutenant (O) at Malta in February, 1931. 'We felt we were the *avant garde*, the forward lookers, the pioneers.'

In 1924 the newly-completed and trail-blazing *Eagle* took part in several eye-opening exercises in the Mediterranean. '*Eagle* brought off an excellent torpedo-plane attack,' Captain Barry Domvile, Chief of Staff to the C-in-C in *Queen Elizabeth*, wrote in his diary in July, 1924. 'I believe the first or second from a carrier — three hits out of five — then fighters arrived unexpectedly and strafed us — a most amazing spectacle — very enterprising to have eleven machines away together.'

In the Mediterranean in August, 1926, *Eagle*'s aircraft on a sortie which lasted for four hours and twenty minutes located a convoy seventy miles from their carrier. The position they reported was actually only one and a half miles in error. In March, 1927, an exercise report noted that 'all opposing enemy forces were quickly found and reported with accuracy, although visibility was never more than 17,000 yards (8½ nautical miles) and sometimes as low as 15,000 yards.' In the Atlantic the same month an enemy battlefleet was found and reported, within eight miles of its actual position, by aircraft who were then ninety miles from their own carrier and battlefleet — an extraordinary and invaluable piece of reconnaissance for that time. In March, 1928, Bisons from *Furious* penetrated to a distance of 111 miles and sent off their enemy sighting report eighty minutes after leaving their carrier. One Fairey 111F located and bombed *Eagle* at a range of 115 miles.

Successful bombing and torpedo attacks by aircraft were often discounted by the gunnery branch, on the grounds that 'in action' capital ships in particular would put up a volume of defensive fire such as effectively to prevent aircraft pressing home their attacks. Time would show.

Meanwhile, naval thinking in the 1930s as at all other times, and on naval aviation, as on other subjects, was both reactionary and radical. In 1930 Captain Bernard Acworth DSO, an ex-submariner and a widely read if not so widely respected writer on naval affairs, wrote in *The Navies of Today and Tomorrow* that '*Flying, whatever aeronauts may say* (author's italics) *is not in itself a whole-time profession for me*. In peacetime, it may be frankly admitted, seaplanes available for picnics, shooting parties, or as substitutes for captains' galleys when lying at anchor far from shore, would be fun.' On the other hand, the Henry Leigh Carslake Essay Prize, instituted in 1927 in memory of an observer lost when his Bison from *Hermes* failed to return from a flight off Malta on 21 October, 1926, had for its set subject in 1929 'The employment of aircraft as adjuncts to cruisers on trade routes'; in 1931 a forward-looking 'The employment of aircraft in convoy protection from attacks by aircraft and submarines'; and in 1933 a concept relevant in the Second World War, 'The management of large forces at sea involving several carriers'.

After Christmas, 1930, at Malta, *Glorious* embarked her aircraft and sailed on 8 January, 1931, for exercises in the

Adriatic, in rough weather which prevented flying for twenty-four hours. (In those days flying stopped in any sea state which prevented the two attendant destroyers, one stationed on each quarter of the carrier, from lowering a 'crash boat' to recover the crew of a ditched aircraft.)

On passage Flight Lieutenants Duggan and Madden of 447 Fairey 111F Flight carried out night deck landings. These were by no means new in the Navy: the first on any. carrier was by a Blackburn Dart flown by Flight Lieutenant Boyce RAF on *Furious* on 1 July, 1926, and the first fighter landings were by Flycatchers flown by Cathcart-Jones and Flying Officer Geary RAF on *Courageous*, off Malta on 26 November, 1929. 447 Flight had already made night landings at Gosport in 1929 and had just exercised with the flare path at Hal Far.

But flying from the ship was quite different: 'As I hurtled under full throttle up the incline to the forward lift,' wrote Madden, 'and on reaching it being hurled into the air at an accelerating speed, I experienced for the first time the sensation of flying into the blackness of the night ahead of the ship and having nothing on which to orient myself.'

The night was calm and fine and as the 111Fs made steep turns to the right, the brightly-lit carrier came into view below, so that the pilots were able to judge their aircraft's altitude by the ship light. After some 'dummy runs', there came the actual landing. 'The flight deck, with its ten or so floodlights on either side, throwing an ice-cold-looking light over the deck seemed to have another dimension by night. It was like a huge lighted table moving away ahead of one, with complete blackness ahead of it.'

Although Madden had some difficulty reading his instruments in the shaded cockpit light and in judging his height as he approached (he recommended a bright light on the after end of the island, which was later adopted), he and Duggan got down safely. Many 'goofers' expected night flying accidents: 'One of the memories of that night was the sea of faces in the nets either side of the flight deck. One often heard the remark, "Oh hullo, have you come to see the blood?".' But there was no blood. Madden completed more than fifty night deck landings without incident between January, 1931, and the summer of 1933.

Glorious' first major exercise, from 15 to 17 January, was designed to test the fleet's defences in harbour against air attack. This was a scenario which constantly preoccupied the fleet in the 1930s, and it was exercised again and again. Thus, the air attack on the Italian fleet at Taranto in November, 1940, was not a sudden inspiration — although its execution was certainly inspired. A whole naval generation had exercised it many times.

Glorious was 'Blue', and the 'Red' fleet included *Eagle*. There was some understandable rivalry between *Eagle's* 'old hands' and *Glorious'* 'new boys'. *Glorious* closed Zante, on the west coast of Greece, during the night of 14th/15th and flew off 111Fs at dawn to search for the 'Red' Fleet. Her Ripons made a torpedo attack on *Eagle* at 10.20. that morning, which *Eagle* evaded by stopping engines and going full astern.

The 'Red' fleet was discovered, at anchor, in Port Drepano, a narrow bay surrounded by hills, opening off the Gulf of Corinth. *Glorious'* Ripon Flights, 461 and 462, made separate attacks, five minutes apart, unobserved, and claimed seven torpedo hits. The umpires allowed five: two on *Queen Elizabeth*, the flagship, reducing her speed (in the umpires' opinions) by eight knots; one each on *Revenge* and *Royal Oak*, reducing their speeds by one knot; and one on the cruiser *Devonshire*, reducing her speed by four knots. (War experience was to show the optimism of these judgments.) Three Ripons were adjudged 'shot down'.

It was *Eagle* who began the next day, 16 January, with a bombing attack on *Glorious*, which *Glorious* evaded by increasing speed and using full helm. But the rest of the day belonged to *Glorious*. Her Flycatchers strafed *Eagle*'s flight deck, the upper deck and exposed personnel of the battleships, and the fleet observations posts (a primitive substitute for airguard radar) placed around Drepano. Her Fairey 111Fs bombed and her Ripons attacked so successfully that the staff report commented: 'It is doubtful whether gunfire would have been effective before the torpedoes were dropped'.

The flying was watched with admiration by Lieutenant Commander A.F.C. Layard, commanding *Wakeful*, one of *Glorious*' attendant destroyers (the other was *Voyager*, commanded by Commander Tom Troubridge). 'At daylight *Glorious* started flying off,' he wrote. 'They flew on and off all day and every machine went up three times and the last one finally landed on just at sunset and every one a perfect landing. It was most impressive.'

From dawn to dusk was about a twelve-hour flying day. From exercise records it can be deduced that *Glorious* had about thirty aircraft embarked — her full complement, less one Flight of Flycatchers and one of 111Fs. To launch and recover the whole air group three times meant some ninety sorties which in one twelve-hour day was, for 1931, an excellent performance.

On 18 January *Glorious* and her two destroyers arrived at Kotor, in Yugoslavia, for a ten-day visit, *Glorious* herself anchoring in the bay, while the destroyers secured to buoys off the naval base at Trivat. This, the first of many formal foreign visits, had a familiar pre-war agenda: Dashwood Moir and the destroyer captains paid calls ashore which were returned by local dignitaries. The sailors landed to play football and sample the local *ouzo*. There was sailing, fishing, car trips to see the local sights and a parade to pay respects to the local saint. On the last day some hundred Yugoslav naval officers and petty officers came to sea for a 'Shop Window' flying display: the Flycatchers did aerobatics and stunts, the Ripons 'dry' torpedo attacks, the 111Fs bombing runs. The Yugoslavs eventually disembarked, loudly proclaiming the quality of *Glorious*' flying and the potency of her gin.

Flying Officer Peter Cracroft, of 408 Flight, was sufficiently inspired by the Yugoslav visit to land on his Flycatcher attired as his *alter ego*, in false beard and cossack hat, 'Don Pedro Kracovitch'. This appearance was warmly welcomed by the sailors on the flight deck but when Don Pedro reached the bridge (having taken the precaution of first removing his hat and beard) he was told, somewhat stiffly, 'not to behave like that'.

Peter Cracroft was one of many RAF officers who thoroughly enjoyed carrier life. Whatever political thunderings went on over their heads, however Their Lordships might address Their Airships, no matter what Lord Beatty might say to Lord Trenchard, each calling to each like mastodons across the primeval deep, the RN and the RAF on board ship got on extremely well together.

The RAF had to undergo what Cracroft called 'a wonderful course at Leuchars, to teach you how to behave on board', but most RN and RAF, as Cracroft said, 'took to each other as though we were brothers'. There were, of course, some senior Flight Lieutenants who had flown operationally in the war, who used to delight in saying, 'I'm going up to bed now', talking of 'upstairs and downstairs', calling guard-rails 'banisters' and pretending not to know the sharp end of the ship from the blunt. One such was described by a naval observer, Lieutenant M.O.W. Miller, as 'Haddon, who wore a moustache to make certain he wasn't mistaken for a naval officer. Gosh! How that chap loathed the Navy! He always referred to his cabin in the ship as his "cell", and called a cruise "three months' hard"'. When standing drinks to celebrate his newly-born son, he told a crowded wardroom bar, 'If the little beggar misbehaves himself, I know what I'll say to him. "You little beggar," I'll say, "if you do that again I'll send you to Dartmouth," and if that doesn't shut him up I don't know what will!'

But there were many more Cracrofts than there were Haddons. The RAF might have been excused for gently nudging some of their weaker brethren towards service afloat, especially as it involved some financial penalties such as loss of marriage allowance in certain cases. But the RAF officers in the fleet were, as their naval colleagues said, 'the pick of Cranwell', and they were not above leg-pulling their own side. RAF officers in the fleet wore a distinctive badge, an anchor surrounded by a wreath, on their left sleeves. Wearing this badge was known, as Cracroft put it, as 'gaining the feathered arsehole'. One RAF officer, challenged on parade by an air marshal, looked down and saw that his anchor had dropped out. 'That's quite in order, sir,' he said. 'We always unship the anchor when we're ashore!'

Glorious returned to Grand Harbour on 30 January, 1931, very well pleased with events, and held a celebration 'Gala'. The officers had a dance on 27 February, the ship's company the following night, for which both hangars were transformed, with a ballroom, palm court and lounge in the lower hangar, and 'Shoat Street' (after Malta's hybrid sheep-goats) with a theatre, the 'Glory Arms', a police station in the upper hangar and side-shows. According to Layard, 'Every officer in the ship was either running a side-show or acting as waiter and the whole organization was superb, and it was undoubtedly the outstanding social event of the year.'

On 13 March *Glorious* arrived at Gibraltar for the combined Atlantic and Mediterranean Fleet exercises in which nearly a hundred ships (a not unusual number in those days) were to take part. The Atlantic Fleet was led by its C-in-C, Admiral Sir Michael Hodge, flying his flag in *Nelson*, with *Rodney*, *Warspite* (flag of Rear-Admiral C.J.C. Little) *Malaya* and *Valiant* of the 2nd Battle Squadron. The Battle cruiser Squadron was commanded by Vice-Admiral Dudley Pound, flying his flag in *Renown*, with *Repulse* and *Tiger*. There were also *Courageous*, with destroyers *Tetrarch* and *Sesame*; four cruisers of the 2nd Cruiser Squadron; seventeen destroyers of the 5th and 6th Flotillas; the 2nd Submarine Flotilla, of five boats, with the depot ship *Lucia*; and *Snapdragon*, the fleet target recovery vessel.

The Mediterranean Fleet was led by Chatfield in *Queen Elizabeth*, with *Royal Oak*, *Royal Sovereign*, *Revenge* (flag of Vice-Admiral Sir William Fisher), *Resolution* and *Ramillies* of the 1st Battle Squadron; also *Glorious*, seven cruisers of the 1st and 3rd Cruiser Squadrons, thirty-one destroyers of the 1st, 2nd, 3rd and 4th Flotillas, led by Rear-Admiral (D) C.M. Forbes in *Coventry*, the 1st Submarine Flotilla, of five boats, with the depot ships *Cyclops* and *Douglas*, the repair ship *Resource* and the hospital ship *Maine*.

Red Land, in the West Indies, with the Azores, Canaries and Madeira as colonies and a base for the Red (Atlantic) Fleet at Funchal, was at war with Blue Land, in the Mediterranean, with a base for the Blue (Mediterranean) Fleet at Gibraltar. Both sides sought to attack the other's vital trade routes and both adopted the convoy system. It is not strictly true, as has been said, that the Navy had no convoy exercises between the wars. Convoy exercises were held most years, but the threat to a convoy was taken to be surface raiders, not U-boats. Aircraft searched for and attacked surface ships with bombs or torpedoes, rather than submarines with depth-charges. Convoys were represented by a single ship or a small group of ships. Exercises involving convoys of several ships in columns, with escorts' defence and counter-attack against submarines, were not held.

Once again, *Glorious* had a good exercise. Her 111Fs found the Red 'raider' *Repulse* only five minutes after she had entered the 'trade route area' and her Ripons, after a flight of an hour and a half through heavy rain squalls and poor visibility, attacked with torpedoes and were adjudged to have scored one hit. While detached for flying, *Glorious* was escorted everywhere by the battleship *Royal Sovereign*. Chatfield and his staff were well aware that a carrier's force was in her aircraft. By herself she was almost helpless. A carrier had to go where the wind took her, which was not necessarily, indeed very rarely, with the rest of the fleet. When she was flying her aircraft on or off, a carrier needed protection from any surface ship larger than a destroyer.

After the exercises, both fleets repaired to Gibraltar where, with nearly a hundred ships alongside or in Algeciras Bay, the bars and sports grounds were soon busy. Exercise results were analysed by the staffs and then explained to ship's officers and petty officers at post-mortems, or 'wash-tips', in the old Coal Shed on the mole. There were staff conferences, exchanges of visits between the ten admirals and one commodore present, parades, regattas, football matches, races on the Gibraltar course, swimming at Rosia Bay, a day out for some with the

Royal Calpe Hunt, picnics in the corkwoods near Algeciras, a point-to-point in which Chatfield, aged 57, rode his first race, (and fell off) and trips across the border to La Linea and the bullfight. Wardrooms dined each other for old acquaintance, while gunrooms raided each other for trophies.

On Sunday, 29 March Dashwood Moir said his farewell to the ship in a speech to the ship's company at Sunday Divisions on the flight deck. He had emerged from his somewhat dour shell in *Glorious*. He liked aircrew and gave them sound advice: to make the utmost use of their spare time from flying duties, so as to fit themselves for wider naval life. For Moir, his leave-taking was an emotional experience and it was Edwards who quickly dismissed Divisions to save his Captain embarrassment. Moir retired, being promoted Rear Admiral and appointed ADC that year. He was promoted Vice-Admiral on the retired list in 1936 and died on 8 August, 1942.

Moir's successor was Charles Kennedy-Purvis, known as 'K-P', who was then 46 years old, with nine years seniority as a Captain. He came of a naval family. His father, Lieutenant Charles Kennedy-Purvis, of HMS *Penelope*, had lost a foot serving with the Naval Brigade in Egypt in 1882. K-P had a technical mind and specialized in torpedoes, getting five 'firsts' in his sub-lieutenants' courses, and coming top of his specialist 'T' course. In those days torpedomen also looked after a ship's electrical systems and K-P, unusually for an executive naval officer of his day, was a Member of the Institute of Electrical Engineers.

K-P was a large, cheerful, red-faced man, whom his Navigating Officer, Lieutenant-Commander Godfrey French, described as 'brilliant and utterly lovable. If he wanted something done, he would tell someone to do it and let them get on with it. He did not, as so many senior officers do, tell them what he wanted done, then tell them how to do it, and then stand over them while they tried to do it.' K-P was equally successful with the aircrew. 'He had a remarkable capacity for being "on our side",' said Gowlland. 'I remember, at the conference in the flagship after a Battle Squadron full calibre firing, K-P took none of the credit accorded to the ship's aircrafts' accurate reporting, but, from his chair in the front row, turned round and gave each of his observers a broad grin.'

K-P's cheerfulness was severely tested on 1 April, his first day at sea in *Glorious*, when she and other ships sailed north-east along the Spanish coast for exercises. There had been some earlier fog, but it had cleared into a beautiful day of sunshine, with the mountains of Andalusia clearly outlined to port, and schools of porpoises gambolling in the ship's bow wave. By 3.50 *Glorious* had twenty-seven aircraft — ten Ripons, three 111Fs and fourteen Flycatchers — in the air.

Glorious was then some sixty miles east of Gibraltar and surrounded by ships: two attendant destroyers astern, three 'C' Class cruisers of the 3rd Squadron on the starboard bow, and, ten miles on the port quarter, four battleships of the 1st Battle Squadron, which the Ripons and 111Fs were to attack. Also on *Glorious'* port quarter, some six or seven miles away, was the French liner SS *Florida*, 12,000 tons, bound from Buenos Aires to Genoa with about 530 passengers, mostly migrants returning to Italy, and a crew of 161. She had been in sight from *Glorious* for some time, steering 0750, which was almost parallel but slightly converging on *Glorious'* mean course.

By 3.55 *Glorious* was steaming at 20 knots so as to provide enough wind over the flight deck to land on five Flycatchers. Abel-Smith reported there was fog ahead and in a short time it came on, in French's words, 'an absolute pea soup'.

Normally a ship slows down or stops in fog. But *Glorious* had twenty-two aircraft still in the air. K-P had to consider them and their crews. He could either steam on to the east, hoping the fog would soon thin, or he could turn back, run through the fog which seemed to be drifting westwards with the wind, turn back into the wind and land the aircraft on.

K-P chose to turn back and ordered the helm hard-a-port (which in those days still meant that the ship turned hard to *starboard*) and the starboard screws slow astern, to help the ship round, only for French (who had himself only just joined the ship and had one previous day at sea with Moir) to point out that the 'C' Class cruisers were on *Glorious'* beam and within her turning circle. K-P at once reversed the turn and *Glorious* steadied on a course of 230° at 9 knots and sounding her fog siren.

The whistle of a steamship was heard about three points (33°) forward of the starboard beam. K-P ordered engines stopped and then, while *Glorious'* fog siren was still sounding, full astern and finally, all engines emergency full astern. But *Glorious* still had way on when SS *Florida* came into view, between two and three hundred yards ahead, on the starboard bow but crossing to port.

Florida's master, Captain Raymond Blanc, said he had entered the main fog bank at about 4.20 and began to sound his whistle. His speed, he said, was about 7 knots. At 4.28pm *Florida's* people heard one long blast on their port bow. Captain Blanc ordered hard-a-port, thus turning to *starboard*. After sounding one short blast, he heard an answering three short blasts and ordered full speed astern. Shortly afterwards *Glorious* came into sight on the port bow, about 100 to 200 metres away.

The collision was at 4.29½pm. *Glorious'* engine-room log recorded 'Slight bump felt'. Fagan, the RAF signals officer, in his cabin aft, also felt a bump and said: 'What ho! Somebody's navigation gone wrong!' Madden was standing on the quarterdeck: 'The air was "thick" with the sound of aero engines diving down or passing low overhead in the fog. Next there was an enormous impact as if the ship had run aground at full speed against a cliff... and then another kind of *ringing* sound, the sound of the metal in the ship's side and the sides of the hangar being compressed and decelerated.'

Glorious' bow inflicted a terrible blow upon *Florida's* port side, cutting a wedge sixty-two feet deep and twenty feet wide at an angle of 6½ degrees. Twenty-two passengers (some reports said thirty-one, and two of the crew), most of them standing by the rail, were killed. *Glorious* suffered one casualty, Ordinary Seaman Ernest John Bicker, the fog lookout on watch on the lower flying-off deck. When he saw *Florida's* bows emerging from the fog, he ran to the telephone to report and was crushed where he stood. *Glorious'* stem was smashed bodily over to port with very extensive structural damage from the flight deck down to the keelson, with buckling of frames aft to No 10 bulkhead, ninety-four feet from the bow.

The noise of engines was from aircraft diving low to attract attention. 'We had seen it all going to happen,' said Lieutenant J.B. Heath, of 441 111F Flight. 'The ships were on a constant bearing... We watched this dreadful thing going on... We tried to get through to the ship... People were diving and firing all the Very lights in the world.'

Cracroft, in his Flycatcher, also saw the collision and, having no means of communicating with ships except visual waving and gesticulating, took even more drastic action. 'I could see other ships heading straight for this collision. So I had to do something pretty desperate. As a last resort I parked my Flycatcher in the sea in front of *Broke*, the leading destroyer. At least it stopped the rest of the ships coming on.' Cracroft was later awarded the AFC.

As the fog shredded away, those on *Glorious*' bridge could look down and see the bows still embedded in the liner's side. Clearly there was extensive damage, and very probably heavy loss of life. 'K-P leaned back against the bridge,' said French, 'put his arms against the guardrail and said, "Well, I've always had a little angel up aloft who looked after me all my life. He seems to have deserted me today." And that was the only recrimination anybody ever heard from him.'

Four Flycatchers ran out of fuel and ditched. Seventeen aircraft flew ashore to Chiriana, near Malaga. The destroyers *Wryneck* and *Verity* took *Florida* in tow, stern first, at slow speed to Malaga, accompanied by *Glorious*, who had *Florida*'s passengers and crew aboard and landed them at Malaga, before returning to Gibraltar on 2 April.

Glorious' damaged bows had been forced so far downwards that she ran aground and divers had to clear away wreckage before she could go alongside. A temporary wooden bow was fitted and a coffer-dam erected across the forward bulkheads, and *Glorious* left on 23 May for permanent repairs in Malta.

The Chief Constructor at Gibraltar evidently had a somewhat sardonic sense of humour. When *Glorious* left he presented her with a small horn of the type fitted on a child's bicycle, which went 'poop poop' when it was pressed. It was mounted on a wooden stand, with the inscription: 'To Be Sounded By *Glorious* When Sighting Any Ship In The Mediterranean'. Later it was silver-plated and used at wardroom guest night dinners instead of the customary mess president's gavel. In those days, as French said, 'it all ran on laughter'.

So, for a second summer, *Glorious* arrived in Malta for lengthy repairs. Her absence from the fleet was a serious setback for Chatfield. Many exercises were forward-looking: 'The attack and defence of a convoy, cruisers searching and shadowing, exercising the disposition of a covering force as convoy escort' and 'To continue the investigation of the attack and defence of a fleet in harbour, including a test of anti-gas organization'. But too many others still had echoes of Jutland: 'Capital ships engaging, with dusk coming on' had an antique ring to it, suggesting the title of a painting of an old sea battle. Exercise programmes with serials such as 'Possible night action between capital ships' and 'Superior force trying to cut off an inferior, including night action between capital ships' badly needed an aircraft carrier to inject some variety.

For *Glorious*, however, there were compensations. Malta has a very pleasant climate in May and June. The spring rains have finished, there is normally a cooling north-westerly breeze and the sun has yet to achieve the torrid heat of August. The island is at its best, with tiny walled fields, parched brown in summer, still bright green, and street flower-stalls piled with red, white and deep purple anemones, arum lilies, violets with their unmistakeable scent, bluebells as big as hyacinths, and great bunches of roses.

Roses of another kind came out every summer from England. Many naval wives joined their husbands in Malta and often brought with them their younger sisters, their cousins or their nieces. The ships were there to dance on and there were plenty of young bachelor officers as partners. Many a ship-born romance turned into marriage, although the Navy had a somewhat bleak terminology for this female influx. The hopeful girls were known as the 'fishing fleet', the ladies' lounge in the Union Club, Valetta, was 'the snake pit', and the ladies' swimming pool at the Sliema Club was the 'Pool of Disillusionment'.

When the ships sailed, wives and 'fishing fleet' went to the breakwater to wave goodbye, but there were still the RAF and the Fleet Air Arm at Hal Far, and the 'brutal and licentious soldiery' to organize swimming parties, or dancing or dalliance. One young RAF officer, who had to go home for a course, proposed to leave his very pretty wife in the charge of a noted Fleet Air Arm philanderer. But first he asked his flight commander's advice. 'Well, put it this way,' was the reply, 'if I had a bag of buns, I wouldn't give it to an elephant to keep.'

Pre-war, Malta had a social whirl which lives on still as a glow in the memories of those who enjoyed it. Valetta, and the three cities of Senglea, Cospicua and Vittorioso, studded with great yellow stone fortresses all built to withstand a siege, looked like the back-drop to an opera. Dawn in Grand Harbour, with early sun on the battlements, church bells tolling and the cries of goatherds, was like the opening of the last act of *Tosca*.

In Malta there was a party, a dance or a reception almost every night on board a ship, or at the C-in-C's residence, Admiralty House in Valetta, or at the Admiral Superintendent's house in Vittorioso, or in the resident regimental garrison mess, dancing at the Sliema Club, dinner and 'cad's bridge' in somebody's house. By day there was football at Corradino, shooting at Ricasoli, swimming in St Paul's Bay, tennis and golf at the Marsa, and polo for those who could afford it. Under Keyes, polo acquired importance for naval officers; everyone knew what was meant by a 'polo promotion'. There were also picnics on the coast, visits to San Antonio Gardens and to the

Opera House in Strada Reale where leading companies from Rome and Naples played; some wardrooms took season tickets. There was always cheap drink: Marsavin, the local wine, or 'Red Infuriator', or, for picnics, 'sloggers' — sloe gin. For the sailor there was cricket or football at Corradino, followed by 'babies' heads' (a particular type of steak and kidney pudding) washed down by Farson's Beer at 2 Vid (old-style pence) a pint. Strada Stretta in Valetta, better known as 'The Gut', with its legendary ladies, was still in full swing, with a second 'Gut' for variety in Floriana.

By September, 1931, *Glorious'* bow had been repaired and the ship sailed for exercises with the fleet off Cyprus on the 21st. There had been a few fatal flying accidents, but on 2 October, off Famagusta, a Ripon flown by Lieutenant-Commander A.G. Elliot, commanding 461 Flight, dived vertically into the sea from level flight. There was little wreckage and no sign of Elliot or his observer, Lieutenant-Commander Bennie. Soon afterwards there was a similar accident when a Ripon flown by Lieutenant M.T. Cowin made a fast, shallow dive from about 1,000 feet towards its hangar at Hal Far, as though to signal that it was about to land. But the aircraft dived vertically into rocky ground outside the airfield boundary.

Investigation showed that a Ripon's tailplane ailerons could 'wind' themselves forward into a 'dive' position. Once a dive had begun no amount of pulling back on the joystick could correct it. A pilot would need thousands of feet in height to give himself time to wind back the controls.

Neither Elliot nor Bennie nor Cowin wore parachutes, which until 1931 had no quick-release gear, making them unpopular with aircrew who might have to use them over the sea, because there was a danger of being encumbered by the harness in the water. After years of requests and complaints by naval aircrew, a quick-release harness was fitted in 1931, but only two parachutes per aircraft were issued, even for 111Fs which had a crew of three. (No official guidance was given on which crew member was supposed to descend without a parachute; aircrews presumed it would 'probably go in order of seniority').

On 24 October, off Cape Elephanisi on the north coast of Crete, the three Ripon Flights, 461, 462 and 460, escorted by two of the Flycatcher Flights, 405 and 406, made a Class 'A' torpedo attack, dropping real torpedoes set to hit (but with collapsible heads), on the 1st Battle Squadron of *Ramillies*, *Royal Sovereign* and *Resolution*, (the flagship *Queen Elizabeth* was at sea but was not to be attacked).

As the Ripons spread out for their attack, the Flycatchers were ordered ahead at about four miles' range to strafe the battleships' upper decks and keep their gunners' heads down whilst the Ripons closed. The Flycatchers were some twenty seconds too late, but the Ripons' attacks were still effective. Fourteen torpedoes were dropped within the space of two minutes, thirteen aimed at *Resolution*, the leading ship, and one at *Ramillies*, the middle ship.

The battleships were making 19 knots, and still working up to full speed, when they took avoiding action, alternate ships turning 45° to port or starboard. The Ripon pilots actually saw the signal flags for this manoeuvre being hoisted one minute before it was executed and were able to exploit the information, although several pilots could not reach the best position to release torpedoes because of the screening destroyers of the 4th Flotilla, and there was some overcrowding among the aircraft, especially on the starboard side.

Nevertheless, of the torpedoes aimed at *Resolution*, four hit her port side, three her starboard side, four missed ahead and one astern. The one torpedo aimed at *Ramillies* hit her port side. The thirteenth torpedo aimed at *Resolution*, which had been dropped unaimed and very high, to avoid risk of collision between aircraft, ran on well and was recovered with a crushed head, having apparently hit *Royal Sovereign*, a mile on *Resolution*'s starboard side.

Although surprise had been lost, as Kennedy-Purvis later wrote in his report, because the Ripons had been sighted while they were circling over Cape Elephanisi, 'The attacks had been well pressed home and there was a high percentage of hits'. In war *Resolution* would have been sunk and *Royal Sovereign* and *Ramillies* damaged, in what would have been a major success for the aircraft. However, aircrew knew from bitter experience that much of their achievement would be discounted. 'Our dropping range was eight hundred yards, our height fifty feet,' said Lieutenant A.S. Bolt, who joined *Glorious* as an observer in January, 1932. 'But it didn't matter how many hits you achieved on the battleships, they always said, "Oh it'll be quite different when all the guns are firing at them, they'll never come as close as that".'

Glorious returned to Grand Harbour on 26 October, again well pleased with events, as indeed was the whole fleet. Chatfield had just directed his subordinate admirals to address their commands, ship by ship, to express his appreciation of the fleet's steadiness under the severe test of discipline caused by that year's cuts in pay. This was a pointed reference to events at Invergordon in September, 1931, when, after one weekend of increasing uncertainty and unrest during which proposed cuts in service pay were announced, a proportion of the ship's companies of the Atlantic Fleet at Invergordon refused to take their ships to sea.

The cuts proposed bore particular hardly on the lower rates. An able seaman's pay was to be cut from four to three shillings a day. For many men, paying rent for their homes and having many goods and furniture on hire purchase, such a savage cut in income represented ruin. The pay cuts were a gross and cynical breach by politicians of firm undertakings previously given to the Navy, but they were promulgated to the fleet by the Admiralty in such a feckless and insensitive manner as to exacerbate the situation.

It was a very polite mutiny and no violence was offered, although it sent a seismic and long-lasting shock throughout the Navy and the country. But there was no unrest of any such kind in the Mediterranean.

In the rigid, inward-looking, hierarchical and fiercely conservative Royal Navy of 1931, every sailor abided within strict limits of what he might and might not do, and where and when he might do it. For work, sport, welfare and ceremonial, the ship's company was divided, literally, into 'divisions', each with divisional officers and chief petty officers. In *Glorious*, the seamen were divided into Fo'c'sle, Top and Quarterdeck Divisions (names which dated from the days of sail). There were also a Boys' and Gunnery Ratings' Division; Torpedo and Electrical Artificers; a Central Division, of regulating and sick berth staff; quartermasters and artisans, who included such as the blacksmith, coppersmith, plumber and the shipwrights; a supply Division, of writers, stores assistants, cooks and stewards; the Engine-room Department; the Fleet Air Arm, headquarter and flights; and the Royal Marine detachment, under their own Corps officers and NCOs. RAF personnel formed a separate Division, again with their own warrant officers and senior NCOs.

Shipboard life followed a time-honoured routine, with a series of rituals and procedures. Watches changed every four hours, except between 4 and 8pm, when the First and Last Dog watches were only two hours each. 'Up spirits' for rum was piped at 11.30, hands to dinner (*not* lunch) at noon. Evening quarters was at four, rounds at eight and pipe down at 9.30pm. Divisions were held on the flight deck on Sundays, and Captain's rounds. Make and mend, when the ship's company secured from work at dinner time, was on Thursday. Clean hammocks were slung on the first and third Fridays of every month. The ship's company was paid at a formal pay parade, held once a fortnight on Thursdays at midday in the lower hangar or on the battery decks.

The rum issue was a daily ritual. The tot was one gill, an eighth of a pint. Chiefs and petty officers had theirs neat, leading rates and below had 'grog', two parts of water to one of rum, a mixture which was supposed to go sour in time and thus prevent hoarding. A tot was powerful currency on a man-o'war. A sailor would do another's day of duty, keep his watch, dhoby his clothes, cut his hair, mend his shoes, all for a tot. There was a sliding scale of rewards, from 'sippers' (a self-explanatory term), through 'gulpers' to the whole tot. Many married men preferred the threepence a day, paid in lieu of the tot. It was also a sad fact, for which every commanding and divisional officer would vouch, that more rates and good conduct badges were lost, more prospects spoiled and more careers ruined, over rum than any other single cause.

Tobacco was issued, in half-pound tins, or in leaf, every fortnight. In the 1930s there were still many sailors who could make up their own leaf tobacco for their pipes, or roll their own cigarettes, or 'ticklers'. The tobacco was excellent and duty-free, one shilling and tenpence the pound. Sailors could only smoke in prescribed places (not normally their messdecks) and at prescribed times; in *Glorious*, until 'Out Pipes', on the fo'c'sle, the upper hangar deck, the flight deck in harbour, the ship's company recreation space, and beside the guns. Officers could smoke on the battery deck aft, on the seaplane platform and on the quarterdeck at certain times. The after lift-well could be converted into a 'cinema', with a hole cut in one bulkhead for the projector and smoking was normally allowed during the film-show.

For every eventuality there was a drill — for the guns, torpedoes, the flight deck, the sea-boat, fire-fighting, for entering and leaving harbour — and for retrieving a crashed aircraft from the sea. The sea-boat (whose crew, for this drill, had to include a Fleet Air Arm officer) took a large 5" grass rope (which floated) which was bent on to some protruding part, normally the tailplane. The sea-boat towed the still-submerged aircraft to a 'salvage position' at the forward end of the starboard battery. The grass was replaced by a steel wire which was rove through the head of the starboard forward crane and then led to a winch on the port side of the lower flying-off deck. Very slowly, to avoid doing any further damage, the winch hauled the aircraft out of the water to the cranehead which then swung and allowed the aircraft to be lowered down on to the deck.

There was a drill for abandoning ship. At the pipe 'Both Watches for Exercise, prepare to abandon ship', the officer of the watch would inform the engineroom and the main switchboard. Boats' crews would run out and lower their boats. Seamen stationed in the Carley Floats would trice up and lower floats. The quartermasters would provide boats' compasses, and the side party (responsible for the upkeep of the ship's boot-topping near the waterline) would hoist out their copper punt. The Supply Department would supply corned beef and biscuits. The Royal Marines, the Band, and stokers longest off watch would provide timber from the ship's stowages, the fo'c'slemen mess stools and tables from the Fleet Air Arm messdeck, the shipwrights would construct rafts and the torpedo party man the winches, while the engine-room department provided hydraulic pressure for cranes and lifts. The remainder of the ship's company, meanwhile, would fall in abreast their manning positions. On the command 'Abandon ship' the officers were to get men down into the boats and floats, taking care that they went down ladders and lifelines in an orderly manner, to prevent accidents.

Glorious spent Christmas, 1931, at Malta. K-P and the other officers did the traditional rounds, to admire the range and ingenuity of the messdeck decorations, and to accept, albeit gingerly, gifts of figgy-duff and cake. By some quirk of naval history, the sailors' menu in *Glorious* that day has survived: Breakfast. Porridge, bacon and eggs, butter and rolls, coffee. Dinner. Tomato soup, roast turkey, sausage meat, stuffing, new potatoes, cauliflower, Christmas pudding, apples, oranges, nuts. Tea. Iced Christmas cake, bread and butter. Supper. Cold roast pork, pickles, mince pies, bread and butter, cocoa.

On 16 January, 1932, Rear-Admiral R.G.H. Henderson arrived in Malta, flying his flag in *Courageous*. Henderson had been appointed the previous June as the first Admiral Aircraft Carriers (RAA) with responsibility for 'the tactical operations of the carriers and carrier-borne aircraft in the Atlantic Fleet' and to be the 'recognized adviser to other Fleets in all matters connected with the Fleet Air Arm'.

Reginald Henderson was one of the ablest officers of his generation. Though not a pilot, he had commanded *Furious* in a most successful commission in 1926-28, in which he had taken an enlightened view of the possibilities of aircraft at sea, realizing early on that many of the counter-claims by the gunnery branch were exaggerated or unrealistic. He was junior to many of the admirals then at sea, especially in the Mediterranean, but he argued the Fleet Air Arm's case with great skill and tact. Later, as Third Sea Lord and Controller, he did much to accelerate the carrier-building programme in time for war.

As RAA Henderson was an inspired choice and as he began to operate his two carriers in tandem, both ships keeping station 1½ miles on each other's beam and turning in and out of the wind together, it was no wonder that *Glorious* and her aircrews were very much on their mettle.

The carriers sailed from Malta on 19 January, 1932, for another exercise attack on the fleet, anchored in Vatika Bay, in southern Greece. In two days *Glorious*' Ripons and *Courageous*' Blackburn Darts dropped the staggering number of fifty-seven torpedoes, claiming seventeen hits. Eleven hits were allowed under exercise rules:

> Target: *Queen Elizabeth*, No of Torpedoes: 9, Hits: 2, % Loss of Speed: 15, Speed (kts) Remaining: 20.
>
> Target: *Resolution*, No of Torpedoes: 27, Hits: 7, % Loss of Speed: 30, Speed (kts) Remaining: 14
>
> Target: *Ramillies*, No of Torpedoes: 4, Hits: 2, % Loss of Speed: 10, Speed (kts) Remaining: 18
>
> Target: *Royal Oak*, No of Torpedoes: 6, Hits: 1, % Loss of Speed: 10, Speed (kts) Remaining: 18
>
> Target: *Devonshire*, No of Torpedoes: 9, Hits: 1, % Loss of Speed: 10, Speed (kts) Remaining: 30
>
> Target: *Sussex*, No of Torpedoes: 1, Hits: 1, % Loss of Speed: 10, Speed (kts) Remaining: 30

Target: *Curlew*, No of Torpedoes: 1, Hits: 3 [2 aimed at Resolution], % Loss of Speed: 100, Speed (kts) Remaining: SUNK

In the light of war experience, the staff assessment of speeds remaining after torpedo hits seems highly optimistic, while the notion that *Resolution* would still make 14 knots after *seven* torpedo hits was taking wishful thinking into the realms of fantasy.

The programme included 'anti-gas' exercises, when the aircraft sprayed ships with a mixture of ten pounds of flour, ten pounds of Duresco and half a pint of Izal to eight gallons of water. This fearful drench was invented in the fleet because the official 'Vanillin' supplied by Porton Down used commercial instead of pure methylated spirits and affected ships' paintwork. Comments afterwards resembled those of many a post-World War Two anti-nuclear fallout exercise: 'Failure to take cover in good time', 'Lack of care in cleansing', 'Failure to observe proper decontamination procedures'.

Both carriers practised night-flying in company, and with destroyers attacking the fleet. The 111Fs dropped calcium flares to mark the point of departure, and to indicate where enemy ships had been sighted. Night-flying, especially off Malta, was not for the faint-hearted. 'I remember the appalling qualms I had,' said French, 'doing perhaps 25 knots, in a westerly wind, heading straight for Malta, no arrester gear, no radar, in dim lighting, while these gallant pilots tried to touch down. I had to say to the Captain, "We've *got* to turn, *whatever* happens, in 2½ minutes time!" K-P had to decide whether to let the aircraft land on or risk running ashore. His ability to do that, when he still had that collision hanging over his head, was a measure of his courage.'

At the 'wash-up' both carrier captains said they would prefer to give up the element of surprise in exchange for accurate information about the fleet anchorage. To Henderson, this was 'peacetime thinking'. War proved him right. Thus, in the use of surprise from the air, torpedo strike, night-flying and chemical warfare, these now forgotten pre-war exercises in remote Mediterranean bays were all in their own day like blazing signs and tokens in the sky, pointing the future to come.

When *Glorious* returned to Malta on 29 January, 1932, a new aircraft, the Hawker Nimrod, was waiting to join. The Nimrod was a single-seat fighter, the naval counterpart of the RAF Hawker Fury, but a distinct marque of its own, with greater wingspan and special equipment such as flotation boxes in the wings and behind the pilot's seat. The Nimrod had a Rolls Royce Kestrel 11.S engine, giving a maximum speed of 195 mph at 14,000 feet, a ceiling of 26,000 feet and an endurance of 1.65 hours. It had two fixed synchronized Vickers guns firing forward, and could carry four 20lb bombs. The Nimrod was brand-new, the first production aircraft having flown in October, 1931. 408 Flight had reequipped with Nimrods in November and, after operational training and workup, was ready to embark.

Both carriers sailed on 22 February for Gibraltar. The Nimrod I was a lively machine and difficult to land on for anyone heavy-handed. The first landing, by Flight Lieutenant J.G. Bryant, commanding 408, ended in the palisades, under the watching gaze of the Admiral.

On 25 February nine Darts with torpedoes and fourteen Ripons with bombs attacked *Warspite* and *Malaya*. It was a beautiful day, with visibility so clear that *Warspite* had *Glorious'* Ripons in sight for over an hour as they closed her. The two battleships took violent avoiding action, which disconcerted the Darts, who scored one hit on *Warspite* and two on *Malaya* (the torpedoes being set to run 'deep'). The Ripons, who should have attacked simultaneously, were about a minute late, but made bombing runs over both ships, who retaliated with over 200 rounds of 4", over 150 rounds of 6" and 8,000 rounds of Lewis, much of it outside effective range. Both sides thought it a draw. After wash-ups at Gibraltar, *Courageous* sailed for home.

Exercises that spring continued to show a carrier's strengths and weaknesses. *Glorious* had to go where the wind took her, regardless of fleet formations. As Chatfield said, 'It was never likely that a carrier operating aircraft would be able to avail herself of an anti-submarine screen.' There was also the danger of surface attack. *Glorious* once had to steam for twenty-three minutes at high speed to fly off aircraft, on a course heading for the enemy, and came under fire from battle cruisers. On another occasion, the cruiser *Sussex* closed to within 13,000 yards of *Glorious*, whose destroyers laid smoke screens, but *Glorious* was judged to have been damaged by 8" shell fire (realistically, she was very probably sunk).

Having only one flight deck made for slow reaction times to a sighting: 'Sixty-six minutes passed between my order to fly off an air striking force and the departure of the force from the carrier.' Arrester gear to shorten the turn-round time was, in Chatfield's view, 'an urgent necessity'.

On the other hand, shadowing and reporting by 111Fs was excellent. In one exercise, shadowing and attacking 'an enemy who endeavours to break off a fleet action at dusk' (again, echoes of Jutland), one 111F made four reports in just over an hour: the greatest error in target course was fifteen degrees, and two courses were reported within five degrees.

There were no Combined Fleet exercises in 1932, under the shadow of Invergordon and 'O.U.N.E.' (Owing to the Urgent Need for Economy). As though to expunge even the memory of Invergordon, on 12 March, 1932, the Atlantic Fleet was renamed the Home Fleet. In the Mediterranean the Battle Squadron was reduced from six battleships to five.

Glorious returned to Malta late in April and on the 25th there was another fatal accident. A Ripon piloted by Lieutenant P.L.H.D. Irven took off from Hal Far for a flight in the L.F.A. (Local Flying Area). When the aircraft became overdue, three Flycatchers searched along the west coast and sighted a crowd of Maltese standing on cliff tops, trying to reach the wreckage of the Ripon with ladders and ropes. The aircraft was smashed against the rocks and by the time the duty destroyer arrived from Sliema Irven and his passenger, Midshipman A. Hamilton, were both drowned.

Hamilton had been on a three-week 'air acquaintance course'. In 1931 the Navy suffered yet another shortage of volunteers for aircrew. The air branch was still regarded as being uncertain for promotion, by having to serve two masters: pilots' promotion depended upon their naval rank, decided by the Admiralty, and on their air rank, decided by the Air Ministry. The Admiralty had introduced a compulsory course for all junior officers, hoping to 'sell' the air branch to likely young lads.

On 29 April *Glorious* gave another of her famous parties, for 768 guests, including the recently-deposed King Alphonso XIII of Spain. There was a palais de dance, and long bars in the lower hangar, shops, two restaurants and a night-club in the upper. The party went on until 2am, when food, drink and hosts were all giving out. Decorations were left up for the ship's company's dance the next night.

In June Vice-Admiral Roger Backhouse, Flag Officer Second in Command, came on board for a two-day inspection. It was a nervous time, in which an already tautly organized ship was wound a few notches tighter; promotions could depend upon the results of admirals' inspections. Backhouse inspected the ship's company by divisions on the flight deck, and then went round the messdecks, the upper deck and the hangars. After lunch he inspected ship's books and store-rooms. The next day the ship's company went to General Quarters for drills. All went well, except that some maniac or malcontent turned on a drencher valve, designed to spray the lower hangar in the event of fire. All 441 Flight's 111Fs except one, which happened to be in a separate bay, were thoroughly soaked in salt water. Also, somebody in a hurry to finish had left a paint pot at the bottom of a ladder and K-P, descending before the Admiral, put his foot in it; it was the only time anyone ever heard K-P swear.

On 23 June *Glorious* sailed with the fleet for the main summer cruise to Argostoli in Greece, Valona in Albania, Corfu, Venice, Split and Kotor, with the usual intensive exercises. Winds were generally light and *Glorious* had to steam at high speeds. A special system was evolved, an interesting forerunner of methods refined by American carriers in the Pacific in the Second World War, where the flagship *Queen Elizabeth*, with her numerous signals staff and signalling projectors, acted as 'link ship', to keep ships informed of the carrier's movements and the carrier herself in visual touch with the screen and the rest of the fleet.

There were the same problems arising from one flight deck. It took an hour and fifty-minutes to range and launch three Flights of Ripons. Meanwhile, the deck was out of action for returning aircraft, or for flying off reliefs. However, the shadowing was once again magnificent. On a dark night between Argostoli and Valona, with visibility down to a mile, one 111F found and correctly identified *Queen Elizabeth*, *Revenge, Resolution* and a cruiser, and in one hour's shadowing spotted and reported three out of four changes of course and speed, estimating speeds within two knots of the actual speeds, and getting two out of three courses exactly right, and the third within ten degrees.

One 111F flew over Valona, while Gowlland took oblique photographs of the battle fleet, using 4" and 5" glass plates which Gowlland developed in the cockpit during the return flight. The sixteen plates were delivered on board 'in a canvas pochette', said Gowlland, looking 'as if a flourishing crop of lichen was obscuring a few lozenge-shaped blemishes — but the enemy was there!'

Gowlland himself, who had passed a course in air photography at the RAF School at Farnborough, had an RAF Corporal (Photographer) and two Airmen (Ph) to handle the excellent modern equipment on board for processing and printing film stills and moving pictures. A film was taken of every deck landing during training and shown to the pilots later while the events were fresh in their minds. After gunnery spotting, films of fall of shot could be shown to guns' crews, control teams and target-towing aircrew within a couple of hours. Visiting VIPs liked to be presented with a photograph of themselves arriving on board by air.

K-P, the Wingco, French and other officers had to go to London in July for the enquiry into the *Florida* collision. Hearing the case in the Admiralty Division from 12-18 July, 1932, Mr Justice Bateson commended the way naval and RAF officers gave evidence (French's evidence alone took more than five hours) and apportioned blame: two-thirds to *Florida*, one-third to *Glorious*, Decision and award were upheld in the Court of Appeal in December. The career of none of the officers concerned was harmed by the collision.

K-P and the others rejoined in Venice and the ship sailed for Kotor in Yugoslavia, arriving on 5 August. The fleet pulling regatta was to be held over two days, 10 and 11 August. This was the most important sporting occasion of the year and the great golden 'Cock' awarded to the ship whose crews won most points was by far the most coveted trophy.

There were races for squadrons and races for flotillas, races for officers and for stokers, for cutters and for gigs, races of every kind. For weeks past every boat in *Glorious* had been lowered at every opportunity for the crews to train. For the regatta *Glorious* with her complement of some 1,200 men was classed with the Battle Squadron.

The large ships with bands embarked them in motor boats. Those ships (the majority) with no bands had 'chucking-up parties': sailors with trumpets, horns, drums, biscuit tins, anything that could be blown or beaten. When the gun went for a race, the bands all played and the chucking-up parties all blew, pounded or shouted, in time to their own boats' oars.

For the regatta bookmakers set up their boards along the battery deck, on the only occasion when gambling was (officially) permitted, except for weekly tombola sessions. In the Battle Squadron betting, *Revenge*'s crews soon dropped away. The main struggle developed between *Glorious* and *Queen Elizabeth*, *Glorious* doing well with her cutters, the flagship with her gigs, until the last race on the second day, when the flagship won by a single point. But evidently the result was controversial: Midshipman J.R. Gower noted bleakly in his Journal: 'It was a very "Shaky" win and Q.E. did not hoist up the coveted "Cock".'

Glorious won five fleet and three squadron Cups, including 'nearly all the best ones', as Lieutenant A.D. Torlesse, one of the ship's observers, noted in his private journal, 'the Duke of Edinburgh Cup, the *Illustrious* Cup, the Evan-Thomas and the Fiume' (even their names now have a nostalgic ring to them). Next day squadron cups were presented by Backhouse on the quarterdeck of *Revenge*, fleet cups on board *Queen Elizabeth* by the C-in-C himself. *Glorious* would have been the first aircraft carrier to have won the Mediterranean Fleet regatta and it was disappointing to have come so close and failed. However, the pinnace came back to the ship loaded with silverware and a crew wreathed in smiles.

On 13 August the fleet moved to an anchorage north of Corfu for a Royal Visit the next day. When King George V spent three days in the Royal Yacht with the Home Fleet in July that year, the First Lord, Sir Bolton Eyres Monsell, had mentioned to the Prince of Wales, accompanying his father, that the Mediterranean Fleet was taking 'a poor view' of the King's visit to the Home Fleet. 'They argue that, since they did *not* mutiny last year, why are the mutineers being thus honoured while they are ignored? I know the King cannot go, but could you?' Thus it was arranged, although Queen Mary was not at all happy about her sons, the Prince of Wales and Prince George, flying from an aircraft carrier.

The fleet put to sea on 16 August. The man from the *Daily Mail*, one of five reporters embarked, was vastly impressed: 'in line ahead, four miles long, a majestic spectacle of power, slowly treading the blue pathway of the Mediterranean'. Some miles off shore the Princes were transferred from *Queen Elizabeth* to *Glorious* by cutter and, after divisions on the flight deck, there was flying.

Eighteen Ripons armed with torpedoes were flown off, followed by Flycatchers, Nimrods and most of the 111Fs, thirty-six aircraft in all. The Princes themselves went up in 111Fs, the Prince of Wales with Lieutenant 'Dago' Kennedy, and the ship's senior observer, Lieutenant-Commander Gerald Langley. Prince George was piloted by Flying Officer J. Constable-Roberts RAF, with Geoffrey Gowlland, who had been in the Prince's Hawke Term at Osborne and Dartmouth, as observer.

All went well and the aircraft headed back for *Glorious*, led by the Prince of Wales' 111F. He had barely landed on when the ship ran into sudden thick fog. Extra lookouts climbed up to the crow's nest and the First Lieutenant stationed himself in the eyes of the ship.

Suddenly an aircraft flashed over the bridge, its pilot barely visible in the murk but clearly pointing urgently ahead. With *Florida* so fresh in his mind, K-P ordered full astern all engines. 'All those without duties ran to the side and peered ahead,' wrote the *Daily Mail* man, apparently the only person unconcerned, 'But even then, in what was really the supreme moment of this adventure, the human current of confidence never flickered.'

This human current of confidence was certainly not felt by K-P nor by the pilots still aloft. The ship was asking for directions. Gowlland signalled that he had the masthead in sight above the fog. 'Nearest clear space from you is about six miles 295 degrees true. I am two miles astern of you, at 3,000 feet. HRH quite relaxed, I thought I could hear his snores.'

'The pilot we had feared as a messenger of danger was really a herald of deliverance,' wrote the *Daily Mail*. 'He had meant to indicate a clear sea ahead. A minute later, engines running dead slow ahead again, we came to it. We were through the fog bank... and there, blessed sight, were the lost planes still circling the widening horizon. In less than five minutes Prince George was aboard again. At regular intervals the rest followed. Not one was lost. Not one failed to make a good landing in its proper turn.'

The Princes went down to the wardroom for half an hour, where they made light of their adventure, before returning to the flagship. All on board *Glorious* were mightily relieved, and delighted to get a graceful signal from the C-in-C, who for some time had not known himself whether the Princes had landed safely, and a signal of thanks and congratulations from the Prince of Wales.

All aircrew complained of lack of air time, so when, in September, 1932, *Glorious* reached Alexandria, twelve 111Fs, nine Ripons, three Flycatchers and three Nimrods, with all spare seats occupied by engine fitters and riggers, flew off for a cruise of their own around RAF airfields in the Nile Delta.

There was much to see and do: the Great Pyramids and the Sphinx from the air; the 1882 battlefield of Tel-el-Kebir, used as an emergency landing field; Lake Timsah, where some swam across the canal from Africa to Asia; the mooring mast at Ismailia ready for the airship R.101, had she ever reached Egypt; and sand yachting at Abu Sueir, where there was a 26-mile track straight out into the desert.

Some pilots misjudged their height when landing on flat desert sand and bounced badly. At Ismailia they were greeted by an RAF sergeant pilot who had taught the first naval pilots at Netheravon. 'I taught you to fly eight years ago, sir,' he said, 'and the next time I see you, you show me a landing like that!'

At Ismailia No 6 Squadron, a very famous fighting unit, then equipped with Fairey Gordons, found 'some special gin which they thought the Navy would like'. The RAF entertained

Glorious' teams at football, hockey, golf, boxing and tennis in Cairo and in Alexandria. In return the ship held an 'At Home' for the RAF, many of whom had never seen an aircraft carrier before. As the ship sailed on 24 September an RAF Vickers Victoria flew overhead and dipped its wings in salute. Once again the RN and the RAF had got on together surpassingly well.

Glorious sailed for home on 1 November, 1932, and arrived at Devonport to pay off on the 10th. From 24 February, 1930, until 24 October, 1932, when she arrived back in Malta after her last cruise, *Glorious* had spent 207 days at sea. Her aircraft had flown 19,625 hours, 737 hours by night, and 892 by floatplanes. There had been 5,659 deck landing by day and 296 at night. There had been forty-four major and twelve minor flying accidents. The ship had consumed 34,809 tons of oil fuel, her aircraft had used 229,369 gallons of petrol and 5,500 gallons of castor oil. The aircraft had dropped 406 torpedoes during exercises, and her guns had fired 1,541 4.7" shells, with another 116 star-shells and sixteen smoke-shells.

K-P left the ship on 11 December. He was made CB in April, 1933, and promoted to Rear-Admiral in September. In 1934 he was Assistant Chief of the Naval Staff, with special responsibility for Fleet Air Arm affairs. From 1936 to 1938 he was back in the Mediterranean commanding the 1st Cruiser Squadron. In March, 1940, he became C-in-C America and West Indies Station and was promoted Admiral in February, 1942. Later in the war he was appointed Deputy First Sea Lord, to take some of the administrative burden off the First Sea Lord himself. *Glorious* was sorry to see him go. 'His leadership and inspiration were magical,' wrote Gowlland. 'We loved that man.'

CHAPTER 3: CRISIS IN ABYSSINIA

K-P'S SUCCESSOR WAS Guy 'Ginger' Royle, who had been gunnery officer of the battleship *Marlborough* at Jutland and fleet gunnery officer of the Atlantic Fleet after the war. He was promoted Captain in 1923 at the early age of 37 and came to *Glorious* after two years commanding the gunnery school HMS *Excellent*. He was a keen rugby footballer and captained the Navy side. He was a high-flyer in the gunnery branch, but in spite of his talents he was a most unassuming man. He and his wife Elizabeth became very popular on board and with the *Glorious* wives. Lieutenant Gerry Rotherham, who joined as a 'makee-learn' observer in August, 1933, said Ginger Royle 'was one of nature's gentlemen, and his wife was in the same league'.

The ship recommissioned at Devonport with a new Commander, Charles Daniel, on 6 January, 1933, sailed on 25th, and arrived at Malta on the 31st. The new C-in-C, Chatfield having become First Sea Lord, was Admiral Sir William Wordsworth Fisher, known as 'W.W.', or, because of his extreme height, 'Agrippa' (from the *Struwwelpeter* rhyme, 'Now tall Agrippa lived close by — so tall, he almost touched the sky'). Fisher, though now almost totally forgotten (he died in June, 1937, aged 62, and never commanded a fleet in war), was a most able, far-sighted and energetic C-in-C.

Glorious flew off her aircraft to Hal Far and for a month exercised off Malta, going to sea several days a week for flying training. On 1 March the Home Fleet arrived with two carriers, *Furious* and *Courageous*, and all three carriers, who had a hundred aircraft embarked between them, took part in a series of fleet exercises to investigate the use of massed air striking forces, led by Henderson, flying his flag in *Courageous*.

The first was on 8 March, on passage to Palma, Majorca, when the carriers flew off twelve Darts from *Courageous*, ten Ripons from *Glorious* and nine Ripons from *Furious*, all carrying torpedoes. The carriers then formed the targets, steaming in line ahead, with the cruisers *Curlew*, *Ceres* and *Delhi* in the rear.

It was another brilliant day of maximum visibility, no clouds below 20,000 feet and therefore no chance of surprise. The striking force was sighted from *Courageous* as they approached at 6,000 feet and scattered into 'open crescent' formation. The three leading flights attacked alternate ships, *Delhi*, *Curlew* and *Furious*, the other three, following a minute later, *Ceres*, *Glorious* and *Courageous*.

All six ships were attacked, within the space of 3 minutes, by four to six aircraft, but a high target speed of 24 knots and violent avoiding action using full rudder about thirty seconds before the torpedoes were dropped were good defences; of thirty torpedoes dropped (one 'hung up'), six hit, twenty-one missed (fifteen astern of their targets) and three did not run properly. The attack on *Furious* was frustrated and she was not hit. No hits were obtained at dropping ranges of more than 860 yards. In return the targets fired 154 rounds of various calibres from 6" to 3", with 1,645 rounds of pompom and 1,590 rounds of Lewis.

The targets for the next exercise, which followed at once, were *Nelson* and *Rodney*, and the cruisers *Dorsetshire*, *York* and *Exeter*, all steaming at the much lower speed of 13 knots. The striking force, twelve Darts from *Courageous*, ten Ripons each from *Glorious* and *Furious*, had been ordered to 'carry out a crippling attack' on the opposing fleet. The first wave of eighteen aircraft dived at angles of between 35° and 45° at speeds of 160 knots on *Nelson*, *Dorsetshire* and *Exeter*; the second, of ten aircraft, on *York* and *Rodney*; and the remaining four aircraft attacked *Exeter*.

The first wave made their attack at ranges of about a mile and had dropped all their torpedoes within forty seconds. Each aircraft was 'down on the water' for only ten seconds and each escaped low in the direction of the sun. Some passed very close to their targets without a finger being laid on them. Of thirty-two torpedoes dropped, twenty-one hit (thirteen from the first wave), one ran deep under *Rodney*, one missed because of a bad drop and nine were badly aimed. In war it certainly would have been a 'crippling attack'.

Yet Henderson later criticized the striking force for attacking too soon. Having sighted *Nelson*, the strike leader had assumed that he must also have been sighted and attacked from 5,000 feet instead of climbing, as Henderson said he should have done, to 10,000 feet. Post-mortem comments showed what high standards were now being demanded; even such a patently successful exercise was subjected to fierce scrutiny and praise was always very well deserved.

In the third exercise thirty-three aircraft attacked *Resolution*, cruisers and destroyers with dummy torpedoes, so it was a long day's flying. But the constant complaint, especially by the Flycatcher Flights who, with their short endurance, were always last off and first back, was lack of flying. 'When Commander (Flying) came into the wardroom,' said Lieutenant R.H.S. Rodger, of 461 Ripon Flight, 'we used to stand on chairs and jump off and pretend to crash on the deck, having forgotten how to fly! It took me all my flying career to qualify for the Perch Club.'

The 'Perch Club' members were those who had completed one hundred deck landings. 'There was the "Seven League

Boot Club", for those who plotted their speed wrong,' said Rotherham, 'the "Where It Listeth Club" for those who worked out wind speed and direction wrong, and the "Rat Club" for those who bailed out of an aircraft before it went over the side after landing on. A.St.J. Edwards, one of our 'O's in *Glorious*, bailed out, but then his pilot gunned the engine hard and took off. When he landed on again, he found his Observer already there! There was one member of the "Trapped Rat Club", an Observer who was still in the aircraft after the pilot, realizing that he was going into the drink, had himself bailed out! If you were a member of several clubs you became a "Man About Town".'

There was a certain antagonism, not always concealed, between pilots and observers. Observers, who all had ship's duties and normally stayed on board in harbour, thought of themselves as the 'brains', and the pilots as the 'brawn', the mere 'chauffeurs' who flew ashore and only flew back on the first day at sea. The observer branch had been created first and for some time had better promotion prospects. Some pilots even had to leave the Fleet Air Arm (R.H.S. Rodger was one; when he left *Glorious* in October, 1933, he also left the Fleet Air Arm) because their naval and RAF ranks had got badly out of step, through no fault of their own. It was possible for a Lieutenant-Commander still to have the RAF rank of Flying Officer.

Ship's officers complained that pilots, when they flew back after their 'jaunts' ashore, always made the wardroom seem overcrowded; in their hordes, pilots created shortages — of cabins, stewards, hot water for shaving, armchairs in the ante-room. One recognized 'battleground' between ship and air group was the 'Line Book', a large scrapbook with the ship's badge embossed on the front cover. *Glorious*' Line Book, started in 1931 (and almost certainly lost with the ship), was a highly idiosyncratic commentary on the commission, with signals, newspaper cuttings, daily orders, cartoons, lists of names, sporting results, verses of songs, anecdotes and a running diary of places and events. There were photographs of flight deck crashes and of ship's personalities. One early picture was a carefully-posed 'Stamping Club', formed 'to stamp out virginity in the Mediterranean'. Another was contributed by Commander A.W.La.T. Bisset, known irreverently as 'Big Bum' Bisset, who relieved Edwards in the first commission. It was a picture of the rear view of his four very small daughters disporting themselves in a state of nature on a beach; the caption, 'Can You Beat It?' Four aircrew officers took up the challenge and replied with a picture of themselves similarly attired — 'Yes We Can!'

The Line Book that summer of 1933 recorded the arrival on board of the Hawker Osprey, the deck-landing version of the RAF Hawker Hart day-bomber. With twin floats, it was also widely used in battleship and cruiser ship's flights. It was a two-seater fighter-reconnaissance aircraft, with a 640 hp Rolls Royce Kestrel V engine, a maximum speed of 176 mph, a service ceiling of 25,000 feet, and an endurance of 2¼ hours. It had one fixed Vickers gun firing forward and a moveable Lewis gun aft. In carriers, Ospreys flew with Nimrods, one Osprey to three Nimrods.

On 3 April, 1933, the old Flights were abolished and amalgamated into Squadrons with new numbering. In *Glorious* 408 Flight became 802 Squadron, with nine Nimrods and three Ospreys. 462 Flight, of twelve Ripons, became 812 Squadron. Six 111Fs of 441 Flight, with six of 448, became 823 Squadron. Six 111Fs of 460 Flight, with six additional 111Fs, became 825 Squadron, one of the most famous of all Fleet Air Arm units.

These squadron numbers, 802, 812, 823 and 825, were to be associated with *Glorious* for the rest of her life.

Glorious arrived back in Malta on 27 April, when the social season was once again getting under way. Admiral Backhouse gave a dance in *Revenge*; the 4th Destroyer Flotilla gave a dance at the Marsa; Rear-Admiral Brownrigg gave a small dance in *Delhi*, and there was a dance at Bighi Hospital. There were three Malta Amateur Dramatic Society shows. Wives, and the fishing fleet, arrived in shoals. A reasonable house could be rented at £6 a month. Two rooms could be had at the Imperial Hotel, Sliema, for 15/- a day, all in.

But there was more serious business. Malta's pre-war defences are often criticized. Certain measures, such as the construction of bomb-proof submarine shelters, were not carried out. But Malta was not entirely defenceless, nor were her defences entirely ignored. On 25-26 May, 1933, the island's invasion defences were tested. The attackers were the 2nd Battalion The Worcestershire Regiment, some 1,300 officers and men of the Malta Security Force and Royal Navy and Royal Engineers demolition parties, who were landed at various points around the coast from *London*, *Shropshire*, *Sussex* and *Devonshire*, and destroyers of the 3rd Flotilla. Defending were the 2nd Battalion The Cheshire Regiment and one Rifle Company, RAF, at Hal Far and Kalafrana seaplane base. The exercise gave garrison planners food for thought. All the landings, except one at Marsa Scirocco, were held to have been successful.

'Goofing', or watching the flying, was always a popular pastime. In *Glorious* 'goofing' positions were the forward control position (but not the director tower), and in the nets abaft No. 2 W/T mast on each side (but not, for safety reasons, in the nets immediately under the palisades). On 26

June, when *Glorious* was flying on her aircraft, Lieutenant B.J.C. Wise flying a Ripon of 812 Squadron misjudged his approach, tried to go round again and hit the starboard palisade. The Napier Lion engine, torn by the impact out of its mountings, and the rest of the Ripon went separately into the sea, the engine actually hitting the water first. Wise was picked up unhurt, but there were some thoughtful faces among the goofers.

The next day *Glorious* sailed with the fleet for a cruise and exercises. Places and events had a reassuring familiarity in those pre-war days, when the fleet moved about the Mediterranean like a Tudor court on a royal progress. The regatta was held in August over the same course. *Revenge*, last the previous year, won the Cock. *Glorious* finished fourth out of five in the Battle Squadron and had one of her boats disqualified. 'Lost all our regatta cups, alas!' Torlesse noted in his journal. Most of the cups went to *London* 'who did very well in cutter races with a stroke they learned from the Yugoslavs, quite short, never falling back beyond the vertical, about 40 to the minute'.

The fleet wasted none of its sea time and always exercised on passage between ports. Leaving Kotor after the regatta, five submarines attacked the fleet through a destroyer and aircraft screen. The conditions, with a clear sea and good visibility, were ideal for *Glorious'* aircraft. *Regulus* was streaming an oil slick which made her visible for miles, but the others were also detected easily. Light-coloured paint on their hulls and conning towers enabled aircraft to see them without difficulty at periscope depth. One aircraft, which already had *Thames* in sight, was able to follow her even when she was at a depth of 150 feet.

The next day, 16 August, was a long one of exercising attacks for *Glorious*. It was a day of mishaps. The Ripons could do nothing right. While waiting for a smoke screen which was never laid, they approached their targets too low, circled too near, and when they eventually closed, at thirty feet above the sea and spread well apart, they were easily picked off. In a bizarre accident on deck, a Very light round, a 'Negative' to warn an incoming aircraft to go round again, was accidentally fired into a Ripon, igniting the wood and fabric and eventually the petrol in its tank. The aircraft burned out.

After docking in Malta in August, *Glorious* sailed at the end of the month for the eastern Mediterranean, to Limassol and Alexandria where the 111Fs and Ripons flew ashore to renew their friendships with the RAF. Returning on 23 September, Lieutenant L.C.B. Ashburner of 823 Squadron landed his 111F too fast and drove full tilt into the island, breaking off both wings and pushing the engine back on its mountings. The RAF adjutant, Squadron Leader Hill, was hit by a wing-tip and knocked out, and two of the flight deck party were injured.

Glorious arrived back in Grand Harbour on 23 October to spend the winter in Malta. Malta had a 'hothouse' effect upon romance. The naval custom was to hoist a green garland for a ship's officer's marriage. There were several *Glorious* garlands that autumn. Naval officers had to organize their matrimonial affairs according to the exigencies of the service, which sometimes called for nice timing. Torlesse, for example, returned to Malta in *Glorious* one Thursday that year and was married in the Anglican cathedral on the Saturday.

Like many other officers, Lieutenant Ben Bolt had his wedding reception in the wardroom, after his marriage at St. Paul's, Sliema, in November, 1933. In a pleasant gesture, the ship's TAGs harnessed themselves to the bridal car and hauled

Bolt and his bride away from the church. Not all wedding arrangements went smoothly. Another of *Glorious'* observers, Lieutenant B.E.W. Logan, was married in London on a day when, as it happened, one of the ship's engine-room artificers died in the hospital ship *Maine*. Logan's wedding garland was mixed up with the funeral wreaths and nearly went off to the cemetery.

The Combined Fleet Exercises of March, 1934, which once again involved nearly 100 ships, were held in the Atlantic. The Home (Blue) Fleet was led by Admiral Sir W.H.D. Boyle, and included *Furious*. The Red (Mediterranean) was led by Fisher and had *Courageous* (flag of Rear-Admiral Hon Sir Alexander Ramsay, who had relieved Henderson as RAA the previous September) and *Glorious*.

A war between Atlantis (Blue) and Great Britain (Red) had been going on for some time. The Blue fleet commander was under political pressure to 'do something'. His response was to try and pass a convoy of 'forty' transports (actually represented by two submarine depot ships, *Lucia* and *Cyclops*, the net-layer *Guardian* and the Royal Fleet Auxiliary *Serbol*), with a powerful escort, from the Azores to a port somewhere along the Iberian coast-line of neutral 'Eastland'. Red, based at Gibraltar, had to intercept convoy and escort.

A full Force 9-10 gale blew from the north-west, with very heavy seas, throughout the four days, 11-14 March, of the exercise. All Blue's destroyers except five actually in company had to run to the east and take shelter in Lagos Bay. Red's destroyers, plugging into the teeth of the gale, were reduced to five knots and kept in touch by flashing their masthead lanterns at intervals. The submarine *L.27* had her fore hydroplanes carried away. *Devonshire* had to return to Gibraltar with defects. The battle cruiser *Renown's* boats were all carried away and a length of anti-torpedo bulge torn from her hull so that she had to reduce speed. *Lucia* broke down for thirty-eight hours and drifted seventy miles, under improvised sail.

Glorious took no part. The weather was too bad for peacetime flying. On the night of 11/12 March a giant wave 'dished in' the forward lower flying-off deck and smashed through the hangar doors. Six Ospreys and Nimrods were 'concertina-ed' into the space of two. One sailor was pinned down in the forward liftwell by a reel of wire which, fortunately for him, snagged on the side of the well, or he would have been crushed to death.

The exercise was a triumph for Fisher. Aided by some admirable scouting and reporting by *Shropshire*, and by destroyers led by Rear-Admiral (D) Andrew Cunningham in the cruiser *Coventry*, Fisher caught up with his opponent on the night of 13 March. The convoy had disintegrated and consisted only of *Serbol*, around whom Boyle, lacking destroyers, had disposed his battleships and cruisers as escort. Shortly after midnight Fisher's battleships in battle order closed to within 7,000 yards of their unsuspecting enemy and then suddenly switched on their searchlights and fired star-shell. Boyle was caught utterly by surprise. 'The moment was spectacular,' wrote one press correspondent, 'beyond even the dreams of the most ambitious Hollywood producer.'

Glorious left Malta 0023 April, 1934, and arrived at Devonport on 1 May to pay off. In refit, her quarterdeck, which had been liable to flooding in rough weather and at high speeds, was raised one deck to be flush with the main battery deck. The flight deck was extended aft, the extra length being supported by large tubular struts in a characteristic letter 'W' (which the sailors insisted stood for 'Work').

The major improvement on the flight deck was the fitting of Mark III arrester gear. Henceforth, Fleet Air Arm aircraft would be fitted with a trailing hook which, on landing, would (the pilot hoped and intended) engage in one of four wires stretched transversely across the flight deck. The energy expended in drawing out the wire, against hydraulic resistance, would bring the aircraft more rapidly to a standstill. The Mark m gear provided an easily-controlled arresting force throughout the wire's travel. It was readily adaptable for aircraft of various weights. It was simply reset, using part of the energy destroyed on landing to reset the gear. It automatically adapted itself to varying entry speeds. The gear worked through the controlled discharge of hydraulic fluid through orifices of variable size to regulate the 'run out' of the wire. It was designed to arrest 8,000lb aircraft landing at 70 knots, with a deceleration no greater than 1.5, for a 'pull out' of 140 feet. The gear was first fitted in *Courageous* in 1933 and, after successful trials, Henderson recommended it be fitted in all carriers.

Ginger Royle left the ship in Devonport and went in September to be Naval Secretary to the First Sea Lord. He was promoted Rear-Admiral in July, 1935, and continued to be involved in the Fleet Air Arm. He was RAA from July, 1937, to July, 1939, and, in November, 1939, became Fifth Sea Lord and Chief of Naval Air Services. His successor in *Glorious*, who joined on 1 May, 1935, when the ship was still refitted, was Captain H.C. Rawlings DSO. Clive Rawlings was a destroyer man who had won his DSO for distinguished service as Senior Officer of Advanced Patrols in the Baltic in 1919. He had some ten years' seniority as a Captain and much experience of the air world, having commanded the seaplane carrier *Pegasus* and served in the Air Ministry. He came to *Glorious* from the Admiralty where he was Director of Naval Air Division.

Glorious recommissioned at Devonport on 23 July, 1935, and sailed on 19 August to embark three Ospreys and nine Nimrods of 802 Squadron, under Squadron Leader Hanmer, from Netheravon. She then went to Portsmouth where at sea on 21 August she embarked six Fairey Seals of 'B' Flight, 823 Squadron from Gosport. The Seal was the naval version of the RAF's Fairey Gordon. Its dimensions and armament were much the same as the 111F, which it superceded, but its 525 hp Armstrong Siddeley Panther 11A engine gave it a slightly higher maximum speed, of i38mph, a longer endurance at 4½ hours, but a lower ceiling at 17,000 feet.

Glorious' final fitting out and departure were hurried, because there were rumours of unrest in the-Mediterranean. On passage the usual deck landing training soon showed that Bobbie Hanmer, C.O. of 802, was no deck-lander. 'He finished in the drink twice out of three,' wrote Geoffrey Eveleigh, then a Flying Officer in 802, 'which the Observers' Union thought a shade over the odds, as they had to fly behind him. Miraculously he had not hurt himself or his observers but his Ospreys were write-offs. On the last occasion, he was hauled on board and went up to the bridge to apologize to Captain Rawlings for knocking his ship about. The Captain made sympathetic noises and suggested Bobbie go down to the wardroom for a stiff brandy. Bobbie thereupon saluted, turned about, tripped over the hatch coaming, fell down the bridge ladder and gashed his shin, requiring three stitches. Which all goes to show the fates will get you in the end!'

Squadron Leader F.E. Bond took over 802, and Flight Lieutenant George Stainforth, of Schneider Trophy fame, who set a world speed record of 407.5 mph in September, 1931, became Adjutant.

After a quick passage, *Glorious* arrived in Malta on 28 August, 1935. There was no time for renewing old acquaintances or for parties. The ship refuelled and restored and on 2 September embarked twelve Blackburn Baffins of 812 Squadron and twelve 111Fs of 825, all from Hal Far, having previously been in *Eagle*, and sailed next day for Alexandria.

812 Squadron, first under Squadron Leader B.B. Caswell and then under Squadron Leader N.A.P. Pritchett, was the first to be equipped with Baffins, which were enlarged and updated versions of the Ripon; many latter Baffins were in fact converted from Ripons. With a 565 hp radial air-cooled Bristol Pegasus I.M.3 engine, the Baffin had a higher speed than the Ripon, at 136 mph, an increased range of 4½ hours and 2,000 feet higher ceiling at 15,000 feet. It could carry the heavier Mark VIII or Mark X torpedo, or one 2000 lb bomb.

Glorious now had five different types of aircraft embarked: Nimrods, Ospreys, Seals, Baffins and Fairey 111Fs. This multiplicity of types, complicating the Fleet Air Arm's flight deck handling, maintenance and spare parts problems, was to persist through and beyond the Second World War. In 1945 the British Pacific Fleet operated Seafires, Fireflies, Hellcats, Corsairs, Avengers and the Walrus. Meanwhile the US Navy's Fast Carrier Task Force had one fighter, the Hellcat, and one bomber, the Avenger.

The squadrons flew off to Aboukir and the ship herself entered Alexandria on 5 September, to find a large part of the fleet already there, in the midst of an ever-deepening crisis over Abyssinia. The second summer cruise had been drastically curtailed, and — the surest sign of the extreme gravity of the international situation — the fleet regatta had been cancelled.

The fleet at Malta had begun to prepare and store for war on 12 August. Leave and drafting cycles were halted. Full complements of stores and provisions were embarked, shell rooms cleared of practise ammunition and wartime outfits replenished. Four battleships of the 1st Battle Squadron, with Fisher flying his flag in *Resolution*, the 1st and 3rd Cruiser Squadrons, the 1st and 4th Destroyer Flotillas and the fleet repair ship *Resource* sailed on the 29th and reached Alexandria on 2 September. Fisher and Cunningham, flying his flag in the cruiser *Despatch*, went on to Port Said, as Cunningham said, 'to get away from fleet routine and distractions for a short time to enable us to draw up plans for possible war'. The Vice-Admiral Second in Command, Sir Charles Forbes, was left in command of the ships at Alexandria.

Fisher's and Cunningham's staffs planned that on the outbreak of war the immediate response would be, on the very night following, a sweep by a strong force of cruisers and destroyers up the east coast of Sicily and into the southern entrance of the Straits of Messina, to bombard harbours and port installations and generally, in Cunningham's phrase, 'make ourselves obnoxious'.

Meanwhile some two or three Italian troopships a day were passing close across the bows of *Resolution* and *Despatch* on their way to the Suez Canal. The Italian soldiers all cheered and shouted, '*Duce! Duce! Duce!*', and sometimes a party of local Italians would shout back, '*Abyssinia a noi!*' During the dinner hour one day a large transport with two or three thousand soldiers on board steamed close to *Resolution*. The Italian troops all broke into the Fascist anthem '*Giovinezzia*'. But, as Cunningham noted, they 'were considerably put out by the loud shouts of "Encore!" from the hundreds of sailors on the forecastles of *Despatch* and *Resolution*. It is impossible to describe the withering contempt the British bluejacket can put into his applause if he dislikes the entertainment or entertainer.'

Benito Mussolini had begun preparations for an invasion in 1933, but the present crisis had broken on 5 December, 1934, with a frontier incident between Italian and Ethiopian troops at a place called Wai Wai, on the border between Italian Somaliland and Ethiopia. The incident was trivial and nobody was even sure whether Wai Wai was in Italian Somaliland or Ethiopia. But the pretext was enough. By February, 1935, large numbers of Italian troops had been despatched to Eritrea, and by the summer Italian troopships were passing through the Suez Canal in a steady stream.

There was immediate international concern, expressed mainly through the League of Nations, which Mussolini ignored or derided. Many nations which said they were in favour of imposing sanctions on Italy lacked the will or the means to do so. The French were consistently uncooperative and never actively gave any support to sanctions.

In fact, the Royal Navy was the only practical means in the Mediterranean of enforcing sanctions. Fisher was confident that his fleet could defeat the Italians, blockade Italy and prevent her sending more troops or bringing any troops back. He and Cunningham were infuriated by 'a very pessimistic, not to say defeatist, view of the Mediterranean Fleet' held by the Chiefs of Staff Committee.

Without the use of the French bases at Toulon and Bizerta, the Royal Navy had to fall back on Gibraltar and Alexandria, 2,000 miles apart. Fisher wanted to stay at Malta but was overruled by the Admiralty Board. Malta was sixty miles — about twenty minutes flying time for a fighter — from Sicily. The Regio Aeronautica was still largely an unknown quantity, but there were already rumours of Italian suicide squadrons. Malta had no anti-aircraft defences at all, and there was a shortage of anti-aircraft ammunition in Malta, at Aden and in Egypt; it was calculated that the fleet had only enough for each long-range gun to fire for twenty-two minutes and each short-range gun for thirteen minutes. Fisher suggested using naval aircraft to defend Malta, but Chatfield replied that there were only enough to defend the carriers. So Fisher had to move to Alexandria, which did at least control the Suez Canal, although it had no docking facilities for anything larger than a 'C' Class cruiser.

To avoid a 'mad dog' attack by Italy, there was a general world-wide movement of warships towards the eastern Mediterranean. The Home Fleet gathered at Portland on 29 August and ships began to sail the next day. *Courageous* and fourteen destroyers of the 2nd and 5th Flotillas steamed to Alexandria, darkening ship passing through the Straits of Gibraltar and the Malta Channel and maintaining twenty knots until east of Malta, arriving at Alexandria on 7 September. Some of the destroyers, with the cruiser *Ajax*, went to Haifa. Other cruisers went to Aden, with the depot ship *Lucia* and four 'L' Class submarines from the Home Fleet. At Alexandria Fisher's fleet was joined by seven minesweepers of the 1st M/S Flotilla, cruisers from South America and China, and *Sussex* from the Royal Australian Navy. The Battle Cruiser Squadron of *Hood* and *Renown*, with cruisers and destroyers, arrived at Gibraltar.

Resolution and *Despatch* arrived at Alexandria on 15 September and the whole fleet put to sea the next day to start a period of intensive exercises and weapon training. The sweep up to Messina was rehearsed and there were exercises in which an 'Italian fleet' was encountered by day and by night. 'A' Flight of 823 Squadron Seals had come out in *Courageous* and joined *Glorious*, to bring her air group to full complement. Carrier aircraft exercised long-distance reconnaissance, night shadowing and torpedo and bombing attacks. All worked very hard but Lieutenant-Commander Robertson, C.O. of 825, was an especially severe taskmaster; 825 called themselves the 'Chain Gang'.

Intensive flying meant long hours for the flight deck personnel, but they worked willingly. Stoker Bill Collier thought the flight deck 'was the best job I had in the Navy. Coming up from the bowels of the ship into the sun and fresh air was like a holiday.' The only disadvantage was having to clear lower deck to hoist in bombing targets 'which seemed to be on the end of miles of wire cable towed astern. Most times this job would coincide with meal times. We would gallop fore and aft along the flight deck to the strains of "Here we are, here we are, here we are again" played in double time whilst our dinners were cooling off nicely down below!'

Just after the war one air marshal had told Admiral Keyes that if the Navy 'were going to make difficulties, the Air Ministry would maintain its own seagoing carriers'. Lieutenant Crichton, an observer in *Courageous*, wrote to Keyes in December, 1935, that this awful prophecy had come true. In October RAF Scapa and Singapore flying boats arrived in Alexandria, with a British-India liner of some 12,000 tons, chartered by the government, as depot ship. 'At her stern she flies the RAF ensign,' wrote Crichton. 'I believe the Captain nearly had an apoplectic fit when told he had to fly the RAF ensign.'

Crichton then made a point of real insight. 'One can't help thinking what a wonderful instrument the whole thing (flying boats and depot ship) would be in the hands of the Admiralty, with sailors running the power boats and a Naval Complement in the ship… These flying boats can go over a thousand miles non-stop and this makes one realize what a powerful reconnaissance instrument they would be to a Commander-in-Chief if they were only properly run.'

Should Italian bombers flying from Libya make Alexandria untenable, the fleet would have to find another base. It was proposed to construct a mobile fleet base in a suitable bay (Navarino in Greece and Suda Bay in Crete were both considered). In October and November, 1935, a train of merchant ships, with the Cunard liner *Lancastria* and the troopship *Neuralia*, arrived with antitorpedo nets and baffles, mines, moorings, guns, searchlights, communications staff and headquarters units. The mobile base was never built and these elements were used to reinforce Alexandria, but the concept surfaced again during the Second World War and this exercise was useful experience.

Italy invaded Ethiopia on 5 October. The Mediterranean Fleet, still not quite knowing whether it was at peace or at war, responded by holding the postponed regatta in Alexandria harbour on 8 and 9 October. The next day the refitted *Queen Elizabeth* arrived with the C-in-C designate, Admiral Sir Dudley Pound. But because of the crisis the Admiralty decided to leave Fisher in command. Pound then, quite unprecedentedly, offered his services as Chief of Staff, which Fisher gratefully accepted, and hoisted his flag in *Queen Elizabeth* on the 12th.

The League of Nations decided on 11 October to impose sanctions on Italy and, on the same day, to celebrate King Fuad of Egypt's accession day, and, as a show of strength, the fleet landed Royal Marine bands and detachments of marines, with platoons of seamen and stokers, to march through the streets of Alexandria, watched by the Egyptian Prime Minister, the High Commissioner and Fisher himself. Whether or not the march had any effect on the Italians, it was much enjoyed by a highly enthusiastic crowd and by Alexandrian pickpockets, who had a field day.

Fisher knew that all work and no play was not good for a fleet. At sea his ships exercised intensively, with ship's companies in 'war routine', keeping watch and watch, half the complement closed up at all times. 'But all is well,' he wrote to Chatfield at the end of October. 'Very well I think in spite of restricted leave, and a great deal of hard work, poor recreational facilities and fabulous price of beer. There has been no grumbling, on the contrary great keenness. Every day and most nights squadrons and flotillas are at sea... Yesterday I counted eighty-four ships and vessels under my command in Alexandria alone. Air attacks on the fleet in harbour and at sea, day and night, all days except Saturday and Sunday.'

These attacks were by *Courageous'* and *Glorious'* squadrons, but the possibility of Italian air attack was ever-present. Ship's companies remained in two watches even in harbour. 'Crash darken ship' was exercised often, and the defence watch closed up for anti-aircraft drills. There was no all-night leave for ship's company or officers.

Anything Italian was looked upon askance and all telescopes were trained upon the Lloyd-Triestino liner *Ausonia* when she entered Alexandria at 8am on 18 October and anchored near *Queen Elizabeth*. But when at about 9am clouds of dense black smoke began to billow from her funnel and superstructure, all thoughts turned to sabotage. She might be a floating bomb. If she grounded in the entrance the harbour might be blocked.

Queen Elizabeth, *Glorious* and other ships sent boats across with firefighting and rescue teams. It was a genuine accident, caused by a flash-back in a boiler room. Four engine-room staff were badly burned and taken to *Maine*, where two of them died.

The Fleet Constructor W.J.A. Davies (a notable fly-half who with C.A. Kershaw formed a famous halfback partnership for the Navy and England) decided it was unsafe to leave the ship burning so close to the battleships. She was towed towards the inner breakwater where, due to the quantities of water pumped into her, she ran aground and remained, a partly burned-out hulk, until she was towed back to Italy in December.

Economic sanctions against Italy came into force on 18 November but it was soon clear they would have little effect. Leave at Alexandria was extended to midnight for ratings, 1am for officers, but ships remained at four hours' notice for steam. The training programme continued. The Navy, as so often in its history, watched and waited and trained, while the politicians talked interminably.

Glorious returned to Malta for docking and Christmas, 1935. 'Malta is very depressing,' Crichton wrote to Keyes. 'All lights are shaded and the dockyard covered in notices showing the way to the nearest air-raid shelter.' But it was not all gloom. The two straight streets in Valetta and Floriana dedicated to relieving the bluejacket of his money and his tensions were open for business and the lights were anything but shaded. 'The girls would stand in doorways of each bar shouting "Inside Navy, singing and dancing", or "Inside Lofty/Shorty, your ship's company inside, both pissed",' wrote Bill Collier. 'They lifted their skirts as further attraction. Inside, a girl would rush over saying, "I love you buy me a drink" all in one breath. If you did, her sherry was cold tea and if you insisted she should drink it, her love for you died and she went looking for another mug. But it was all fun.'

Beards at that time were rare in wardrooms, having been jibed out of fashion by schoolboy shouts of 'Beaver', a craze of the mid-Twenties. But some *Glorious* aircrew disembarked to Aboukir, to defend Alexandria naval base, commanded by Rear-Admiral Brownrigg. Wearing khaki and conforming to an RAF existence, they had proclaimed their naval identities by growing beards. At Rexford's, a celebrated watering hole in Malta, a party of 'Brownrigg's Light Horse', as these bearded aircrew were known, caused a sensation. '*Ah, la barbe!*' cried one middle-aged hostess. '*C'est un peu demodée, mats c'est une attraction sexuelle superbe!*'

When *Glorious* returned to Alexandria on 3 January, 1936, training went on as before, but more was done for the sailors' recreation ashore: football and hockey at Mustapha Barracks, rugby at Smouha, and a Fleet Club, largely instigated by Tubby Clayton, of 'Toe H' fame, at the Claridge Hotel, where up to 4,000 sailors every evening could buy beer and a meal, write letters, go to a dance and play games.

On 20 January the fleet heard of the death of King George V. He was greatly loved by the Navy, having been a professional naval officer himself. Ship's companies went to Divisions next day, and a Royal Salute was fired to the new King, Edward VIII. On 28 January, the day of the funeral at Windsor, the fleet observed Sunday routine, with memorial services and flagships firing minute guns, one for each year of the late King's reign. At 1.30pm two minutes' silence was observed (also observed at that moment all over the Empire). Court mourning, with the wearing of black arm bands, was in force for six months.

The shadow of a future war came closer on 7 March when Germany, aware that British attention was fixed on the east, reoccupied the Rhineland. But the crisis was deemed to have eased enough for Fisher to leave and on 18 March he took his fleet to sea for the last time, on a day of display and exercises laid on for distinguished guests, including the High Commissioner and several Egyptian politicians. After a farewell dinner in *Renown*, Fisher returned to *Queen Elizabeth* in a galley rowed by admirals, escorted by a double-banked cutter rowed by captains. Next morning *Queen Elizabeth* steamed slowly out of harbour, with Fisher standing on top of 'B' turret. Guards and bands were paraded, sailors manned the side and cheered Fisher out to sea. He had led his fleet surpassingly well, through a period of great political and personal strain (his son Nevill, who had joined the RAF, was killed in a flying accident on 17 October at the height of the crisis).

On 2 May, 1936, the Emperor Haile Selassie left his capital, Addis Ababa, and on the 5th Italian troops entered the city, while the Emperor, accompanied by some seventy relatives and followers, and with ten tons of baggage, embarked in HMS *Enterprise* at Djibouti, bound for Haifa. Sanctions against Italy had been useless and were ended on 15 July. The fleet was informed on 9 July that it would return to its normal stations and duties on the 18th.

By that time the fleet was holding one of its biggest regattas ever, lasting a whole week. On Monday, 13 July, a final week of parties and farewells began, with *Glorious* giving one of her own special parties on the Thursday for 2,000 guests, to repay hospitality shown to the sailors ashore.

In Abyssinia Mussolini's bluff had succeeded. The British government, as Churchill said, had had a chance of 'striking a decisive blow in a generous cause with the minimum of risk'. But this failure of nerve, or its sincere love of peace, was to play a part in leading to an infinitely more terrible war. There were interested spectators in Germany and Japan who drew their own conclusions from Abyssinia.

But none of this concerned the sailors of the fleet, as the ships began to leave, to east and west, each cheered out of harbour. The main fleet, leaving only *Valiant* and *Repulse* as guard ships in Egyptian waters, sailed on 18 July for Malta. Just before midnight on the 20th a signal was received that there had been rioting in Spain. The Abyssinian crisis was over, but the Spanish Civil War was about to begin.

CHAPTER 4: THE SHADOW OF WAR — FROM SPAIN TO ALEXANDRIA

IN JULY, 1936, there were many warships on passage westwards across the Mediterranean, on their way home to the United Kingdom after the Abyssinian crisis, who were available to lend a hand in Spain. By 24 July every major Spanish harbour, as well as Palma, Tenerife and Tangier, had a British man-of-war as guardship. By the end of the month there were thirty-six British warships in Spanish ports, or at Gibraltar.

The political and military situation in Spain during the Civil War was never clear-cut until the final victory of the Nationalists in March, 1939. But, broadly, the Republican Government, with its capital in Madrid, was supported by Soviet Russia, by international Communism, by socialists, liberals and those who later formed the International Brigades, and by poets and romantics. Italy and Germany supported the Nationalists (or rebels) under General Francisco Franco. In the Spanish Navy, the officers generally supported the Nationalists, while the lower deck remained loyal to the Republican government. The result was a breakdown of discipline in many Spanish warships.

The Royal Navy's tasks throughout the Civil War were humanitarian and the first was to evacuate British tourists and British residents and businessmen who wished to leave. But tourists and nationals of many other countries also asked for refuge. Thousands of Spaniards were fleeing their own country: priests and the wealthier professional classes from ports held by the Republicans, which were often ruled by mobs, and members of the Popular Front and known left-wing activists and politicians from ports held by the Nationalists. By October, 1936, 11,195 refugees (35% of them British) had been rescued by British warships, who had made 220 voyages and steamed 75,724 sea miles. No discrimination was made between nationalities. On one trip by the hospital ship *Maine* there were refugees of thirty-nine nationalities.

Conditions were always confused, and sometimes dangerous. Everything depended upon the good humour and willingness of the sailors and the initiative and good sense of their officers. Many difficult decisions had to be made quickly and correctly by quite junior officers commanding small warships, such as destroyers, which often carried well over a hundred refugees. The women were accommodated in the wardroom or in cabins, the men on the upper deck, except in bad weather, when they went down below to the crowded messdecks. The sailors took absolutely everything in their stride, acting as nurses, midwives, baby-sitters, dog-minders, tailors, cooks and father-confessors.

British ships often found themselves in the position of mediators and were fired on, or bombed, by both sides. British destroyers, which looked similar in silhouette to Spanish (being designed and built by the same firm), were regularly bombed by Nationalist aircraft, while British merchant ships were bombed by Republican aircraft in mistake for Nationalist troop transports. On 21 July, in the Straits of Gibraltar, the destroyer *Wild Swan* was bombed by Nationalist aircraft, fortunately without damage. On 5 August, when a Nationalist convoy was bringing troops and supplies across from Morocco to Algeciras, the destroyer *Basilisk* was straddled in error by the Nationalist gunboat *Dato*. Recently, during a throw-off shoot,

Basilisk herself had accidentally straddled a flotilla mate, who now signalled sharply: 'Now you know what it feels like'.

Glorious was not immediately involved in the Spanish Civil War. She spent the summer of 1936 at Malta and, except for exercises and a cruise to Greece and Crete in September and October, stayed there until February, 1937. Clive Rawlings left the ship on 22 May, 1936 and went on the Retired List, being promoted Rear-Admiral in June. (He did not have another active appointment and died on New Year's Eve, 1965).

The new man, who commanded *Glorious* for the final months of the crisis, was Captain B. A. Fraser, OBE, ADC, one of the most remarkable naval officers of the twentieth century. Bruce Fraser had, as they say, God's thumb-print on his forehead and seemed destined for the highest promotion since his earliest days. He had been Gunnery Officer of the cruiser *Minerva* at Gallipoli in 1915, and then of the new battleship *Resolution*. In 1920 he led a party of fifty sailors ashore from *Resolution* who went by train to Baku, the oil port on the Caspian Sea, to support anti-Bolshevik forces. But the town declared itself for the Bolsheviks and Fraser's party was imprisoned for eight months; it was Fraser's personal qualities and leadership which kept his little band together, in body and in spirit.

After the war Fraser went from one promising appointment to another and he came to *Glorious* after two years in the Admiralty as Director of Naval Ordnance. He was a first-class seaman and an excellent ship-handler. Bringing an aircraft carrier into Grand Harbour with a strong cross-wind at the entrance required great skill, but Fraser could slip *Glorious'* great bulk between St Elmo and Ricasoli even in a December Force 7 wind. He abhorred so-called 'shiphandling' where hauling and pulling on wires compensated for a faulty approach. No buoy-jumper ever got wet with Fraser.

Fraser possessed the common touch to an unusual degree and from the start established a close rapport with his aircrew, RN and RAF. In July, 1936, 815 Squadron was equipped with the new Fairey Swordfish torpedo-bomber reconnaissance aircraft, the first squadron to fly them. 'Fraser got on with the RAF extremely well,' said Flying Officer Les Levis, of 825, 'and had a wonderful impish sense of humour. As we were the first squadron to have Swordfish, we were doing "consumption trials", to see how far they would go on how much fuel. Some of us RAF were inclined to have more than our fair share of spirits in the wardroom. Fraser sent for us in his cabin, lined us up, and said, "I know you're doing these consumption trials, but I wished to draw your attention to the fact that your mixture in the wardroom is perhaps a little too rich!" Enough said! Point taken!'

The fighter squadron, 802, was pressed very hard. 'We had twelve aircraft,' said Flying Officer John Shepherd, 'and we could land them all on in nine minutes — exactly the time it took the forward lift to go up and down!' Almost everybody in 802 had one accident. There were two fatalities, due to engine failures and ditching in the sea. The accelerator, fitted in the 1934/35 refit, was often used. 'I blacked out every time,' said Shepherd, 'until well after clearing the ship. On that accelerator, just after dawn, it was like going off into a bowl of blue soup!'

Great emphasis was placed on night flying. 'We started with a very faint flood-lighting and very small pea-lights delineating the centre line of the flight deck, with the rest of the ship darkened,' said Geoffrey Eveleigh, also in 802. 'Given a starlit night and the ship's phosphorescent wake, you could manage well enough, but the floods were too bright for the Captain's liking. On dark nights you plunged into inky blackness on leaving the ship, before your meagre air-driven flying instruments had settled down. The solution was to station our "attendant" destroyer ahead with its topmast light on, to give us a lead.'

One night-flying device was the 'Pillar light', made on board, of opaque glass, internally illuminated. 'Four were spaced along the deck up to the island on either side. If you approached at too low an angle, they overlapped. If too high, there was a vertical gap between them. At the correct angle they appeared to be on top of each other.'

A third solution was 'Sector lights, made on board, from the Schoolies' magic lantern. Amber, green and red slides were projected from lanterns either side of the flight deck. The green sector showed the correct approach, red and amber were too low or too high.'

Night-fliers were also driven hard. 'We were out each week and all week, back on Friday night,' said Levis. 'We flew days and we flew nights, using Filfla, a little island off Malta as a bombing range, one end the bows, the other the stern. We made night torpedo attacks, we came in on the bow, from each side. We were always supposed to break off by flying aft. Once, the ships brought their searchlights into action and waved them about the sky. We found this very disorientating, particularly when we were close to the water. One night off Alex (in February, 1937), there was a mid-air collision. Gerry Vardon was lost. The other pilot, Harry Newcombe, managed to put his aircraft down in the water.'

On 24 November, 1936, *Glorious* was alongside Parlatorio Wharf and her squadrons were ashore when, at Hal Far that afternoon, according to Don Donovan, a telegraphist-air-gunner, 'we gradually became aware of a strange moaning sound... Then quite suddenly it grew louder and up over the nearby cliff edge swept a big cone-shaped cloud which reached high into the sky. It was spinning on its axis point downwards and swaying from side to side.'

The 'footprint' of the local cyclone was about a hundred yards wide, but took a diagonal path along the line of hangars, badly damaging them. 'Airmen working in the cockpit of one Baffin ended up under the aircraft, wedged in the torpedo crutches!' said Eveleigh, another eye-witness. 'Tool boxes which weigh very heavily were flung about and I remember seeing a refuelling tanker spinning along the tarmac with its terrified driver hanging on to the wheel, unable to do anything.' 'Another sight I shall never forget,' said Donovan, 'was of three aircraft lifting straight upwards off their chocks, slowly rotating in unison at shoulder level, then dropping back heavily to earth shedding odd bits as they landed. Perhaps clearest of all I can still hear the squadron chief's stentorian bellow, way above the roaring wind and the cacophony of bangs and crashes, "That bloody hangar's taking off without permission!".'

Violent though the storm was, the squadrons attributed to it unlikely powers. 'The Stores Officer,' said Donovan, 'flatly refused to believe that the aero watches issued to us on personal loan could in any way have been blown off our wrists'. Lieutenant Commander Buckley, Senior Pilot of 802, also tried unsuccessfully to have a metal vice, weighing some yolbs, written off charge as having 'been blown away'. Squadron Leader N.A.P. Pritchett had been just about to sign for 812 Squadron when he heard the commotion. 'Not yet,' he said to his predecessor, putting his pen down. 'I'll leave you to sort this out.'

Beppo's survived the cyclone unscathed. Beppo's was a bar in a stone building on the airfield, where officers could sign chits for drinks, charging them to their messbills. Everyone who had been in a squadron at Hal Far for a year worked his name in a length of wire and hung it up on the wall. There were some famous names, going back many years: Caspar John, Izzy Grant, Robin Kilroy, Monkey Bryant, Rastus Carnduff, Bruin Purvis, Keighley-Peach, George Pickering, Jeudy Jeudwine, Scotty Pryde, Micky Bramwell, Jimmy Nares, Drunkie Lewin, Cracksie Crawford, Tiffy Torrens-Spence, 'Dal' Dalyell-Stead, Jimmy Buckley and many more. Beppo, a taciturn Maltese who had originally farmed Hal Far, knew everybody's names and a great deal more about them than they suspected.

On Sunday 27 December, 1936, there was a Boxing Day Meet of the Hal Far Foxhounds. Every pi-dog which strayed near the airfield was impounded to form the pack. The fox was made of parachute material filled with raw meat and placed in the 'covert' — three trees in one corner of the airfield — with a Royal Marine to drag it on a line.

Lieutenant The Hon Peter Carew, of 812, was Master, with Flight Officer Leonard Pankhurst as 'Terrier Man'. As Whipper-In and Fieldmaster, Les Levis hired fifty donkeys for the field to ride. He attached no significance to the Maltese donkey-master's warning that the donkeys would not all be of the same sex. The Meet was attended by many officers' wives, a brace of admirals, and several distinguished guests, including Sybil Thorndike, the actress, who was spending Christmas in Malta with her son, Lieutenant John Casson, of 802.

It was not until the covert had been drawn, the Marine had set off at the double and the field trotted past the front of the Officers' Mess, every male donkey in a state of high and visible excitement at the close prospect of females, that Les Levis recalled the donkey-master's warning. The Meet was reported next day in *The Times of Malta* under the discreet headline 'High Jinks at Hal Far'.

Fraser ran his ship with a light touch. That Christmas of 1936 the naval 'powers that be' had, for some reason, refused an offer from NAAFI to issue every sailor with a free bottle of beer — a decision not well received on the lower deck. The ship's company could have foliage and green garlands to decorate their messes and the best-decorated mess on Captain's Christmas Day rounds would win a prize cake. 'My messmates ignored this olive branch,' wrote Bill Collier, 'and instead hung up an outsize pair of ladies green unmentionables. Where they came from, I tremble to think. We awaited the rounds with bated breath. Along they came. On reaching our mess, there was a pregnant pause. Then Captain Fraser chuckled and his entourage fell about in fits of forced laughter. They had gone just a moment when a very red-faced Chief Stoker rushed back and told us (not very kindly) what to do with the bloody things! We did *not* win the cake.'

'Fraser, of course, was the most magnificent man ever, and relations on board were always very good,' said Flying Officer George Seymour-Price, a Nimrod pilot of 802, who served in *Glorious* from September, 1936, to January, 1938, and made fifty-seven deck-landings in that time. 'It was like going on a Mediterranean cruise and being paid for it. The thing that always amazed me was that when I got ashore I would say, "I must go and get something from my cabin," which on an *air station*, of course, you were laughed out of church! It became second nature to use naval jargon because we lived with the Navy and worked with them. I had a very *very* happy time and I thought the Navy, and the Fleet Air Arm in particular, were super chaps.'

But Fraser was not always sweetness and light. A notable personality in *Glorious* was Lieutenant-Commander E.B. 'Rastus' Carnduff, who was Lieutenant-Commander (Flying) — 'Little F' in FAA parlance — and the Wingco's right-hand man. Little F's duties involved more administration and less flying than Rastus wished, and he protested vigorously to Fraser. The details are lost now, but Fraser's clinching retort was: 'If you don't like me and you don't like my ship, you will go, and I will see to it you are not promoted.' (Nor was Carnduff promoted; he remained a Lieutenant-Commander, although he did achieve War Service Rank of Commander.)

There was a huge and almost unbridgeable gap between the wardroom and the lower deck, still 'one law for them and another for us', as Leading Torpedoman 'Ginger' Le Breton, who joined *Glorious* in June, 1935, recalled: 'On the same day as a young O.D. (Ordinary Seaman) was mulcted 4½d (about 2p but a large sum for an O.D. in the 1930s) for losing a hand-scrubber over the side, we proceeded to sea to enable a pilot to land on a new 111F he had collected from shore. Because he had forgotten to switch something on, the pilot ditched just astern of the ship. We thought it unfair that it cost him nothing. I suppose he got a bollocking.'

The Combined Fleet exercises of March, 1937, were moved into the Atlantic because of the situation in Spain. All ships taking part had three identification stripes, red, white and blue, painted across a forward gun turret, clearly visible from the air, and, for defence patrols flown over the fleet, aircraft front guns were loaded with live ammunition.

Once again over a hundred ships took part, including ten capital ships, the carriers *Courageous* (flying the flag of Vice-Admiral N.F. Laurence, CB, DSO) and *Glorious*, three cruiser squadrons, five destroyer flotillas and submarines. The Home

Fleet was led by Admiral Sir Roger Backhouse, the Mediterranean by Pound.

One object was to make a thorough test of the full fleet action W/T organization, including 'enemy' jamming of wireless traffic. Unknown to the fleet, the German B-Dienst Wireless Intelligence Service was also taking part, and making that close study of British naval wireless traffic, routines and vocabulary which led to their later success in breaking British naval cyphers.

For the carriers, the emphasis was on night operations, with aircraft identification exercises by night, a night torpedo attack (one of the first, if not the very first, in the Royal Navy), night shadowing and reconnaissance. In one serial, aircraft guided a destroyer flotilla through a smoke screen, and there were also a torpedo attack on the capital ships, long-range reconnaissance, high-level and dive-bombing, and experiments to determine the safest position in the fleet for an aircraft carrier at night.

The weather, as usual, was appalling, but Fraser decided his striking force would fly off and attack the Home Fleet. With *Glorious*' stern rising and falling thirty-six feet in the swell, the problem for pilots was, as Seymour Price said, 'When did you take off, when you could see the sea or when you could see the sky?' The weather worsened and Fraser recalled his aircraft. He, and they, were all very relieved when they landed on safely, and glad to get a signal from Pound congratulating them for having at least had a try.

On 5 May *Glorious* and her attendant destroyer *Comet* arrived in Portsmouth to take part in the Coronation Review at Spithead later that month. Her squadrons flew off to RAF Gosport to rehearse for their 'Fly Past'. This was the first Coronation Review since 1911 and the first to include aircraft carriers. There were 141 Royal Navy or RFA ships: eight battleships, two battle cruisers, six large cruisers, ten light cruisers, five carriers (*Courageous*, *Glorious*, *Furious*, *Hermes*, and the Reserve Fleet seaplane carrier *Pegasus*), sixty destroyers, twenty-two submarines, two netlayers, five escort vessels, thirteen patrol vessels, the gunnery training ship *Iron Duke*, four depot ships, two surveying vessels and the oiler *Brambleleaf*. There were also seventeen foreign warships, from the U.S. battleship *New York* to the Estonian submarine *Kalev*, each with a British ship as host. *Glorious*' charge was the Cuban escort vessel *Cuba*, a somewhat accident-prone vessel: she had collided with a merchant ship at Lisbon on her way to Spithead and had another collision in the Thames, after she left.

All the carriers' squadrons had practised intensively for their fly past, which took place on the evening of Review Day, 20 May, after the Royal Yacht had moored. The squadrons flew past, from east to west, intending to return after some twenty minutes, to dive down from 1,500 feet to 500 feet in salute. Because of misty weather the return flight was cancelled and the dive-salute was made on the first run. Unfortunately, two of *Courageous*' aircraft touched wings and the TAG in one of them, who had neglected to fasten his 'dog-lead', securing him to the airframe, was tipped out and fell to his death.

After the Review *Glorious* went to Devonport to give summer leave, returned on 24 June to embark her squadrons, and arrived on the 26th at Falmouth, her 'home base', for a series of Trade Defence exercises in the Western Approaches. Great Britain (Red) was at war with a Blue power whose main naval forces were safely contained by the British fleet in a distant area. However, intelligence had reported that a Blue 6" gun cruiser and an armed merchant raider had escaped and were threatening British trade routes.

Glorious was Red flagship, flying the flag of Rear-Admiral T.H. Binney, CB, DSO, with the 6" gun cruiser *Newcastle*, and the destroyer *Brazen* representing a second 6" gun cruiser. Red also had 201, 209 and 228 Flying Boat Squadrons, under the orders of the Air Officer Commanding 16th Reconnaissance Group, based at RAF Mount Batten, Plymouth, and in the Scilly Isles.

The Blue flagship was the 6" gun cruiser *Southampton*, flying the flag of Rear-Admiral T.F.P. Calvert, CB, CVO, DSO, with the RFA oiler *Prestol* who was, for exercise purposes, disguised as an armed merchant ship raider, with four 6" guns and two 4" AA guns.

The exercise was planned to last eight days, but *Glorious'* aircraft were so successful in sighting and attacking that the exercise was cycled twice. On the first day, 28 June, *Southampton* sank three merchant ships, while *Glorious'* aircraft looked for her all day without success. But at 4pm *Glorious* launched twelve Swordfish to fly a diverging search, in pairs between 185° and 255°.

Southampton sighted two Swordfish to the north-west at 5.15. One flew close overhead, apparently to examine the flags *Southampton* was flying (which closely resembled *Newcastle*'s recognition signal) and was almost certainly shot down. The second Swordfish shadowed from astern. The sighting report, although *Southampton* tried to 'jam' it, was received in *Glorious* at 5.26pm.

Two relief shadowers were flown off and a striking force ranged on deck, of twelve Swordfish of 823 Squadron (which had been re-equipped with Swordfish 1s in November, 1936), armed with torpedoes, and six Swordfish of 825, each armed with 250lb bombs. This force had flown off by 6.30 and attacked at 7.21. Torpedo bombers and dive-bombers brilliantly synchronized their attacks to the nearest second, and *Southampton* was judged completely disabled.

Binney always had in mind the possibility that *Glorious* might be surprised by a powerfully-gunned surface vessel at a time when she was unprotected. He had kept *Brazen* in company as escort until Blue raiders were definitely located. With *Southampton* disabled, he could release *Brazen* to search for *Prestol*.

Prestol was found and bombed by a London flying boat from the Scillies just after midday, but claimed the aircraft would have been shot down. *Prestol* evaded all searches until 30 June when she encountered *Newcastle* in fog and, after trying to escape, was judged sunk. This ended the first part of the exercise.

The second phase began on 1 July when *Prestol* sighted *Queen Mary* and 'captured' her. *Southampton* also sank one merchant ship, whilst on that day and the next *Glorious'* aircraft and the shore-based flying boats were hampered by poor visibility. *Prestol's* day was Saturday 3 July when, continuing to wipe the Royal Navy's eye, she sank or captured seven ships.

At about midday on 4 July *Southampton* sighted two aircraft on the starboard beam, quickly followed by four more, and deduced correctly from their presence that *Glorious* must be quite close. Calvert decided, as *Southampton* could not hope to outrun an air striking force, to turn towards and try and sink *Glorious* before she could launch the strike. But to achieve this *Southampton* had first to engage *Newcastle*, who was positioned to meet this very contingency.

Although *Southampton* could actually see *Glorious* flying off her aircraft only some seventeen miles away and pressed towards her, she found herself having to repel a bombing attack at the same time as she began her gun duel with *Newcastle*. In a short but hectic engagement in which the gun ranges came down from an opening 18,500 yards to 6,000, *Southampton* was attacked by dive-bombers and torpedo-bombers. She took violent evasive action, stopping inner shafts and using full rudder to speed up her turns, and made smoke, but was eventually overwhelmed and judged sunk.

Meanwhile *Prestol* had sunk another three ships, but she was sighted and bombed that evening by a Scapa flying boat from Mount Batten, which stayed to shadow. She was also found by one of *Glorious'* aircraft and finally bombed and sunk by eight Swordfish out of a strike of ten (the other two bombed a friendly merchantman in error).

The exercises had shown once again how vitally necessary it was to give a carrier close support. In Binney's opinion, when *Southampton* decided to sell herself dearly and turned to engage *Glorious*, had *Newcastle* not been there *Southampton* might well have come close enough to have sunk *Glorious* before she could launch her strike.

For the flying boats the Scillies had proved unsuitable for landing and taking off, even under quite average sea conditions. At Mount Batten fog, mist and rain had prevented flying boats taking off at the proper times. For the carrier aircraft, although it was high summer, bad visibility had prevented flying on three out of seven days. Admiral Backhouse said that *Glorious'* flying was a credit to all concerned. The Admiralty was less impressed, questioning the efficiency of aircraft making bombing attacks in pairs against targets who were forewarned and armed with more AA guns. The 1937 Fleet Air Arm bombing results had shown that, without opposition, eleven bombs in dive-bombing attacks and thirty bombs in level bombing attacks from 10,000 feet were needed to register just one hit on a cruiser-sized target. The

Admiralty pointed out that *Glorious'* aircraft should have sighted *Southampton* twice more and *Prestol* three times more than they actually did, given the visibility at the time.

Fraser commented that *Glorious* had twenty-six observers and observers' mates on board. On a typical day they would fly two searches, each of three hours, and might also fly on a strike, making a total of seven and a half hours flying — a long day, especially as observers were often required to stand by for long periods between flights. Fraser recommended six more observers, to make nine per Swordfish squadron and four per Nimrod/Osprey squadron, with a Commander (O) and two more observers for signals and plotting duties.

Glorious' aircraft had flown ten searches, two strikes and one special shadowing. The average depth of search was 105 miles; the average visibility had been ten miles, the average course error reported was 7°; the average speed error reported was about 3 knots. In seven days the Swordfish had flown 295 hours, a distance of 26,580 miles, and used an average of 3,500 gallons of petrol a day (4,839 on the heaviest day). *Glorious* carried 26,955 gallons of petrol which at this rate was enough for only about five or six full flying days. As a result of this exercise the Admiralty noted that petrol capacity, as well as stowage for pyrotechnics such as smoke-floats and smoke-puffs for navigation and marking, should be increased in the new carrier *Ark Royal*, then building at Cammell Lairds.

When *Glorious* returned to Malta on 16 July, 1937, there was a sense of change in the air. It seemed that at last the Navy was about to regain control of its air arm. The system of 'dual control', set up in 1923, whereby the Admiralty and the Air Ministry both shared to some extent in administering the Fleet Air Arm, had never worked satisfactorily; that it had worked at all was almost entirely due to the professional talents and the good will of RAF officers, embarked in carriers, or ashore. 'Dual control' was well summed up by Flight Lieutenant Nigel Blair-Oliphant, who joined *Glorious* as Armaments Officer in January, 1938: 'Their Lordships and Their Airships were continually at one another's throats and the Admiralty's attitude was nicely illustrated by a slip of paper pasted inside the RAF Technical and Tactical manuals, which were necessarily used on board, saying in effect, "Their Lordships do not necessarily agree with anything contained in this book".'

By the mid-1930s naval flying had progressed so far and improved so much that 'dual control' was not just inconvenient and inefficient, it was actually beginning to affect the country's security. 'Dual control' brought anomalies in every field but especially in training. There was a perennial shortage of pilots, because naval officers continued to doubt their promotion prospects. The Navy would have liked to get more pilots from the RAF but having fought so hard to establish the 70-30 ratio of RN to RAF, the Navy could hardly admit that it could not maintain even this quota. Meanwhile the RAF refused to train ratings as pilots. Yet, through an anomalous quirk, the Navy always had and still could train its own observers (in dual conjunction, of course, with the RAF). In 1935 ratings could qualify as observer's mates, through a simplified form of the officers' course, lasting twenty-two weeks (later extended to seven months). There were nine vacancies for the first course which joined the RAF School of Naval Co-operation, Lee-on-Solent, on 15 July. Observers' mates could reach warrant rank as Boatswains (O).

But the best argument against 'dual control' was put by Chatfield himself. If war came, and it was looking more likely every month, and if the Fleet Air Arm failed in war, it would be the Navy, not the RAF, which would be blamed. It was only just and right therefore that the Navy should have control over its own air arm. Chatfield's first battle was to get the debate reopened at all. He succeeded, and his campaign, for which the country and the Navy should ever be grateful, took two years and two months, survived two Prime Ministers and three First Lords, before on 21 July, 1937, the Cabinet agreed to two main recommendations put by Sir Thomas Inskip: that ship-borne aircraft were to be administered by the Admiralty, but for shore-based aircraft the present system would continue. There was much bargaining still to be done and it would be another two years before the Navy regained the full control over its air arm. But, to the amazement and rage of 'Their Airships', the main battle had been won.

Bruce Fraser played a part in this victory. Sir Samuel Hoare, the then First Lord, (who had been Secretary of State for Air when 'dual control' was set up and was therefore considered by the Navy to be very much 'on the other side') came out in the Admiralty yacht *Enchantress* to visit the Mediterranean Fleet in the summer of 1936. Determined to impress, Pound and his staff laid on a full programme: a tour of Malta's defences, visits to the dockyard, Bighi Hospital, *Repulse* and *Severn*, a march past at which the First Lord took the salute, a large official cocktail party in *Queen Elizabeth*, dinner with the Governor, dinner at Admiralty House, tennis, a picnic and swimming party. The fleet put to sea; *Glorious* did her dive-bombing, torpedo dropping and aerobatic routines.

On Sunday 30 August Pound took Hoare for a cruise round Malta in the destroyer *Grenville*. He invited Fraser, as the fleet's carrier captain, to come too. Fraser had an hour's talk with the First Lord which, in its own way, encapsulated current political views and prejudices about the Fleet Air Arm.

Hoare asked Fraser what *were* all these difficulties about 'dual control'? Fraser explained the difficulties of working under several authorities, of fixing responsibility and of getting anybody to make a decision. Hoare said that surely there were ex-naval officers in the RAF who were qualified? Fraser pointed out that the more senior RAF officers had not been to sea for very many years.

Then, taking the bull by the horns, Fraser asked Hoare what were the *disadvantages* of the Navy taking over the Fleet Air Arm. Hoare said that that had failed in the last year of the war and it would lead to duplications of aerodromes and so on. He said that more and more shore-based aircraft would be built and such aircraft must all be under one control.

To that Fraser replied that the last years of the war, when an entirely new service had had to be organized, could not be compared with the present day, when the Navy knew what was required. Fraser pointed out that *Glorious* carried some thirty RAF officers and 250 men who could not be used for ship's duties at sea. There were two systems of stores accounting which could be greatly simplified.

Hoare said he would bear all this in mind. Maybe he was playing the part of devil's advocate to see what Fraser would say. But, when the party went on to Comino Island for a picnic and a bathe, Fraser was left feeling that he had failed to convince. Reporting later to Pound, Fraser said that the First Lord still seemed to believe that the Navy had failed in the air in the last war and that once a carrier had landed her aircraft they became shore-based aircraft. He could not seem to grasp that they were only landing for training, and when the carrier could not go to sea; they were still *naval* aircraft and their training was still *naval* training. The First Lord seemed to believe that if the Navy was once allowed to take control of the

Fleet Air Arm, the Army would then demand to be allowed to control army co-operation flights, and there would be much 'duplication' in 'shore aerodromes, personnel and plant'. But possibly Fraser had been more persuasive than he gave himself credit for.

In July, 1937, when *Glorious* returned to Malta, the season was picking up after a slow start. The ships, which had gone home for the Coronation, had been badly missed. But there had been the spring spate of weddings, polo (Tigne Tigers versus The Eligible Bachelors), the Army beat the Navy by two wickets at the Marsa and in the football final at Corradino the Rifle Brigade beat the Destroyers four goals to three.

But this year there was a sombre undercurrent. In March a mobile gas chamber had been set up in Palace Square, Valetta, and children from five years old queued up to try the new toy. The respirators were imported (supposedly enough for the whole population) during the Abyssinian crisis. Other anti-gas appliances were on show and pamphlets were distributed.

The 1937 Air Estimates proposed to build a new airfield at Luqa, about three miles N.E. of Hal Far. In the House, Vice-Admiral E.A. Taylor, Member for South Paddington, advocated underground hangars and oil storage tanks in Malta. In June there was a full-scale exercise for Passive Defence Class 'A' Reservists, who had been mobilized some days earlier. Three RAF bombers attacked Valetta. The streets were cleared. Unwary stray pedestrians were rounded up and shepherded into shelters. Smoke candles and tear-gas generators were used and there was a simulated water-main burst outside the main G.P.O. First aid and decontamination squads exercised gear and procedures, with Boy Scouts as 'casualties'. Later in the month there was a practise 'black-out'. Attacking parties landed at St Paul's Bay, with defenders occupying the surrounding high ground. Search-lights caught and held aircraft overhead. All this activity had an authentic air about it, which, according to the local press, 'brought back to many of the older generation unpleasant memories'.

On 24 August *Glorious* sailed for a major fleet exercise which, as the staff at RNC Greenwich candidly said later, represented 'roughly conditions which might arise in a war with Italy'. The familiar Red Fleet was to pass a heavily-escorted convoy the 320 miles from Malta to Argostoli, whilst Blue, based at Navarino, tried to stop it. The orders spoke of the 'skeleton forces' available, but Pound, leading Red, flew his flag in the battleship *Barham*, and *Glorious*, with *Comet*, was part of 'Force F', with *Hood*, *Repulse*, three 8" gun cruisers and a flotilla of destroyers. Force F was in fact a balanced task force, with heavy guns and aircraft, similar to those employed in the war to come, which was strong enough to engage anything Blue could field and fast enough to ensure that Blue could not escape.

But one old problem remained. On the first evening the westerly wind dropped away and when *Glorious* began to land on her aircraft she rapidly fell astern of the rest, who were steering east. *Glorious* was engaged, and very probably sunk, by *Despatch*. The fleet had still not grasped the truth, so well exploited by the US Navy in the Pacific, that the task force must conform to the movements of the carriers and not vice versa.

Glorious returned to Malta on 17 September, 1937, for one day to refuel before sailing west to Gibraltar to take part, at last, in the naval operations of the Spanish Civil War.

Although in general the sympathies of officers and men were with the 'White' Nationalist Navy rather than the 'Red' Republican, the Royal Navy had continued to act as peacekeepers, helping refugees of both sides and remaining impartial, even under provocation: the destroyer *Hunter* was mined and badly damaged (the ship was torn almost completely in two) while lying off the southern port of Almeria on 13 May, 1937. Eight men were killed and fourteen injured. But the Navy continued to resist attempts by both sides to impose blockades on British and international shipping. The arrival of such ships as *Hood* and *Repulse*, with 15" guns, cooled several inflamed situations.

But in August, 1937, the Italians began a campaign of submarine warfare which was, in a word, piracy. Mussolini lent four 'legionary' submarines which, with Spanish liaison officers on board, operated under Nationalist colours from Malaga. On 11 August two Italian destroyers torpedoed a Republican tanker, *Campeador*, in a disgracefully inhuman and treacherous manner.

The campaign was indiscriminate in area and in nationality: the French ship *Parame* was sunk off Tunis on 13 August, a Spanish ship off Tenedos on the 15th, a Republican destroyer torpedoed off Cartagena, two Russian ships sunk in the Aegean and one off Algiers. On 2 September the British tanker *Woodford*, with a cargo of oil for the Republicans, was torpedoed and sunk without warning and with no subsequent attempt to pick up survivors on the high seas off Valencia.

By then the Admiralty had authorized counter-attacks on submarines which attacked British merchant ships and Pound had issued rules of engagement to his fleet (which, however, were cautious and complicated enough to make any captain pause before engaging).

On the night of 31 August the destroyer *Havock*, on passage in the western Mediterranean, suffered a near-miss from a torpedo which crossed her wake close astern. *Havock* turned towards the track and soon gained an asdic contact. A submarine was sighted on the surface. It dived, but contact was lost at a range of about 400 yards. *Havock*'s Captain decided not to use the submarine's point of dive as his attack datum (for which he was later criticized) but to try and regain asdic contact. Three hours later *Havock* got another asdic contact and carried out a deliberate depth-charge attack. Intelligence later reported that the submarine, almost certainly the Italian *Iride*, was badly shaken and 'nearly had to come up'. Rear-Admiral (D) Somerville in *Galatea* and five destroyers later reached the scene and searched for some hours, attacking one possible contact.

Piracy demanded retaliation. The Foreign Secretary, Anthony Eden, proposed the sinking of the Nationalist cruiser *Canarias*, an act of open warfare. The Admiralty preferred evasive routing of merchant ships along fixed lanes patrolled by ships and aircraft (a measure, one would have thought, most bloodily discredited in 1917). Pound proposed convoy, accepting the enormous maritime, legal and practical difficulties of convoying the world's merchant ships in peacetime.

In September, 1937, Eden and Chatfield attended an international conference at Nyon, a village near Geneva, where it was agreed that Great Britain would be responsible for waters around Gibraltar, Malta, Cyprus and part of the Aegean; France, the area around Tunis and the Gulf of Hammamet; and Greece for the Gulf of Corinth. Ironically, Italy (who, with Germany, boycotted the conference) was allocated the Tyrrhenian Sea, if she agreed, which she never did. The Admiralty knew through intelligence that the Italians had already called off their submarine campaign. The Nyon Conference's object had been achieved before it even met.

Glorious arrived at Oran on 22 September, flew off some of her aircraft to a desert airfield to carry out reconnaissance flights, whilst their crews lived under canvas, and sailed next day. Anti-submarine patrols were flown for several days but, despite the recent issue of polaroid sun-glasses, none of the aircrew saw a submarine.

The only excitement was on 4 October when the destroyer *Basilisk* reported that a torpedo had been fired at her (eight of her sailors later said they saw the track passing down the starboard side). Lieutenant David Buchanan-Dunlop, one of *Glorious'* observers, was officer of the watch and 'turned full wheel towards the bearing of the torpedo, sounded off "Close watertight doors" and "Action Stations". Bruce Fraser appeared on the bridge, quite unruffled, and apart from turning the ship 180°, approved all action taken.'

Basilisk delivered a depth-charge attack upon an asdic 'echo', firmly classified as a submarine. Contact was lost, regained an hour later, and a second attack made. The contact faded, but there was no oil, debris or any other evidence.

Basilisk was newly out of refit and her asdic team were considered inexperienced. A very experienced asdic team present, in the destroyer *Boreas*, had had no contact at any time. There were inconsistencies in *Basilisk*'s eyewitness accounts, inaccuracies in her track charts and asdic records. The official verdict was that there had been no submarine.

But the incident caused a stir in the press and had serious implications for the Navy. Good results were being obtained with asdic at the anti-submarine training school at Portland and asdic was thought to be an almost fool-proof defence against submarines. The *Basilisk* incidents, like *Havock*'s earlier affair with *Iride*, showed that there was a deal of difference between exercise and war. But Pound said, 'If a submarine was depth-charged by *Basilisk* it ought to have been destroyed and if there was no submarine we cannot say so without acknowledging the unreliability of asdics.' Chatfield finally minuted the *Basilisk* docket: 'No action is required since the *Basilisk* incident did not take place.'

Nobody at the time stopped to consider the implications of sending *Glorious* and destroyers to search for submarines in this manner. There might have been no submarine and no torpedo this time, but two years later, almost to the month, when *Courageous* and her attendant destroyers were searching in an identical way off the Western Approaches, a U-boat and its torpedoes were there and *Courageous* was sunk.

Glorious flew off 812, 823 and half of 825 Squadron to Hal Far when she returned on 18 October. On the 25th the bands played 'Rolling Home', the crowds gathered on the Baracca and on the breakwaters to wave goodbye as *Glorious* sailed for Devonport to pay off. Fraser left the ship. Everybody (possibly excepting Rastus Carnduff) was devoted to him. 'Nobody who heard it will ever forget Bruce Fraser's farewell speech at the dinner held in his honour in the wardroom,' wrote Buchanan-Dunlop. 'To riotous applause he mentioned every one of the wilder young officers, both RN and RAF, by name, making it clear that he knew exactly what they got up to in their off-duty moments.'

Glorious expected that Fraser would be promoted Rear Admiral (as indeed he was, in January 1938) and on to Admiral. A Rear-Admiral's flag has two red balls on its cantons, a full Admiral's none, so the toast at dinner that night was 'No balls at all!' The wish was more than fulfilled. Fraser, as C-in-C Home Fleet, planned and executed the sinking of *Scharnhorst* in 1943 and later became C-in-C British Pacific Fleet, First Sea Lord, Admiral of the Fleet and Lord Fraser.

He was relieved on 7 December, 1937, by Arthur Lumley St George Lyster, a gunnery officer and a senior Captain, having been promoted in 1928. He won a DSO as gunnery and executive officer of *Cassandra* in the 6th Light Cruiser Squadron and was made CVO in 1936, when, as Captain of the Chatham Gunnery School, he organized King George V's funeral, including the traditional hauling of the gun-carriage by a party of blue-jackets. He came to *Glorious* from the Admiralty, where he had been Director of Training and Staff Duties.

Glorious commissioned, for the last time, at Devonport on 4 January, 1938. She sailed on the 15th in a gale (the sailing was cancelled, but the ship was already on her way) with a tug at bow and stern. Passing Devil's Point, the bow-wire parted and wrapped itself around the tug's propeller. Only by emergency astern power was *Glorious* herself prevented from going aground near Drake's Island.

802 Squadron's Ospreys and Nimrods were flown on from Abingdon, then six Swordfish of 825 from Southampton on 17 January, and *Glorious* sailed for Malta. In deck-landing practise on passage, a Nimrod flown by Pilot Officer Heber-Percy spun into the sea. The destroyer *Comet* could find no sign of aircraft or pilot.

Despite this start, *Glorious* had a most successful eighteen months under Lyster. She was, as Blair-Oliphant said, 'An extraordinarily happy ship, due very largely to her Skipper, who was an ideal choice to command a combined service unit'. 'Pilots from both services flew together, respected one another professionally and were united in the job they did together.' On the Navy's side, 'One wonderful thing about *Glorious* when I joined her in '37,' said Buchanan-Dunlop, 'was the marvellous quality of the RAF pilots still serving in her. Those left were THE PICK of Cranwell and among them I found some of the best friends I've ever made anywhere.'

The Commander, who had served for the last six months of the previous commission, was Edward Evans-Lombe, a gunnery officer and a most able man, later Fraser's Chief of Staff in the Pacific, and a Vice-Admiral. The air group showed a changing Fleet Air Arm. 'Wings', for the very first time, was a Commander RN, Guy Willoughby. The Senior Observer was Commander (O) L.D. Mackintosh (relieved in June, 1938, by J.F.H. Sawyer). 802 Squadron was commanded by Lieutenant-Commander (P) J.P.G. Bryant, 823 by Lieutenant-Commander Robin Kilroy and 825 by Lieutenant-Commander A. Brock (relieved in August, 1938, by J.W. Hale). The one remaining RAF squadron commander was Squadron Leader J.H. Hutchinson of 812 and he was relieved by Lieutenant-Commander J.D.C. Little in November, 1938.

The only RAF who had mixed feelings about *Glorious* were the skilled airframe riggers and engine fitters, of whom there were still over two hundred embarked. For regulating duties, they had a senior RAF warrant officer who was equivalent to (but often did not see eye to eye with) the ship's Master at Arms. To their disgust RAF NCOs lived in a cramped mess which was nothing like the Sergeant's Messes they were used to, and, worse still, there was no beer. Many RAF personnel strongly objected to slinging hammocks, and some refused point-blank, preferring to sleep on messdeck benches and tables, or on campbeds. When squadrons flew ashore to live under canvas, sailors were paid extra 'hard-lying' money. The RAF were not.

But relations between sailors and the RAF were usually very good and, as Blair-Oliphant said, 'Arguments were confined to good-natured ribbing, mainly about naval terms. Once, when some equipment was being lowered from a stowage in the hangar roof (sic), an airman remarked provocatively, "Lower away beautifully", to which a sailor replied "Not beautifully — *handsomely*", to receive the airman's response "I knew it was something f...g lovely!".'

Grand Harbour, where *Glorious* arrived on 24 January, 1938, was full of ships. Beppo's, Rexford's, and the Gut were open for business. But everybody's main task was to work up the ship and the air group for the combined exercises off Gibraltar in March. These took up most of the month and, although the Navy still had commitments around the coast of Spain from Bilbao to Perpignan, involved over eighty ships.

There were twelve serials, exercising various tactical situations, from dusk attack to convoy escort, from night encounters to massed destroyer and air attacks on the battle fleet. Old lessons were relearned. 'Once more,' wrote Cunningham, now commanding the Battle Cruiser Squadron, in *Hood*, 'I learnt the unwisdom of one's aircraft carrier operating apart from the fleet.' *Glorious* and *Courageous* were both sunk by each other's aircraft in one early exchange, drawing from Pound a most perceptive post-exercise comment: 'Armoured carriers may be the only satisfactory solution to the problem of bomb attacks.'

Two serials showed again the deadly threat to capital ships posed by airborne torpedo strikes. On 10 March *Courageous* flew off a strike including twenty-four Swordfish with torpedoes, to attack the battle fleet steaming at 19 knots. 821 Squadron got four hits on *Warspite*, Pound's flagship (and another two aimed at her ran on and hit *Nelson*); 820 got three hits on *Revenge* and 810 five on *Royal Oak* — fourteen hits in all.

Glorious also flew off eleven fighters of 802, ten Swordfish of 812 to make a 'light torpedo' attack, and nine Swordfish each from 823 and 825 carrying torpedoes, to attack *Hood* and *Repulse*, steaming at 26 knots. 802 achieved three dive-bombing hits on *Hood* and two on *Repulse*, while 812 had three 'light' hits on *Hood*. Of eighteen torpedoes actually fired, two did not run and one 'hung up'. Lieutenant Paul Compton of 823 had one hit on *Repulse*, Lieutenants Dobbs and Newcombe and Flying Officer Rankin of 825 one hit each on *Hood*.

On 17 March both carriers launched a combined strike of forty-six Swordfish and eleven fighters of 802 Squadron against all seven battleships steaming at 19 knots. 812, 810 and 820 achieved seventeen torpedo hits on the flagship *Nelson*, leading the line, for the 'loss' of one Swordfish each from 810 and 820. Meanwhile 825 scored two hits on *Rodney*, losing one Swordfish, and 823 one hit on *Malaya*, losing two Swordfish. *Royal Oak* was also hit by one torpedo. Of forty-six torpedoes fired, twenty-one hit, for the loss of five Swordfish.

Battleship staffs continued to denigrate and discount these results. Hits scored by aircraft which had been 'shot down' were disallowed, although in war torpedoes might well hit after the aircraft had been lost. However, the results were taken very seriously by Ginger Royle, now RAA in *Courageous*, and conferences were held to consider the relative merits of torpedo-bombing, divebombing and high-level bombing.

Of the three, high-level bombing was the weakest. Not surprisingly, accuracy diminished markedly with height. Exercises over the years had shown that above 10,000 feet, no matter how carefully and steadily a pilot flew, no matter how expert his observer in wind-finding and spotting, hits were very rare.

When *Glorious* returned to Malta at the end of March, 1938, exercises were held with *Centurion*, an old (1911) battleship converted as a target ship for shells up to 8" calibre. She was radio-controlled from her specially-equipped attendant destroyer *Shikari*, so that her helm could be put over and sprayers on her boilers turned on or off to alter her course and speed. So long as *Centurion* held her course and speed steady, *Glorious*' Swordfish had reasonable results. But when *Centurion* began to take evasive action, directed by Commander Sawyer in *Shikari*, bombing accuracy fell away dramatically. High level bombing played less and less part in the Fleet Air Arm training programme.

As the tempo of operational training increased throughout 1938 more and more emphasis was laid on night-flying, night torpedo attacks, night shadowing and all the basic flying practices such as taking off, forming up, keeping station, flying steady courses and landing on in very low or no lighting. *Glorious*' squadrons pioneered dawn or dusk attacks, in which enemy ships were silhouetted against a rising or setting sun. A night search pattern was evolved, in which six Swordfish flew in line abreast. Above them, on a parallel course, flew six more, dropping flares at intervals, against which the lower Swordfish could spot ship silhouettes.

After Abyssinia and Spain, *Glorious* expected an 'autumn crisis'. In 1938 it was Munich. The Mediterranean Fleet, in traditional style, was holding its regatta in Alexandria harbour on the day Neville Chamberlain returned. To *Glorious* beating *Warspite* was more important than Munich.

Ever afterwards *Glorious*' sailors were convinced that this regatta victory over the flagship made Pound dislike them and their ship. There might have been a grain of truth in it, although Bruce Fraser had returned as Pound's Chief of Staff in January, 1938, and would surely have put in a good word for his old ship. It is hard at this distance of time to assess Pound's views on the Fleet Air Arm, and on *Glorious* in particular, without seeming unfair. Certainly, he underestimated capital ships' vulnerability to torpedo attack and overestimated their ability to defend themselves against air attack by their own gunfire.

Dudley Pound was a difficult man to serve. Aloof and reserved, with a temper always liable to erupt, he still had a great many friends. He drove himself as hard as he drove his fleet. He adored fishing and shooting, and after anchoring off one of the Greek islands after a full day's exercises at sea, he would ask if anybody was interested in shooting quail. He would leave the ship at 5am, shoot for a couple of hours, return on board, bathe and have breakfast and then do a day's work, after which he would go to a party or a dinner, come back on board and work until 2am.

He was tremendously sociable. He and Lady Pound were seen everywhere. He attended every large wedding, and on occasions even gave the bride away. He loved dancing into the small hours. The C-in-C quick-stepping with the Governor's lady was said to be an 'awe-inspiring spectacle' and there were some, with Pound's best interests at heart, who sometimes wondered if such exertion was wise, for a man of his age, in the heat of a Maltese summer.

On Sunday 29 January, 1939, *Warspite* was alongside in Alexandria, with *Glorious* moored to two anchors in the harbour. *Glorious'* sailors were convinced that, while they went to sea every week from Monday to Friday, the flagship stayed in harbour grounding on her own beer bottles. They also knew that Pound had been duck-shooting that weekend. When

Warspite sailed for Malta that evening she passed close to *Glorious* on her way out to sea.

What happened next has lost nothing in the telling over the years, but it seems that some of *Glorious'* sailors on the flight deck indulged in what is known in naval parlance as 'chiyacking'. References to 'f***g ducks', accompanied by loud quacking noises, were audible on *Warspite*'s flag-bridge. As *Warspite* passed through the breakwater, her largest signal projector began flashing furiously: 'DISGRACEFUL SCENES... DISRESPECT TO THE FLAG... PROCEED TO SEA AT ONCE... REPORT WHEN PASSING THE BREAKWATER.'

When Bolt, who was 'Day On' as duty lieutenant commander, passed the message to Lyster, dining ashore, Lyster enquired what *Glorious'* notice for steam was, and when told it was four hours, said, 'We pass through the breakwater four hours from the time on the C-in-C's signal'. By 8.45 *Glorious'* hands were unmooring ship and the ship sailed just after midnight, to anchor again at 1.25am. She was due for a full day's flying on Monday in any case and sailed again at 5.25am.

825 Squadron had some new pilots and when some Swordfish flew off at 9.20pm that evening for night deck landing and formation training, they had newcomers as passengers. Visibility was not good but the aircraft could be seen from the ship. Leading Seaman Birch, one of four fire-fighters on the flight deck, saw one flight of three Swordfish 'dive across the bow. They made their climb but the centre aircraft veered to the left. The left-hand aircraft rose up underneath the centre one. There was a flash of flame and both planes locked together and plunged into the sea about half a mile from the ship.'

Glorious anchored, some twelve miles off Ras el Tin, and lowered boats. The search was joined by *Boadicea* and *Wren*, and later by *Ark Royal*, recently arrived to work up her squadrons. The search was abandoned and all boats hoisted at 2.30am. Three aircraft from Dekheila, a desert field a few miles west of Alexandria, took up the search at 7.15. *Ark Royal*, *Boadicea* and *Wren* closed *Glorious*, and at 9.30 a burial and memorial service was held.

The dead were Lieutenants Richard Dobbs and Gordon Newcombe (his second and last mid-air collision), their passengers Flying Officer Henry Bridger RAF and Lieutenant John Lincoln, and the TAGs in both aircraft, Leading Signalmen RJ. Peerman and B.A. Coughlin. At Malta a somewhat conscience-stricken Pound, it was believed, sent *Warspite* to sea for an extra day as penance.

In 1943 the HMSO publication *Fleet Air Arm* reported that in 1938 Pound had asked Lyster to prepare a plan for *Glorious'* highly-trained night-flying squadrons to carry out an attack on the Italian fleet at Taranto. The idea had been floated in the fleet during the Abyssinian crisis, but was not fully investigated until much later, as Ben Bolt, who was involved from an early stage, recalls: 'Lyster spoke to Dudley Pound at Alexandria about the projected attack on Taranto and said that *Glorious'* Swordfish squadrons were sufficiently trained in night torpedo work and night formation flying to carry out such an operation. Dudley Pound agreed in principle. Lyster then had a meeting in *Glorious* with Commander Flying (Willoughby), Senior Observer (Paul Slessor) the three Swordfish squadron C.O.s and myself, as I had been made a night operations co-ordinator to develop night tactics and training. We were told to maintain complete secrecy but to train the Swordfish squadrons with this end in view. Nothing was ever written down and nothing ever reached the Admiralty about this plan, as I was to discover later'.

Dudley Pound himself was quite explicit about Taranto and his view of *Glorious'* future in wartime, writing on 18 August, 1939 (when he was First Sea Lord) to Admiral Cunningham, who was C-in-C Mediterranean: 'When we attack Italy itself (in which I include Sicily) then I think there is a great deal to be said for making an attack by air on the Italian fleet at Taranto. One reason for this is that I do not believe the *Glorious* will be able to remain in a serviceable condition in the Mediterranean for very long, what with air and submarine attack, and it might be a good thing to get the most one can out of her before she is placed *hors de combat.*

However, air attacks on a fleet in harbour had dropped out of exercise schedules in the late 1930s. Certainly they were not included in the strategic and tactical exercises for the Combined Fleets off Gibraltar in February and March, 1939.

Normally a press description of such exercises was issued, but in 1939 everything was withheld. The greatest secret was Type 79 radar — known in the Navy by the initials RDF — fitted to *Rodney* in August, 1938, and to *Sheffield* in November, and now being used by them for the first time in fleet exercises.

When the fleets assembled *Glorious* had to anchor out in Algeciras Bay for the third year running (utterly convincing her sailors that Pound did not like them) while *Ark Royal*, flying the flag of Vice-Admiral Aircraft Carriers, berthed alongside the Main Wharf. But *Glorious* had the satisfaction of surprising and 'sinking' *Ark Royal* with four torpedo hits in an early serial on 1 March. Neither carrier's torpedo-bombers had such good results against the Battle Squadron. Evidently the battleships had learned something about evasion and aerial defence since the previous year.

By April *Glorious* was back in Alexandria, where she now spent more time than in Malta, and which was one of the sailors' favourite runs ashore. Like their forefathers in the Victorian navy, *Glorious*' sailors made pious pilgrimages to Pompey's Pillar, eighty-eight feet high and nine feet round, erected by the Emperor Diocletian in AD 297. It was the largest single piece of red granite in the world and the sailors loved to be photographed beside it.

A sailor's favourite excursion was the three-day trip under the aegis of Mr William Johnson ('Official Guide No 2 & Contractor to HBM's Navy Ships') to the Great Pyramids, the Sphinx, the Cairo bazaars, Joseph's Wall and the Mameluke Kings' tombs. The round trip cost £2.6s (Egyptian) (about £2.90) for men, £2.11s (£3.20) for officers, which included the return train fare, with lunch baskets, two nights in a hotel, meals, motor-car, carriages, entrance fees to mosques and tombs, camel and donkey, guide and tips.

The Royal Navy resumed control of its own air arm on 24 May, 1939, when Rear-Admiral Richard Bell Davies, VC, DSO, AFC hoisted his flag at Lee-on-Solent as Rear-Admiral, Naval Air Stations. The RAF stations at Lee, Ford, Worthy Down, Donibristle and in Bermuda became HMS *Daedalus*, *Peregrine*, *Kestrel*, *Merlin* and *Malabar*. Dual RN and RAF ranks, and RAF commissions, were cancelled.

The Navy had two problems; to assimilate the Fleet Air Arm and to increase its size from a 1939 strength of about 3,000 to 10,000 by 1942 (this figure was, of course, overtaken by the war). In February, 1938, the Admiralty introduced short (seven year) service commissions in the Air Branch, open to candidates aged between 17½ and 23 years; those under 22 were Midshipmen (A), being promoted to Sub-Lieutenant (A) at 22 or at any age over 20 if they had completed their training. Promotion to Lieutenant (A) was after two years as a Sub-Lieutenant (A). There was a shortage of more senior officers, so Commanders and Lieutenant-Commanders with Fleet Air Arm experience who had been 'passed over' for promotion in the normal course were promoted to Captain (A) and Commander (A). Allowances were made for previous flying experience. Eugene Esmonde, who won a VC leading 825 Squadron against *Scharnhorst* and *Gneisenau* in February, 1942, joined the Navy as a Lieutenant-Commander (A) on 14 April, 1939, with seniority back-dated to 1 January, recognizing his 5,000 flying hours with the RAF Reserve and Imperial Airways.

A number of RAF officers transferred to the Navy on seven-year commissions, with appropriate naval ranks. The first was Flight Lieutenant A.J.D. Harding, who was appointed to *Glorious* as Lieutenant (A) on 1 April, 1938.

The (A) Branch had its own distinctive badge: an 'A' in silver within a laurel wreath of gold, worn above the rank stripes. On 6 April, 1939, the Fleet Air Arm was granted its own badge: wings of gold embroidery with, in the centre, a silver anchor and cable surrounded by a gold-embroidered wreath and surmounted by a crown.

In March, 1938, naval ratings became eligible to qualify as pilots. They were selected between the ages of 21 and 24 from the seaman, signal and telegraphist branches, but men from other branches could volunteer. Their initial training was one year ashore and eight weeks in a training carrier. Their flying pay was 2s 9d a day and 5s a day when they had their wings, in addition to their normal pay. On getting their wings, they were automatically rated petty officers. The first twenty began training in May, 1938.

There were changes, high and low. The Fifth Sea Lord was officially designated Chief of Naval Air Services. Two new Admiralty Departments, Air Material and Air Personnel, were created, with experienced air officers such as Commanders Caspar John and J.B. Heath on their staffs. Technical officers were recruited from the Engineering Branch and given two years specialist aeroengineering training. An RNVR Air Branch was instituted, and ex-RNR officers were also eligible to specialize as pilots or observers. New categories of naval ratings, Air Artificers, Air Fitters and Riggers, and Air Mechanics, were established, and a new Flying Branch, with substantive ratings of Chief Petty Officer Airman, Petty Officer Airman, Leading Airman and Naval Airman.

The first forty candidates for 'A' Branch commissions joined *Hermes* at Devonport on 19 April, 1938, to begin their training. They were all very young indeed, only thirteen of them having reached the age of 22. None of them had, of course, gone through normal naval training at such establishments as Dartmouth. Briefly, they knew how to put on their uniforms, how to salute and how to fly, but very little else about the Navy at large. When they reached their first wardrooms in the fleet, therefore, the cultural shock on both sides was sometimes very great.

War was coming; nobody now doubted it. That was the sombre theme running beneath the hilarity of Evans-Lombe's speech of farewell to Lumley Lyster when the wardroom dined him out. A relief had been appointed on 19 May, 1939, and Lyster himself left at Alexandria on 15 June.

Lyster went ashore in the 1st Motor Boat, manned by all the ship's Commanders and the Major of Marines, escorted by the 1st cutter, pulled by an officers' crew, as detailed by Lieutenant-Commander Nicholson the First Lieutenant, and the 2nd cutter, pulled by a volunteer crew from the Petty Officer's Mess. Lower deck was cleared ten minutes before the Captain was due to go over the side and hands mustered on the lower flying-off deck where Master at Arms Fred Woodcock led three cheers. Officers mustered on the quarterdeck, where Lieutenant-Commander (O) Paul Slessor likewise led the cheers.

Lyster had been a very popular Captain and the ship's company wanted to show what they thought of him. Away went the 1st Motor Boat to ringing cheers from forward and aft. The cutters' crew tossed their oars in salute and cheered as the motor boat went past. A car waited for the Captain on the jetty, and two sailors to handle his personal luggage. The motor boat and the cutters returned to the ship. Officers and ship's company then turned to regard their new Captain.

CHAPTER 5: GUY D'OYLY-HUGHES

THE NEW CAPTAIN was Guy D'Oyly-Hughes, who was a celebrity in the Royal Navy. He was a submariner whose famous captain, Martin Nasmith, had won the Victoria Cross. D'Oyly-Hughes himself, as Nasmith's First Lieutenant, won the DSC for his services in the same patrol in the Sea of Marmara and went on to win two DSOs. He was tall, dark, good-looking, fearless, a forceful leader of men. He was marked for promotion; some said he would be First Sea Lord. He was, as Commander Hugh Haggard, an equally distinguished submarine commander of the Second World War, summed him up, 'The sort of fellow senior officers like to have at their tables'.

Glorious had looked forward to his coming. After two such captains as Fraser and Lyster, when, as Buchanan-Dunlop said, 'we heard that no less a person than Dunbar-Nasmith's old First Lieutenant was to command us hopes ran high that, if we continued to give all we had, he would prove another "winner". But such was not to be.'

The trouble began almost at once. 'I do recall that after witnessing our first dummy torpedo-attack on his ship our new Captain gave us a harangue (in the absence of Commander (F)) in which he informed us that dropping ranges were not to exceed 200 yards in future. This met with complete silence — an embarrassed one, if I remember right, since I imagine compliance would have entailed, *inter alia*, modifying the ship's torpedoes. Looking back, I cannot help wondering if our failure to produce a single insincere "Aye aye, sir" was not mistaken for a collective sign of what came, much later, to be called l.m.f. [lack of moral fibre].'

Ben Bolt was another shocked witness of that scene. 'Although this was more than forty years ago, the substance and manner of his talk made the most vivid impression on me and on all the other responsible officers, both ship and air, who were present, and there were very few absentees. He said in effect that he disagreed with all the doctrine about training in the FAA, particularly on the amount of time spent in reconnaissance training and that as far as air antisubmarine operations were concerned, no aircraft had ever sunk a submarine nor ever would. I remember thinking that if I ever became a senior officer, I would remember this talk as a classic example of how not to speak to one's officers, particularly those engaged in such a hazardous occupation as carrier flying was in those days. He showed contempt for the Fleet Air Arm and for everything that had been achieved in training for the war which we all knew was inevitable. He turned down proposals made by Willoughby and Slessor for future training programmes and would brook no discussion. In a few days the morale of the ship was reduced to a level I had never known when serving under her three previous Captains.'

The change in the ship was all the more remarkable because it seemed to be the result of a change in D'Oyly-Hughes himself. Buchanan-Dunlop had been a submariner before joining the Fleet Air Arm and 'early in 1935 D'Oyly-Hughes was briefly my Captain (S) in the Mediterranean Flotilla when I was Third Hand in *Otway*. He appeared to me to be a perfectly reasonable sort of chap then, and I was all the more surprised at his almost immediate and extremely sad impact on the *Glorious* aircrews, of whom I was one, four years later.' Several officers who knew D'Oyly-Hughes earlier in his career were surprised to hear what happened in *Glorious*. Their feelings were summed up by Captain St. J. Fancourt, who had served with D'Oyly-Hughes in *Courageous* nearly ten years earlier; 'Something must have happened in the meantime to change him.'

Guy D'Oyly-Hughes was born on 1 August, 1891, the eldest son of Dr D'Oyly-Hughes of New Milton, Hants. His upbringing was unusual. According to 'Fellow Student', writing in *The Times* of 6 July, 1940, he was born 'in a cattle-ranching neighbourhood of Colorado' and inherited from his father 'a fine independence of character which was moulded and fortified among that forthright but kindly race, the cowboys'. He lacked childhood companionship but that 'was amply replaced by this association, in a community where he learned to stand on his own feet and where no man was another's master except by virtue of physical or moral force. Until he was ten years old he had no knowledge of discipline as we understand it in this country. At age 10 he crossed the Atlantic unaccompanied, to go to school and Osborne.'

At Osborne, which he joined as a Naval Cadet on 15 May, 1904, D'Oyly-Hughes did not shine. In fact he was on the list of those to be discarded, but fortunately for him his tutor, Mr Ranson, saved him by declaring that there was more to him than met the eye. He volunteered for the submarine service as a sub-lieutenant in June, 1913, and came top of his training class. He was promoted Lieutenant on 30 September and served in 'The Trade', as it was called, continuously until the end of the First World War.

D'Oyly-Hughes' DSC was gazetted on 25 June, 1915, after that epic patrol in *E.11*, on the same day as his Captain won the VC, another Lieutenant the DSC and every member of *E.11* ship's company the DSM. *E.11* returned on patrol in the

Marmara in August, 1915. By the 20th *E.11* was patrolling off the Gulf of Ismid, at the eastern end of the Marmara. The main railway line to Scutari ran along the northern shore of the Gulf. In the early hours of the 21st, in an exploit straight out of *The Boy's Own Paper*, D'Oyly-Hughes swam ashore from *E.11*, pushing in front of him a raft loaded with guncotton, with the object of blowing up a railway viaduct. Although disturbed and actually chased by Turkish guards, he blew up a portion of the line and, after several adventures, swam off again to *E.11*. His DSO for this was gazetted on 28 October, 1915.

By 1916 D'Oyly-Hughes was in command of his own submarine *E.35*. On 2 May, 1918, *UB.31* and *UC.78* were sunk by mines and depth-charges while trying to get through the Straits of Dover. From one of the sunk U-boats information was recovered revealing that *U.153* and *U.154* were to rendezvous off the Spanish coast on 11th May. *E.35*, then at Gibraltar, was ordered to intercept and was waiting at the rendezvous when *U.154* arrived shortly after 4pm and began to patrol up and down. This frustrated D'Oyly-Hughes and prevented him reaching a good firing position until 6.18 when he fired one torpedo which ran under the target. At 6.25 he fired two more, aimed at bow and stern, from a range of 500 yards. Both hit and one detonated with such violence it broke electric light bulbs in *E.35*. *U.154* sank in a broad lake of oil, leaving three or four survivors. *E.35* surfaced but a periscope was soon sighted. *E.33* dived at once and heard through hydrophones the sound of a torpedo, obviously fired at *E.33* by *U.133*. Fortunately for D'Oyly-Hughes and his crew the torpedo missed. He was awarded a Bar to his DSO on 14 September, 1918.

In another incident in *E.11*, at about 6.30am on 20 July, 1915, a stoker called Maine was washed off the submarine's casing in choppy seas about 130 miles from Malta. D'Oyly-Hughes jumped after him but failed to reach him before he sank. For the attempt he was voted the Silver Medal of the Royal Humane Society. Thus he emerged from the First World War as one of the most decorated junior naval officers. It could be said he had everything but the VC, and it was this omission (as some in *Glorious* were later only too ready to point out) that he was trying to rectify in the Second World War.

For eighteen months after the war, D'Oyly-Hughes was Flag Lieutenant to Commodore J.S. Dumaresq, commanding the Australian Squadron and flying his broad pennant in the battle cruiser *Australia*. He came home in 1920 to do the staff course and to get married to Ann Margaret, daughter of J.A.D. Crawford of County Down, Northern Ireland.

In the Navy an officer's appointments tend to spell out his destiny. D'Oyly-Hughes' were full of promise. In 1921, as a newly-promoted Lieutenant-Commander, he went to *Queen Elizabeth* on the staff of Admiral Sir Charles Madden, C-in-C of the Atlantic Fleet, and from there to the staff at *Dolphin*, the submariners' main base and *alma mater*. He was appointed in command of the large steam-driven submarine *K.12* in July, 1924, and in November, 1925, to Chatham Dockyard to stand by the building of the new submarine *O.1* (renamed *Oberon*). On 31 December he had early promotion to Commander, being only just in the 'zone' for promotion.

But by the late 1920s he seemed to weary of the Navy. He felt that advancement in peacetime was too slow. In 1929 he went on half-pay and became a land-agent. He spent some time at Charborough Park, the home of Admiral Sir Reginald Plunkett-Ernle-Erle-Drax, who was and remained one of his greatest friends. D'Oyly-Hughes later stood godfather to Drax's son Walter. However, as Drax wrote, D'Oyly-Hughes' 'heart was in the Navy, he pined to be back in it and soon returned to us, plunging back with his accustomed vigour'.

In July, 1930, D'Oyly-Hughes was appointed to the Admiralty 'for Miscellaneous and Special Services' in which he was lent to the RAF. Basil Embry, then an instructor at the Central Flying School, taught him to fly, which he did with an enthusiasm which caused his friends some concern, flying 'fast RAF machines' as Drax said, 'for which both his age and his reckless courage rendered him rather unsuitable'.

In 1934 he spent eleven months as Commander and Executive Officer of *Courageous* in the Atlantic Fleet and from there he went to the Air Ministry, on the Directorate of Air Training, where he was very well liked and respected. It is the great paradox of *Glorious*' last year that a Captain who knew so much about aircraft and air affairs, and who had taken the trouble to learn to fly, could so quickly and almost wilfully antagonize his own aircrew. D'Oyly-Hughes was by no means an ignorant 'fishhead' whom aircrew loved to scorn. As a submariner he should have had an extra affinity with the Fleet Air Arm, both being branches standing somewhat apart from the main 'gunnery' stream of the Navy.

He was promoted to Captain on 31 December, 1932, and returned to the Submarine Service in May, 1934, as Captain (S) of the 1st Flotilla at Malta. In complete contrast to his remarks in *Glorious*, he showed himself aware of the dangers of aircraft to submarines, carrying out trials to establish how visible dived submarines were from the air. Yet, even then, he had bitter critics. 'At that time,' said Haggard, 'he was unstable. He did not trust his officers. He was still living on an 1914-1918 war escapade. He did his best to make our lives tedious and did nothing to gain our confidence and fit us for the war years ahead of us.'

In November, 1936, he came home to be Chief of Staff and Maintenance Captain to his friend Drax, who was then C-in-C Devonport. He did a year's course at the Imperial Defence College and was then unemployed until his appointment to *Glorious* in May, 1939.

In many ways D'Oyly-Hughes was a brilliant man. He was a very good shot, a scratch golfer, an expert fly-fisherman. He could, and did, design his own house. He drove cars very fast. He loved to recite poetry and to read aloud to his two small daughters. He was extremely attractive to women and was not above propositioning his junior officers' wives. He once said of the midshipmen in his own ship, 'It was easy to pinch their bits of fluff from them.'

With such a record in peace and war, and with his known interest in and deep knowledge of the air, D'Oyly-Hughes was the obvious, indeed the perfect, choice of captain for *Glorious*. Such a well-known naval personality could do much for his ship's company, with a word or two in a senior officer's ear. He had enormous personal charm, and what would now be termed 'charisma'. The lower deck undoubtedly liked him. His somewhat unconventional dress — he would often wander around the flight deck, while they were playing deck hockey, wearing plus-fours — and his war decorations gave him what they called 'that little bit of mystique' which they admired.

Yet there must have been a flaw in him. Even at Osborne he had an independence which he showed, as his old captain, Nasmith, wrote, 'to the discomfiture of the authorities'. As Drax said, 'He was not built to be set under the authority of others. He always chafed to be running a show of his own, and the bigger it might be the better he would like it.' In certain circumstances, under certain stresses, such a determination to be independent and to bind others to his will might easily turn to megalomania, and such overwhelming self-confidence could quickly decline into paranoia.

The main brunt of D'Oyly-Hughes' personality, if it can be called that, fell upon his Commander (F), Guy Willoughby, who 'very soon got the impression that D'Oyly-Hughes thought he had been sent to the ship to teach the airmen their job. Whenever we went to sea for exercises, he used to send for me and instruct me to carry out exercises with both squadrons which he had designed with a view, as he said, to further their efficiency. These exercises were mainly rubbish, but I had the Squadrons carry them out when I considered none of the aircraft taking part were endangered; when I did think these exercises were dangerous I modified his orders accordingly, without, of course, his knowledge.'

Later in the year, when Mrs D'Oyly-Hughes came out to Malta, Willoughby met her and came to know her 'very well, and on one occasion she said to me, "Be forebearing with Guy, won't you? For sometimes he does things which seem quite mad." I found myself closely in agreement with her.' Many years later Guy Willoughby considered that D'Oyly-Hughes was not just 'quite mad' but 'mad as a hatter. We could control him while Evans-Lombe was there, but when he got another submariner as Commander we no longer could. He *wouldn't* take advice.'

Evans-Lombe had been promoted Captain in June, 1939, and had been in the ship for two years. He was relieved in July. He was very popular on board and had learned much from his time in *Glorious*, having been constantly confronted by novel situations where aircraft, and especially the RAF, had intruded into naval tradition. For example, Blair-Oliphant's armaments section went ashore to Hal Far with the squadrons, leaving their armoury on board locked. But, for Commander's rounds

Blair-Oliphant and his armoury sergeant, Flight Sergeant Wagstaff, would be summoned back on board to open up for inspection.

On one occasion, after Blair-Oliphant and his section had been ashore for some weeks 'the hallowed brasswork round the scuttles had become dim with neglect. The Commander was mortified and remained so even when our situation was explained to him. "What," he asked Sergeant Wagstaff, "are you going to do about it?" "Well sir," Wagstaff replied, with reasonableness and an expression of innocence, "perhaps the best thing would be to paint the brasswork." *Paint* the brasswork! There was a terrible pause, during which Wagstaff's appalling suggestion struck at the very depths of the Commander's soul. Then, to his enormous credit, he remarked, "I think, Sergeant, you are probably right".'

Evans-Lombe's relief was A.E.D. Lovell, who had been D'Oyly-Hughes' submarine staff officer in Malta. Two gunnery officers had been exchanged for two submariners. Lovell is remembered as 'somewhat colourless', 'a cypher' who 'did his best to keep the peace'. Clearly Lovell owed his appointment to D'Oyly-Hughes. In a sense he was D'Oyly-Hughes' man. But, unfortunately for the ship, as second-in-command he could not provide the counterweight D'Oyly-Hughes' personality needed.

In 17 May, 1939, the last Osprey was paid off from 802 Squadron, who reequipped that month with twelve Sea Gladiators, which were RAF Gladiator Mark 1 is, converted for FAA use by fitting catapult points, arrester hooks and fairings between the undercarriage legs for stowing collapsible dinghies. The Sea Gladiator was a single-seater fighter, with a 840 hp Bristol Mercury V111A radial engine, a top speed of 260 mph at 14,600 feet, an operational ceiling of 33,500 feet and a normal range of about 444 miles. It was armed with two .303 Browning machine-guns fitted one on each side of the front fuselage and one beneath each lower wing. The Sea Gladiator was a delightful aircraft, easy to fly, easy to deck-land and very manoeuvrable. As Petty Officer Dick Leggott, one of *Glorious'* rating pilots in 802, said, 'It was always springtime in a Gladiator cockpit'. But the Sea Gladiator, like all biplanes, was obsolete by May, 1939. 800 Squadron in *Ark Royal* and 801 in *Courageous* both had the new two-seater, fighter-dive bomber monoplane Skua 11.

The Mediterranean Fleet moved to Alexandria after the Italian invasion of Albania in April, 1939, which had wound up international tension by several more notches. *Glorious* arrived on 28 April and alternated between Alexandria and Malta for the rest of that summer, disembarking her aircraft to Hal Far as usual or to Dekheila, where the aircrew lived under canvas.

Flying training, already intensive, increased in tempo. The aircraft flew by day or night whenever the weather permitted. These final peacetime months of hard training consolidated the work of the pre-war years and applied the finishing touches to that high professional competence which was to serve the nation and the Navy so well in operations at home and in the Mediterranean, including the strike at Taranto, in the wartime months to come.

On average aircrew flew some 130 hours per month by day and another twenty or more by night. Despite Willoughby's difficulties with D'Oyly-Hughes, there was a very wide range of flying exercises. The TBR squadrons practised constantly by night, to locate and attack targets. Flares were first dropped to search for a target. Once found, the target was shadowed, flame floats being dropped at intervals to indicate the target's position. The shadowing aircraft was in radio touch with the strike force commander and, on the order from him, would illuminate the target with flares, whereupon the strike force would attack.

In an average week's flying the squadrons would carry out dusk torpedo attacks on the flagship *Warspite* and other ships, squadron torpedo and divebombing attacks on *Glorious* herself, fighter strafing of personnel on the bridges of the battle and cruiser squadrons, patrols over Alexandria to test the searchlight batteries of the Egyptian army, flights over the fleet to exercise the anti-aircraft gunners in height estimation, inner and outer anti-submarine patrols for the fleet at sea, gunnery spotting for shoots, reconnaissance flights over Alexandria harbour to practise drawing sketches of the defences and shipping, air-to-air fighter interception and, in June and July, accelerator trials which were, for not a few aircrew, a new experience. Also catapulted from time to time was an old obsolete 111F, filled with concrete and radio-controlled, which acted as a target. (It was eventually shot down by the fleet).

Ashore at Dekheila living conditions were somewhat primitive, but there were compensations. Everybody worked a Mediterranean 'hot weather' routine, turning to very early at 6am, but securing for the day at one pm, leaving the afternoons free. Nearby was one of the best bathing beaches in the Mediterranean and many of *Glorious'* officers and ship's company had their wives living in hotels and *pensions* in Alexandria.

That summer of '39 there were enough '*Glorious* wives' in Alexandria to form a small community. They even had a loosely constituted 'club', so that they could keep in general touch, which normally met on Saturday mornings in a room at the English Girls' School in Alexandria where Hope Slessor, wife of Lieutenant-Commander Paul Slessor, the senior ship's observer, taught during the week.

All the *Glorious* wives were constantly hampered by shortage of money. They were entertained on board HM Ships as often as possible and practicable, and they lived in the cheapest possible lodgings, but they sometimes felt dowdy compared with the colossal *chic* of the Alexandrian women, of whom even the most naturally ill-favoured always appeared *svelte* and impeccably turned out. The Alexandrians even had a phrase, *les Anglaises toujours sans bas*, which, politely translated, means English women never wear any knickers.

At that time the Navy barely recognized that its officers and men even had wives. The Admiralty paid no marriage allowance to any officer under 25 years of age, presumably on the principle that premature wedlock was to be discouraged. One very young officer Sub-Lieutenant (P) Roy Baker-Falkner, joined *Glorious* (his first ship) and 812 (his first front-line squadron) early in 1939. He brought his even younger wife Naomi out to Alexandria and on a basic salary of about £250 a year, even with extra flying pay, they had great difficulty in making ends meet.

Wives were never told that summer when the ship would sail, to what destination, and when she would return. Although there were naturally rumours, sometimes accurate, one morning the ship would be gone. On another she was back. In August, while the ship was away, Naomi Baker-Falkner and another *Glorious* wife accepted a lift in a private civil aeroplane to visit Cyprus. They were surprised and annoyed to look down and see the familiar shape of *Glorious* leaving Limassol as they flew over.

Glorious had sailed on 4 July for her last peacetime period of exercises and visits, to Phaleron and Milos in Greece, to Suda

Bay in Crete and to Limassol in Cyprus, returning to Alexandria on 15 August. D'Oyly-Hughes had been very generous to all with leave at Limassol, remarking that 'they might as well make the most of it as they wouldn't get much leave when the war came.'

War was now very close but it still came as a surprise to some. 'I certainly had no thoughts whatever about there being a war in the offing,' said David Jolliff, a Leading TAG with 812, who had been in *Glorious* since July, 1937. 'Nor did I ever hear any officer or rating even mention the word war.' But Jolliff, with many of the ship's company, had certainly noticed the effect of the change of captains. 'One noticed the change almost immediately. I cannot tell you what happened on board *Glorious* from here on, but the feeling was different. Whether it was the new Captain's first address to the ship's company or not I do not know. All I can say is that whereas the whole ship's company looked forward to an address by both the previous C.O.s, not so now.

'*Glorious* was in Alexandria with her squadrons embarked on the day war was declared. The ship's programme was to sail next day for Malta to carry out self-refit. I was having a cup of tea in the mess when Captain Hughes came on ship's broadcast system and told us that a very important broadcast was to be made from London. Almost immediately Big Ben struck and was followed by Mr Chamberlain's broadcast telling us we were at war with Germany. Shortly after, the Captain came on the system and told us that the ship was not immediately affected, the crew could go on normal shore leave and ship would sail for Malta as per programme in the morning.

'From the ship being almost "still as the grave", she suddenly became full of life and conversation. There were only a handful on board who had been involved in the 1914-18 war, and things had changed so much in that twenty years that we could only guess what was going to happen. The only thing to do was to go ashore and have a skin full which most of us did, and of course the whole of Alex were informed that *Glorious* was going to Malta next day.'

In fact *Glorious* sailed on 11 September, not for Malta, but for five days' exercises in the eastern Mediterranean, during which her squadrons' misgivings about their new Captain increased. It was later said by D'Oyly-Hughes' elder daughter, in mitigation of her father, that when he took over *Glorious* 'he found her to be neither a happy nor an efficient ship, and his impatience with some of her officers was the measure of his determination to improve this'. There is no evidence that *Glorious* was an unhappy or an inefficient ship, indeed quite to the contrary; the successes achieved and the string of decorations later won by aircrew officers who were serving in *Glorious* when D'Oyly-Hughes arrived refute his criticism.

Nevertheless, D'Oyly-Hughes did have to deal with a most difficult manning and morale situation on board. With the new *Illustrious* Class of carrier building and about to be commissioned, and a greatly increased training programme to be planned and staffed, there was an insatiable demand for experienced aircrew officers. The quality of his squadrons was steadily diluted during the whole period D'Oyly-Hughes was in command. On occasions whole squadrons left the ship together. Nearly all the replacements were the extremely young fledgling pilots and observers of the new (A) Branch, keen but inexperienced, and others who knew not Joseph. There was also an inevitable wastage through accident or sickness. Ben Bolt was one of the most experienced observers on board and on 10 June, 1939, he became C.O. of 812 Squadron, one of the very first naval observers to achieve a squadron command, but he was invalided home with tonsilitis in November, 1939. This was a blessing in disguise for him, though it was well disguised at the time. However, 'this probably saved me from going down in *Glorious*,' he said, 'or being sent for court-martial with J.B. Heath, as I could see the new Captain was off his head.'

D'Oyly-Hughes' immediate response to the outbreak of war was certainly idiosyncratic. 'When war was declared, D'Oyly-Hughes brought out one of those little glass-fronted boxes containing revolvers,' said Lieutenant G.R.M. ('Grubby') Going, an observer in 825. 'Suddenly one of these boxes appeared on the back end of the bridge. Guy Willoughby asked D'Oyly-Hughes what it was for. He said it was to shoot any of his officers who failed to do his duty in action! As Guy Willoughby was hanging out flags from the Flying Position, and I was running up and down the deck as flight deck officer at that time, we reckoned we would be the first two to be killed by winging shots by this gallant man! He really didn't enamour himself to anybody very much.' Grubby Going left the ship in December, 1939, and later flew on the Taranto Raid. 'I always say, thank God I got out of that ship in time!'

Glorious returned to Alexandria on 16 September. The war had lasted nearly a fortnight and nothing much had happened. In the heat and summer lassitude of Alexandria harbour it all seemed very far away and remote. But soon news arrived which shocked everybody on board. *Courageous* had been sunk, torpedoed by a U-boat in the Western Approaches on 17 September.

Courageous and four destroyers had formed a 'hunter-killer group' to search for U-boats. In spite of the bitter and bloody experience of the First World War which should have taught everybody that the best place to encounter and kill U-boats was around their prey, the convoys, the notion of 'hunter-killer groups' died hard. The idea was that the groups should plunge around the oceans, casting about them like nautical cavalry. (In fact the First Lord, Winston Churchill, who very much favoured these tactics, actually used the phrase 'like a cavalry division' to describe them.) *Courageous*' task had been to find U-boats. She had certainly found one. But it might have been worse. On 14 September *Ark Royal*, engaged upon an exactly similar task, had been narrowly missed by a torpedo from another U-boat. These hunter killer tactics were discontinued. But meanwhile, it could be said that *Courageous* had been not so much lost as thrown away.

Glorious and *Courageous* were sister ships. 'Hope you didn't get mixed up with *Courageous* and *Glorious*,' wrote *Glorious*' Master-at-Arms, Fred Woodcock, on 26 September to his wife who was still living in Malta. 'A hard knock, heavy loss of life too, the chances of war, I suppose.' Many in *Glorious* knew their counterparts in *Courageous* and some had served in *Courageous* themselves. 'I see Jefferies, MAA, is missing from *Courageous*,' Woodcock wrote. 'Hard on her [Jefferies' wife], but fortunately still young in years and attractive, bitter blow for her, to think this time last year we met them for the last time.'

It was a bitter blow for everybody. Later it was revealed that *Courageous*' Captain, W.T. Makeig-Jones, and 518 of her people had gone down in her. *Courageous* had been *Glorious*' sparring partner, friend and rival for almost a decade. For nearly ten years they had played football against her, run, swum, shot, rowed against her, bombed and torpedoed her, strafed her and 'beat her up', dined in her wardroom and punched her sailors on the nose. Now she was gone. Suddenly, the war came very close indeed.

Late in September there were more rumours of a return to Malta. 'Just returned from a couple of days at sea,' wrote

Woodcock on the 26th, 'so now I can only eagerly await our return to Malta. I pray it will be soon.' One Sunday two weeks later D'Oyly-Hughes came back on board from a visit to *Warspite*, cleared lower deck and announced that the ship was going to Malta for docking, although this information was to be kept secret. On 9 October *Glorious* sailed and for some hours steered west. But shortly after midday the ship altered course through 1800 and steered for the Suez Canal, passing through it that night. She reached Aden on the 13th, fuelled and sailed again, anchoring that evening in Ghubbet Shoab, a bay on the almost barren island of Socotra, off the entrance to the Gulf of Aden.

The German pocket battleships *Admiral Graf Spee* and *Deutschland* had sailed from Wilhelmshaven before the outbreak of war, *Graf Spee* on 21 August, 1939, *Deutschland* three days later. While *Deutschland* operated in the North Atlantic, *Graf Spee* headed south, where the first definite confirmation of her activities was on 1 October, when the surviving crew members of the British ship *Clement*, sunk off Pernambuco on 30 September, landed in South America.

The Admiralty set up hunting groups to cover the North and South Atlantic and the Indian Ocean. *Glorious*, based on Socotra, with the battleship *Malaya*, the attendant destroyer *Bulldog* and a *Daring* Class destroyer from the China Station, searched southwards into the Indian Ocean. 'We flew searches the whole time, out to extreme limits and back again,' said Lieutenant Norman 'Blood' Scarlett, one of the ship's observers. 'We investigated every ship we saw. Nothing exciting happened. It was utterly uneventful, except for this mad Captain we had. Mad as a hatter. He relieved Lumley Lyster, who was an excellent old boy. Then we had this chap

D'Oyly-Hughes, who overrode his air staff. He was *always* interfering.'

However, the ship's company, by and large, were all for a quiet life. 'I'm going on grand,' wrote Woodcock, 'the ship too is as strong and swift as ever, also our pilots with their birds. Really our job is certainly monotonous, as we see nothing out of the ordinary, just our party. The planes do all the necessary observations; luckily we still have cinema aboard, wireless programmes and other pastimes, also various officers give lectures at evenings, all very interesting but no one can say when we shall leave this area which is really safe. Fortunate in that, honey.'

Between 5 and 10 October *Graf Spee* sank or captured three more British vessels on the trade routes to Cape Town, off St Helena or Ascension Island. Later, acting on a suggestion from Admiral Raeder, *Graf Spee* headed for the Indian Ocean, passing off the Cape of Good Hope in the early hours of 4 November. On the 15th she sank the small British tanker *Africa Shell* in the Mozambique Channel.

The ship's company were not alone in hoping that *Glorious* would see no action. 'I was really glad of the excuse to get the *Glorious* out of the Mediterranean,' Pound wrote to Cunningham on 24 October, 'as I do not think her efficient life will be a very long one.' But this was, of course, unknown to D'Oyly-Hughes, on whom the news of *Africa Shelf so* comparatively close, had a galvanic effect. He alarmed his officers by his apparent belief that he could handle *Glorious* like a capital ship, heading directly and without support, accompanied only by *Bulldog*, to confront the enemy. 'He was obsessed with the idea he wanted to win the Victoria Cross,' said 'Blood' Scarlett. 'I'm absolutely convinced of it. He said, more or less, "This ship won't open fire until we see the whites of their eyes." He had revolvers on the bridge, to shoot the first man who did the wrong thing.'

The ship's company were just as apprehensive. 'Captain Hughes had left us in no doubt of his war tactics,' said David Jolliff. '"If we meet the whole German Navy we go straight at them with all our guns firing". Our ship's armament consisted of 4.7" anti-aircraft guns and some Oerlikons. You can well imagine the thoughts of the squadron of highly trained and very efficient aircrews. I dare not put them into words.'

The only excitement, according to 'Blood' Scarlett, was the occasional aircraft which 'used to get lost because the ship's position wasn't always correct, because of all the currents off Socotra. She'd be about twenty miles out.' And, of course, there was always D'Oyly-Hughes: 'He had this idea that you could come straight up the lift and take off straight away, and then the next aircraft would come up and away. Crazy idea.' (In fact Scarlett 'actually rather liked D'Oyly-Hughes. He passed on my resignation from flying. I wanted to be in destroyers, not bloody aircraft.' But Scarlett's application was delayed and he was told to wait. He left *Glorious* in January, 1940, flew on the Taranto Raid and was shot down. By the time his application was approved he was in an Italian prisoner-of-war camp and was a PoW for the next five years.)

While D'Oyly-Hughes impatiently waited to encounter the enemy, and his ship's company as fervently prayed they would not, the uneventful weeks passed. The sole emergency was down below where the ship was suffering from a severe bout of 'condenseritis'. The main condensers, situated under the main turbines, condensed steam into fresh water, which was then pumped back to feed the boilers. The condenser coolant was sea water. If any one of the thousands of small-bore tubes in the condensers leaked, the salinity of the boiler feed water (normally kept down to a minute level) would rise, with disastrous effects on the boilers.

In peacetime the ship would have gone alongside for such repairs. Instead, thousands of new condenser tubes were brought on board and stowed in one of the hangars before the ship left Alexandria. Every evening, after the flying programme had been completed, one shaft was stopped and locked overnight while the engine-room staff worked in the only partly-cooled condensers, replacing forty tubes every night. Thousands of tubes were replaced while the ship was in the Indian Ocean and not one day's flying was missed. It was a tremendous achievement by the engine-room department, who worked long hours in very hot and cramped conditions.

D'Oyly-Hughes himself realized, none better, that it was not only the condenser tubes which needed replacing. He was well aware that his ship had been in continuous commission for near two years and the ship's company, who had worked very hard and long, needed a rest. He knew that his sailors, who had served together for so many months of peace, had not yet adjusted to the added uncertainties and mental stress of war. Uncertainty has always been a feature of naval life; 'Haven't You 'Eard, It's All Been Changed', posted over a hundred ship's notice boards, has been a naval motto since the time of King Alfred. But D'Oyly-Hughes sensed that something more was needed. He organized and encouraged sport wherever and whenever possible, gave leave as generously as he was able, allowed trips and visits ashore at every opportunity. As his elder daughter Bridget said, her father 'did his very best to brighten things up for the sailors'.

D'Oyly-Hughes was as concerned as any of his sailors about his family at home. Like many seventeen-year-old girls, Bridget 'slouched her shoulders'. He sent her a photograph of himself with a Socotran native chieftain and wrote on the back, 'Look how straight *he* holds his shoulders'.

Colombo, where the ship arrived on 10 December, 1939, seemed like paradise after Socotra to everybody on board, and especially to Lieutenant-Commander Paul Slessor, the staff officer (air). After weeks of close daily proximity to the Captain, and daily chivvying and criticism of himself and Guy Willoughby by the Captain, Slessor's nerves were beginning to fray. He had been in the ship since July, 1937, and was hoping, indeed longing, for the relief which was now some months overdue.

Paul Slessor was to play the intermediary part, like a buffer, almost a catalyst, in the events to come in *Glorious*. He was a sensitive, gifted man, painstaking in his work and very popular in the wardroom, but his personality was not powerful enough to make any dint upon D'Oyly-Hughes. He was the first of his family to join the Navy. (His father Philip was a well-known broadcaster.) He had not enjoyed his time at Dartmouth and had tried to leave the Navy soon after. He had 'Outside Interests' — a phrase which could and often did wither promotion prospects in the pre-war Navy — in the theatre, painting and music. He was a talented pianist and *Glorious* cabarets, with Paul Slessor playing songs and sketches composed by himself, were famous.

His wife Hope, from Western Australia, was an actress and, as a producer, could hold her own with professionals. The Slessors were permanently short of money, although like many naval couples they had compensations in travel and companionship, with new places and new faces every year. Hope had £50 a year of her own, but they married on Paul's pay of less than £400 a year, which included 5/- a day flying pay. Paul had joined the Fleet Air Arm as an Observer, not from any burning urge to fly, but mainly for the extra money. For the same reason, the small additions to his pay, he qualified as an Interpreter in French and German.

Paul Slessor was not forceful enough, not 'pushing' enough, to win promotion to Commander in a fiercely competitive Service. In fact, promotion was a taboo subject. 'We never mentioned it,' said Hope, 'because we were sick of some of the other wives, with "promotionitis", always talking about it.' In Alexandria, on the night the half-yearly promotions of 30 June, 1939, were to be promulgated, Paul and Hope went to an open-air cinema. They had told the ship of their whereabouts so that a messenger with good news would be able to find them. Throughout the show Hope steeled herself not to look behind her and, of course, neither of them mentioned the subject. The film they saw was *The Postman Always Knocks Twice*, but no postman knocked for Paul Slessor that night.

Slessor had been one of the handful of officers who had known the ship's true destination when she sailed, ostensibly for Malta but actually for Suez, in October, 1939. He had, in fact, been the only officer with a wife in Alexandria who knew the truth and naturally he longed to tell her something, even if it was only a hint of the wrong story, just to put her on her guard. But, knowing the information was confidential, he refrained. He was therefore furious when Hope wrote to tell him that at a drinks party that weekend D'Oyly-Hughes had told the wives of officers in other ships that *Glorious* was sailing for the Mediterranean the following morning. 'But of course,' he wrote to Hope on 9 November, 'the man's a double-crosser of the deepest dye.'

In that letter Slessor had guardedly referred to the Captain as 'that certain gentleman you mention'. Common sense, and wartime censorship which was now enforced, demanded discretion. Nevertheless, Slessor's letters become increasingly desperate. 'I haven't had much trouble with our friend lately, mostly because I have been at pains to keep out of his way,' he wrote on 16 November. 'No doubt it will be my turn again in due course. But I feel this life is quite near enough to *cafard* without going out of one's way to meet trouble and consequent irritations to the nerves.' 'The cove has been playing up again,' he wrote on 30 November, 'which is not only unkind but very foolish under the circumstances. I have written dear old "Lumley" a line for Christmas, and couldn't refrain from the obvious remark — or at least a hint.'

Colombo was a blessed change. 'We have had a whole week's rest, and I have given myself a treat by going ashore often. Toby [Watkins], Norman Quill and I got a whole day off and took a car for a famous expedition I have done before. Once again I was astonished at the intense beauty of this place. It is paradisal. And the people are so happy and kindly. I suppose their wants are very few; they live in the midst of all this loveliness and are contented by nature.'

But by the end of that week, when Slessor wrote on 17 December, the shadows were gathering again. 'The boyfriend has been very trying. I dread to think what will happen when Guy goes. We are just about as different, temperamentally, as we could be, but we have stuck together staunchly in the face of adversity — and now I shall feel dreadfully on my own. Excuse my dull letter. I am in a badly depressed mood just now, which I suppose is wrong, observing the rest I've had and the pleasant surroundings. But oh, when, when, when?'

The demands of war recalled many retired officers to active service. Lieutenant Commander (Flying) in *Glorious* was Lieutenant-Commander William Parkin, a pilot who had served in *Courageous* and *Hermes* and had retired in 1934 to run an airline in the Far East. One officer who joined *Glorious* in Colombo was Lieutenant-Commander Rupert Hill, who had retired some years earlier to become a tea-planter in Ceylon. But the most noticeable arrivals in the wardroom were the 'A' Branch aircrew officers. At times some of the staider wardroom members must have thought there were hordes of them and there were even mutterings, among some of the oldest and boldest, that 'subs and snotties live in the gunroom'. They took some convincing that Sub-Lieutenants and Midshipmen (A), very young and very inexperienced as they were, were not still under training and were entitled to the privileges and status of wardroom life.

The newcomers did have a 'Snotties' Nurse', to use the term loosely, in 'Blood' Scarlett, who was told off to look after their welfare generally and to act as their advocate with Father. 'Blood' organized a 'beard-growing competition' to while away the tedium of the days spent looking for *Graf Spee* and took his charges' part when necessary. 'There was one young Midshipman (A) called Franklin, who knew a lot of songs which the older members didn't. Quite near the knuckle, some of them. One morning after they'd all had a party and singsong the Commander, Lovell, sent for me. He said, "I'm absolutely horrified to hear that you allowed a Midshipman (A) to lead the singing of dirty songs in the wardroom." I said, "There were a lot of officers senior to me there and if they were going to be led by a Midshipman (A) it's them you ought to be seeing, sir, not the Midshipmen (A) nor me who was in charge of them." He was a miserable man, Lovell. Always praying. Very religious. He was a submariner. He wasn't frightfully inspiring.'

The new (A) Branch in *Glorious* (which included Sub-Lieutenant (A) Rupert Davies, the future TV 'Maigret' actor) had to make enormous adjustments to their new life. Midshipman (A) Roy Hinton joined 823 as an Observer in November, 1939, having taken passage from Aden to Socotra in the battleship *Ramillies*. 'In 823 in *Glorious* we had a marvellous crowd. They accepted us, although when we were sent out we had very, very, *very* little experience; in fact it horrified the senior officers in *Glorious* when they heard how very little experience we had. We were shoved out there because they wanted people desperately, even though we were only half-trained. In those days you had, literally, the two services, the Fleet Air Arm on one side, the RN executive types on the other. They certainly weren't a closely-knit service, as it subsequently became.'

Midshipman (A) John Michael Franklin of the extensive musical *repertoire* was the son of a naval officer. His father, Commander Cyril Franklin, had won a DSO for minesweeping operations in the previous war. Franklin joined *Hermes* as a Probationary Midshipman (A) in July, 1938, and won his wings as an Observer on the 34th Naval Observers Course which qualified a year later. *Glorious* was his first ship, 823 his first squadron. He kept a photograph album, which survives. It is now a nostalgic document, with the faces, ships and images of the time preserved, as in amber.

Franklin collected pictures, of Gibraltar and Ras-el-Tin, of Limassol in August, 1939, and the Suez Canal. There are 'penny-divers' at Malta, Arab dhows, natives in canoes alongside the ship, elephants washing themselves at Kandy. There is a picture of Franklin himself, in shirt, shorts and trilby hat, at Dekheila, and others in 823, sitting on the flight deck, sun-bathing on the quarterdeck, showing off their beard-growing prowess, bartering for pearls on the beach at Socotra. There are *Glorious*, *Bulldog*, *Malaya* and *Ramillies* at Ghubbet

Shoab, the cruisers *Kent* and the French *Suffren* in Colombo, the armed merchant cruisers *Cathay* and *Carthage* at Trincomalee, where *Glorious* went to spend Christmas, 1939.

At Christmas everyone on board received a Royal Christmas card: 'With Our Best Wishes for Christmas, 1939. May God Bless You and Protect You. Elizabeth R. George R.I.' Franklin pasted his in his album, along with a snapshot of Sub-Lieutenants and Midshipmen (A) drinking what was evidently a quantity of champagne on Christmas Day, and a record of a visit to the sailors' graveyard on Sober Island, with one *memento mori*: a gravestone 'To the Memory of Douglas Baxter, Ldg Seaman, HMS *Retribution* aged 30 Years, Who Was Killed by Falling from Aloft, 13 July 1860, In the Midst of Life We are in Death'.

Glorious sailed from Trincomalee on 29 December, with *Kent* and *Suffren*, convoying three small ships carrying French troops from Indo-China. The Swordfish flew reconnaissance flights every day on passage across the Indian Ocean. *Glorious* reached Aden on 7 January, 1940, where the new Commander (F), Guy Willoughby's relief, who had been appointed on 1 December, was waiting to join. Willoughby stayed on board until the ship reached Malta on 17 January for her much delayed docking and refit. On the 24th he and about 300 ship and squadron officers and men embarked in the liner *Duchess of Atholl* which took them to Marseilles. After an eventful three-day train journey across France they all eventually reached home.

The new Commander (Flying), 'Wings' as he was always known, was Commander J.B. Heath. He was one of the most experienced Fleet Air Arm officers in the Navy. He had virtually grown up with the naval air service, having qualified on one of the earliest flying training courses, and having been one of the first naval officers to command a flight (in *Glorious*, in an earlier commission). He had commanded 800 Fighter Squadron, of Ospreys and Nimrods, in *Courageous* from 1935 to 1937»one of the first naval officers to command a squadron. He was one of the first naval pilots to achieve the rank of Commander and, coming as he did from the Admiralty with the latest doctrine on tactics, material and personnel, he was one of the first naval officers to be appointed Commander (Flying) of a carrier.

In temperament J.B. Heath was the most gentle and pleasant of men, good-humoured, very hard to ruffle or to make angry. He was almost too placid: Leggott of 802 said, 'He was a nice old cup of tea'. He was approachable, even by midshipmen (A). 'He was an extremely charming chap,' said Roy Hinton. 'He was a senior officer, in our eyes, who would chat to a midshipman. He was very easy to get on with. He accepted your point of view, listened to what you said, whereas some of the executive officers were very difficult to get through to.'

J.B. Heath should have been a good choice for *Glorious*. In practice his appointment could only have been arranged by some malignant fate. He and D'Oyly-Hughes should never have been appointed to the same ship. Heath was a much more cautious man than D'Oyly-Hughes and had a much greater knowledge of aircrafts' capabilities. Whenever D'Oyly-Hughes wanted to reach out for some spectacular and dramatic coup, Heath would bring him down to earth. While D'Oyly-Hughes wanted to soar, Heath kept both feet firmly on the ground. At last D'Oyly-Hughes came to see Heath's caution as wilful and even shameful obstruction. The two men rubbed each other the wrong way from the very first. They might have been specially selected to set each other's teeth on edge. Heath himself said of his very first meeting with D'Oyly-Hughes that the Captain's reaction to him 'was instant dislike'. 'Almost from the date of my joining HMS *Glorious*,' Heath wrote later, 'the Captain showed, by his manner and bearing towards me, an open hostility which early destroyed all regard and mutual confidence. At the same time, he never at any period informed me in what respect I was failing or had given him cause for dissatisfaction, demonstrating it only in extreme rudeness to me, often in the presence of junior officers and even of the lower deck.'

It is psychologically feasible that D'Oyly-Hughes did make up his mind about J.B. Heath, irrevocably for the worse, in that very first exchange of glances. D'Oyly-Hughes' main fault, if it was a fault, was an excess of zeal. He was not a man who would ever do less than his utmost best at all times, regardless of what others thought of him or what he said or did to offend them. It may be that in that first moment he sensed that here was a man who might oppose him, who might urge caution when D'Oyly-Hughes wanted to throw caution to the winds, who might bring his high-flying ambitions down to earth with hard, cold, practical facts. Certainly D'Oyly-Hughes had the sudden suspiciousness of an oriental despot, and could be as suddenly lavish with his charm and his affections. Vernon Donaldson, the Torpedo Officer, who had been promoted to Commander in the most recent half-yearly lists on 31 December, 1938, and left the ship with Guy Willoughby, had had ample chances to study D'Oyly-Hughes. Apart from concurring that the man 'was as mad as a bloody hatter', Donaldson said that D'Oyly-Hughes 'could be absolutely charming. But he gave you the feeling that it didn't take very much to topple him one way or the other'. His antipathy towards Heath was a double tragedy. It ruined Heath's career directly and indirectly lost D'Oyly-Hughes his life and the ship.

Most of the wives had already arrived in Malta from Alexandria, their husbands having succeeded in sending some form of coded message. Lieutenant-Commander J. W. 'Ginger' Hale, C.O. of 825 Squadron, had sent his wife a telegram: 'Suggest you see Tony soon,' Tony being their landlord in Malta. Mrs D'Oyly-Hughes was also in Malta. The Slessors were invited to dinner. It is a measure of the state of Paul Slessor's feelings by that time that he took the almost unheard-of and barely credible action by a junior officer towards his Captain and his wife of refusing the invitation, and he forbade Hope to accept on their joint behalf.

There was an edgy atmosphere in Malta, with practice blackouts and air-raid precaution exercises. But the war still seemed far away. The *Altmark* Incident, in some remote Norwegian fjord, might have happened on some other planet. *Ark Royal* had arrived in the Mediterranean again to work up her squadrons. She sailed with *Glorious* for Alexandria on 31 March, 1940, arriving there on 4 April. Both ships were at sea on the following Monday, the 8th, to begin a week of intensive training, when a signal arrived cancelling the exercise programme and ordering both ships back to harbour. The Phoney War was over at last. Germany had invaded Denmark and Norway. Both ships sailed for Malta on 9 April.

Ironically *Glorious* was on her way to war, but without many of the aircrews who had trained so hard in her. '*Glorious* had a tremendous spirit,' wrote Lieutenant A.W.F. (Alfie) Sutton, an Observer of 812 who, with Lieutenant M.A. Torrens-Spence, also of 812, flew on the Taranto Raid, 'marred only by a growing apprehension as to the stability of the new Captain. But whilst I was in the ship there were enough of the old commission to hold us all together, and the approach of war gave us all a firm purpose to bring ourselves to the greatest efficiency. We were front line squadrons and we reckoned that we were the elite of the Navy on whom the brunt of the war would fall in the early stages.' Of all the prophecies made about the Norwegian campaign to come, Alfie Sutton's was one, perhaps the only one, which came true.

CHAPTER 6: INVASION IN THE NORTH

THE GERMAN INVASION of Denmark and Norway came as a complete surprise, although there had been signs which, with the benefit of hindsight, would seem to have indicated that something was afoot. But at the time they were discounted or disbelieved. In mid-March, 1940, the U-boats abruptly stopped attacks on convoys on the trade routes, which suggested they were being withdrawn for some other purpose. Minelaying by U-boats and destroyers also stopped. On 4 April, for the first time ever, a German reconnaissance aircraft, probably on a photographic flight, flew over the west coast of Norway. On the same day *Scharnhorst* and *Gneisenau* were sighted in Wilhelmshaven roads. On the 6th diplomatic sources in Copenhagen warned of a German invasion of Narvik, but sceptical Foreign Office officials minuted 'surely out of the question' and 'I wish I could believe this'. From the evening of the 6th onwards there was unusually intense German radio activity from Wilhelmshaven and on the night of the 6/7th several aircraft reported equally intense activity on wharves and jetties in Kiel, Eckernforde, Hamburg and Lubeck, with many lorries travelling with unshaded headlights and whole areas of the docks brilliantly lit by arc-lights. On Sunday the 7th Captain Henry Denham, Naval Attaché in Copenhagen, sat on a Danish beach looking over the Great Belt and saw the German cruiser *Blücher* and another warship exercising or on passage in the sound and reported the sighting to the Admiralty. Earlier in the day a reconnaissance aircraft reported a cruiser and two destroyers about 150 miles south of the Naze. This report was later amended to one *Nurnberg* Class and six destroyers. (They had an air escort of eight fighters which drove the shadower away.)

The Admiralty, which was still preoccupied at that time by the possibility, not of an invasion but of a break-out of heavy German warships into the Atlantic, signalled the C-in-C Home Fleet, Admiral Sir Charles Forbes, at Scapa Flow at 2.20pm on the 7th: 'Recent reports suggest a German expedition is being prepared.' The signal also mentioned the Copenhagen report of the movement of one division of troops in ten ships by night to Narvik, with simultaneous occupation of Jutland. However, the last paragraph of the signal concluded, most unfortunately, 'All these reports are of doubtful value and may well be only a further move in the war of nerves.' Forbes ordered the Home Fleet to one hour's notice for steam.

Finally, just after 5pm, another Admiralty signal was received: 'At 1.25pm an aircraft sighted two cruisers, one large ship possibly of *Scharnhorst* Class and ten destroyers, all steering north-west, about eighty miles south-west of the Naze'. The heavy ships of the Home Fleet, *Rodney*, *Valiant* and *Repulse*, with the cruisers *Sheffield* and *Penelope* and ten destroyers, sailed from Scapa Flow at 8.15 that evening. Vice-Admiral Edward-Collins, with the cruisers *Galatea* and *Arethusa*, and destroyers, sailed from Rosyth an hour later. The Home Fleet's course was north-east, Forbes being intent on searching for German heavy units escaping into the Atlantic, although, on the morning of the next day, 8 April, there was a most significant event. The Polish submarine *Orzel*, patrolling the Skagerrak, sank the German SS *Rio de Janeiro* off Kristiansand. A Norwegian destroyer and local fishing vessels rescued hundreds of German soldiers in uniform, who said they had been on their way to protect Bergen from the Allies. This news reached the

172

Admiralty but was not passed to Forbes until late that evening, by which time the German invasion was well under way.

The German invasion plan depended upon surprise. It was to be carried out by seven army divisions commanded by General von Falkenhorst — three divisions in the assault phase, four in the follow-up. One division would carry out the invasion of Denmark. The troops would be supported by some 800 operational aircraft and between 200 and 300 transport aircraft, to supplement the initial seaborne landings which were to take place simultaneously at Oslo, Arendal, Kristiansand, Egersund, Bergen, Trondheim and Narvik.

Plans for the naval side of the operation, which was code-named *Weserubung* (Operation Weser), were first issued by Grand Admiral Raeder on 6 March, 1940. They, too, were a calculated risk, relying upon initial surprise. They would involve almost the entire German Navy which would have to operate without command of the sea, except locally in the Kattegat and Skagerrak, and against much more powerful Allied naval forces. Nevertheless the German Navy expected that the most dangerous phase of the operation would be the return to Germany, after the landings had taken place, when the Royal Navy would have had time to react.

The German ships were divided into eleven groups, Groups I and II in the north, Groups III to VI in the south, against Norway, and Groups VII to IX, which were very much weaker, against Denmark. Group I had *Gneisenau*, flying the flag of Admiral Günther Lütjens, the Deputy C-in-C (the C-in-C himself, Admiral Wilhelm Marschall, being sick) and *Scharnhorst*, with ten destroyers under Commodore Friedrich Bonte, which would land 2,000 mountain-warfare-trained troops under Major-General Eduard Dietl at Narvik. The destroyers would then rejoin the battle cruisers. Group II, for

Trondheim, was commanded by Captain Hellmuth Heye in the 8" gun cruiser *Admiral Hipper*, with four destroyers carrying some 1,700. troops. Group II after the landing was also to join Group I. These two Groups were to be the main covering force for the whole operation. After joining, both Groups were to create a diversion in the North Sea, then to patrol the southern area of the Arctic off Norway, and finally to cover the return of other warships to Germany.

Group III, with the light cruisers *Köln* (flag of Rear-Admiral Hubert Schmundt, Flag Officer Scouting Forces), *Königsberg* and *Bremse*, seven E-boats of the 1st Flotilla, the two torpedo boats *Leopard* and *Wolf*, the depot ship *Karl Peters* and some minor vessels, was to land 1,900 troops at Bergen. Group IV, to land about 1,100 troops at Kristiansand and Arendal, was led by Captain Rieve in the light cruiser *Karlsruhe*, with three torpedo boats *Luchs*, *Seeadler* and *Grief*, and seven E-boats of the 2nd Flotilla and their depot ship *Tsingtau*. Group V, for Oslo, carried 2,000 troops in the cruiser *Blücher* (flag of Rear-Admiral Oskar Kummetz), with the pocket battleship *Lützow*, the cruiser *Emden*, three torpedo boats *Möwe*, *Albatros* and *Kondor* and some smaller vessels. Lastly, four mine-sweepers of the 2nd Flotilla, in Group VI, were to land 150 men to occupy the cable station at Egersund. Groups VII, VIII, XI, X and XI, which included the aged battleship *Schleswig-Holstein*, landed troops at Korsoer, Nyborg, Copenhagen, Middelfart and Esbjerg.

While Groups I and II patrolled the Arctic, twenty-eight U-boats were disposed in a great arc stretching from Narvik to the Shetlands, to the Kattegat and down to the eastern approaches to the English Channel. Minefields were to be laid on the day of the landings in the Skagerrak and in Scapa Flow (although this operation was cancelled, without consultation with the Navy, by Reichsmarshal Goering.) But the Luftwaffe was to provide air reconnaissance and CAPs in daylight and anti-submarine patrols in the Kattegat, Skagerrak and the North Sea.

Although, for reasons of speed and safety, the initial assault troops were carried in warships, the follow-up troops for Bergen and the ports south of it, including Copenhagen, were transported in fifteen steamships of the 1st Sea Transport Division. These ships, disguised as ordinary merchantmen and sailing singly and inconspicuously so as to arrive at their destinations on the day of the landings, carried between them 3,761 troops, 672 horses, 1,377 vehicles and 5,935 tons stores. Weapons and ammunition for the northern ports of Narvik, Trondheim and Stavanger were to be carried in seven steamships of the so-called 'Export Group' which sailed from Hamburg, disguised as normal traffic to Murmansk, to arrive at their real destination actually ahead of the warships carrying the assault troops.

The main port for the occupation was, of course, Oslo, where eleven more ships of the 2nd Sea Transport Division carried another 8,450 men, 969 horses, 1,283 vehicles and 2,170 tons of stores two days after the landing. Twelve ships of the 3rd Division delivered another 6,065 men, 893 horses, 1,347 vehicles and 6,050 tons of stores four days after the landing. Another 40,000 men, 4,000 horses, 10,000 vehicles and 40,000 tons of stores were shipped in later journeys.

Fuel for the army and the Luftwaffe locally and for the return voyages of the warships was a major problem. Three tankers were to carry 21,000 tons of fuel, *Kattegat* and *Skagerrak* from Wilhelmshaven to Narvik and Trondheim, and *Jan Wellen* from the 'Northern Base' (Murmansk) to Narvik. Of these only *Jan Wellen* arrived, with serious consequences later for

Commodore Bonte's destroyers. (Of the 'Export Group' only one, *Levante* for Trondheim, reached her destination, three days late.)

Theoretically the German Navy did not have enough warships with enough speed, weight of shell and striking capacity for such a bold, wide-ranging and complicated operation as *Weserubung*. Yet, with some errors and omissions excepted, it succeeded brilliantly. *Scharnhorst*, *Gneisenau*, *Admiral Hipper* and the destroyers of Groups I and II sailed in two groups shortly before midnight on 6 April and joined each other at 3am on the 7th. The German forces were at sea by the 7th and by the 9th the landings were taking place.

At Trondheim Group II's landing was practically unopposed. At Bergen the troops were unopposed, but *Königsberg* was hit by three 8" shells from the shore battery at Kvarven; the damage was serious enough to make her Captain decide not to put to sea and return to Germany that evening, as planned, but to stay in harbour. *Bremse* was also damaged.

Group IV met resistance at Kristiansand where shore batteries on Odderoy Island fought off four attempts to enter the fjord and a German ship steaming ahead of the Group's ships was hit and set on fire. There was further delay, here and at Arendal, because of mist, but eventually both places were seized before noon. At Narvik Group I had arrived off Vest Fjord entrance on the evening of the 8th. Bonte's destroyers parted company with the battle cruisers and steamed up the fjord, arriving off Narvik in a snowstorm at dawn. Two Norwegian coast defence vessels, *Eidsvold* and *Norge*, were outnumbered and overwhelmed and both were sunk with heavy loss of life. The destroyers went alongside and Dietl's troops landed unopposed.

Only at Oslo was there serious opposition. Group V's ships reached the entrance to Oslo at about midnight on 8 April and steamed up the fjord at high speed. They reached Drobak, some eighteen miles from Oslo, where the fjord narrows to some six hundred yards in width, at about 3.40am on the morning of the 9th. There, the gun batteries on the island of Oscarsborg opened fire and, with torpedoes fired from Kaholm, damaged *Blücher* so badly she had to anchor some distance up the fjord. With internal fires burning so fiercely they could not be brought under control, *Blücher* eventually heeled over and sank. The troops were landed some ten miles to the south.

The setback was only temporary. The landing force had overwhelming air support from the Luftwaffe and by midday on the 9th most of Oslo was in German hands. However, the delay had been long enough to allow the Norwegian Royal Family, the Government and Parliament to leave the city, taking with them all the gold in the Bank of Norway. However, within forty-eight hours of the first landing all the main objectives had been achieved. By 10 April all airfields and the main seaports of Norway were in German hands. *Weserubung* had been an astounding, an almost complete, success.

Ironically the Allies also had plans for operations in Norwegian waters which would have begun on almost the same date as *Weserubung*, but as the saying went, the bear blew first. Mr Churchill had long been pressing for an operation, given what he himself called the 'minor and innocent' codename of WILFRED, to lay minefields in the Norwegian Leads so as to force German ships, carrying vital iron ore south from Narvik, out of Norwegian territorial waters.

Three areas were to be declared dangerous, one off the eastern shore of Vest Fjord, the second off Bud, and the third off Stadtlandet (although no mines were actually to be laid off Bud). The minelayer *Teviot Bank*, escorted by the destroyers *Inglefield*, *Ilex*, *Isis* and *Imogen* of the 3rd Flotilla, sailed from Scapa on 5 April to lay the minefield off Stadtlandet. Four minelaying destroyers, *Esk*, *Impulsive*, *Icarus* and *Ivanhoe* of the 20th Flotilla, (Captain J.G. Bickford) escorted by four destroyers, *Hardy*, *Hotspur*, *Havock* and *Hunter* of the 2nd Flotilla, (Captain B.W. Warburton-Lee) sailed to lay the minefield off Vest Fjord.

Such minelaying was a clear violation of Norwegian neutrality and the Norwegian Navy could be expected to react. Four coastal defence vessels were supposed to be in northern ports (*Eidsvold* and *Norge* were, in fact, at Narvik). Admiral Forbes therefore sent *Renown* (flag of Vice-Admiral W.J. Whitworth), screened by *Greyhound*, *Glowworm*, *Hyperion* and *Hero*, to support the Vest Fjord minelayers. This force left Scapa on the evening of 5 April and was joined on the morning of the 6th by Bickford's and Warburton-Lee's destroyers.

On the 7th, in very heavy seas and poor visibility, *Glowworm* lost a man overboard and while turning to try to pick him up lost touch with *Renown* and the other destroyers. At about 8am the next day *Glowworm* sighted two German destroyers, which were actually part of the Trondheim invasion force. The two German ships were supported by *Admiral Hipper* which opened fire and badly damaged *Glowworm*. *Glowworm* fired a salvo of torpedoes which all missed and from a protecting smokescreen steered towards *Hipper*. *Glowworm* was sunk but not before she had rammed *Hipper*, torn away 130 feet of the armoured belt on her starboard side and her starboard torpedo tubes. The story of *Glowworm*'s last fight was not known until after the war, when her forty survivors, including one officer, returned from PoW camp in Germany. *Glowworm*'s Captain, Lieutenant-

Commander Gerard Roope, was then awarded a posthumous Victoria Cross, the earliest-dated of the war.

Renown and the Vest Fjord minelayers arrived off the mouth of the fjord on the evening of the 7th. The minelayers were detached to lay their mines, which they did between 4.30 and 5.30am on the 8th. *Renown* now had only one destroyer escort, *Greyhound*; *Hyperion* and *Hero* had left to fuel and then to pretend to lay mines off Bud. When *Glowworm*'s signals reporting an enemy force were received, Admiral Whitworth turned *Renown* and *Greyhound* south to support her, but soon had to slow down because of heavy seas. By 10am it had to be assumed, from her silence, that *Glowworm* had been sunk. At 10.45 the Vest Fjord minelayers and escort were ordered direct from the Admiralty to rejoin Whitworth, which they did on the evening of the 8th. In the event this meant that Vest Fjord was unwatched and deserted when Group I arrived that evening and Bonte's destroyers went up to Narvik.

From the entrance to Vest Fjord *Scharnhorst* and *Gneisenau* steered northwest towards their patrol position in the Arctic. At 3.37am on the 9th, they were sighted from *Renown*, broad on her port bow and rather more than ten miles distant. *Renown* was then steering on an almost opposite course, with her destroyers astern of her. *Renown* was the first to react by hauling round to port until she was steering a course roughly parallel to her enemy and her 'A' arcs were open (i.e. all guns in all turrets could bear on the target). *Renown* opened fire first, at 4.05am at a range of 18,600 yards. *Gneisenau* replied after six minute's delay, and *Scharnhorst*, who had not sighted *Renown* until she opened fire, followed later. Both sides exchanged fire for the next ten minutes, *Gneisenau* and *Scharnhorst* both firing at *Renown* with their main 11" armament, *Renown* firing her main 15" at *Gneisenau* and her secondary 4.5" at *Scharnhorst*. *Renown*'s destroyers also opened with their 4.7"s, although their fire was hardly effective at that range.

Renown sustained two hits without any serious damage. At 4.17am at a range of 14,600 yards *Renown* obtained a much more important hit herself, on *Gneisenau*'s foretop, destroying her main fire control equipment and temporarily putting her main armament out of action. *Gneisenau* broke off the action and retired behind a smokescreen laid astern of her by *Scharnhorst*. *Renown* began to chase her enemies to the north, steaming up into a rising wind, a heavy swell and huge seas. *Gneisenau* fired with her after turret, while *Scharnhorst* slewed from side to side to fire broadsides. *Renown* continued to engage *Scharnhorst* without hitting her. But shortly after 4.30 she obtained two more hits on *Gneisenau*, on 'A' turret and aft on the port side.

Both German ships disappeared in a rain squall just before 5am. When the weather cleared twenty minutes later they were even further from *Renown*, but *Renown* once again gave chase, straining herself 'to the maximum' and for a short time achieving 29 knots. The last sight of the enemy was at 6.15, far ahead and well out of range. *Renown* stood on until 8am, when Whitworth gave up the chase and turned to the west, still hoping to intercept. But the action was finally over. The Admiralty had ordered Whitworth to maintain a patrol off Vest Fjord. *Renown* and her destroyers closed the Norwegian coast and were joined later on the 9th by *Repulse* and *Penelope*, escorted by the destroyers *Bedouin*, *Eskimo*, *Punjabi* and *Kimberley*, which the C-in-C had originally detached to support *Glowworm*.

Whitworth set up the Vest Fjord patrol on the 9th (although by then the ten German destroyers under Bonte had already gone unnoticed up to Narvik) with *Renown* and *Repulse* out to sea, *Penelope* closer in and Bickford's destroyers, less *Impulsive* who had gone home with a damaged paravane boom, but with *Greyhound* added, close in to Vest Fjord. Whitworth also ordered Warburton-Lee to join him with his destroyers. But, not for the first or last time in the Norwegian campaign, orders from the man on the spot were countermanded from afar.

Since leaving Scapa on the evening of the 7th the major ships of the Home Fleet under Admiral Forbes ('Wrong Way Forbes' as he was sometimes cruelly called) continued to steer north-east, anticipating action with the main German warships breaking out into the Atlantic. But on the forenoon of the 8th Forbes received the Admiralty signal ordering the Vest Fjord minelaying force and their escort to join Whitworth. This signal, which left Vest Fjord uncovered at a critical time and had, as Forbes said, 'far-reaching effects', gave Forbes food for thought. But the general situation was unclear. He assumed the Admiralty had information not available to him and he did not wish to break radio silence because the enemy was very likely to be somewhere between his ships and Whitworth's. But on the afternoon of the 8th another Admiralty signal was received which did surprise Forbes greatly. The Plan codenamed 'R.4' was to be abandoned and the troops which were to carry it out were ordered to 'march ashore'.

Under R.4, the military plan associated with WILFRED, the Allies had decided to hold troops ready to occupy Bergen, Stavanger and Trondheim, and ready to land at Narvik. But no troops would actually be landed until the Germans had violated Norwegian neutrality or there was clear evidence that they were about to do so. Two battalions each for Bergen and Stavanger were to be embarked in cruisers, with one battalion for Narvik embarked in a transport, accompanied by two cruisers, under the command of Admiral Sir Edward Evans

(Evans of the *Broke*). The Narvik force was to be followed by an oiler, the rest of a brigade and further French troops, bringing the force up to a total strength of about 18,000 men.

By 7 April six battalions had actually embarked: 1/5th Royal Leicestershire Regiment in the cruiser *Devonshire*; 1/4th Battalion, Royal Lincolnshire Regiment in *Berwick*; 1/4th King's Own Yorkshire Light Infantry in *York*; 1/8th Battalion Sherwood Foresters in *Glasgow*. These four cruisers were all at Rosyth under Vice-Admiral John Cunningham. At the Tail o'the Bank in the Clyde were the Hallamshire Battalion of the York and Lancaster Regiment in the Polish liner *Chrobry*, and the 1st Battalion Scots Guards in *Batory*. While the troops in the Clyde watched the cruiser *Aurora* and the rest of their escort sail for Scapa, the troops in Rosyth began to disembark in considerable confusion which is not adequately described under the phrase 'marching ashore'. As a result of this Admiralty decision to disembark all troops and send their ships north to assist Forbes, the battalions for Norway were ashore, some with their stores and equipment, but most without, while the very invasion they might have helped to forestall was actually beginning to take place in Norway. The cruisers which should have carried them were, instead, steaming north to join Forbes (although Forbes already had enough cruisers at his disposal, and the initial concept for R.4 must have assumed that Forbes would not need these four troop-carrying cruisers in order to defeat whatever force the German Navy could put against him).

At 2pm on 8 April an RAF Sunderland of 204 Squadron reported a battle cruiser, two cruisers and two destroyers ahead of the Home Fleet west-northwest of Trondheim, well out to sea and steering west. This could be the enemy Forbes was seeking. It was in fact *Hipper* and four destroyers of the

Trondheim invasion force cruising to and fro until the time for invasion. Their westerly course was irrelevant. But, understandably, Forbes altered course to the north-north-west to intercept. By the time a second Sunderland and *Rodney*'s Walrus had investigated, the German ships had turned back towards Trondheim and neither aircraft sighted anything.

Forbes now appreciated that there might be an enemy battle cruiser to the north, and another battle cruiser and possibly two pocket battleships, to the south, in the Kattegat or Skagerrak. He therefore sent *Repulse*, *Penelope* and the four destroyers on to join Whitworth and turned south himself at 8pm on the evening of the 8th.

Warburton-Lee had been ordered to join Whitworth but on the morning of the 9th Forbes ordered him to 'send some destroyers up to Narvik to make certain that no enemy troops land' and two hours later the Admiralty signalled him direct that one German ship had already arrived at Narvik and landed a small force. He was to 'proceed Narvik and sink or capture enemy ship'. It was left to Warburton-Lee's discretion whether to land a force and, if he could, recapture Narvik.

Warburton-Lee had been joined by a fifth destroyer, *Hostile*, but he learned from a pilot station on his way up Vest Fjord that this reinforcement would not be nearly enough. The pilots said they had seen 'six ships larger than the *Hardy*' going up to Narvik and Warburton-Lee would need twice as many ships. He signalled this to the Admiralty, to Forbes and to Whitworth, adding that the harbour entrance was mined and Narvik was held by a strong force of Germans. Nevertheless he intended 'attacking at dawn high water'.

This put Whitworth in a quandary. Warburton-Lee clearly needed reinforcement, but his intended time of attack, in the early hours of the 10th, left no time for reinforcement. Besides, the plan had been made with forces ordered by the Admiralty. Order had already been followed by counterorder. More orders might mean disorder. So Whitworth decided to leave matters as they stood. But evidently even the Admiralty (in the person of the First Lord) had misgivings, signalling eventually: 'You alone can judge whether in these circumstances attack should be made. Shall support whatever decision you take.'

By then Warburton-Lee's ships were making their way up Vest Fjord in snow squalls and very poor visibility, arriving off Narvik at about 4am. In three attacks Warburton-Lee's ships sank six German merchantmen and one destroyer, and damaged six other destroyers with torpedoes and gunfire (Commodore Bonte was killed). Whilst retreating down the fjord they also sank the German ammunition ship *Rauenfels*. However, they were cut off by three remaining German destroyers. *Hunter* was sunk. *Hardy* was disabled and drifted ashore. Warburton-Lee was killed. He was posthumously awarded the Victoria Cross, the earliest-gazetted of the war.

The German Navy had anticipated losses during the withdrawal phase and so it proved. On 9 April off Kristiansand the cruiser *Karlsruhe* was torpedoed by the submarine *Truant* and so badly damaged that she had to be dispatched by torpedoes from *Grief*. On 10 April, in the early hours, the cruiser *Königsberg*, lying damaged alongside in Bergen, was dive-bombed by sixteen Skuas flying to the limits of their endurance from Hatston in the Orkneys. The Skuas, led by Captain R.T. Partridge, Royal Marines, (800 Squadron) and Lieutenant W.P. Lucy (803 Squadron) scored three direct hits with 500lb bombs and several near-misses. *Königsberg* caught fire, capsized and sank. This sinking, although announced by the BBC that evening as 'The RAF do it again' was an historic naval event, being the first time a major warship had been sunk by air attack. To complete an uncomfortable few days for the German Navy, *Spearfish* badly damaged *Lützow* with one torpedo off the Skaw on n April, and British submarines sank several other merchant ships.

Admiral Whitworth shifted his flag to the battleship *Warspite*, which had recently joined the fleet, on the night of 12/13 April and the next morning, the 13th, *Warspite* and the destroyers *Icarus, Hero, Foxhound, Kimberley, Forester, Bedouin, Punjabi, Eskimo* and *Cossack* went up Vest Fjord and in a brisk day's work sank or drove ashore the eight remaining German destroyers. *Warspite*'s own Swordfish particularly distinguished itself by spotting German destroyers lying in wait for the British ships in time for action to be taken, and by bombing and sinking *U.64*. As Whitworth himself said, 'I doubt if ever a ship-borne aircraft has been used to such good purpose.'

The same could not be said of all ship-borne aircraft during the Norwegian campaign. Off Norway the Royal Navy had its first real experience of sustained air attack. Some bitter lessons were learned. For years before the war one of the main strands of the Navy's argument for control over its own air arm was that air power was indivisible from sea power and that the aircraft carrier, entirely manned and controlled by the Navy, should be an integral part of the fleet. Yet, ironically, the Home Fleet had sailed without an aircraft carrier. *Courageous* was already gone. *Ark Royal* and *Glorious* were in the Mediterranean. *Eagle* was refitting at Singapore and *Hermes* was in the south Atlantic. The nearest carrier was *Furious*, who had just finished a short refit at Devonport and was in the Clyde, but with her Swordfish squadrons, 816 and 818, disembarked at Campbeltown on the Mull of Kintyre and her Skua fighter squadron, 801, at Evanton, near Invergordon.

Nor, at first, was there any great pressure for an aircraft carrier to join the fleet. Certainly, as a fleet commander, Forbes did not have progressive views on airpower. When the fleet, including *Ark Royal*, was attacked from the air on 26 September, 1939, *Ark*'s Skuas were struck down below and their tanks drained of petrol against the risk of fire, while the fleet relied upon anti-aircraft guns for defence. *Ark Royal* was near-missed by one large (2000lb) bomb and it was very fortunate for her and for the Navy that the only damage done was to crockery. By the time the Norwegian campaign opened *Ark Royal*'s Skua squadrons, 801 and 803, were protecting, not *Ark Royal* or the fleet, but the fleet base at Scapa, being disembarked to Hatston (from where they flew to sink *Königsberg*).

Forbes does not appear to have regarded *Furious* as part of his fleet. But her Captain, T.H. Troubridge, cancelled all leave, brought the ship to one hour's notice for sea and warned the squadrons at Campbeltown to be ready to embark, all on his own initiative, and signalled Forbes on 7 April asking permission to join his flag. Before Forbes could reply the Admiralty signalled direct to *Furious* ordering her to sail. *Furious* flew on 816 and 818 after dark on the 9th and sailed at 27½ knots north to join the fleet. 801, meanwhile, was a hundred miles away on the other side of Scotland. Troubridge asked if they should be embarked, but the Admiralty replied not. So the fleet was at least to have a carrier, but no fighters.

Meanwhile the fleet had just had its first taste of air attack. A force under Vice-Admiral Geoffrey Layton, of the cruisers *Manchester*, *Southampton*, *Glasgow* and *Sheffield*, with the destroyers *Afridi*, *Gurkha*, *Sikh*, *Mohawk*, *Somali*, *Matabele* and *Mashona*, detached from the main body at 11.30 on the 9th to attack German forces at Bergen, and principally a *Köln* Class cruiser (actually *Königsberg*) which had been reported there. But Layton's force had not reached Bergen before the Admiralty intervened directly, once again, to cancel the operation.

German aircraft had been shadowing the fleet since about 8am that morning. At 2.30pm they attacked and for the next three hours there was hardly a moment when some ship somewhere was not being attacked. Near-misses slightly damaged *Southampton* and *Glasgow*. *Gurkha*'s Captain, Commander Anthony Buzzard, it was said, became so enraged by the close attention of the Luftwaffe and so anxious to clear his arcs of fire that he allowed his ship to become separated from the main body and *Gurkha* was sunk. With the fleet, *Valiant*, *Berwick*, *Devonshire* and several destroyers had near misses and at 3.30 a Junkers Ju.88 dive-bombed *Rodney*, Forbes's flagship, and hit her with one sizeable bomb which luckily did no serious damage. The fleet put up prodigious amounts of anti-aircraft fire (Layton's ships used 40% of their AA outfit). In all forty-seven Ju.88s of Kampfgeschwader 30 and forty-one Heinkel H.11 is of Kamfgeschwader 26 took part. Four Ju.88s were shot down.

Furious joined the fleet at about 8am on 10 April. For the whole of that day the fleet steered north so as to be in position about ninety miles north-west of Trondheim early the next day. From there *Furious'* Swordfish were to fly on an historic occasion: the first co-ordinated air torpedo attack in naval warfare. Reconnaissance had reported two cruisers, one of the *Admiral Hipper* Class, destroyers and some merchantmen in Trondheim. For nearly two decades, on dozens of occasions, the Fleet Air Arm had exercised torpedo attacks on ships in harbours from Argostoli to Invergordon. Now, at last, the moment had come to make a real attack.

But, as so often in life, reality was nothing like the rehearsal. The Swordfish took off at 4am but the cruiser (it actually was *Admiral Hipper*) had already sailed, with one destroyer, leaving three destroyers in harbour. The Swordfish attacked these, but their torpedoes, set to run at a depth of twenty feet, grounded on shallow banks and no hits were achieved. It was a very disappointing result. Worse still, the Luftwaffe retaliated that afternoon. The destroyer *Eclipse* was hit and her engine-room flooded. She was towed to Lerwick by *Escort*.

The failure of the Trondheim strike was not the fault of the aircrew who carried it out, but it did cause Forbes and his staff to consider whether bombing would be more effective than torpedo attack. On the morning of 12 April Forbes met Whitworth and the fleet steered north for an area off the Lofoten Islands. By this time the fleet strength was being steadily shredded away, to escort *Eclipse*, to meet the first of the troop convoys taking the hastily organized Allied expedition to Norway, and to search the Inner Leads from Trondheim up to Vest Fjord. By the evening of the 12th, when the fleet reached the position from where *Furious* was to launch a bombing strike and photo-reconnaissance flight over Narvik, Forbes had with him only *Rodney*, *Warspite*, *Renown*, *Furious* and six destroyers, with another twelve destroyers operating in the southern approaches to Narvik.

Nine Swordfish of 818 Squadron, armed with four 250lb and four 20lb bombs, took off at 4.15pm, followed fifty minutes later by nine Swordfish of 816. They had a flight of some 150 miles to their target. Weather conditions were the worst possible: storms of snow and sleet, winds of 35 to 45 knots, an average cloud ceiling of 1,000 feet reducing suddenly and without warning to a hundred feet. The aircrews had no proper maps, only photographic reproductions of Admiralty charts, with no contours.

816 Squadron, feeling their way almost blind up the fjord, ran into a snowstorm with ceiling of less than a hundred feet and were forced to turn back. They landed on just before dark, with one Swordfish plunging over the side; the crew were recovered by *Hero*. Meanwhile 818 pressed on to bomb five destroyers alongside or at anchor in Narvik from heights between 400 and 1600 feet. They claimed four hits, but the Germans reported only splinter damage. They also took vertical and oblique photographs of the harbour and approaches. Two aircraft were lost but their crews were picked up by *Punjabi* and *Penelope*. The rest landed on in darkness. Six aircraft had been damaged by gunfire and the crew of one wounded.

The next day, as *Warspite* and her destroyers were carrying out the second battle of Narvik, accounting for eight remaining German destroyers, ten of *Furious*' Swordfish (the only aircraft still available) 'fought their way,' as Captain Troubridge said, 'through the narrows into Ofot Fjord with a ceiling of 500 feet and snow squalls that occasionally reduced visibility to a few yards.' The weather improved as they reached the open fjord and the Swordfish carried out a well-synchronized attack, diving from 2,000 to 900 feet to drop about a hundred bombs, thirty of them 250-pounders. They claimed two hits but in fact they were both near-misses. Two aircraft, with their crews, were lost.

Meanwhile, as these events unfolded, like the rumble of distant gunfire in the north, *Ark Royal* and *Glorious* were at Gibraltar, where they had arrived, after a breathless dash westwards across the Mediterranean, on 13 April. For their sailors Norway was still not much more than a country in the

189

atlas, and names like Narvik and Bergen and Vest Fjord, which now filled the signal pads and the BBC broadcasts and the newspapers at Gibraltar, meant no more than Kamchatka or Katmandu.

On Sunday, 14 April, a signal arrived ordering Vice-Admiral L.V. Wells, CB, DSO, the V.A.A. (Vice-Admiral Air), to shift his flag from *Ark Royal* to *Glorious* and proceed to join the Home Fleet. Wells suggested that *Ark Royal*, not *Glorious*, return to the U.K., but this was not approved. *Glorious*, flying Wells's flag, sailed from Gibraltar escorted by *Stuart* at 9.30pm that evening. *Ark Royal* was left behind to exercise, somewhat disconsolately, off Gibraltar for a day and a half before she too received the joyful summons to come and join the war.

Vice-Admiral Lionel Victor ('Nutty') Wells was a peppery little gunnery officer, red of face and short of temper. His Secretary, Captain (S) Jasper Parrott, called him 'the last of the "awful" admirals'. It was not wise to approach him before breakfast for any reason, and not with paper-work to sign at any time. He had a good deal of experience of the air world, having commanded *Eagle* during a successful commission in the early 1930s (in which one of the officers was Paul Slessor).

Nutty Wells would have to have been peculiarly insensitive not to have noticed the unhappy atmosphere in *Glorious*. In fact he had not only noticed, he had enquired. 'J.B. and I dined with Nutty one night,' Paul Slessor wrote to Hope on 12 April, 'He *is* an extraordinary little man. This was one of the occasions when he was at his best and most likeable. He was so kind to me. He had heard one or two things, and after dinner led me aside. I wouldn't open my mouth until he promised to forget for the moment what we had on our respective sleeves, and also that he would keep everything under his hat. I can't of course tell you the story. But he was most sympathetic and reassuring, "One of my old officers…" etc. His last words, seizing me by the arm, were "Don't worry, old Paul".'

The attitude, amounting to antagonism, which D'Oyly-Hughes exhibited to J.B. Heath had deteriorated over the previous few weeks. The two had first met at a bathing party in Aden and D'Oyly-Hughes continued to treat Heath, in Heath's phrase, as though 'I might have been another bit of sand to be kicked around'. In a letter to his predecessor and good friend Guy Willoughby, J.B. Heath 'just unburdened my heart. I made no cover-up. I said I simply couldn't handle the situation as it was. Overruled. Stamped on. Total rudeness, and intolerance. You had the sensation of total ignorance of air affairs. Just because he'd flown a Moth.' A great burden also fell upon the ship's Executive Officer, Commander A.E. Lovell. 'I spoke to Teddy Lovell,' said Heath, 'before it all blew up. I said, "Well, how does it go with you?" He said, "I can't do anything right." Poor Teddy Lovell, he was put in a very difficult position.'

Also in a very difficult position, in *Glorious* as in any carrier in those days, were the rating pilots. In the early days, because rating pilots lacked the necessary security clearances, they were forbidden access to the air operations room and not allowed to see the plot. But a pilot's lack of knowledge of the ship's latest position and movement could, and did, result in the aircraft being lost, with fatal results. Rating pilots, though they were petty officers and thus members of the ship's company, occupied a somewhat awkward anomalous position between the officers and the lower deck. As Dick Leggott said, 'We were neither fish nor fowl nor good red herring'. In the squadron a pilot's status depended upon his flying ability rather than his rank or rating. At briefings petty officer pilots received information which was confidential and could not be passed to other ship's petty officers. This reserve was bound to distance the pilots from the rest of the ship's company, who, for their part, knew that rating pilots spent much time perforce in officers' company, and therefore they treated pilots with a certain reserve.

When Leggott joined *Glorious*, with another petty officer pilot, A.G. Johnson, they were summoned to the bridge to meet the Captain. 'D'Oyly-Hughes greeted us *very* kindly indeed. He liked his fighter squadron. There was never a difficult word between the fighter squadron C.O. (Lieutenant 'Ginger' Jack Marmont) and D'Oyly-Hughes. Slessor and J.B. Heath were also on the bridge, standing on one side. "I'm very pleased to see both of you," D'Oyly-Hughes said to us. "I know you've had a certain amount of experience in an operational squadron and have seen something of the enemy. You two will be much more valuable than those two standing there" — he pointed at Slessor and Heath. I thought he was *joking*! I was about to give a polite social laugh when I saw Heath and Slessor looking so hangdog and dejected. I thought, Christ, what's going on? I was amazed Heath didn't say to the Captain, "Hey, steady on," or something. But he didn't. He just stood there, like a small boy. They were extremely nice people, both of them, Heath and Slessor. Maybe they were too nice to be in a situation like that.'

Glorious steamed north, up the 150 meridian, round the north coast of Ireland, through the North Channel and into the Clyde, arriving late on 18 April. While she was on passage, the naval staff had decided that *Glorious* should retain only enough aircraft, one squadron (802) of fighters and one Swordfish squadron (823), for her own protection. 812 and 825 were therefore flown off on the 21st to Prestwick, and thence to minelaying and convoy escort on the east or south coasts and,

192

eventually, to operations during the Dunkirk evacuation. 'By the time I flew off the ship for the last time,' wrote Dave Jolliff, who was one of those who left on the 21st, 'morale amongst squadron ratings was at an all-time low, even taking into effect the way the war was going against us, and I know that not one of 812 Squadron air gunners was sorry to have left her.' Meanwhile the space in *Glorious* was to be filled with RAF fighters, urgently needed in Norway. Much had happened in the north while *Glorious* had been on passage.

Barely had most of the troops for R.4 been bundled ashore, less much of their equipment and stores, than plans were hurried forward to mount an expedition to Norway using the same troops. (In fact the Scots Guards in *Batory* and the Hallamshire Battalion in *Chrobry* were still embarked.) But since the abandonment of R.4 the situation in Norway had changed utterly. The troops in R.4 had been expected to land without any opposition. The Germans now occupied Bergen, Stavanger and Trondheim, and had forces at Narvik. R.4 had no air cover, because no air opposition had been expected. (For some curious reason the Allied planning staffs continued to think for some time that the Luftwaffe would confine itself entirely to troop-carrying and would eschew bombing.) But now the Luftwaffe was present in force. Land-based air power was already affecting the battle at sea. Forbes was already being forced by the threat of air attack to alter the dispositions and movements of his ships.

The Allies had two main objectives in Norway — Narvik and Trondheim — and nobody was ever sure which was the more important and should have priority. On occasion an expedition would be launched against one and diverted to the other in passage. In the event expeditions were mounted against both. In the event neither object was achieved. For this and other reasons the Norwegian campaign has been called 'ramshackle' and criticisms have been made of the inadequate forces dispatched to carry it out. In fact, considering the circumstances of the time and the British army's existing commitments in France and in the Middle East, the wonder is not that the forces were so small but that they were as large as they were and the surprise is not that the campaign was a failure but that anything at all was achieved.

The first ships of the troop convoy NP.1, *Empress of Australia* with the K.O.Y.L.I. and the Lincolnshires, *Monarch of Bermuda* with the 1st Battalion, Irish Guards, and *Reino del Pacifico* with the 2nd Battalion South Wales Borderers, sailed from the Clyde on 11 April and were joined the next day off Cape Wrath by *Batory* and *Chrobry* from Scapa Flow. The convoy was escorted by the cruisers *Manchester* (flag of Vice-Admiral Layton), *Birmingham* and *Cairo*, and the destroyers *Witherington*, *Volunteer*, *Vanoc*, *Whirlwind* and *Highlander*, and the netlayer *Protector*. The convoy steered for Vest Fjord at 14 knots, the escort being strengthened on the 14th by *Valiant*, the repair ship *Vindictive*, with the destroyers *Codrington*, *Acasta* and *Ardent* from Scapa, and *Fearless*, *Griffin* and *Brazen* from Sullom Voe. The landing at Narvik, Operation RUPERT, was under way.

Meanwhile, on 12 April, Major-General P.J. Macksey, who was to command the land forces, and two companies of the Scots Guards, embarked in *Southampton* and sailed from Scapa. On the same day the naval force commander, Admiral of the Fleet the Earl of Cork and Orrery, hoisted his flag in the cruiser *Aurora* and sailed from Rosyth.

But on the evening of the 14th the plan was changed. The Government had decided that, because only 'reduced opposition' was expected at Narvik, some of the forces should be diverted to seize Trondheim (which certainly was the key to the Norwegian campaign and strategically a much more important objective than Narvik), beginning with a landing at Namsos to the north of Trondheim. An outright frontal assault on Trondheim, Operation HAMMER, (in which *Glorious* was originally scheduled to take part) was also planned.

Chrobry, with the Hallamshires, and *Empress of Australia*, with the K.O.Y.L.I. and the Lincolnshires, these three Territorial battalions comprising the 146th Infantry Brigade, were detached from the convoy for Namsos, escorted by *Manchester*, *Birmingham*, *Cairo*, *Vanoc*, *Whirlwind*, and *Highlander*, the rest of the convoy, escorted by *Valiant* and ten destroyers, continuing towards Vaags Fjord. Unfortunately, and perhaps typically of the whole Norwegian campaign, Brigadier C.G. Phillips was in a different ship to his troops and, while the 146th Brigade headed for Namsos, their commanding officer was carried willy-nilly to the north.

The first Allied troops actually to land in Norway were 350 seamen and marines from *Sheffield* and *Glasgow* who were landed from destroyers at Namsos on the evening of 14 April in Operation HENRY. They soon discovered, as did everybody who landed in Norway that spring, that deep snow made any movement extremely slow and difficult without special ski equipment and training, and that everything in the open was highly visible and vulnerable to air attack.

The destroyers which took part in HENRY were harassed by a score of enemy bombers off Aalesund on the 13th. They managed to beat them off without damage to themselves, but the ever-present threat of air attack and the inadequate harbour facilities at Namsos caused the ships carrying the main force for Namsos (Operation MAURICE) under Layton to go to Lillesjona, one hundred miles north of Namsos, to transfer the troops from the transports to the destroyers which were to take them inshore.

Every day there were ominous signs of increasing air attacks. On the 15th, as the Sunderland flying boat carrying General Carton de Wiart, VC, who was to command the land forces in Namsos, touched down in the fjord, it was attacked by aircraft who had been bombing the destroyer *Somali*. Carton de Wiart was untouched but one staff officer (his *only* staff officer, as it happened) was wounded. *Somali* was attacked three times in all and had sixty bombs aimed at her. She was not actually hit but fired off her entire outfit of anti-aircraft ammunition and at the end was reduced to firing practise rounds 'for moral effect'.

Chrobry and *Empress of Australia* were bombed while the destroyers *Afridi*, *Nubian*, *Sikh*, *Matabele* and *Mashona* were alongside them but the Lincoln-shires and two companies of the Hallamshires were landed in Namsos on the night of 16th/17th, the other two companies of the Hallamshires being taken to Bangsund. The K.O. Y.L.I.s should also have transferred into destroyers, but the risk of air attack while the troops were still in *Empress of Australia* forced a change of plan. The battalion and all but 179 tons of their stores were shifted to *Chrobry* which took them in under destroyer escort to Namsos on the night of 17th/18th. The K.O.Y.L.I.s disembarked but left another 130 tons of their stores in *Chrobry*.

The following day, 19 April, three battalions of French Chasseurs-Alpins arrived at Namsos in four troopships. They were led up the fjord by the cruiser *Cairo*, one of two ships (the other being *Curlew*) specially fitted for anti-aircraft defence. *Cairo*'s expertise was needed, because the French were attacked from the air just as the British-had been. The French flagship, the cruiser *Emile Bertin*, was hit and badly damaged.

The original 'Mauriceforce' which had been intended for Namsos left Rosyth on 17 April, but for Aandalsnes and Molde, not Namsos. The troops were the 148th Infantry Brigade; of two Territorial battalions, the 5th Leicestershires and the 8th Sherwood Foresters, embarked in the cruisers *Galatea*, (flag of Vice-Admiral Edward-Collins) *Arethusa*, *Carlisle*, and *Curacoa*, with the transport *Orion* and the destroyers *Arrow* and *Acheron*, and arrived at their destinations of Aandalsnes and Molde on the 18th. This operation, codenamed SICKLE, took place without any interference from the air, probably, as Edward-Collins said, because there were no troop transports to give the force's purpose away.

But 'Sickleforce' was not the first on the scene. On the night of the 17th/18th, in Operation PRIMROSE, the sloops *Black Swan*, *Bittern*, *Flamingo*, and *Auckland* landed at Aandelsnes some forty-five officers and 680 Royal Marines, a force which had recently been assembled from all over the country, with detachments from *Hood* (at Plymouth), *Barham* (at Liverpool) and *Nelson* (from Portsmouth), an anti-aircraft battery from Tynemouth and a searchlight regiment (although unfortunately, due to another 'Norwegian slip-up', not the searchlights) from Yeovil.

With 'Mauriceforce' at Namsos to the north, and 'Sickleforce' and 'Primrose' at Aandalsnes and Molde to the south, the German position at Trondheim was threatened from both sides. But it remained to be seen how the Allies would fare under the onslaught from the air which was about to fall upon them. Meanwhile on the 15th the 24th Brigade, of the Guards and the South Wales Borderers, landed not at Narvik but at Harstad to the north. The ships were harassed by German aircraft but no serious damage was done and on the approach to Vaags Fjord the destroyers *Fearless* and *Brazen* achieved a major coup by blowing U.49 to the surface. Her crew abandoned ship and 'started screaming in the most dreadful fashion'. *Brazen* picked most of them up, and with them a most interesting document giving the whole of the U-boat dispositions for the coast of Norway.

The growing power and ferocity of Fliegerkorps X's bombing attacks in Norway had to be experienced to be believed, and it seemed to have been Admiral Forbes's opinion that the Admiralty, having never experienced them, did not believe them. 'It was only in the Fleet,' he wrote, 'which had practical experience in the matter, that the scale of air attack which could develop on the Norwegian coast was properly appreciated.' But on 18 April, the day *Glorious* arrived in the Clyde from the Mediterranean, there was another brutal reminder of the effect of air attack when the cruiser *Suffolk* struggled into Scapa Flow with her quarterdeck literally awash. It seems, paradoxically, that *Suffolk* made a much bigger impact by surviving than by being sunk. Out of sight at sea was out of mind, but the sight of *Suffolk*'s splinter-riddled hull, beached ashore at Longhope (as she had to be for temporary hull repairs) seems to have concentrated the minds of the naval staff.

Suffolk, with the destroyers, *Kipling, Juno, Janus* and *Hereward*, had sailed from Scapa on the afternoon of 16 April to carry out Operation DUCK, which was a bombardment of Sola airfield at Stavanger, in support of the PRIMROSE landing at Aandalsnes. The bombardment began just after 5am on the 17th, at a range of about ten miles. *Suffolk* had launched both her Walrus aircraft for spotting but due to meteorological conditions was not able to get in touch with either aircraft by wireless. So the bombardment was much less effective. *Suffolk* fired 202 rounds of 8", destroyed four seaplanes and two petrol dumps, and did other damage.

The damage done to the enemy seemed hardly worth the risk to the ships involved, especially as the Luftwaffe could be expected to come after *Suffolk* like a swarm of hornets. The original plan had been for the ships to retire westwards at high speed under RAF fighter cover. But an Admiralty signal timed 11pm the previous night ordered *Suffolk* to sweep northwards after her bombardment 'to intercept enemy destroyers'.

This change of plan was popularly supposed to have been an intervention by the First Lord, one of the so-called 'Midnight Follies' when operations were ordered after Mr Churchill's nightly visit to the Admiralty war room after dinner. Whatever its origins, the change put *Suffolk* in grave danger. The first bombers found her at 8.05am and she was subjected to continuous air attack for the next six hours and forty-seven minutes. She had to endure thirty-three attacks, twenty-one of them high level bombing and twelve dive-bombing, during which eighty-eight splashes of near-misses were counted.

Whether or not enemy destroyers had ever been present, the search for them quickly became irrelevant. *Suffolk*'s main concern was survival. At 10.37 she suffered the most dangerous and accurate attack of all and was hit by a large, possibly 1,000lb, bomb abreast 'X' Turret. The damage was very severe. Some of the main machinery and both 'X' and 'Y' turrets were put out of action. Some 1,500 tons of water flooded the after-part of the ship within twenty minutes. Speed was reduced to 18 knots.

As she struggled westwards, still under constant air attack, *Suffolk* signalled frantically for fighter cover, giving her position (which, of course, the enemy already knew only too well). The RAF fighters failed to find her, explaining later that they had expected her to be much closer inshore. In the afternoon Skuas from Hatston arrived but the attacks went on. In fact four of the most dangerous attacks of all were carried out in the presence of nine Skuas.

When eventually *Suffolk*, escorted by *Renown* and *Repulse*, reached Scapa late on the 18th so much water had flooded in aft that her hull was at a grotesque angle, with water lapping over her quarterdeck and her fore-foot level with the waterline. Her steering gear was wrecked and she had been steering on main engines for the last 164 miles. Her survival had been a triumph of damage control. The only comfort to be drawn from her appearance was that Fliegerkorps X could not be quite as deadly as was feared. Given the chances they had had that day, they should have sunk *Suffolk* early on.

Operation HAMMER was cancelled, wisely, on 19 April. Admiral Forbes had never been enthusiastic about its chances of success. One of his main reservations had been about air cover. Even the forty-five naval fighters promised, from *Ark Royal* and *Glorious*, had not been enough in his opinion. But it was now high time, and past high time, that fighter cover was provided for the ships inshore and the troops on shore. Here, at last, *Ark Royal* and *Glorious* were to play their parts.

CHAPTER 7: CARRIER TASK FORCE OFF NORWAY

AS EXPECTED THE Luftwaffe reacted to the Allied landings at Aandalsnes and Namsos with an even more ferocious air assault. Aandalsnes was bombed every day from 20 April onwards. The troops had to take shelter in forests nearby during the day and work at night. Eventually the town, which was largely made of wood, was destroyed. At Namsos bombing began on the 20th only a few hours after the last French troops had disembarked. Of the scene at Namsos on the night of the 20th, Commander R.W. Ravenhill, commanding the destroyer *Nubian*, wrote that 'The whole place was a mass of flames from end to end, and the glare on the snows of the surrounding mountains produced an unforgettable spectacle'. The next day General Carton de Wiart, already thinking of withdrawal from Namsos, signalled to the War Office that 'enemy aircraft have almost completely destroyed Namsos, beginning on railhead target, diving indiscriminately... I see little chance of carrying out decisive or, indeed, any operations, unless enemy air activity is considerably restricted.'

Admiral Forbes had returned to Scapa on 17 April but *Warspite* and *Furious* were operating west of the Lofotens. *Furious*, though still with no fighters, was carrying out a variety of roles, including army liaison, with her Swordfish. She was an extremely lucky ship. Coast-watchers, including lighthouse keepers, gave warning of the approach of German aircraft from the south in time for *Furious* more than once to efface herself inside a providential snowstorm.

But on the 18th, the day of *Suffolk*'s ordeal, *Furious*' luck ran out. A single Heinkel He.111 bomber approached her at a height of some 15,000 feet when she was in a narrow fjord at Tromso. Flying carefully, well out of range of *Furious*' 4" high-angle guns, the bomber deliberately dropped two small bombs which, as the Navigating Officer later wrote, 'burst on the rocky foreshore three or four hundred yards on our starboard beam, and the uninitiated laughed at the poorness of his aim'. However, these two were for wind measurement. The next two bombs were very much larger and one of them detonated only thirty feet from *Furious*' port side, shaking her shafts out of alignment and stripping some of the turbine blades of her port main engines. Her speed was reduced to 20 knots. But she stayed off the Norwegian coast, operating under Lord Cork's orders, although she only had half of her Swordfish still serviceable, until the 26th when she left for the Clyde for repairs.

Furious had done marvellously well. Withdrawing on the 26th, Captain Troubridge made a general signal that 'since leaving the Clyde on 8 April, *Furious*' aircraft have flown 23,870 miles, dropped eighteen torpedoes, 15½ tons of bombs, lost 50 per cent of planes, and had seventeen hit by enemy fire, taken 295 photographs. Casualties — three killed, seven wounded, two missing feared dead.' The ship well deserved the commendatory signals from the Fifth Sea Lord, from Churchill and from the Chief of the Air Staff, and her air group in particular merited their Captain's comment in his report: 'Their honour and courage remained throughout as dazzling as the snow-covered mountains over which they so triumphantly flew.'

It was now up to *Ark Royal* and *Glorious* to take over the torch carried so gallantly by *Furious*. *Glorious* had sailed from the Clyde for Scapa on 21 April and next day flew on eighteen Gladiators of 263 Squadron RAF. These were flown on by naval pilots. As Heath said, 'All old hands rushed in for the job and ferried back to shore again.' The C.O. of 263, Squadron Leader J.W. ('Baldy') Donaldson and seventeen of his pilots, including five sergeant-pilots, embarked at Scapa. They had previously been based at Filton, near Bristol.

On 23 April *Glorious* sailed from Scapa with *Ark Royal* (once more flying Wells's flag), *Berwick*, *Curlew* (to provide radar cover) and *Hyperion*, *Hereward*, *Hasty*, *Fearless*, *Fury* and *Juno*, all forming the first carrier task force in the Royal Navy's history, to carry out Operation D.X. whose objectives were to reach a position approximately 120 miles distant from Trondheim, Namsos and Aandalsnes and carry out air operations on all three places, in particular to provide fighter protection for Namsos and Aandalsnes, to attack enemy aircraft, aerodromes and shipping at Trondheim, to disembark 263 Squadron from *Glorious* and to carry out reconnaissance at Jonsvatet, a frozen lake five miles south-east of Trondheim, where bombers had been reported.

The sixty-nine aircraft in the two carriers was the largest number so far fielded in the Fleet Air Arm's history at sea. *Ark Royal* had twelve Swordfish of 810 Squadron, nine Swordfish of 820, nine Skuas and two Rocs of 800, nine Skuas and three Rocs of 801 and one Walrus. *Glorious* had disembarked 823 on the 22nd and had no Swordfish on board, but had eighteen Gladiators of 263 Squadron, nine Sea Gladiators of 802, nine Sea Gladiators of 804 and eleven Skuas of 803.

This was the first time *Glorious* had had the Fleet Air Arm's first monoplane embarked. The Blackburn Skua was a two-seater fighter-dive-bomber (an almost impossible design requirement to fulfil satisfactorily). In the event the Skua was too slow for a fighter and had too small a bomb load for a bomber. Its Bristol Perseus XII radial engine gave it a top speed of 225 mph, which was slower than all the bombers it was supposed to shoot down except the Junkers Ju.87 'Stuka', and over 100 mph slower than the opposing fighter, the Messerschmitt Me 109. The Skua had a maximum service ceiling of 20,500 feet which was, again, very low for a modern combat aircraft. The Skua was in fact obsolete even before the Norwegian campaign began, but the skill, experience and courage of its crews made up for its deficiencies.

The two carriers shared the flying duties, *Ark Royal* maintaining two Swordfish on anti-submarine patrol and *Glorious* three Gladiators on fighter CAP, with another three Gladiators on deck instantly ready to fly off. *Ark Royal* also kept Rocs on short notice to join patrols if necessary. The Gladiators were briefed to remain near the task force and not to chase enemy aircraft after they had withdrawn, and to keep a special lookout for enemy flying boats, shadowing the carrier task force and usually flying close to the water at a range of seven to ten miles. The anti-submarine and fighter patrols were relieved simultaneously at two-hour intervals and all pilots were briefed to close their carriers to land on as soon as they saw their reliefs taking off.

The first sorties of Operation D.X. had been timed to begin at 2pm on the 24th, but, half-an-hour before, the task force ran into a snowstorm which reduced visibility to two to three miles and flying was postponed. But at 2.20 a 'Most Immediate' signal was received from *Curacoa* that the army required air cover at Otta, which was some twenty-five miles south-east of Dombaas. This was precisely what the task force had come to do and six Skuas were immediately ranged in each carrier to wait for the weather to improve. By 4.35 the storm clouds had lifted and at 4.36 the first aircraft from *Glorious* to fly an operational sortie over enemy territory took off.

It was a Skua of 803 (a squadron more associated with *Ark Royal* than *Glorious*) flown by the squadron C.O., Lieutenant W.P. Lucy, with the squadron observer, Lieutenant M.C.E. Hanson, leading Blue Section of three Skuas. The three Skuas of Red Section were led by Lieutenant Harris, Royal Marines. Their brief was to fly to Aandalsnes and then up the Romsdal valley to Dombaas and Otta and drive off enemy aircraft.

After an hour's flight they crossed the coast at 6,000 feet over Bjornsund, climbed to 8,000 over Aandelsnes, sighting a British cruiser and two escort vessels in the fjord, and then up the valley. At 5.55 they sighted a Heinkel He III flying towards and below them. Lucy led both sections down to attack and the Heinkel was seen to lose height and crash. Fifteen minutes later they saw another Heinkel flying up the valley and several Skuas made individual attacks as the Sections had become somewhat split up. Their pilots said they saw hits and the Heinkel finally dived away after jettisoning its bombs. Finally, at 6.20, Lucy and Lieutenant Christian in his flight attacked a Dornier Do. 17. They had all expended their ammunition and reformed at 6.25 for the long flight of 180 miles back to the carriers, and landed on at 8.30 after a round flight of 400 miles. Their appearance must have been an unpleasant surprise for the Heinkels which had been bombing the railway to Aandalsnes and the airfield at Lesjaskog with impunity. 'This was a very hazardous flight,' wrote Wells, 'most gallantly carried out.' Lucy's Skua had been hit five times and Lieutenant Harris' three times. Two of *Ark Royal's* Skuas on the same sortie ran out of fuel and ditched. The crews were picked up by destroyers.

Before the Skuas left on their sortie, another 'Most Immediate' signal had been received from the Admiralty ordering 263 Squadron's Gladiators to be flown off forthwith. The Gladiators were ranged as soon as the Skuas were clear and flew off, led by Donaldson, in two sections of nine aircraft, at 5.25 and 6.05pm, each section guided by a Skua. Neither Donaldson nor any of his pilots had ever taken off from a carrier before, but the fly-off went safely and all eighteen Gladiators arrived at their new 'airfield' which was in fact the frozen Lake Lesjaskog, in the Romsdal valley, some thirty miles south-east of Aandalsnes.

The experience of 263 Squadron on 'Gladiator Lake', as it was called, was typical of the whole Norwegian campaign. Organizationally it was an almost complete disaster, mitigated only by individual acts of bravery and dedication by some of its participants. Apart from the first, incident-free landings, almost everything else that could go wrong did so.

Lesjaskog itself is a long narrow lake some eight miles long by half a mile wide, bounded by woods. By the time the Gladiators arrived a runway about 800 yards long and seventy-five yards wide had been cleared of snow, which was between two and three feet deep, by a working party of 200 Norwegians who had also swept the snow from a track leading from the main Aandalsnes road to the edge of the lake.

An advance party for Lesjaskog, under Wing Commander Keens, landed at Aandalsnes from the cruiser *Arethusa* on the night of 22 April. The party consisted of five officers, a servicing party of one officer and seventy men (most of whom did not belong to 263 Squadron), a naval battery with two oerlikon anti-aircraft guns, and a platoon of marines. The stores, which included a deck cargo of forty-five tons of petrol, were landed quickly but with a certain amount of confusion because there was no Sea Transport Officer to take charge of unloading on the jetty. As Admiral Edward-Collins said, 'The old proverb of more haste, less speed has been very much in evidence.'

A portable W/T station, with its personnel and equipment, was landed on the 23rd. Meanwhile, for the main party, difficulties continued to mount. Petrol and stores were first placed in a railway tunnel (the line being out of action). Two lorries ran a shuttle service up to the lake while the advance party themselves marched by road. Stores had to be loaded into three horse-drawn sleighs for the last half-mile from the end of the swept track across the lake, in a foot of snow, to the runway. No stores were labelled or listed and all had to be unpacked in the open on the lake. There were no petrol bowsers; petrol was carried in four-gallon drums and then in tins, jugs, or any other available containers, to dumps beside the runway. The starter trolley batteries were flat and had no acid in them. There was only one trained armourer to service the seventy-two Browning machine guns in the Gladiators. There was no early warning radar system. By the time the Gladiators actually arrived the heaped-up snow was melting, covering the icy lake surface with trickling water. There were shortages of ammunition, of tools, even of forage for the sleigh horses. However, the two oerlikon guns were in position and the marines were guarding the petrol supply.

An unidentified aircraft was reported overhead almost at once, but it was Norwegian (although possibly flown by the enemy). The eighteen Gladiators were, with difficulty, refuelled and looked forward to flying patrols over Dombaas the next morning, starting at 3 am. But overnight, in the bitter cold, engines and carburettors froze; joysticks and elevator pedals were immovable; wheels were stuck to the ice. Because of the cold and the lack of proper starting equipment, the first two Gladiators were not airborne until nearly 5am, when they shot down a Heinkel He.115 seaplane but could not prevent the enemy dropping bombs on the lake.

Two more Gladiators were airborne by 7am, but the ground crews were still struggling to start more engines when a heavy bombing raid developed at about 9.30. Heinkel bombers, approaching in threes, split up near the lake to bomb and machine-gun the Gladiators stranded out on the open ice. Two more Gladiators got up in time to engage one of the earliest and biggest bombing attacks but another five were destroyed almost at once and by midday ten Gladiators were wrecked.

The bombing and machine-gunning went on almost incessantly all day. The naval gunners did their best with the oerlikons and some borrowed Lewis guns, but the ground crews deserted their posts and ran into the woods and stayed there. These men had just been landed in a foreign and hostile country in a bitter climate, and put to work in a strange squadron with unfamiliar aircraft under intense enemy attack. Those who have suffered a similar experience can judge them. But it did seem a shameful neglect of duty. They watched from the trees while their officers and sergeants laboured to rearm and refuel the aircraft and restart engines. Unsurprisingly, it took over an hour to rearm and refuel a single Gladiator and many of them were bombed and set alight or destroyed by blast while waiting on the ice.

It was a miracle that any sorties were flown at all. In fact, 263 Squadron flew forty sorties that day, engaged thirty-seven separate enemy aircraft, shot down six confirmed, with another eight probables unconfirmed. Their mere presence also gave tremendous encouragement to Allied troops on the ground who up to then had seen nothing but hostile aircraft. But, by the end of the afternoon, there were 132 bomb craters in or around the lake. There was no more belted ammunition and unarmed Gladiators were taking off in the hope of somehow distracting enemy bomb-aimers with their feint attacks.

That evening Donaldson took the only five remaining Gladiators to Setnesmoen, a peacetime Norwegian army camp just outside Aandalsnes, where the parade ground had been converted into a temporary landing strip. From there the Gladiators flew over and around Aandalsnes the following day but by the evening only one was still serviceable. That never flew again and was abandoned in Norway.

On 27 April Squadron Leader K.B.B. ('Bing') Cross landed at Aandalsnes in a flying boat to reconnoitre the general situation and to choose possible landing areas for his own No 46 Hurricane Squadron. Cross urged that 46 be landed at once, with the ground crews and servicing equipment in flying boats, but the Air Ministry rejected the suggestion. Although the Navy had brought further reinforcements, the fighting on land had been bogged down and the decision had been made to evacuate. But 46 Squadron's chance would come.

As for 263, the Lake Lesjaskog party were embarked in the sloop *Fleetwood* and in destroyers on the 29th for passage to the UK. The pilots embarked the same day in the freighter *Delius* and, after being bombed continuously from 8am until 2pm, eventually reached Scapa Flow on 1 May. So ended, after forty-eight hours, the first attempt to base fighters ashore in Norway.

Meanwhile, at sea on the 24th, after the Gladiators had departed the carriers recovered their last Skua patrols by 9pm and steered north to clear the coast. At 11 pm a signal was received from Admiral Forbes that, even if the Gladiators could operate from shore the next day (a doubt which, in view of what was to happen next day on Gladiator Lake, was well expressed) the task force was to continue to provide fighter cover for Namsos and to strike at targets already allocated at Trondheim. At midnight the carrier squadron altered to the southeast to close the flying-off position which was about 120 miles distant from both Namsos and Trondheim.

The first range flew off at 3am on the 25th: from *Ark Royal* six Swordfish of 820, to bomb Vaernes airfield, eight Swordfish of 810 to bomb Jonsvatet Lake and Vaernes, seven Skuas of 801 and two from 800 to attack shipping in Trondheim harbour, including a cruiser which was supposed to be alongside Bratora Wharf. From *Glorious*: five Skuas of 803 to bomb seaplanes at their moorings and shipping in Trondheim harbour, six Skuas of 803 to search fjords around Trondheim for enemy warships and to reconnoitre for possible enemy landing grounds, including the race-course. The Skuas were briefed to stay in the area after their bombing to cover the Swordfish. *Ark Royal*'s Skuas also maintained a patrol of three over Namsos, while *Glorious*' Sea Gladiators flew CAPs over the task force. Swordfish were armed with four 250lb bombs and eight 20lb bombs, Skuas with one 250lb and eight 20lb bombs.

The second range was away at 4.30am. It was a moderately fine day, with cloud at about 5,000 feet and patches of broken cumulus at about 1,000 feet with fair visibility, for the carrier task force's first large strike of the war. 820 and 810 destroyed two hangers and a petrol dump at Vaernes and damaged a large bomber sitting outside on the tarmac. 801 and 800 saw no warships but attacked two 5,000 ton merchant ships, hitting one on the stern. 803 bombed nine seaplanes in Trondheim harbour, got a direct hit on one and near misses on several others. They also bombed a large supply ship in the outer basin, which replied with anti-aircraft fire. Other Skuas searched the fjords. There were no warships but two large oilers were set on fire.

Ark Royal lost a Swordfish from 820 and three from 810 (and the crew of one of 810, all the others being picked up). *Glorious* lost four Skuas. One of them, from a Section led by Lucy, was flown by Lieutenant A.B. Fraser-Harris who saw a stream of tracer bullets pass close ahead and felt several hit the fuselage while attacking the seaplanes in the harbour. His oil pressure gauge dropped to zero and he had just reported it to Lucy when his engine cut out. He decided to land in a small fjord, as near as he could to a pier.

The Skua touched down steadily but, being badly holed, began to sink at once. Fraser-Harris and his air gunner, leading Airman G. Russell, had to swim. They were met by hostile Norwegians who had killed two German aviators the day before and now intended to do the same for Fraser-Harris and Russell. But, once identities had been established, Fraser-Harris and Russell were provided with warm Norwegian clothing and, with a Norwegian guide who spoke English, began a 24-hour 70-mile trek by sleigh, by skis (somewhat unskilfully), boat and, finally, by taxi, to British headquarters in Namsos. Fraser-Harris reported intelligence he had gained en route to Carton de Wiart's staff. He also learned from a Norwegian officer that *Glorious'* raid on the seaplanes had destroyed six and the Swordfish raid on Vaernes had set a petrol dump on fire and wrecked five planes. Finally, on the 27th, Fraser-Harris and Russell went on board *Calcutta*, lying at Namsos.

The crews of *Glorious'* other three Skuas were eventually recovered, but it had been an expensive day. One cause was the distance the carriers had to lie off shore for their own protection. After a strike aircraft were faced with a flight of nearly a hundred miles to safety. In one of *Glorious'* Skuas of the second range Lieutenant G.R. Callingham attacked ships in Trondheim harbour through heavy AA fire, flew out to sea, could not find the ship, flew back and then, with twenty gallons of fuel, succeeded in putting his Skua down on a sandy spit of land jutting out into a fjord near Namsos. French troops helped him drag the Skua up above the high-water line and there he left it. There, presumably, the wreck remains. Callingham and his air gunner also went on board *Calcutta*.

Some of the more perceptive ship's officers were very conscious of what Commander William Jameson of *Ark Royal* called 'the contrast between the risks run by the aircrews and by the remainder of the ship's company... It is strange, and very humbling, for a ship's officer to sit at table with a pilot or an observer who, between breakfast and dinner, has flown to the distant shore and been in action over enemy-occupied territory.'

At 7.30pm on the 25th Wells signalled Forbes to report the completion of Operation D.X. and that the carriers were returning to base because the destroyer screen was short of fuel. However, Forbes replied that D.X. was to go on and a fresh destroyer screen would be provided. At 7.25am on the 26th the new screen of *Grenade, Beagle, Fortune, Volunteer, Encounter* and *Escort* joined and the old screen detached to Sullom Voe to fuel.

By this time there were not enough Skuas left in the task force to maintain continuous fighter patrols over both Namsos and Aandalsnes and as there had been several urgent calls from the Aandalsnes area it was decided to fly the patrols there. The carriers reached a flying-off position 120 miles from Aandalsnes at 10am. *Ark Royal* and *Glorious* were ordered to fly off Skua patrols to Aandalsnes at two-hourly intervals. *Glorious* flew off the second of these patrols, three Skuas of 803, at noon. They engaged three Junkers Ju.88s at 11,500 feet over Aalesund. The Skuas were nowhere near fast enough to catch Ju.88s and one Skua was lost. The pilot, Lieutenant C.H. Filmer, was later recovered, but the air gunner, Petty Officer Airman K.G. Baldwin, was killed by an enemy bullet during the action. He was *Glorious'* first aircrew to become a casualty. The two remaining Skuas of this patrol shot down a Heinkel 111 off Aandalsnes while it was bombing a frigate, but both Skuas landed on with bullet damage.

Fighter patrols went on for the rest of the day (one of them being specially flown after two urgent cries for help from the sloop *Flamingo*) and all aircraft had been recovered by 9.10pm. The carriers steered north-west to clear the coast-line and to prepare for the following day.

That afternoon (26th) Admiral Forbes had signalled that it was intended to prepare three aerodromes for RAF fighter squadrons ashore in the Aandalsnes area and proposed that *Ark Royal* maintain continuous fighter patrols over Aandalsnes after *Glorious* had left to refuel. This was taking a very optimistic view of what one carrier could do on her own. Wells replied that it was impracticable for one carrier to maintain continuous fighter patrols, her own anti-submarine patrols and her own CAP overhead. Forbes then said that *Ark* must give the maximum protection she could and carry out further bombing raids on Trondheim.

In the early hours of the 27th *Grenade* had an asdic contact, confirmed as a submarine, and she and *Volunteer* carried out a depth-charge attack with no visible result. *Beagle* also had a contact later in the forenoon. Her depth-charges caused a large disturbance in the water but no U-boat appeared (nor was one sunk).

The first fighters of the day were away at 8.20am but the first real excitement of the day in the air was at 9.30 when four of *Glorious'* Sea Gladiators went out to chase an intruding Heinkel 111K low on the water about fifteen miles from the carriers. The fighters closed to within 200 yards and fired at it, but it was going at full throttle and they were not able to clinch the attack. Sub-Lieutenant R.R. Lamb of 804 reported that the Heinkel actually touched the water three times during the pursuit.

At 10.35 the last four remaining serviceable Skuas in *Glorious* were flown off for a patrol over Aandalsnes. They forced a Heinkel 111 down until it crashed into a hillside and on returning landed on *Ark Royal* because *Glorious* was operating her Sea Gladiators at the time. In the event, they stayed in *Ark Royal*. The original destroyer screen returned from fuelling just after 5pm and the last fighters were recovered by 7.30. *Glorious* left at 9pm on the 27th to refuel and embark replacement fighters at Scapa, escorted on passage by *Hasty*, *Fury*, *Grenade*, *Escort*, *Encounter*, *Volunteer* and *Beagle*, leaving *Hyperion*, *Hereward*, *Fearless* and *Juno* with the carrier squadron.

After *Glorious* had left, *Ark Royal* had another hectic day of fighter patrols and bombing strikes on Vaernes and Trondheim on the 28th, after which Wells decided his aircrews had had enough for the time being. He signalled Forbes that 'The fighter personnel who had been in action for five successive days were showing definite signs of strain', and suggested that *Ark Royal* should withdraw to the north-west for forty-eight hours before continuing operations. This was approved.

Meanwhile, on the 28th, *Glorious* arrived again in Scapa Flow where the bleak landscape must have seemed to *Glorious'* ship's company, so recently in the sun and blue skies of the Mediterranean, like a vision from Mars. Most of them had spent more than two years in the ship in a warm climate and their blood was running thin for service in the Arctic, especially after the coldest winter for over a century. Of the officers, Paul Slessor had been on board nearly three years and was almost the only wardroom survivor of the old commission, but he probably spoke for everybody on board when he wrote home on arriving at Scapa on the 28th, 'I am very well but rather cold. We are on very active and strenuous operations, and I don't expect much shore-going for some little time yet... Toby Watkins [Lieutenant-Commander R.D. Watkins, another observer] has been relieved, which may indicate that I shall be relieved at three years — which would mean June or July... Toby's going was quite out of the blue, and I really felt that he was the last link with the old times. I have no real intimates left. I have had a good deal to do lately with a certain red-faced Captain of mine [Wells], and he has been *most* awfully good to me. I can't tell you the full story here but will do so one day. My sole shore-going since leaving Alex has been two hours in a very dour, grey place [probably Greenock] a charming first arrival for an exile like me. I am longing to hear from you. God knows when I shall.'

Glorious was to have sailed from Scapa on 29 April, landed on replacement fighters from Hatston, and then, in company with *Valiant*, rejoined *Ark Royal*. But while *Valiant* sailed as planned, bad weather curtailed flying and when *Glorious* eventually did sail on the 30th she still had not embarked all the replacement fighters. She had on board eighteen Sea Gladiators of 802 and 804, twelve Swordfish of 823, who flew on board on 30th, three Skuas, and one Roc — a fabulous bird, a curious hybrid Skua with a four-Browning-gun turret on top and no forward-firing guns. A fighter with no forward-firing guns was in itself an unsound tactical concept and the turret further reduced the

Skua's low speed to below 200 mph for the Roc, and the ceiling was likewise reduced to 15,000 feet.

By the time *Glorious* sailed it had been decided to evacuate Aandalsnes and Namsos after a short, bitter and utterly futile land campaign, and arrangements were already in hand. The evacuations were carried out by some familiar names, many of whom had carried out the initial landings. Some 5,500 troops were lifted from Aandalsnes and Molde by Admiral Edward-Collins, with *Galatea*, *Arethusa*, *Sheffield*, *Southampton*, and the destroyers *Somali*, *Mashona*, *Sikh*, *Wanderer*, *Walker* and *Tartar*, and the transports *Ulster Monarch* and *Ulster Prince*, on the night of 30 April/1 May, and by Admiral Layton, with *Manchester* and *Birmingham*, the destroyers *Inglefield*, *Delight*, *Diana*, *Somali* and *Mashona* (for the second night), the AA cruiser *Calcutta* and the sloop *Auckland* on the night of 1/2 May.

Edward-Collins' ships were bombed early on the morning of 1 May as they passed through the outer fjords; so too were some of Layton's ships later that afternoon when Aandalsnes suffered the usual attacks. But generally the bombing was comparatively light. It was different at Namsos, where some 6,000 troops, British and Norwegian, were lifted off in the night of 2/3 May by Admiral John Cunningham with *Devonshire* and *York*, the French Cruiser *Montcalm*, destroyers *Afridi*, *Nubian*, *Hasty*, *Imperial* and the French *Bison*, the transports *El d'Jezair*, *El Kantara* and *El Mansour*, the AA cruiser *Carlisle* and additional destroyers *Kelly*, *Grenade*, *Griffin* and *Maori*. Not a man was lost until aircraft bombed and disabled *Bison*, out to sea, on the forenoon of the 3rd. Her survivors were taken off by *Afridi*, *Imperial* and *Grenade*, whose Captain, Commander R.C. Boyle, put his ship alongside *Bison*. *Bison's* wrecked hull had to be sunk, but in the afternoon *Afridi* was herself hit by two bombs and eventually capsized, losing about one hundred killed, including some of *Bison*'s people and some men of the York and Lancaster Regiment. These were the only army casualties incurred during the evacuation from Namsos. Carton de Wiart's much-quoted tribute to the Navy deserves quoting again: 'In the course of that last endless day I got a message from the Navy to say that they would evacuate the whole of my force that night. I thought it was impossible, but learned a few hours later that the Navy do not know the word... It was a tremendous undertaking to embark that whole force in a night of three short hours, but the Navy did it and earned my undying gratitude.'

The heaviest brunt of the air attack fell on the smallest ships, the antisubmarine trawlers, who lost eleven out of twenty-nine ships, sunk or driven ashore. 'Despite these arduous and hazardous conditions,' wrote Admiral Forbes, 'the morale and gallantry of officers and men remained magnificent.' One example was the trawler *Arab*, whose crew spent a most hectic five days at Namsos fighting fires and the Luftwaffe alike, finally shooting down a Heinkel as *Arab* went down the fjord for the last time. *Arab*'s Captain, Lieutenant R.B. Stannard RNR, was awarded the Victoria Cross, the third naval VC of the Norwegian campaign.

Glorious, escorted by *Acheron*, *Antelope* and *Beagle*, rejoined the task force just after 10am on 1 May. Her reappearance could not have been more welcome or timely. Her destroyers joined the screen and her Sea Gladiators took over the fighter defence of the squadron. The ships evacuating Aandalsnes and Molde were at sea and under threat of air attack, and the task force itself had been shadowed by a Heinkel 115 seaplane since 7am that morning. Two or three of these aircraft continued to shadow from the horizon throughout that day.

Skuas of 801 from *Ark Royal* had flown patrols over Aandalsnes, to cover the evacuation convoys or in response to calls for help, from 4am. One section, on their way back, chased a Ju.88 which has just bombed *Ark Royal* but failed to catch it. But it was already clear that a day of intense air activity lay ahead. At 7.51 a Heinkel 111 or a Junkers Ju.88 (nobody was sure) approached *Ark Royal* unseen out of the sun and dropped one or perhaps two small bombs just astern. The aircraft made off, pursued by somewhat ineffective AA fire from *Ark Royal*. Only four minutes later a Ju.88 dive-bombed *Ark Royal* and dropped a single large bomb which exploded fifty yards astern. As Jameson said, 'An officer standing at an open scuttle admiring the sparkling sea was so surprised that he almost swallowed his after-breakfast cigarette.'

The early morning patrols had reported Aandalsnes quiet and, as RAF Bristol Blenheim patrols had been organized for the area from 6am, the carriers began to work to the northward to give fighter support to Namsos, where the evacuation was due to begin that evening (though it actually took place the following evening because Carton de Wiart signalled that he could not disengage his troops in time). But progress to the north was very slow because the wind was light and southerly and the carriers had to steam at high speed to the south to fly on and off aircraft. Two Swordfish flew anti-submarine patrols and *Glorious*' CAPs were double-banked; *Glorious* maintained a Sea Gladiator patrol of six aircraft constantly in the air, with another three standing by on deck, from 11am until 9.30pm that night.

Main attacks developed in the afternoon. *Valiant*'s radar gave warning of enemy aircraft but the carrier squadron was still taken by surprise. The ships were steaming in line ahead, in the order *Ark Royal*, *Valiant*, *Glorious* and *Berwick*, with seven destroyers in the screen. They were executing a standard zigzag pattern but were actually steering on their M.L.A. (Mean Line of Advance) with the sun dead astern of them when, at 3.21pm, the first salvo of bombs dropped only a hundred yards to starboard of *Glorious*, followed a few minutes later by a second salvo just to starboard of *Valiant*. Until then nobody had been aware of four heavy German bombers approaching down sun from astern at 17,000 feet.

This was the first time *Glorious* had been fired on since November, 1917, and, when her 4.7" HA/LA guns replied, the first time they had ever fired in anger. Midshipman (A) Roy Hinton, of 823, was standing on the quarterdeck: 'This was the first action that any of us had been involved in. It was a tremendous spectacle. The Gladiators were up and everybody was opening up on the enemy bombers. We were standing watching when they decided to open up with *Glorious'* 4.7". There was one on either side of the quarterdeck. We weren't given any warning that the guns were going to fire. One moment we were standing there watching the aircraft having a dogfight up topsides and the next a great flash of flame, an *enormous* great noise! We all thought, God, a bomb on the ship, and we all went flat on the deck!'

Marine Ronald Healiss, the fuse-setter on the Royal Marine-manned P.7 gun, the aftermost but one 4.7" on the port side, took a professional pride in the sound of his gun: 'Tray back. Breech-block back. Ready for firing — automatic firing now we're on remote control.

'The majesty — the sheer bloody majesty — of that noise!

'It cracks your eardrums and the smoke swirls around the gun platform. The recoil comes out. As it goes past the breech-work, a long arm comes out, swings open the block and takes out the red-hot relic.

"*Fuse* 040... 04 *and a half*..."

'Something's moving in on us pretty darned quick, but now we've begun firing a few rounds we feel better. It's that waiting which hurts.

'You seldom see anything as pretty as gunfire, especially when it's a clear morning and you can watch the whole length of a shell's flight until it bursts in a plume of purple smoke. In with the rammer. Up the spout. Then we stand tense as the layer swings his handles like a crazy mangle, and black pointer follows red in a wild and waving pattern.

'There's a thirty-knot wind which the speed of *Glorious'* passage is flooding back down the flight deck and curling over to our gun position three decks below on the port side; and this wind — now seeming like a gale when the guns are bellowing — kills our words.

"*Enemy in sight*," rattles the metal voice of the Transmitting Station [T.S.] over the earphones and all eyes start looking for the target. No, not all. Trainer is staring at his pointers. If that bloody aircraft comes right over the ship, we'll have to bring our fuses down 050... 030... 020...

"*Local fire*..."

'The *Glorious* moment we've been waiting for. On the wheel that the layer turns is the trigger for firing, when T.S. have switched us over from remote control. Squeeze that trigger. Squeeze that Hun aircraft out of the sky. Squeeze it hard, boy. And again P.7 gives a billowing violence of sound. As the roar begins to fade, the echo is taken up with the ugly rattle of the multiple pom-poms.

'Then silence, broken only by spews of spray on the gently heaving deck. We wait — that fretful waiting. Well, at least we had a crack at it.'

Unfortunately the 'cracks' of the squadrons' combined gunfire were not effective. 'At 1520 we observed HA fire over the fleet,' wrote Lieutenant R.M. Smeeton, of Blue Section 804, 'and we climbed to 12,000 feet, the height of the bursts, but did not sight enemy aircraft. The Section remained at 12,000 feet and at 1540 HA fire was again observed. A Heinkel 111K was sighted well above this fire, and the Section climbed to intercept. The enemy aircraft had released its bombs and was retiring on a course 120, at 16,000 feet. BLUE 2 and 3, who were stepped up on BLUE 1, managed to get in some short bursts from an almost stalled position under the enemy aircraft. Section then chased on a course 120, but were unable to close, due to the enemy's superior speed, and the chase was broken off.'

Two more exactly similar bombing attacks were made, presumably by bombers which had failed to drop their bombs on the first run, at 3.44 and 4.05pm. The bombs fell 'unpleasantly close' ahead of *Ark Royal*, so that she steamed through the spray of the explosions, and about 800 yards on her port beam. Once more Smeeton's Section tried to intercept: 'At 1600 I observed a Heinkel 111K approaching the fleet from about 030, some 2,000-3,000 feet above the Section. I altered course to intercept. The enemy released his bombs at 17,000 feet; I was then about 800 yards astern and saw the bombs released. BLUE 2, again being stepped up, managed to get in some bursts from about 450 yards. It was immediately after this that the enemy released his bombs and, opening out his engines, went into a shallow dive; his speed was then too great for the Gladiators to attempt a chase.'

There was a lull for two hours until just after 6pm when *Valiant*'s radar again detected a large formation of enemy aircraft, range thirty-forty miles, bearing 220 (indicating that the enemy had flown out to seaward of the squadron to attack with sun behind them). With such advance warning, the ships were aware and at their highest state of readiness when at 6.23 three Junkers Ju.87 Stukas broke formation at about 8,000 feet on the squadron's port bow and dived, one of them on *Ark Royal*, one on *Glorious* and the third on *Valiant*, in an obviously well rehearsed and practised tactic.

The Stukas were intercepted by Yellow Section of 804. 'At 1823 six enemy Junkers 87K dive bombers were sighted three miles ahead, on an opposite course, in open "V" formation,' reported Lieutenant-Commander J.C. Cockburn, Yellow Leader and C.O. of 804. 'The order to open fire was given and the Section half-rolled individually on to the tails of the enemy aircraft, each pilot attacking one enemy. Fire was maintained in short bursts, as the enemy twisted and turned, until the final bombing dive was commenced. The attack was broken off at this point as I imagined, quite erroneously, that the pom-pom fire would take effect below this.'

Lieutenant Jack Marmont of Blue Section 802 pursued the Stuka which had chosen *Ark Royal* and shot it down. Its crew were picked up by *Encounter*. In all twelve Ju.87s took part, supported by five Heinkel 111Ks making a synchronized attack from high level. The ships put up a very heavy volume of gunfire and in the 'ensuing melee' the Gladiators were lucky not to be hit and seriously damaged or even shot down; some were certainly peppered. At the height of the action the situation was 'noisy and confused', wrote Jameson, 'with bombs falling all round the ships and every anti-aircraft gun blazing away. Columns of dirty water from exploding bombs shot into the air to twice masthead height and the sky was full of puffs of shell-smoke. Skuas from *Ark Royal* and Gladiators from *Glorious* dived and twisted among the enemy aircraft.'

On breaking away after their dives, some of the Stukas attacked destroyers in the screen. Two or three attacked *Fury* with machine guns and small bombs. One of the Swordfish on anti-submarine patrol was also attacked with front and rear guns by a Stuka and the surprised pilot, Captain N. Skene, Royal Marines, had to extricate himself with a steep climbing turn, but suffered two hits.

At least one of the squadron's losses was self-inflicted. At 6.05 Lucy had led four Skuas of 803 to patrol over *Devonshire* (in the Namsos evacuating force) who had reported enemy aircraft. There was fog in the area and the visibility was patchy. At one point two Skuas found themselves directly over the ships they had come to protect, and were subjected to heavy AA fire, although they had fired the proper recognition signal and flashed the reply letters over an Aldis lamp. The ships were understandably in a highly sensitive state approaching an enemy coastline. They kept up an intense fire and eventually shot down one of the Skuas, piloted by Sub-Lieutenant G.W. Brokensha. He and his crew, Petty Officer Andrews, were picked up by *Nubian*. Problems of firing at friendly aircraft were to plague all carriers throughout the war; guns crews tended to open fire first and consult their aircraft identification manuals later.

By 7pm the last Stuka had gone and the last CAPs were preparing to land on. It had been a long day. For one Marine, Charles Hodgson, one abiding memory of *Glorious* off Norway was 'the sight of a Royal Marines ammunition supply party, recently emerged from the ship's magazine, looking up at the stars and vowing never to take for granted even the most basic ingredients of life'.

No ship had actually been hit, though several had been near-missed. But if the Luftwaffe kept up this rate of attack, and it seemed they would, Admiral Wells did not consider the risk to the ships was worth the amount of air support they could give to the troops ashore. He signalled Forbes that evening that 'he did not consider he was able any longer to maintain a position from which aircraft could give support to our forces and stated he was withdrawing to the north-west'. This signal actually crossed one from Forbes ordering the carrier squadron to move northwards to provide fighter protection for Namsos and to continue bombing attacks on Trondheim. Wells replied at 10.30pm that night, reporting the continuous shadowing and bombing the carrier squadron had experienced during the day and saying that the operations the C-in-C had just ordered 'were no longer practicable by a carrier force in this area'. In other words, the Luftwaffe had won.

There were other lessons to be learned. Brokensha's was the only aircraft actually to be shot down by its own side, but there could so easily have been more. 'High Angle fire from *Glorious* and *Valiant*,' reported Cockburn of 804, 'was concentrated chiefly on our own Gladiators. Fortunately it was grossly inaccurate.' Jack Marmont reported that his Section 'was subjected to heavy pom-pom fire which fortunately had no effect,' (although, on landing, one of his Section was found to have been hit by a fragment 'presumably from an H.A. gun'). Lieutenant R.H.P. Carver, of 804's Red Section, said they were 'fired at continuously by all ships' pom-poms and 4" from H.M.S. *Berwick*'.

Neither carrier was fitted with radar, but the squadron did have a radar-equipped ship in company for much of the time: the cruiser *Curlew*, with her Type 79Z, able to detect aircraft at ninety miles and 20,000 feet, until 11.30am on 28 April when she was relieved by *Sheffield*, with her older Type 79 (fifty miles at 10,000 feet). *Sheffield* left at 9pm on the 29th to take part in the evacuation from Aandalsnes, but *Valiant* arrived at 11am on the 30th equipped with the improved Type 279 (100 miles, 30,000 feet).

The radar guard-ship passed ranges, bearings and estimated heights of incoming aircraft to the carriers who informed the CAPs by R/T. This was a primitive form of fighter direction, although it was to be improved and refined, as the war progressed and carriers were fitted with their own radar, into the highly-skilled techniques, which almost reached the status of an art form, practised by the fighter direction teams in the carriers of the British Pacific Fleet in 1945.

But off Norway in May, 1940, the system was still in its infancy and the multiplicity of radar echoes led to confusion on who was friend and who was foe. 'Various reports of aircraft were passed by R/T, the height given in each case being not more than 5,000 feet,' reported Smeeton of 804. 'It became clear to me that we were the aircraft in question on several occasions. Enemy reports were passed to us and in several cases it was apparent that we were the cause of the reports.' D'Oyly-Hughes himself commented, 'There was such a constant stream of bearings and distances from *Valiant*, many of which looked as though they were our own fighters, that it was extremely difficult to decide what pieces of information to give our Gladiators and what to give to my own lookouts and Gun Control Officers.'

The aircrews also had useful comments to make about the close formation of the carrier squadron, which made it a good target for 'stick bombing', the zigzag pattern, which was too short to disturb a bomb-aimer's aim, and the excellent aiming marks the ships made, up to heights of 20,000 feet when they were silhouetted against the western sky at sunset.

But the most important lesson to be learned off Norway was that the Fleet Air Arm's Skuas, Sea Gladiators, Rocs and Swordfish were simply out-performed by the Luftwaffe's Messerschmitts, Junkers, Heinkels and Dorniers. Time after time the CAPs would climb to engage a target, only to see it give 'a startled puff of brown smoke' from its engines and accelerate away to safety. Throughout that long day of 1 May only one enemy aircraft was officially noted as destroyed: the Ju.87 shot down by *Glorious'* Sea Gladiators.

Officially *Ark Royal's* aircraft were credited with destroying nine Heinkel He.111s, three Junkers Ju.88s, and one Heinkel He.115 floatplane, and badly damaging one 'bomber/transport', eight He.111s, six He.115s and two Ju.88s. *Glorious* was credited with destroying four He.111s, one He.115, one Ju.88 and one Ju.87, and badly damaging another three He.115s. Ships' gunfire was credited with one Heinkel He.111 shot down, off Trondheim on 28 April. This was a total of twenty-one enemy aircraft shot down or destroyed on ground and twenty badly damaged.

Against that, the carriers had lost (apart from 'own goals') four Swordfish from *Ark Royal* force-landed in the sea, and three of her Skuas force-landed and one shot down. From *Glorious* five Skuas force-landed in Norway and two were unserviceable. The task force therefore lost nine Skuas, and another two unserviceable, and four Swordfish. This seemed a reasonable rate of exchange, but in fact the figures are probably too optimistic. Fleet Air Arm aircraft were inferior in every department — speed, range, endurance and fire-power.

Evidently gritting his teeth while he penned his report in *Glorious*, Cockburn recorded that his squadron were heavily handicapped operationally because they had to fly at dangerously low revolutions to make their petrol last out their patrols. Even then, the times on patrol were often half an hour longer than the 'safe' endurance recommended in Gloster's aircraft manuals and test-pilots' reports. In Cockburn's view, combat had shown (1) that the Gladiator had 'insufficient performance to chase and hold the aircraft employed by the enemy'; (2) 'the time between sighting the enemy by our own pilots and the time the enemy drops his bomb is very short; therefore a high concentration of gunfire is required and Fleet Air Arm fighters should have at least eight front guns'; (3)'to save the fleet turning into wind frequently the Fleet Air Arm fighter should have a reasonable endurance, e.g. five hours'.

Waxing caustic, Cockburn concluded: '(1) and (2) above can be complied with by giving us Spitfires; (1), (2) and (3) can be complied with by giving us practically any U.S. Navy fighter'.

The carrier squadron was ordered to withdraw by the C-in-C late in the evening of 1 May. On Friday, 3 May, five Rocs from *Ark Royal* and one Roc from *Glorious* were flown off to Donibristle and the six remaining Skuas in *Glorious* were flown off to *Ark Royal*. *Glorious* and *Ark Royal* arrived at Scapa later on the 3rd. *Glorious* sailed again at 4.30pm and arrived at Greenock the following day, 4 May. That day Slessor wrote to Hope again: 'J.B. [Heath] is showing signs of wear and Parkin and I have rather a job with him — to make him use himself properly. Parkin is a treasure. The man [D'Oyly-Hughes], though exceedingly trying, has on the whole been quite pleasant to me lately. I rather think he has taken to heart what a certain red-headed Captain wrote about me, and has come to the conclusion, at last, that there may be something in it. He is perfectly foul to the chum [J.B. Heath] and to others, but we battle through somehow.'

Now that the pressure of operations had been lifted, *Glorious'* perennial domestic problems came to the fore again.

CHAPTER 8: D'OYLY-HUGHES AND J. B. HEATH — THE GREAT FEUD

IN THE LATTER days of *Glorious* there were serious doubts on board over the mental stability of D'Oyly-Hughes. The 'revolvers on the bridge' incident at the outbreak of war had been followed by others: Paul Slessor was once ordered by the Captain to flog a young observer for some alleged failure of duty. Among papers preserved by Commander J. B. Heath, a marginal note has the authentic ring of D'Oyly-Hughes: 'If you are content to run your Department in such a smug and complacent way,' runs the quote, 'it may be all right for you but I intend to teach that pilot a lesson and make him an example.' The incident which provoked the remark is not recorded, but it sounds like D'Oyly-Hughes. Eventually, according to Heath, some wardroom officers went so far as to say to the ship's P.M.O., Surgeon Commander Howard Douglas, 'Look here, we think your attention is needed here'. Douglas refused, perhaps sensibly, to take any action and asked to be relieved from the ship. Very probably D'Oyly-Hughes was not schizophrenic in any clinical or diagnostic sense, but there is no doubt he was one man on board and quite another ashore.

D'Oyly-Hughes had always had the respect and affection of the ship's company. 'Up forrard,' said Dick Leggott, 'the men thought the world of him. He had that little bit of mystique, his DSO from the First World War. The men liked that. Give him a *battleship* and I couldn't think of anybody not wishing to sail with him.' D'Oyly-Hughes had the right attitudes in every way towards the lower deck. He knew when to stand on ceremony and when to be informal. He was understanding and painstaking over the sailors' welfare and matrimonial problems. At the defaulters' table, he was fair, punctilious and just.

But towards the end D'Oyly-Hughes fell out even with the sailors. The details are obscure now, but it seems it was a question of leave, and particularly leave to those whose families lived locally, when the ship arrived in the Clyde. Many of the ships' company, especially the Chiefs and petty officers, had their families up to see them while the ship was in harbour. Mrs Grinter, wife of Chief Mechanician Ernest Grinter, travelled up from Plymouth with her small son Roy, who recalls the visit: 'On arrival we learnt there had been a certain amount of trouble on board amongst the crew, generated by the Captain refusing to grant leave to the lower deck or to allow their families in the area. It culminated in a member of the crew dropping pamphlets round the ship endorsed "No leave — no work". A change of mind obviously took place but not before twenty-six crew members were disciplined and sentenced to cells/detention.'

Many officers' wives travelled up to Scotland, among them Mrs Steel, the wife of Instructor Lieutenant Guy Steel, the ship's meteorological officer. They had been married in Malta in November, 1938, and Mollie Steel was actually pregnant when she last saw her husband. Guy Steel had been on board since the commission began in January, 1938, and was due for relief. But, as a considerable athlete, a Navy rugger and cricket player, he was an invaluable asset to the ship's teams and was, besides, an experienced met. officer, so D'Oyly-Hughes was understandably reluctant to let him go. Mollie Steel found a 'tense uncomfortable atmosphere' on board. Her husband 'was a very unhappy man' and 'in a very low state'. D'Oyly-Hughes, she said, 'treated everybody as underlings'.

Yet, ironically, in spite of the furore over leave, each watch got four days while the ship was at Greenock and when D'Oyly-Hughes himself went down to his home in London his main preoccupations were the ship and the welfare of her sailors. He was also preoccupied by speed and he took with him an official letter to the Admiralty suggesting that, to improve the ship's speed, the guns and ammunition should be landed. The episode is remembered contemptuously by Heath: 'He was going to allow us to have some petrol. So we were lucky. We were going to have some oil fuel. That was lucky, too. He solemnly wrote this letter out, propounded this theory, and he shot off to London from the Clyde with this. Nobody thought it peculiar. He wanted the world to be made up of ships which went like a fart in a gale of wind, and forget the armament. He used to get these extraordinary brainstorms.'

But there was no brainstorm about D'Oyly-Hughes' concern for his sailors. He was met off the overnight train at Euston by his elder daughter Bridget who noted that he had with him all his dress uniforms in trunks and his canary and his chihuahua dog; D'Oyly-Hughes, like everybody else, was landing inessentials in wartime. Bridget found him as usual, her father 'going out of his way to recognize that I was no longer a schoolgirl'. Admiral Drax came to lunch at their house in Hesper Mews, off the Gloucester Road (which D'Oyly-Hughes, who had some talent as an amateur architect, had improved and enlarged). Bridget overheard her father telling Drax, with some heat, that his ship 'was in no state to do any more'. He had told his ship's company they would have some proper leave the next time they arrived in harbour and a chance to do some urgent work on the main machinery. 'I told them, and now I find I'm having to break my word to them.

I'll risk my bloody neck once more, but I'm not going to risk this ship once more.'

Bridget had just passed her seventeenth birthday and was learning to drive. But when she drove her father to the Admiralty, he made her take her 'L' plates off the car because he was going to call on Churchill. No doubt D'Oyly-Hughes made his points about his ship to Churchill with his customary force, but Churchill had weightier matters on his mind. On the Friday of that week, 10 May, he became Prime Minister. D'Oyly-Hughes also met Commander Fancourt, whose back-seat passenger he had often been in flights from *Courageous* in 1931. Fancourt found D'Oyly-Hughes the same confident, ebullient self. 'He took me to lunch at his club. He said, "Look here, I want you to come to the *Glorious*." I said, "I can't do that. I've got this job in London [Deputy Director of Personnel]. I should like to, very much. If only I could get rid of this bloody desk." He said, "Oh we'll see what we can do about that." He was that sort of chap. Of course if I had gone to the *Glorious*, I might not have been here now. I rather liked D'Oyly-Hughes and he liked me. There's an affinity between submariners and flying chaps.'

Bridget saw her father off at Euston. D'Oyly-Hughes had an Austin car, which was to be landed at Greenock, and he promised it to Bridget if she passed her driving test. She never saw the car, or her father, again.

Glorious was due to sail that weekend for Norway with six Sea Gladiators of 802 and six Swordfish of 823 for her own protection. Her main task was to transport a squadron of Hawker Hurricanes and fly them off to a landing ground prepared in Norway for the air defence of the expeditionary force ashore.

Glorious' new RAF guests were 46 Squadron, who had been commanded since October, 1939 by Squadron-Leader Bing Cross. 46's pilots were highly experienced (*'very* professional' Cross called them) and had been flying Hurricanes since March, 1939; they all had between 300 and 600 flying hours on the type. Based at Digby in Lincolnshire, 46 had been flying fighter patrols over the East Coast convoys throughout the bitter winter and had fought one of the earliest aerial engagements of the war, when they had shot down several Heinkel He.115s attacking a convoy. They had been expecting to go to France to operate alongside 73 Squadron near Rheims. Cross and Flight-Lieutenant 'Jamie' Jameson had in fact been across to France to survey possible landing fields.

Then, suddenly, 46 were issued with arctic equipment and, on 9 May, in a state of high excitement and anticipation, flew to Abbotsinch, near Glasgow. Next day they taxied through fields to Messrs Blackburn's wharf on the Clyde, where the Hurricanes were to be loaded on to barges for the twenty-mile journey down river to *Glorious.* Eight Hurricanes were loaded that day, the other ten on 11 May. It was a tricky operation, with the risk of the Hurricanes' wing-tips striking the overhang of the ship's side as they were hoisted. 'The sight of our beloved Hurricanes being hauled up on the end of a rope,' wrote Jameson, 'swinging around, wings and tails nearly hitting the side of the ship, was sickening'. (Cross insisted that each pilot accompany his aircraft in case of damage by slings. But, in spite of this precaution, it was found, when the ship sailed, that the wing mainplane locking bolts for four or five Hurricanes had been taken ashore in error by the slinging party. Those Hurricanes were unflyable. 'When the ship's engineers heard about this, they simply said, "Not to worry, we will make some;

send a sample down",' wrote Jameson. 'We did this and in no time at all our Hurricanes were serviceable again.')

46 Squadron's ground crews and advance parties embarked in *Batory* at Glasgow on 13 May. Cross and his seventeen pilots, who included five sergeant pilots, sailed in *Glorious* on the 12th. The ship returned next day and finally sailed on the 14th. *Furious* had also sailed with a refurbished 263 Squadron, still under Squadron Leader 'Baldy' Donaldson (now with a DSO) but with new Gladiators, also bound for Norway.

Glorious was suffering from an epidemic of leave-breaking and desertion and sailed minus some dozens of absentees. 'We have had lots of chaps failing to return from their leave,' Master at Arms Woodcock wrote on 9 May. 'Just don't try, put on the wrong train, got lost. Can you believe such stories of men? Wonder what the Commander thinks in his head at times at the excuses. Senior rates, too.' The destroyer *Diana* stayed behind in the Clyde to pick up as many of *Glorious'* leave-breakers as turned up. She caught up with the carrier out to sea and transferred them by whaler. *Glorious* and *Furious*, escorted by *Diana*, *Veteran*, and *Viscount*, sailed for Norway, intending to fly off the Hurricanes to Skaanland and the Gladiators to Bardufoss.

Cross knew very little about the Navy or naval officers 'except those I played rugger against at Twickenham'. 'My immediate boss was J. B. Heath, who welcomed me on board and said come and meet the Captain. D'Oyly-Hughes was a very formidable-looking man. We got no welcome from him. He looked at me, and nodded. He never asked to meet the other pilots. So I thought, well, this is the way they went on in the Navy.'

Other passengers in the ship to receive a cool welcome were 701 Squadron, newly formed on 8 May with six Walrus amphibians under Lieutenant H.H. Bracken. D'Oyly-Hughes pronounced Walrus as unsuitable to operate from his ship, as Bracken later said, 'all because of some relatively minor shortcomings'. (Thus, a month later, when Bracken was given the choice of *Ark Royal* or *Glorious*, to take passage home from Norway, nothing would have induced him to choose *Glorious*. He thereby saved his own and his squadrons' lives and aircraft.)

The six Swordfish of 823 remaining on shore were fitted with long-range fuel tanks and flown up to Hatston, from where they carried out minelaying sorties off the Norwegian coast. The first of these, on the night of 17/18 May, was in the narrow Inner Lead channel south of Haugesund, between Bergen and Stavanger. Another of *Glorious'* pilots, Sub-Lieutenant (A) Harry Mourilyan, was lost on this operation. 'The memory of that is still with me,' said Roy Hinton. 'The aircraft were lined up on the airfield. We were going off that night. We were checking our aircraft to see everything was all right. I still remember walking past Mourilyan and I said, "How are you doing?" He said, "I'll never get back; this wretched aircraft, the engine is losing oil." I said, "For God's sake tell them and don't go!" He said, "No, I can't do that, I must go." We were flying in Vic formation coming back. Mourilyan was on our port side. All we saw was a ball of flame and the whole of the aircraft began to sink into the sea. I didn't actually see it go in. When we got back I tried to pinpoint the position. He went straight in, never seen or heard of again. He was the first of my close friends to be lost in the war.' (Mourilyan's air gunner, Naval Airman Roy Parkinson, was also lost.)

While *Glorious* and *Furious* steamed north, every news bulletin brought graver news from the south. On 10 May Germany invaded the Low Countries, using infantry, armour, the Luftwaffe and paratroopers. On the 14th the Luftwaffe bombed Rotterdam, and the same day Holland capitulated. By the 15th German armour had broken through between Namur and Sedan and by the 18th they had reached St Quentin. Antwerp fell on the same day and on the 20th panzers reached the English Channel at Abbeville. Against this darkening international background, the campaign in Norway was beginning to seem more and more remote and less and less important to the Allied cause.

But to the ship's companies of the carriers the events in France seemed no more significant than the muttering of distant guns. *Glorious* and *Furious* met *Ark Royal* off Norway on 18 May, the first time three aircraft carriers had operated together during the war. The ships exchanged identities and intelligence information. *Ark Royal* flew a Swordfish across to *Glorious* with photographs of the airfield proposed for the Gladiators at Bardufoss. But neither that nor the field intended for the Hurricanes at Skaanland was ready.

Ark Royal had returned to Norway on 6 May and had been flying fighter patrols and mounting bombing attacks on targets ashore whenever the weather (which, though better than in April, was still bad) permitted. *Ark Royal*'s aircraft covered the naval bombardment of Narvik of 13/14 May and the landing of two battalions of the French Foreign Legion from *Effingham* and *Aurora* at Bjerkvik, north of Narvik on the 14th.

The Luftwaffe remained a constant threat. They sank the Polish destroyer *Grom* in Ofot Fjord on 4 May, damaged *Aurora* on the 7th, the destroyer *Vansittart* off Narvik on the 10th, *Somali* off Bodo on the 15th and hit the battleship *Resolution* with one large bomb on the 18th. On the 14th the Luftwaffe had an important success when they caught the troopship *Chrobry* in the middle of Vest Fjord, bombing her and setting her on fire. Her escort, the destroyer *Wolverine* and the sloop *Stork*, took off over 1000 men, but the ship had to be abandoned and she was eventually sunk, with the loss of all the tanks, guns and equipment still on board her, by *Ark Royal's* aircraft on the 16th. The Luftwaffe constantly threatened the main Allied fleet anchorage off Skaanland. On the 13th, while driving off an attack by Heinkel He.111Ks, Lucy was shot down; he and Hanson his observer were both killed. On the evening of the 17th, while taking the South Wales Borderers to Bodo, *Effingham* took a short cut between Briksvoer and the Terra Islands. She and her escort, *Matabele*, ran ashore. *Matabele* escaped with slight damage, but *Effingham* was a total loss.

Thus, by the 18th, when *Glorious* and *Furious* arrived, everyone on the Allied side, ashore and afloat, was badly in need of some good news and some RAF fighters. Bracken and his Walrus flew off *Glorious* to Harstad on the 18th where, until 6 June, they flew anti-submarine patrols, escorted convoys and provided airborne taxis for senior officers, flying 250 sorties. On their last day, before embarking in *Ark Royal*, the five Walruses still serviceable carried out a splendid bombing raid on German troops and installations at Solfolla. (Some of Cross's Hurricanes of 46 Squadron provided fighter escort, in an almost unique fighting combination of RN amphibian/RAF fighter.).

But Sunday, 19 May brought only bad weather, with low, racing clouds, thick mists and driving rain. Vice-Admiral Wells suggested *Glorious* should leave for the United Kingdom at once after Flag Officer Narvik had signalled that the Gladiators from *Furious* would disembark on the 21st, but *Glorious'* Hurricanes could not be received until the 26th.

On Monday the 20th the weather cleared enough for flying. At 10.30 *Glorious* flew off a reconnaissance flight of three Swordfish. The ship's engine fitters had been having problems with sparking plugs for the Swordfish engines. No spare plugs could be obtained. Used plugs had to be taken out again and again, cleaned and replaced. Even so, and not for the first time, the third Swordfish of that flight took off with an ominous 'spitting' sound from its engine. Heath gave orders that the aircraft was to land on again at once and sent a messenger down to find out what the trouble was.

The messenger had hardly left when D'Oyly-Hughes asked Heath what was wrong. Heath said he had sent down to find out. If possible, the Swordfish would take off again: if not, another would be ranged and flown off in its stead. D'Oyly-Hughes approved, but barely five minutes had passed when D'Oyly-Hughes asked Heath 'very abruptly', in the words of a bystander, 'what the delay was'.

The bystander was Lieutenant-Commander W.G.D. Blakeney, an officer of the Emergency Reserve, and a Master Mariner in the Merchant Navy, who had rejoined the Navy for the duration. He was interested in watching the flying and was, quite simply, goofing. It seemed to Blakeney, in a letter he later wrote and handed to Heath, that 'your reply was given at once, and in a manner which I submit, with all due deference and respect to yourself, was given with every courtesy'.

D'Oyly-Hughes' response astounded Blakeney and everybody who heard it. 'I was dumbfounded at the Commanding Officer's reply,' he wrote. 'I regret that I cannot recall the exact words he used on that occasion, but have no hesitation whatsoever in saying that, in the course of over eighteen years at sea, I have never heard an Officer spoken to in similar fashion, more especially when not only Junior

Officers, but (and this makes it worse) ratings were present as well and could hear every word that was said.'

'He went on and on,' said Heath. 'I shut my ears. Otherwise there might have been an explosion.' It was a trivial incident in itself, though profoundly shocking for Heath and disturbing for everybody who witnessed it, but it showed that the time was fast approaching when no rational conversation could be carried on with D'Oyly-Hughes and no suggestion or proposal of his or of anybody else could be discussed with him in a sensible manner.

That evening there was an increasingly urgent exchange of signals about the Gladiators which ended with Wing Commander R.T. Atcherley, in charge at Bardufoss, being asked at 7.30pm, 'Can you receive aircraft in three hours time? Reply, urgently, in clear, yes or no.' Later, at 9pm, Flag Officer Narvik (Admiral of the Fleet The Earl of Cork and Orrery) signalled to *Furious* to land her Gladiators immediately. But bad weather prevented any flying until the forenoon of the 21st when, in appalling conditions of low cloud and rainstorms, 'Baldy' Donaldson led his Gladiators ashore for the second time, guided by a Swordfish. However, in mist and low visibility, the guiding Swordfish and two of the Gladiators flew into a mountainside and were lost.

All three carriers withdrew from Norway and by the 22nd were steaming back to Scapa in thick fog. *Glorious* arrived at Scapa on Thursday, 23 May. Thursday night was Guest Night in the wardroom and that night the wardroom dined their guests, 46 Squadron. The ship was refuelling until noon on the 24th and sailed again, in thick fog, at 1.15pm, escorted by *Wren*, *Arrow* and *Highlander*. That same day the decision was taken to evacuate the Narvik area and end the Norwegian campaign (Operation ALPHABET). The decision was kept secret not only from the Germans but from the Norwegian government and armed forces. Only Coastal Command was told unofficially. But before Norway was finally abandoned, Narvik was to be taken and the iron ore and harbour installations there destroyed. That at least would impede the German war effort. But the date of the Narvik attack was postponed. It depended upon the arrival of 46 Squadron's Hurricanes.

46 Squadron had now been in *Glorious* for a fortnight, but Cross's relationship with D'Oyly-Hughes had not improved on longer acquaintance. On 26 May, when the landing strip at Skaanland was finally reported to be ready to receive the Hurricanes, there was a disagreement between Cross and D'Oyly-Hughes over the procedures for flying-off. Cross knew what had happened to 263 at Lesjaskog and was determined that nothing similar would happen to his Squadron.

At first D'Oyly-Hughes wanted 46 to fly ashore in pairs. Cross demurred at that: 'I thought we'd get written off in detail if we did that.' A signal from Rear-Admiral Narvik (who was actually Lumley Lyster) proposed that if six Skuas were available to lead, 46 should land in sections of three aircraft. 'If short of Skuas, Squadron Commander prefers three groups of six aircraft, first section to patrol aerodrome 15,000 feet until second section arrives and takes over patrol. First section then lands. Not less than three aircraft maintaining patrol over aerodrome whilst previously arrived aircraft land. Interval between arrival of first and second groups to be 20 minutes, between second and third groups 40 minutes.' The signal went on to warn that 'pilots should not brake too hard while taxiing on wire section of runway. Runway appears unfinished but is serviceable'.

In fact *Glorious* had no Skuas at all and, as the signal said, Cross much preferred to fly ashore in sections of six. This was agreed but first he had to endure a lecture from D'Oyly-Hughes 'with two main themes. The first, people at a distance who thought they knew better than people on the spot. The second, young chaps (like me, Cross) who thought they knew better than their elders and betters.'

The goofing galleries were unusually full that evening when the first six Hurricanes were ranged on deck. It was an historic occasion: the first time single-seater, high-performance monoplane fighters had ever taken off from a British carrier. 46's Hurricanes had had their two-bladed wooden propellers replaced by heavier three-bladed, metal variable-pitch propellers. These would help them get off the deck but there would be a greater risk of propellers' tips striking that ramp, two-thirds of the way up the flight deck. The Hurricanes would need 272 feet of deck to take off, with a wind speed of 30 knots. By 'Sod's Law' the winds became much lighter towards the evening, but *Glorious'* engine-room department again did their best. The Engineer Commander, Commander (E) Michael Goodman, said later that the ship touched 30 knots, the highest speed since her trials years before. It was enough. Cross went first and, as he said, his Hurricane 'just leaped off the deck like a bird'. The rest of his section duly followed him with no mishaps.

Guided by a Swordish, Cross's section flew to Skaanland and, when the second section had arrived, Cross was the first to land. The runway was about 700 yards long and had steel-meshed Sommerfelt tracking laid on bare earth. The snow, some two feet deep, had only recently been cleared and the ground was pulpy. The warning in Lyster's signal was good advice. Cross's Hurricane landed and, as it began to slow up, tipped over on to its nose. Cross jumped out 'in a white-hot rage' and berated the nearest ground staff, telling them the place was not suitable for Hurricanes. However, the next two landed on perfectly and only one more Hurricane, flown by Flight-Lieutenant Stewart, tipped on to its nose. But Cross had seen enough. He climbed back into his cockpit and instructed Jameson, who was overhead, on his R/T to fly to Bardufoss. When Cross's propeller tips had been hammered back into shape, he took his section to Bardufoss. There the runway was even shorter than at Skaanland, but only one Hurricane overshot 'into the scenery'. It was hauled back undamaged. From then on Cross's Hurricanes operated with Donaldson's Gladiators from Bardufoss.

The last of 46 Squadron's Swordfish guides landed on just after midnight on the 26th. J.B. Heath saw it on and then went down to his cabin to turn in. About ten minutes to two he was shaken awake by the Paymaster Commander, C.S. Bishop, who was duty cypher officer, and shown a copy of a signal sent the previous evening by Flag Officer Narvik to *Glorious*, inviting consideration of the possibilities of attacking enemy troops and transport on the Mosjoen-Jamo road and at Mosjoen aerodrome.

After the collapse of the Allied campaign in central Norway and the evacuations from Aandalsnes and Namsos in April, further landings on a small scale were made north of Namsos at Mo and Mosjoen in an attempt at least to delay the German advance to the north and especially to try and prevent them establishing new airfields and extending the range of their air cover. The destroyer *Janus* landed a hundred French Chasseurs-Alpins at Mosjoen on 2 May. Three hundred men of the 1st Independent Company (forerunners of the Commandos) landed from the transport *Royal Ulsterman*, escorted by *Mohawk*, at Mo, forty-five miles north of Mosjoen on 4 May. Eventually four more Independent Companies were landed, two at Mosjoen from *Ulster Prince* on the 9th, and two at Bodo, in the *Royal Scotsman* on the 9th and in *Royal Ulsterman*, escorted by *Matabele*, on the 13th or 14th. By the 21st Brigadier Gubbins, in area command, had some 4,000 troops under command.

But by then the Germans also had 4,000 troops in the area, with ample artillery and tanks and, of course, air cover. German reaction had been swift. Troops landed from seaplanes and a transport at Hemnes, fifteen miles west of Mo, on the 10th and Mosjoen had to be evacuated on 12 May. Mo was also evacuated on the 18th and by the 26th, when *Glorious* arrived, the picture around Bodo was of steady German reinforcement and complete control in the air. In the fortnight after the bombing of *Chrobry* on the 14th, the Luftwaffe sank or damaged a dozen warships, transports and storeships, and after *Ark Royal* left on the 21st they had no opposition at all. On the 26th the fleet suffered a very serious loss with the sinking of *Curlew* and her priceless radar set in the main fleet anchorage off Skaanland. It was understandable that Lord Cork should turn to *Glorious* for help.

Heath, in his dressing gown, went to Slessor's cabin to find a bridge messenger there telling Slessor that the Captain wished to see him. Heath himself had not been so summoned but because of what the signal said and because, as Commander (Air), he was bound to be involved Heath told Slessor he would go with him. Heath dressed and went up to the bridge, pausing at the Intelligence Office on the way to pick up a map.

They found D'Oyly-Hughes in bed in his sea-cabin. Together the three discussed a possible 'operation' based on the signal. It was D'Oyly-Hughes who said at the beginning that this, as Heath remembered him saying, 'was not proper employment for F.A.A. aircraft'. But Slessor volunteered to collect all the available intelligence and, when he and Heath had been through it, they would come back.

The Allies had suffered throughout the campaign from a shortage of good maps of Norway. Admiralty charts, though they had no contours in any proper cartographical sense, did show any prominent cliffs, hills, mountains or features which were conspicuous from the sea. They and the volume of the Norwegian pilot also gave drawings of the appearances of coast-lines from the sea. Bomber Command, it has been noted, used the town plans in Baedeker's *Scandinavia* (revised 1912); the implication is that these plans were inadequate. In fact, allowing for housing development, the plans are excellent, as is the rest of this splendidly informative book.

Heath and Slessor got out all the available maps and charts of the Mosjoen area. They also had the Intelligence Notes, the latest Weekly Intelligence Report, dated 17 May, 1940, and the Scandinavia Intelligence Report. They were unable to find 'Jarno', mentioned in the signal. (Nor is it in the gazetteer of the 1912 Baedeker). It seems very probable that 'Jarno' was an error of encrypting or decrypting. The message should simply have read 'the Mosjoen-Mo road'.

The pair went back to D'Oyly-Hughes to report what they had found. Slessor asked if further Intelligence might be requested from Flag Officer Narvik. D'Oyly-Hughes replied 'categorically' (Heath's word), 'No'. Heath and Slessor both gave their opinion that troops and transport on roads were not targets which Fleet Air Arm flying personnel had had any training in recognition or attack, and that an aerodrome was the only suitable target, provided its position was known within reasonable limits. It was significant that the crews of the Swordfish who had gone to Skaanland the previous evening had reported that if they had not had exact information on where the airfield was they would have great difficulty in finding it. In this case the position of Mosjoen aerodrome, mentioned in the signal, was completely unknown. 'We held the view,' said Heath, 'that an air operation without an objective clearly defined and accurately located is fundamentally unsound for low-performance aircraft.'

According to Heath's account, D'Oyly-Hughes agreed with this statement. He ended by saying that he wished Heath and Slessor to give a decision, that the point on which he wanted advice was the feasibility of the operation. It seems that Heath and Slessor had won the argument for the time being. Otherwise a man of D'Oyly-Hughes' impatient temperament might have insisted that orders be made out then and there, intelligence or no intelligence, for an operation first thing in the morning. It was, after all, not strictly true that, as Heath and Slessor had said and as D'Oyly-Hughes appeared, to agree, troops and transport on roads were not targets for F.A.A. aircraft. *Ark Royal*'s Skuas, albeit of much higher performance than Swordfish, had been attacking those very targets in support of the assault upon Narvik only a few days before. However, D'Oyly-Hughes appeared content, remarking that there would be plenty of time in the morning. But, ominously in view of what was to come, he also added that he thought 'we might let them have a smack at it'. Heath and Slessor left the Captain's sea-cabin at about 3.30am and Heath turned in again.

At 9am Heath joined Slessor again in the Plot and again they went over all the intelligence they had. They reconsidered the performance and endurance of Swordfish and the distance a Swordfish could fly in a given time. Once again they reached their former conclusion: the operation 'was inherently unsound'.

At 9.30 they both went to the bridge where D'Oyly-Hughes greeted them with the remark: 'We must think about sending fighters'. It seemed that D'Oyly-Hughes might have had a change of heart during the night. Had Heath and Slessor been dealing with Tom Troubridge in *Furious*, or Arthur John Power in *Ark Royal* (just recently relieved by Cecil Holland), all would have turned out differently. But with Guy D'Oyly-Hughes in *Glorious* such an atmosphere of tension and suspicion had been generated over the previous months that almost nothing could any longer be judged on its merits. Heath and Slessor were very old friends; they had been cadets together and knew each very well indeed. But they could not handle D'Oyly-Hughes, either singly or together; he was too much for them both. It seems that D'Oyly-Hughes may have reached the mental stage where he regarded any caution or hesitation on either of their parts as disloyalty. His officers, for their part, had reached the stage where any scheme proposed by D'Oyly-Hughes was likely to be regarded as *de facto* ill-advised and even hare-brained. Whatever the exact psychological explanation, that sequence of events was already in train which was to bring disaster upon the ship.

But at first there was no acrimony. Slessor went over his notes again. D'Oyly-Hughes disagreed with some of his figures, notably the allowance of one hour for investigating and attacking targets. There was unconfirmed intelligence of an airfield at Tjotta and some discussion as to whether this could be the Mosjoen airfield mentioned in the signal. (It was not. Tjotta is on an island at the mouth of the fjord leading up to Mosjoen.) Slessor said that in spite of all the objections he personally could see to the operation, Flag Officer Narvik had asked the ship to consider it and no doubt he had his reasons. Heath agreed and said it was possible Flag Officer Narvik thought *Glorious* had Skuas embarked (as the signal concerning Cross's squadron flying ashore had certainly suggested).

There was more discussion: on the best position for flying off, on the bomb loads (250lb bombs, with four 20lb and four smoke floats) and the time required to fit long-distance fuel tanks to the Swordfish. Heath said this would take twenty-four to thirty-six hours with the men available. D'Oyly-Hughes said that was obviously impracticable. Newnham, the Navigating Officer, said he thought the ship would be likely to be seen by enemy aircraft flying up the coast to Narvik. D'Oyly-Hughes said, 'I can't see why they should at that distance without a search.' Slessor then made the disconcerting remark that one pilot and one observer returning from Skaanland the previous evening had reported seeing the ship at seventy and forty miles respectively. D'Oyly-Hughes replied, 'Well, if they do find us, good luck to them!'

It may have been at about this point that D'Oyly-Hughes' listeners — Heath, Slessor, Newnham, and Lieutenant-Commander C.J.T. Stephens, the C.O. of 823 Squadron of Swordfish — began to have their first inkling of what D'Oyly-Hughes had in mind. Until then the carriers had operated some eighty to 120 miles offshore for their own safety. But now it seemed that, to give the Swordfish more time over their targets, and to compensate for the comparatively low endurance of the Sea Gladiators who would necessarily escort them, D'Oyly-Hughes proposed to take the ship to within forty miles of the shore. Furthermore he had made out a flight plan which was provocative: the Swordfish were to go to Hemnes first, on the coast, and then fly forty miles south to Mosjoen. Heath pointed that if Hemnes was attacked first,

Mosjoen would be forewarned and 'ready for us'. D'Oyly-Hughes overruled the objection, as he had already laid down the approximate track he wanted the aircraft to fly.

By 10.45 D'Oyly-Hughes had decided the times and positions for flying off and landing on, the aircraft to take part and the route they were to take. He told Heath and Slessor to make out the operational orders. Slessor said, 'May I be instructed as to the objects of the operation?' D'Oyly-Hughes replied: 'Bomb anything they can find — roads, aerodromes, or anything else.' Slessor wrote this down on his pad and showed it to Heath 'to ensure that this was implemented in the operation orders'.

Heath and Slessor returned to the Plot and made out draft operation orders. They took them to D'Oyly-Hughes who made certain changes. He said the whole unit must move as one body. Single aircraft would be detailed to attack selected objectives. According to Heath, 'This is in direct conflict with accepted principles of concentration in bombing attack.' Heath pointed out that, to be of any value, the fighter escort should be at 10,000 feet at least or at cloud ceiling. D'Oyly-Hughes said that was not keeping together and Heath 'was again overruled'.

The orders as made out and signed by D'Oyly-Hughes were for five Swordfish, armed with six 250lb C.P. and four 20lb bombs, and three fighters as escort. Their object was 'to bomb any suitable objective that can be found, including troops and transport on road between HEMNES and MOSJOEN, small bridges or viaducts, and enemy aerodromes'. They were to attack nothing north of Hemnes because Allied forces might be there.

The force was to take off at 8pm on the 27th and fly to Hemnes. The whole force was 'to remain as one body throughout'. The primary duty of the fighters was 'to protect the Swordfish and not to be led away by engagements outside this duty. Their petrol must be carefully conserved'. In the event of failing to find *Glorious* at the ETA, 'every effort should be made to land at BODIN (three miles east of BODO)'.

'Up to this time,' wrote Heath a few days after the event, 'although it was clear there was a strong divergence of view, the discussions had been conducted without acrimony. Lieutenant-Commander Slessor and I had made it quite clear that we considered the operation fundamentally unsound. The Captain made it equally clear that he wished and intended, if possible, to carry it out. On this understanding the draft operation order had been made out and had been approved by the Captain. I had no reason to suppose that the Captain was in any way dissatisfied with the manner in which Lieutenant-Commander Slessor and I had acted in our advisory capacity. In spite of the divergence of opinion at no period am I aware of having shown the slightest hesitation, nor was I at any time reluctant to carry out the Captain's orders.'

It was now about 12.30pm. While Slessor went away to get the orders reproduced and distributed, Heath went down to his cabin where he found Stephens, 823's C.O., waiting to see him. Stephens had been in the Plot while the operation was being discussed and, now that he had seen the approved draft of the orders, he requested an interview with the Captain, being the senior officer conducting the operation in the air. Heath asked Stephens if he wished to take this course. Stephens replied that he was sure; he had taken advice about it and he felt it was his duty.

Heath took Stephens up to the bridge and reported to D'Oyly-Hughes in his sea-cabin that Stephens wished to see him about the operation. D'Oyly-Hughes told Heath to wait in the Plot and asked Heath as he left, 'Is this *another* deputation?' Heath replied, 'No, sir'.

When D'Oyly-Hughes appeared Stephens asked and was granted formal permission to state his views on the operation. He said that he was fully prepared to carry out whatever operation was ordered, but he wanted to point out that this operation was, in his opinion, a bad one, on account of the smallness and poor performance of the forces available and the indeterminate objectives. D'Oyly-Hughes then said, 'Will you make out the operation orders, Stephens?' Stephens replied with what Heath called 'some diffidence' that he would try. Finally D'Oyly-Hughes said, 'Go away with the Wing Commander, Stephens, and make them out.' Heath was not asked any question or addressed during this interview.

Heath and Stephens went to the Observers' Office where Slessor had all the maps, charts and intelligence. However, to make out fresh orders was easier said than done. Heath and Slessor had already gone over all the possible alternative courses of action and as Heath said, 'I found extreme difficulty in suggesting any alternatives to Lieutenant-Commander Stephens'.

But time had now run out. At 1.40pm, before Heath or Stephens had come to any fresh proposals, D'Oyly-Hughes sent for Heath, Slessor, Stephens and Lovell, the Commander. They all assembled in the Plotting Office and D'Oyly-Hughes came in. To Lovell he said that he wished him, as Executive Officer, to know what had happened. D'Oyly-Hughes then read from a piece of paper a summary of what he alleged had happened.

He said that when he had received Flag Officer Narvik's signal the night before, he had sent for Heath and Slessor and ordered them to produce a plan. He said that up to this time

(2pm) nothing had been produced. Slessor then pointed out that, on the contrary, orders had been produced as directed and approved by him. D'Oyly-Hughes held up a copy of the orders and said, 'What's this? I don't know anything about it'. He remarked that it bore his signature, but he did not know why. He said that he himself had produced a plan, drawn in red on the Navigating Officer's chart. This, Heath presumed, referred to an outline sketch D'Oyly-Hughes had drawn on the chart of his ordered route for the aircraft to fly.

D'Oyly-Hughes now addressed Heath and 'in great heat' said, 'You have been reluctant all day to produce a plan'. Heath replied, 'Not reluctant, but I found great difficulty in producing a satisfactory one due to the lack of intelligence and the inadequate force available.' D'Oyly-Hughes 'exultantly exclaimed', 'That's what I want!' and ordered Heath to put that statement on paper.

Slessor and Stephens both tried to speak during this interview but were not allowed to. D'Oyly-Hughes addressed them all, Lovell, Slessor, Stephens and Heath, and said he 'was shocked and horrified' to find any ship which he commanded should be reluctant to take part in an offensive operation proposed by a Flag Officer. He said that he intended to make this state of affairs on board known to the 'highest possible authority' on return to the Clyde. He said he had gone into the weather situation at great length with Steel who had told him there would be no fog on the coast that evening, but thick fog about thirty miles off. These, he said, were ideal conditions for a carrier which could run and hide in the fog whenever necessary. He repeated the expressions 'Shocked' and 'Horrified' and said the ship would return to the Clyde. As he left the Plot D'Oyly-Hughes turned back and said, 'One other thing. I want to make the position of the *ship* clear. When I am prepared to risk this ship within thirty-five miles of an enemy coast I do it for people who want it and not for those who don't.'

'Throughout this painful interview,' wrote Heath, 'Captain D'Oyly-Hughes displayed a total disregard of fairness and restraint, and that in thus addressing me before a number of my subordinates his action was calculated gravely to undermine my authority. However, his whole manner and tone were as improper as his insinuations were injurious and entirely without foundation. It is regretted that this incident was by no means an isolated case of disagreement but is, in fact, the culmination of a very distressing relationship.'

Heath went away to write the letter D'Oyly-Hughes had ordered. 'Sir, I have the honour to report that with reference to F.O. Narvik's 2202/26/5 I am unable to produce a plan for offensive operations in which I have any faith in view of the lack of intelligence and inadequacy of the aircraft at our disposal. I have the honour to be, Sir, Your Obedient Servant...' As Heath was later at pains to try and make clear, the 'plan for offensive operations' referred to here was not the original orders, which D'Oyly-Hughes had approved and signed, but orders for the 'alternative' which Heath had been discussing with Stephens when they were both summoned by D'Oyly-Hughes.

This sad little letter was J.B. Heath's last act as *Glorious'* Commander (Air). He was relieved of his duties and went to his cabin. His exact status was not made clear, but he was under no form of arrest though he was likely to be charged with offences under the Naval Discipline Act. Again, these were never precisely formulated, but they would have been for offences such as 'cowardice in the face of the enemy'.

Opinion in the air group was by no means unanimously on Heath's side. At least one pilot who survived, Dick Leggott of 802, who would most probably have been one of the Sea Gladiator fighter escort, said, 'I think we *should* have flown something. I would not denigrate D'Oyly-Hughes as much as many have. When it came to Flag Officer Narvik sending a signal saying we would like you to try and do something to assist the army ashore, the least we should have done was to send off an armed reconnaissance. We had been asked to do something. Three Swordfish and three Gladiators could have carried out the necessary patrol, although it was daylight twenty-four hours a day. It could have been done. There was only a twenty to one chance of anybody even seeing a Swordfish for more than two minutes in that sort of terrain. There weren't German fighters in every square foot of air there. That really to me is where the affair doesn't entirely devolve upon D'Oyly-Hughes. The majority of the pilots in the Swordfish squadron were put out about it. My own squadron C.O. [Marmont] refused to be drawn into it. He was asked to go and see the Captain but he said it was nothing to do with him. It was not good enough. Something could have been done.'

In the event nothing was done. Ironically the strike was never flown. Perhaps D'Oyly-Hughes had another change of mind, or perhaps he was impressed by the weight of air opinion against him. The operation over which there had been so much heart-searching never took place. Instead, the main preoccupation that day was the transfer of Hurricane ammunition by boat to a destroyer for transport to the airfield ashore.

While *Glorious* was racked by internal wranglings, the war at large went on. In France the British Expeditionary Force was falling back upon the Channel coast. On the 24th Hitler and General Rundstedt had halted the German armour and the 'Nine Days' Wonder' of Operation DYNAMO — the evacuation from Dunkirk — began on the 26th. Belgium capitulated on the 28th. During that night Narvik was captured and the situation of German forces in the area put in such peril that it remains a matter for conjecture how much more successful a much bolder campaign by the Allies would have been.

That day, 28 May, three Sea Gladiators from *Glorious* shot down a shadowing Heinkel He.115 floatplane. By the evening the ship was on her way back to Scapa Flow. She spent the 29th fogged off Hoy and entered Scapa Flow with *Highlander* on the 30th. Paul Slessor wrote to his wife on the 29th: 'J.B. and I are in great trouble. I can't tell you the story but you will guess the cause of it. It was bound to come sooner or later I suppose and perhaps it is a good thing. I needn't tell you where *right* lies nor that my conscience is absolutely clear. But we need your thoughts and prayers very much — please give them to us during the next few days. Don't worry — nothing matters but to have done right.'

It is a measure of Paul Slessor's quality as a man and as a friend that he found time, in spite of all his own cares, to think of Mrs Heath. 'Dear Sylvia,' he wrote on 30 May, 'You will probably have heard, by the time this reaches you, of J.B.'s troubles. They are also my troubles — I might almost say *our* troubles. You must not worry. We are all with him. He has acted as a *man* should. All will be well, I feel sure. Speaking quite personally, he can rely on everything I can possibly do, however distasteful it may appear to be. In any case, I beg you not to worry. I must tell you, what you already know — that to work with and under J.B. has given me much happiness and pleasure. I don't know how on earth I'm going to face things now, without him.'

For J.B. Heath that day at Scapa must have been one of the longest of his life. He was not under arrest. In fact, he went across by boat to visit a friend commanding a battleship to seek his advice. But D'Oyly-Hughes carried out his threat in full. He wrote a letter to Wells about Heath in the most derogatory terms, which Captain Jasper Parrott, the Admiral's Secretary, later showed Heath in confidence. At five minutes to six that evening the blow finally fell. A signalling lamp began to flash in the flagship *Rodney*, lying across the Flow: 'From the Commander-in-Chief to *Glorious*, Commander J.B. Heath is to be sent from *Glorious* to *Dunluce Castle* tonight Thursday and is to be temporarily accommodated there until further orders.'

Heath did not leave at once but waited until after midnight. He knew the wardroom was 'seething' with indignation and wanted to avoid trouble. 'I realized that the wardroom were boiling. I had to pack up quick. I didn't dare go into the wardroom. I knew there would be trouble. The ship was near mutiny. I didn't say goodbye to D'Oyly-Hughes. Once I'd left the bridge after that showdown, I never saw him again. The trouble was that the Captain's cabin in harbour was right by the quarterdeck and the gangway came down past it. I dreaded an awful *hurrah hurrah* as I went over the side. I managed to escape. There were a number of chaps there. I *pleaded* with them not to make a noise. I was smuggled out. It was the nearest thing I've been to tears.'

On that last evening, several officers called at Heath's cabin to bid their adieux. Among them was Lieutenant-Commander 'Kit' Wells, the Gunnery Officer, who said to Heath 'that at least I had a chance of letting things be known, for their chances of survival were very small'. But once again opinion among the aircrew was not entirely with Heath. Dick Leggott was among the dissenters: 'Stephens came into the ready room and said, "I want all the aviators to go down to the quarterdeck and cheer off J.B. Heath." Half the aviators said no. Not to Stephens, but after he had gone. They said, "We will not. We don't agree that those Swordfish should not have gone." My own Squadron C.O. said to us, "You do as you please." Half went. Half didn't. I did not go.'

But there is no question that *Glorious* experienced a great surge of sympathy and feeling for J.B. Heath that night. It was then that Blakeney handed Heath his letter, giving his account of the 'Sparking Plug' episode and ending: 'I am quite ready to give personal testimony in Court should you require me to do so and I trust you will not think me too impertinent for addressing a letter of this kind to you.'

The last word on J.B. Heath's time in *Glorious* was said in another letter handed to him that night. It was from a young Sea Gladiator pilot, Lieutenant Nick Ward of 802 Squadron, who had run the organization of the Fleet Air Arm Office under Heath. 'Dear Commander Heath,' he wrote, 'I hope you will not mind my writing this purely personal note to you; but I know if I was to try and say anything to you, I would not be able to do so and would probably make us both extremely uncomfortable.

'I have only just heard that you are leaving, though nothing of the circumstances. However, from what I do know, and from the fact that you are apparently leaving under a most unjustifiable cloud, I can see that a gross injustice is being done. Of one thing you can be quite certain — every single officer and man in the ship will know before long who is to blame. A man who can boast that he will ruthlessly sweep from his path anyone who looks like threatening his own "success" may be able to fool the Admiralty (and possibly a lot of officers) but he will never get past the troops.

'For your own sake, and even more for the sake of the Navy as a whole and the F.A.A. in particular, I do implore you to fight to clear your name; and if no charge is brought against you to demand an explanation.

'I don't know what you will think of this, coming from a young lieutenant, but I hope you will realize (from my normal inability to say what I feel) that it comes from a very deep feeling, and an equally strong desire to see you vindicated. The F.A.A. needs you, and people like you, badly and I only hope that I may serve under you again in the future under more favourable conditions. P.S. I can't think how I had the nerve to offer advice to you; but I know you will take it as from a friend and not as from an impertinent junior officer.'

Sitting alone in a strange cabin in the depot ship *Dunluce Castle*, with such letters, and with all his bags and belongings still unpacked around him, J.B. Heath had now to face a future in which, in due course of time, he would have to try and salvage what he could from the wreckage of his naval career.

CHAPTER 9: OPERATION JUNO — *SCHARNHORST* AND *GNEISENAU*

'THE WHOLE FORCE can talk of nothing else,' wrote Lieutenant-General Auchinleck, the G.O.C-in-C of the Norwegian Expeditionary Force on 2 June, 1940. He was referring to the exploits of the Gladiators and Hurricanes of the Air component of his Expeditionary Force. The Air Component, under the command of Group Captain M. Moore, comprising the two squadrons, 263 and 46 and their ground crews, with No 11 Observer Screen, numbered at their maximum on 4 June seventy-three officers and 940 Other Ranks. But they had an effect out of all proportion to their numbers.

263 had a dispiriting start when two Gladiators flew into the side of a 3,000-foot mountain on the island of Senjen, and one pilot, Pilot Officer Richards, was killed. But 263 began to fly fighter patrols from the time of their arrival at Bardufoss on the morning of 21 May. Their first contact with enemy aircraft was on the 23rd and their star performer was Flight Lieutenant C. Hull who was eventually credited with five victories. On the 25th 263 shot down six German aircraft, including a four-engine bomber near Harstad, at the cost of two Gladiators badly damaged.

On the 26th the army at Bodo asked for fighter cover and three Gladiators flew to an advanced landing ground which had been prepared by an energetic party under Wing Commander Maxton. However, the ground was still so soggy that all three 'bogged down'. One Gladiator crashed on taking off but the other two managed to shoot down four German aircraft between them before Bodo landing ground was bombed into unserviceability, with more than a hundred craters on and around the landing strip. But by then the Gladiators had played an invaluable part in the evacuation of troops from the Bodo area.

The main tasks of the fighters were to defend the main fleet anchorage off Skaanland and the main military base at Harstad and, wherever possible, to give close air support to any sea or land forces in contact with the enemy. Both fighter squadrons kept up a furious pace, 263 being credited with eleven enemy confirmed and five unconfirmed by 28 May. 46 arrived at Bardufoss on the 27th and next day Flying Officer Lydall shot down a Ju.88 over Ofot Fjord, and a flight of Flight Lieutenant P.G. Jameson, Flying Officer Knight and Pilot Officer Johnson destroyed two four-engined flying boats lying in Rombaks Fjord. Meanwhile, three Gladiators shot up a convoy of German lorries and strafed German troops embarking at Beisfjord, near Narvik.

The Hurricanes of 46 won a tactical victory over the Luftwaffe and achieved a local air superiority over Narvik when it was retaken by the Allies on 28 May. In the early hours of the 29th Jameson and Pilot Officer Drummond intercepted three aircraft, two He.111s and a Junkers Ju.88, south-east of Narvik. 'I surprised the rearmost enemy aircraft by climbing up under his tail,' Jameson reported. 'On opening fire at 200 yards, a bright flash appeared from the 88 and my windscreen was obscured by oil. After breaking away, I noticed black smoke was coming from his starboard engine. As I approached again he jettisoned his bombs, so fired another burst at about 250 yards. The starboard engine began to burn and the fire gradually spread to the fuselage. Shortly before the machine crashed on the cliff of a fjord, one of the crew jumped by parachute.' Drummond shot down one of the Heinkels but the He.111s rear-gunners put up a formidable amount of return fire (as Lucy and others had discovered) and Drummond himself had to bale out. He was picked up by the destroyer *Firedrake*.

That afternoon (the 29th) Pilot Officer Banks, a newcomer to the squadron, of whom Bing Cross said, 'Every time he flew he met the Germans', met and shot down a four-engined Junkers. Later, although Flight Sergeant Shackley got another Ju.88, Lydall and Banks were both shot down and killed. Bad weather prevented all but a few sorties by 263 on the 30th but on the 31st 46 patrolled Skaanland and Harstad and, in the evening, covered the evacuation from Bodo.

Everybody who served there agreed that life at Bardufoss had a flavour all its own. The catchphrase, according to Jameson, a New Zealander, was, 'We don't get much money but we do see life'. There was the sheer intensity of the flying: 263 flew over 390 sorties and engaged in seventy-two aerial combats: 46 flew 249 sorties, with twenty-six combats. The sorties generally lasted two hours and were flown in pairs; Cross had begun with sections of three but Donaldson had told him, 'You'll never be able to afford them,' which was true. There was the intense beauty of the scenery, with the mountains changing colour as the sun climbed towards its summer zenith; the nights dwindled away to the merest change of light, like the dropping of a thin veil. There was Dick Atcherley, the station commander, Schneider Trophy pilot and one of the RAF's characters, with his ski trousers and ski boots under his uniform tunic and cap; and the family of elks, in the nearby forest, their coats the same colour, and their way of life apparently as permanently motionless as the tree trunks; and there was life under canvas for 46, in an array of tents on the northern rim near the 'dock golf course'; and the so-called 'Rest House', beside the waterfall two miles away, where pilots went for a night's sleep and a rest; and the air-raid shelters, with their log and stone walls; and the three-storeyed, gaunt-windowed Barrack Block, which had the only telephone for miles and was control tower, operations room, mess-hall and barracks; and the Norwegian labourers, with their curious humming songs, which they sang apparently through their noses; and there was 46 Squadron's mess dinner given for the 6th Battalion of the French Chasseurs-Alpins, when the toast was '*Entente Cordiale*', while everybody, in view of the news, wondered what the future of France would be.

The stream of bad news from home had a depressing effect upon morale, which, when the ground crews first came under air attack, was described as 'somewhat shaky'. Two Leading Aircraftmen of 263 were killed in an air raid on 27 May. There were several cases of 'minor neurosis' among the older men. One statement at the time spoke of 'a large proportion of all ranks being in a state of jitters, resulting in inability to think clearly, issue logical instructions or take energetic measures'. However, spirits began to rise when it was seen how little actual damage was being done t6 the airfield and how well the fighter pilots were doing. Morale soared, along with the tally of kills. Eventually the Gladiators claimed twenty-six aircraft destroyed and the Hurricanes eleven, and 'the general spirit of all ranks in the end was both resolute and confident'.

By 1 June preparations were being made to evacuate Bardufoss, as part of the arrangements to take off the whole Expeditionary Force, some 25,000 men, starting on 2 June (Operation ALPHABET), although the operation was in fact delayed by twenty-four hours. *Ark Royal*, flying Wells' flag, had arrived at Scapa Flow from the Clyde early in the morning of

31 May and sailed again at 8am with *Glorious* (less J.B. Heath) in company, screened by *Highlander, Diana, Acasta, Ardent,* and *Acheron.* The two carriers set course to pass west of the Orkneys, beginning to fly anti-submarine patrols from 9.30. At 10.15 *Ark Royal* began to fly on twelve Skuas of 803 Squadron and two replacement Skuas for 800. The carrier squadron then steered to the north, heading for the Narvik area.

The roles of the two carriers for this final sortie into Norwegian waters were quite different. *Ark Royal* had the fighting element, to carry out bombing and harassing raids whenever possible on the enemy ashore and to provide fighter cover for our troops ashore and for the troop convoys at sea. *Glorious,* meanwhile, with only enough aircraft (802's Sea Gladiators and six Swordfish of 823) for her own protection, was to re-embark the RAF Gladiators if it were possible to do so. She was to act merely as a ferry and was shunted into, literally, a backwater until called forward to play her part. It can only be conjectured what effect the imposition of this comparatively minor and non-combatant role had upon a man of D'Oyly-Hughes' temperament, especially as he had deprived himself of his usual buffer and butt, J.B. Heath.

By 2 June the carriers were off the Norwegian coast. At 5pm that afternoon a Walrus from Narvik landed on *Ark Royal* with the orders for Operation ALPHABET. *Ardent* and *Acasta* were detached to Harstad to refuel (destroyers left in pairs to refuel throughout the operation). At 7.30 on 3 June *Glorious* and *Highlander* were detached to the north-west, in the words of Wells' report, 'to conserve fuel until required for embarking shore-based aircraft'.

In retrospect it does seem strange that *Glorious'* squadrons were not brought up to full or near-full complement, so that her Sea Gladiators and her Swordfish could contribute to a joint effort with *Ark Royal*. The RAF fighters she was expecting to embark amounted, after all, to only one squadron of Gladiators. As it was, the menial task allotted to them must have seemed to Guy D'Oyly-Hughes to reflect upon himself and his ship. To steam innocuously up and down, out of harm's way, to save fuel, must have been very hard to bear for such an aggressive, ambitious and, in his own manner, conscientious man; for, whatever charges may be levelled at Guy D'Oyly-Hughes, nobody could ever accuse him of doing anything less than his very best at all times.

The main evacuation was due to begin on the night of 3 June and Flag Officer Narvik had already signalled, on 1 June, his requirements from the carrier squadron; they were to fly fighter patrols over the embarkation points ashore and over the rendezvous at sea where the ferrying destroyers were to meet the troop transports, to carry out reconnaissance and bombing of enemy troop movements in the Sorfold-Drag area (south-west of Narvik) and bombing of General Dietl's headquarters at Hundallen, which was east of Narvik, on the railway line to Sweden.

Ark Royal began her fighter patrols at 11.30pm on the 3rd and kept them up throughout the night, the following morning and forenoon and into the afternoon. Cloud conditions were unsuitable for bombing, but at 11.15 on the 4th two Skuas were sent to reconnoitre the road between Sorfold and Drag, and one of them managed to bomb the jetty at Sorfold. Fighter patrols began again at 11.45pm on the 4th but had to be called off early on the morning of the 5th because of rain and low cloud. None of the patrols met any enemy aircraft.

Bad weather on the 5th, with patches of fog which thickened later, prevented much flying. *Glorious* rejoined *Ark Royal* at

2.20pm, so that *Highlander* could go in to refuel while *Glorious* remained in company with *Ark Royal* and her screen.

In the early hours of 6 June D'Oyly-Hughes at last achieved his desire and, doubtless after the strongest representations by him to Admiral Wells, was able to mount a bombing raid very similar (except for a more clearly defined target) to that opposed by J.B. Heath. At 2am four Swordfish of 823, led by Stephens, took off to bomb Dietl's HQ at Hundallen. They were led by a Swordfish from *Ark Royal* and escorted by three of *Ark Royal*'s Skuas. But this final effort by *Glorious'* aircraft turned to anticlimax. Low clouds prevented them reaching their target. They jettisoned their bombs into the sea and landed on again at 5.30am. That, in a sense, ended *Glorious'* war effort. At 10.15 *Highlander* rejoined from Harstad, and *Glorious* and *Highlander* were once again detached 'to the north-west to conserve fuel until required for embarking aircraft pm 7 June'.

Ark Royal, by contrast, went on to a very full day's flying. Besides maintaining fighter and anti-submarine patrols and long-range Swordfish searches, *Ark Royal* launched two Skuas to bomb Sorfold and Drag at 12.10pm, six more Skuas to bomb enemy troops around Fauske at 5.10, six Swordfish to bomb Hundallen and Sildvik at 9.05, three Swordfish to search for enemy vessels at 11.30 and one Swordfish at the same time to drop two 250lb bombs near a bridge ten miles south-east of Drag. The last aircraft from the activities of 6 June had hardly landed on when, at 2am on the 7th, *Ark Royal* began fighter patrols again over the transports embarking troops from destroyers at Risoy, and continued the patrols throughout that morning, afternoon and evening of the 7th.

On 4 June, when Mr Churchill announced the successful completion of DYNAMO at Dunkirk, the equally successful but far less publicized ALPHABET was under way in the north. The evacuation of some 25,000 troops of several nationalities, from a main base at Harstad, from Narvik and more than a dozen other embarkation points stretching across Norway from Ballangen, south-west of Narvik on the Ofot Fjord, up to Tromso in the north, required close co-ordination, good planning, bold ship-handling, bad weather and air cover to keep the Luftwaffe at bay, and some luck. For once in the Norwegian campaign it all went right.

The first evacuation, at Bodo, took three nights and was covered by two Gladiators and two Hurricanes until the final stages. On 29 May 1,000 men of the Independent Companies were transported in two destroyers out to the cruiser *Vindictive*, converted pre-war to a cadet training ship and now, with her reduced armament, used as a repair and depot ship who took them to Scapa Flow. The rest were taken off on the 30th and 31st by the destroyers *Firedrake*, *Vanoc*, *Arrow*, *Havelock* and *Echo*, and some smaller craft, to Harstad. The evacuation was assisted by the small Norwegian steamer SS *Ranen*, which was armed with a Bofors, an oerlikon and some machine guns, and renamed as the decoy ship *Raven*, commanded by Commander Sir Geoffrey Congreve. Congreve and his mixed crew of naval ratings, Irish Guardsmen and South Wales Borderers hindered the enemy's advance along the coast from Bodo by bombarding their troops and cutting their telephone lines.

The main evacuation took place over five nights from 3 June, in the words of Lord Cork's dispatch, 'without untoward incident'. Large quantities of material, guns, vehicles, stores and ammunition, (much more than had been expected) was retrieved, including a 'bag' of sixty captured Luftwaffe airmen. In the last few days before the troops began to leave steps were taken to remove or destroy anything that could be of value to the enemy. The iron ore quays, generating plant and two miles of railway in Narvik were destroyed, so that the first iron ore steamer from Narvik did not leave until 8 January, 1941. The Mobile Naval Base depot ship *Mashobra*, which had been bombed and beached on 25 May, was blown up. The 7,000-ton oiler *Oleander*, badly damaged by a near-miss on the 26th, was sunk. Disabled trawlers were sunk or burned. Harbour defence booms and nets were sunk. The landing craft used for transporting tanks and vehicles ashore were scuttled.

For the troops fifteen troopships (of which two eventually took no part) sailed so as to arrive at one of two distant rendezvous arranged some 180 miles from the coast. From there they were escorted in pairs by destroyers closer inshore to outlying fjords or rendezvous forty miles from the coast. Rear-Admiral Vivian (Flag Officer commanding 20th Cruiser Squadron), in general charge of embarkation, met them in his flagship *Coventry* to give them final instructions and to provide anti-aircraft gun support. Three or four destroyers provided anti-submarine protection.

The soldiers embarked at night, although there was no actual darkness at that time of year, when the Luftwaffe were least active. The soldiers embarked, with all their small arms and equipment, at places along Ofot Fjord, in Harstad, in Tjeldsundet and from a dozen tiny fjords in the area, either into Norwegian puffers which took them to destroyers, or directly into destroyers, who ferried them out to the troopships offshore. Two small passenger ships, *Ulster Prince* and *Ulster Monarch*, embarked men and stores in Harstad itself.

The first main group of troopships, *Monarch of Bermuda*, *Batory*, *Sobieski*, *Franconia*, *Lancastria* and *Georgic*, with *Vindictive*, took off nearly 15,000 men in three early-morning loadings between 4 and 6 June. The second main group, *Oronsay*, *Ormonde*, *Arandora Star*, *Duchess of York*, with the smaller *Royal*

Ulsterman, Ulster Prince and *Ulster Monarch,* took off just under 10,000 men on 7 and 8 June.

Group 1, escorted only by *Vindictive,* left the distant rendezvous early on 7 June and was met by *Valiant,* escorted by *Tartar, Mashona, Bedouin* and *Ashanti* at 1am on the 8th. Five destroyers, *Atherstone, Wolverine, Witherington, Antelope, Viscount,* met the Group off the Faeroes that night. *Valiant* and her escort then left and turned north again. The convoy stood on and, except for one German aircraft which was driven off by *Vindictive*'s fire, reached the Clyde uneventfully.

Admiral Forbes had intended to send a much stronger escort of *Renown* and *Repulse* with destroyers, but on 5 June the decoy ship *Prunella* reported 'two unknown vessels', possibly raiders, breaking out into the Atlantic about 200 miles north-east of the Faeroes and steering towards the Iceland-Faeroes gap. Vice-Admiral Whitworth was sent with the two battle cruisers, with *Newcastle* and *Sussex,* and the destroyers *Zulu, Kelvin, Maori, Forester* and *Foxhound,* to intercept. On the 7th Whitworth's force steered for Iceland after a report that the enemy was landing there. But nothing more was seen or heard either of the two 'raiders' or the Iceland invasion. The only result was that the Home Fleet's heavy ships were dispersed at the time of the Norwegian evacuation when the troop convoys were actually, as it transpired, in much greater danger than anybody supposed. On the 8th the Admiralty ordered *Renown* and two destroyers back to Scapa Flow, where there was only *Rodney* and a few destroyers, because it was considered that 'there should not be less than two capital ships available to proceed south in case of invasion'.

On the 7th a 'slow convoy' of the storeships *Blackheath, Oligarch, Harmattan, Cromarty Firth, Theseus, Acrity, Coxwold* and *Couch,* left Harstad escorted by *Stork* and *Arrow* and ten trawlers. The same day another convoy left Tromso, of *Oil Pioneer*, *Vermont* and the ammunition ships *Arbroath* and *Nyakoa* and some Norwegian vessels, escorted by four trawlers. That evening HM King Haakon VII, the Crown Prince and a total of 435 men and twenty-six women — politicians, diplomats, the royal retinue, Norwegian Air Force officers and British officers and other ranks — embarked in *Devonshire*, (Flag of Vice-Admiral John Cunningham) at Tromso. *Devonshire* sailed at 8.30pm on the 7th independently for the Clyde.

To conceal the evacuation from the enemy some troops remained in contact almost until the last moment. Among the last (perhaps the very last) to leave Norway were Wing Commander Atcherley and the RAF ground crews at Bardufoss who, like the aircrews, had one final hectic day after a strenuous week. After bad weather on 1 June, the 2nd was a big flying day. Among many successes that day, the most outstanding *coup* was brought off by Pilot Officer L.R. Jacobsen DFC, a New Zealander in 263, who found himself inside a circle of two Junkers Ju.88s and six Heinkel He.111Ks. Though Jacobsen used every possible device to evade enemy fire, his Gladiator was hit, but he counterattacked with such vigour that three of the Heinkel He.111Ks he attacked were later found crashed in Sweden.

There was bad weather again on the 3rd, 4th and 5th, but patrols were resumed on the 6th when the pilot noticed the lack of enemy reaction over Narvik. But by 7 June, 263 were down to ten serviceable Gladiators (having lost another pilot, Pilot Officer Wilkie, on the 2nd) and 46 also had only ten flyable Hurricanes: four were lost to enemy action and four were irreparable with the equipment available at Bardufoss. By that time the evacuation was clearly very close. At 1.30pm that day *Glorious* and *Highlander* rejoined the flag. It would soon be time for Donaldson's Gladiators to fly out to the carrier, but the problem remained: what was to be done with Cross's remaining Hurricanes?

Cross's day had begun at 3am when he awoke to hear the section of two Hurricanes in readiness taking off. 'I got up to go the Ops tent and asked, "What goes on?" There was a report of something approaching Harstad. I said, "I'll take the next one." I was taxiing down the runway and as I turned at the end I saw four Heinkels dead in line. I took off straight towards them and to the astonishment of me and my number two, Pete Lefevre, they turned away. I climbed after them, but I got hit in the windscreen. No oil pressure. Pete attacked the one on the right. Perhaps I should have waited before attacking. I had enough height to make the airfield. They worked on the Hurricane all day and it was flown out by Sergeant Taylor that evening.'

Sergeant Taylor's flight, with the rest of 46 that evening, was the result of a daring and unprecedented decision taken by Cross and endorsed by Group Captain Moore. It had never been intended that Hurricanes should fly back to *Glorious*, Tests at Farnborough had shown that it was 'impossible' for a Hurricane to land safely inside the limits of a flight deck. But tests by Jameson on the runway at Bardufoss, with a 14lb sandbag in the tail frame, had shown that full brakes could be used with no danger of tipping the Hurricane on its nose.

The obvious course, to Cross, was to try and fly the Hurricanes on to *Glorious*. Fighters were badly needed back home and, in any case, Cross disliked all the alternatives suggested: flying to Skaanland and destroying the Hurricanes there, or flying to some airfield far in the north and dismantling the Hurricanes ('a ridiculous idea' Cross called it).

Somebody even suggested flying out to sea and ditching alongside destroyers.

Cross himself flew out to the carrier squadron in a Walrus to confer with D'Oyly-Hughes, who 'seemed in a much better mood this time'. D'Oyly-Hughes thought Cross's proposal feasible and promised that his ship would once again work up to full speed for the occasion. Cross then flew to *Ark Royal* ('the spirit in that ship was *terrific*, quite different from *Glorious*') whose flight deck was some hundred feet longer than *Glorious*' but whose lifts were smaller. The Hurricanes' wings would have to be removed before they could be struck down in the hanger. It was decided that the Hurricanes would try *Glorious* first and then, if that failed, go to *Ark Royal*.

At 2.30pm on the 7th *Glorious* flew off four Swordfish to Bardufoss to guide the fighter aircraft back to the carriers. *Ark Royal* flew off one Swordfish to Bardufoss at 4.15, with orders for the fighter to embark. Three Hurricanes, piloted by Jameson, Flight Lieutenant Knight and Sergeant Taylor, took off at about 6pm and were over the carriers just after 7. (Cross had asked for volunteers: 'They *all* volunteered, so I chose the ten senior pilots.')

Once again *Glorious*' engine-room department did their utmost (D'Oyly-Hughes himself always thought they 'did marvels') and worked the ship up to some 29 or 30 knots. 'The Captain of the *Glorious* kept his word,' said Jameson. 'When we saw the *Glorious* it was going flat out, with steam pouring out of every rivet-hole. While we were waiting for the signal to land on, Sergeant Taylor went down and made a perfect landing on the carrier. When I tackled him about it later, he said he had engine trouble, but I suspect he really wanted to be the first chap to land a Hurricane on a carrier.' Thus Sergeant Taylor it was who made that historic first landing (although, as he was flying Cross's Hurricane, it was probably true that there was something wrong with the engine, after the combat earlier that day).

Then it was Jameson's turn. 'When I looked at *Glorious* again, her deck reminded me of the back of an elephant — grey, and the flight deck had a rounddown at the stern which was moving up and down like a cantering elephant's backside! We had to touch down as near the top of the heaving rump as possible to minimize the chance of over-shooting. There was quite a swell on and *Glorious* was at full tilt (about 30 knots) which meant that the landing spot was moving up and down at an alarming rate! Before taking off from Bardufoss I had decided that the only way to find out if it was possible to land on *Glorious* was to commit myself completely to the landing... If one got three-quarters of the way along the deck and then realized that one was not going to stop in time, it would be too late to take off again anyway!

'I came in on the approach just above stalling speed, feeling my way because of the sandbag away down in the tail affecting the flying characteristics, when suddenly, as I was getting near the touchdown point, the Hurricane dropped rapidly and it seemed she was trying to land on the quarterdeck. I slammed on full throttle and that beautiful Rolls Royce Merlin engine never faltered. It dragged us up onto the flight deck and the Hurricane and I stopped about a quarter of the way along. All three of us managed to get down O.K., none using more than three-quarters of the deck.'

Safely on board, Jameson drafted a signal to Cross to say all was well, but it was probably never sent; at any rate Cross did not receive it. While *Ark Royal* was landing on the five remaining Walruses of 701 Squadron from Harstad, *Glorious* flew off a Swordfish to Bardufoss with orders for landing on the rest of the RAF fighters. Donaldson's Gladiators and Cross's Hurricanes took off about midnight, having kept up fighter patrols over Narvik and Harstad all day. 'We left at 0045 hours,' Cross wrote to a friend, 'dead beat; and as we left we were pleased to see the Skuas of the Fleet Air Arm coming in to cover the embarkation of our troops who had a destroyer standing by for them at a little fishing village seventeen miles away. We were navigated out to sea by a Swordfish at 100 knots and the old Hurricanes had to do some fairly hearty zigzagging to keep behind. It wasn't a nice feeling knowing that if we couldn't get on the deck there was no way out.'

Glorious began to land on her guests at 1.15am, the ten Gladiators first, followed by the seven Hurricanes. 'I was level with the deck,' said Cross, 'then hoisted the Hurricane over the round-down, cut the engine and came down *bonk*! I broke a strut in the tailwheel. Otherwise a piece of cake. I didn't use more than two-thirds of the deck. There was a hell of a wind over the deck this time.' After the Hurricanes came a Walrus with Group Captain Moore on board and last the Swordfish guide. 'All landings were completely successful,' Wells wrote in his report and sent both RAF squadrons a signal of congratulations.

Cross went up to the bridge to report to D'Oyly-Hughes, who 'was complaining about how long we had taken to do it'. The criticism hurt Cross: 'We had watched how the Fleet Air Arm landed, and we thought we were rather classy, doing it the same way.' Cross also noticed the absence of J.B. Heath and asked Ginger Marmont 'Where's Wings?'. '"The Captain has put him ashore," was all he said. We were all a bit sleepy. We'd been flying for practically twenty-four hours. I had the same cabin as the one I'd come out in. We all had some eggs and bacon and cocoa and then went to bed, absolutely flat out.'

The Walrus took Group Captain Moore to *Ark Royal*, landing on at 2.07am. It was the last aircraft ever to take off from *Glorious*. It seemed that D'Oyly-Hughes had a pressing reason for impatience and was eager to return to Scapa Flow. At about 2.25am Commander Le Geyt in *Diana* noticed a signalling lamp in *Glorious* calling up *Ark Royal*. Out of curiosity he told one of his signal staff, Leading Signalman Harris, to read the message. It was a request from *Glorious*, as Le Geyt recalled, 'for permission to part company and proceed ahead to Scapa Flow for the purpose of making preparations for impending courts-martial. The request was approved'. Thus at 2.53am *Glorious*, with her escort of *Acasta* and *Ardent*, detached from the squadron to proceed independently, speed of advance 16 knots. She was routed to pass through three specific positions (her position and mean line of advance for at least the next twenty-four hours would therefore be known in *Ark Royal*).

Meanwhile, back at Bardufoss demolition (delayed until 12.30am on the 8th to deceive the enemy) had begun and some 120 craters were blown in the runway. The ground crews left the field in small unobtrusive parties to assemble in the woods some distance away. Lorries took them to Sorreisa and a destroyer took them out to the *Arandora Star*. They, and the rearguard party of Royal Engineers and Royal Military Police embarked by *Southampton* at 9am on the 8th, were the last to leave.

Arandora Star was one of Group II which had cleared And Fjord by 11 pm that evening (8th) and left the distant rendezvous early on the 9th, escorted by *Southampton* and *Coventry*, with *Havelock*, *Fame*, *Firedrake*, *Beagle* and *Delight*. *Ark Royal*, with *Diana*, *Acheron* and *Highlander*, provided air cover and anti-submarine protection. At midnight on the 9th/10th, being clear of Norwegian waters, Lord Cork hauled down his flag in *Southampton* and the convoy came under the command of the C-in-C Home Fleet.

The Norwegian campaign had taught many hard lessons. For the army the main lessons were the effect of air power on land operations and the need for proper training, with every man physically hard and fit. The Navy also learned the meaning of air power, that it was not possible to maintain the army ashore, or even to keep ships offshore, in the face of determined air attack, without proper air cover. One other lesson was not so obvious; it was not known until much later how many warships and transports had been attacked off Norway by U-boats and how many times the U-boats had been frustrated by torpedo failures. As for the Fleet Air Arm's experience, nobody put it better than Admiral Forbes: 'Our Fleet Air Arm aircraft are hopelessly outclassed by everything that flies in the air and the sooner we get some different aircraft the better. We have made a "false God" of the business of flying on and off a carrier but now that it has been done by four RAF pilots in Gladiators at their first attempt and ten Hurricanes have been flown on to a carrier the matter should be reconsidered.'

But there was another bitter lesson to be learned, or rather relearned, off Norway: an aircraft carrier's force is in her aircraft and an aircraft carrier who, for whatever reason, fails to operate her aircraft is as helpless as a picket boat. As the expeditionary force made its way back to the U.K. this lesson was about to be demonstrated in a most tragic and dramatic manner.

The Germans were surprised, not to say amazed, by the Allies' withdrawal from northern Norway. General Dietl's forces were hard-pressed and were being driven back towards the Swedish frontier. It must have seemed to the Germans that the Allies had only to persevere to be on the brink of winning a major victory. The secret of the evacuation was well kept. Movements of troops and ships were well disguised with 'conflicting rumours and bogus reports'. Before the Germans properly knew what was happening, they were, most unexpectedly, masters of all Norway.

However, the German High Command had had some anxious moments. The slaughter of German destroyers by Warburton-Lee's ships on 10 April and by *Warspite* on the 13th had kept *Scharnhorst* and *Gneisenau* (still being repaired) in harbour ever since for lack of escort. Early in May, as the German situation in Narvik continued to deteriorate, the German Naval Staff began to consider some form of intervention from the sea. On the 14th the staff decided upon a sortie up the Vest Fjord to Narvik and up Vaags Fjord to Harstad using Trondheim as a base.

Admiral Raeder ordered preparations to be made for the operation, but two days later the plan had to be extended to include Hitler's orders that it should also include the supply of stores by sea for the army, on its way up to Narvik, through the leads from Trondheim to Bodo. Clearly this would be a major naval undertaking and light forces would not be enough. Heavy ships would be needed and they would have to operate off the coast for some time. On 21 May Raeder proposed a task force of *Scharnhorst*, *Admiral Hipper* and three destroyers, which would be available from 27 May, and *Gneisenau*, whose repairs would be complete early in June. On 27 May the German B-Dienst 'Y' Intelligence service intercepted and decoded a British W/T message which gave details of the basic organization of the Northern Patrol south of Iceland. This encouraged the German Naval Staff to plan an ambitious operation, code name JUNO, for an attack on Allied shipping at Narvik, Harstad and Bodo, and a prolonged sortie by German heavy ships in northern Norwegian waters.

The German Naval Staff, the Naval Group Commander (West), General-Admiral Saalwaechter, and the fleet commander, Admiral Wilhelm Marschall, were never entirely in agreement about the principal aim of Operation JUNO. This led to some acrimonious argument later. On 29 May Saalwaechter issued a directive to Marschall that his first and main task was to penetrate And Fjord and Vaags Fjord and destroy enemy warships, transports and bases. However, if reconnaissance showed that a penetration of Ofot Fjord, as far as Narvik, was feasible, then *that* was to become the main task. A further task was to safeguard the army's supply line from Trondheim, up to Saltdal, Bodo and Mo. Trondheim was to be the base, but, to achieve surprise, Marschall's ships were not to go there until they had finished their sortie to Narvik.

Marschall discussed JUNO with Raeder two days later and the record of their discussion in War Diary of the Naval Staff seems to give Marschall much more latitude to act as he thought best. JUNO was designed to meet the requirements of the situation on land. Marschall must make his decisions on that basis. 'Primarily,' the diary recorded, 'the intention is to act against the allied naval forces and transports operating against the German Narvik Group, and secondly to afford relief to our land forces. The control in detail of this operation cannot be undertaken by Group West, but must be under the Commander-in-Chief of the Fleet (Marschall) in consultation with Admiral Norway.'

Meanwhile, Trondheim was strengthened and upgraded as a base. Admiral Norway, Admiral Boehm, Fliegerkorps X and Luftflotte V all moved their headquarters there. The anti-aircraft defences were reinforced by several heavy batteries.

Extra tankers and supply ships arrived in the harbour. Two others, *Nordinark* and *Dithmarschen*, were ordered to take up rendezvous positions in the Norwegian Sea from 4 and 6 June. At the end of May German intelligence assessed that there were, in the area of Tromso, Harstad and Narvik, two British battleships, six heavy cruisers, an aircraft carrier and seven destroyers, also that the battleship *Resolution* and the carriers *Ark Royal* and *Glorious*, with three destroyers, would sail from Scapa Flow bound for Vest Fjord at the end of May and the beginning of June respectively. Also off Narvik German intelligence had identified the flag officers commanding the 1st and 20th Cruiser Squadrons and the 9th Destroyer Flotilla. With this knowledge, *Gneisenau* (Kapitan Harald Netzbandt) flying Marschall's flag, *Scharnhorst* (Kapitan Caesar Hoffman), *Admiral Hipper* (Kapitan Hellmuth Heye), flying the flag of Rear-Admiral Schmundt, with the destroyers *Hans Lody* (Kapitan Erich Bey), *Karl Galster. Erich Steinbrinck*, and *Hermann Schoemann*, and the torpedo boats *Jaguar* and *Falke*, sailed from Kiel for JUNO at 8am on 4 June. The ships steamed in line ahead, at 500-metre intervals, behind a screen of four mine-sweepers. It was a bright sunny day, with a calm sea, marred only by the ominous sights of past wrecks: off Kiel a large ore carrier sunk at the beginning of May, showing masts and upperworks above the water, and in the southern part of the Great Belt the wrecks of several minesweepers sunk by mines.

At noon on 4 June Raeder went to brief Hitler on the progress of JUNO. The ships were at sea. Enemy dispositions were at their most favourable, with several British ships under repair. Trondheim had been furnished with fuel, mines, boom defence vessels, a repair ship, ammunition and heavy AA batteries. At this conference Hitler and Raeder also discussed a possible landing by 3,000 men from the Lloyd liners *Europa* and *Bremen* at Lyngen Fjord, some thirty miles east of Tromso. But this never went past the discussion stage.

Off Korsoer the JUNO force was met by more minesweepers who swept them through the Great Belt and the Kattegat. By 6am on the 5th the ships were rounding Skagen and, although there were a couple of submarine alarms, Marschall released *Jaguar* and *Falke* to return to Wilhelmshaven just after midday, after passing through the Skagerrak minefield. Air cover overhead was provided by Heinkel He.111s from first light onwards. By the evening of the 5th Marschall's ships were steaming north-west at 24 knots through patches of fog. By 10am on the 6th the ships were in the latitude of 65°N, north of Trondheim, about a hundred miles from the coast. So far everything had gone according to plan, although *Scharnhorst* reported an engine defect, reducing her top speed to 29 knots, during the day. At 7.20pm that evening *Dithmarschen* came into sight, disguised as a Russian merchantman. *Admiral Hipper* and the destroyers topped up with fuel from her. The fleet steered north-east at low speed in clear visibility and good weather while fuelling.

By 8pm on 6 June Marschall's ships were in 68°N, 2°30'W, a remote area, some 350 miles west of the Lofoten Islands. While his ships refuelled, Marschall considered the evidence available to him of his enemy's strength and disposition. Air reconnaissance had provided little information on the 5th and 6th but 'Y' intelligence reports had located the following ships on the 6th in the north Norwegian area: *Valiant, Glorious, Ark Royal, Southampton, Coventry, Vindictive* and about fifteen destroyers. Their main base was believed to be Harstad. 'Y' intelligence had also reported the movements of heavy ships from Scapa Flow on the 5th (after *Prunella's* report) steering in a north-westerly direction.

The Germans were particularly watchful for any signs of unusual Allied radio activity which might show that Marschall's ships had been sighted. But later on the 6th Saalwaechter signalled Marschall that British radio traffic had no unusual features. His ships had been at sea for two and a half days and were still undetected. All was going well. The German War Staff Diary for the 7th June noted: 'From radio interception in the Harstad area, it appears that there is a British convoy rendezvous off the entrance to Tromso. At 0700 German air reconnaissance sighted four ships and three escorts on a southerly course, about 360 miles north-west of Trondheim; convoy traffic between England and North Norway is particularly active at the moment.

'Air reconnaissance in the area Harstad-Narvik spotted three groups of vessels between 1235 and 1355, about eighty miles north-west of And Fjord. They consisted of one light cruiser, two destroyers, two large ships on a westerly course, two destroyers to the north-west of these, and further to the north *Ark Royal*, *Glorious* and one destroyer stopped. In the evening three patrol boats were sighted by air reconnaissance, 240 miles north-west of Trondheim, steering south-west. The only British heavy ship in the Narvik area was identified by 'Y' as *Valiant*. Radio traffic between Narvik and England shows nothing unusual. The German battleship formation has not so far been spotted. Thus the prospects for our operation are good.'

Prospects certainly did seem good. Marschall had informed his ships by short-range R/T on the 6th that it was his intention to attack Harstad on the night of the 9th. Marschall received the report of the 0700 convoy of seven ships 260 miles north-west of Trondheim as early as 8.20am on the 7th. Although his ships were only some no miles north-west of the convoy, he decided to stick to his plan to attack Harstad. In his opinion, these ships were 'empties' returning to the west. He did not want to give away his presence prematurely for a minor target.

So far Marschall had been somewhat disappointed by the Luftwaffe's contribution. 'Air reconnaissance in northern area is, as previously, not available,' he recorded, sourly, in his diary on the evening of the 7th. In fact, he was being less than fair. At 11.35am that morning air reconnaissance had reported another convoy, a tanker with an escort, steering south-west 220 miles east of his ships. While it was true that air reconnaissance over Narvik and Harstad in the forenoon of the 7th had been thwarted by bad weather, an afternoon flight over the sea area north-west of Harstad revealed 'one cruiser, two destroyers, two large ships at 1325 in the northern entrance of And Fjord, proceeding west at medium speed, and two destroyers at 1345, twenty-five miles north of Andenes, on a northerly course. Also two aircraft carriers and two destroyers stopped at 1400, about forty-five miles north of Andenes.'

This message was received in *Gneisenau* via Group West at 8.55pm on the 7th, when Admiral Marschall was in conference. Fuelling had been completed at 6pm and, in Nelsonian fashion, Marschall had summoned his fellow captains on board his flagship to discuss with them his plans for the operation against Harstad. Present were the Chief of Staff, Rear-Admiral Otto Backenkohler, and Schmundt; Hoffmann, Netzbandt, Heye and Erich Bey; the destroyer captains, Huberts Baron von Wangenheim (*Lody*), Rolf Johannesson (*Steinbrinck*), Theodor Baron von Bechtolsheim (*Galster*) and Theodor Detmers (*Schoemann*); and several other officers, such as Ulrich

Brocksien, the Operations Officer, and *Gneisenau*'s navigating officer, Commander Hans Eberhard Busch.

The mood of the meeting was generally against the Harstad operation. The captains present were being called upon to venture their ships into the confined waters of fjords with no knowledge of the defences, the mines, nets, booms, shore batteries, ships and shore-based aircraft they might find there. Feelings were running so high that Marschall had eventually to tell Schmundt, rather sharply, 'You can rest assured that I shall not send the ships on any senseless foray'. Nevertheless, Marschall had been ordered to carry out Operation Harstad and it seemed it would go ahead. Lieutenant-Commander Wolfgang Kahler, *Gneisenau*'s second gunnery officer, wrote in his diary: 'It looks as though we may lose the whole Fleet without gaining any appreciable success.'

But the signal containing the new reconnaissance information put a completely different aspect on the situation. The signal had nothing to say about Harstad or Vaags Fjord, but it did show a general westward movement of numbers of British naval units. It now seemed that the main targets were at sea and not in the fjords, and they were all steaming *west*. It was left to the youngest officer on the Admiral's staff and the most junior present, Lieutenant Heinz Kohler, to remark, like the child who pointed out that the emperor had no clothes on, what had escaped his seniors, Group West and the German B-Dienst service: 'Can the British perhaps be pulling out?'

More evidence arrived later that evening which appears to have changed the fleet commander's mind. It was a delayed signal, originated by Admiral Norway at 11.10am that morning, but not received in *Gneisenau* until 11.30pm. It was a report from a reconnaissance aircraft which had flown over Harstad and had been fired at in Vaags Fjord by one gunboat. It was hardly dramatic evidence, but it did suggest that enemy reaction was now light. Maybe, if Marschall's ships did penetrate the fjords, they would find their birds had flown.

By midnight Marschall had made his decision and at three minutes past he broadcast to his ships by short-range R/T that their objective would now be the convoys which had been reported. Ships would go to Battle Order 2 at 2am and to Battle Order 1 (full action stations) at 4am. Battle speed was 28 knots. This was a most fortunate change of plan for the Germans. By luck Marschall's powerful force was squarely athwart the homeward route of the convoys and the Kriegsmarine could be on the brink of inflicting an appalling catastrophe upon the Royal Navy.

Nevertheless, this possibility was not grasped in Germany. When Marschall signalled his new intentions at 4am that morning, the response from Saalwaechter at 5.58am was discouraging: 'Failing important reason not known here for attack on convoy proceed with main task, Harstad.' And later: 'Convoy attack to be delegated to *Hipper* and destroyers. Further target Trondheim. Main objective remains Harstad.' But Marschall was already committed. As he said himself, 'It seemed an attack on Harstad would be like beating the air.' Furthermore, targets were already appearing.

Marschall's ships spread out in line abreast, in a broad search formation, steering east-north-east at 15 knots. The wind was light to moderate force 4 from the west-north-west, with a long swell, and, as it was for most of this period of operations, visibility was exceptionally good. (One of the most disconcerting aspects of the proposed Harstad operation, for Marschall and his captains, had been the knowledge that their ships would have been visible more than twenty-five miles offshore.) At 5.55am *Hipper* first, and then *Gneisenau* soon after, sighted a British tanker, *Oil Pioneer* (5,600 tons), escorted by the anti-submarine trawler *Juniper*.

Juniper challenged *Admiral Hipper* by light: 'What ship?' To confuse matters and to delay the possibility of *Juniper* broadcasting an alarm, *Gneisenau* replied '*Southampton*', before what the Germans called 'an annihilating fire' was poured upon *Juniper* by *Hipper*. Meanwhile *Oil Pioneer* was under fire from *Gneisenau*'s secondary armament and was soon on fire and sinking. Her crew abandoned her and she was finally sunk by a torpedo from *Hipper*. Neither ship was able to transmit any signal. Twenty-nine survivors were picked up.

But these two were only small fry and clearly not the convoy reported the previous day. Marschall's ships altered course to north-north-west shortly after 8am. The Arado Ar 196 floatplanes from *Scharnhorst* and *Admiral Hipper* were both launched at 8.26, *Scharnhorst*'s to search to the north, *Hipper*'s to the south.

Hipper's Arado reported first, at 9.26: one heavy cruiser, one destroyer and a cargo ship, steering north. At 10am *Scharnhorst*'s plane reported an auxiliary ship of some 10,000 tons steering south-west. In the very clear weather *Scharnhorst*'s lookouts had already sighted one ship at 9.44, range 37,500 metres (twenty-three miles) and sighted another at 10.23.

The first ship was the hospital ship *Atlantis*. She was not attacked; she respected her side of the Geneva Convention and made no wireless transmissions. The second ship was the 19,000-ton troopship *Orama* who had sailed from Norway the day before. She had not had enough fuel or fresh water to wait for the rest of Group II and had sailed alone and empty, except for about a hundred German PoWs. *Hipper* and the destroyers were dispatched to sink her. *Hipper* opened fire at 10.58 and finally sank *Orama* with a torpedo at 11.21. She and the destroyers picked up 275 survivors and rejoined. All *Orama*'s attempts to send an SOS message were jammed by *Gneisenau*.

Scharnhorst and *Gneisenau* meanwhile had been searching unsuccessfully for the ships reported to the south. Both ships steamed south-east at 25 knots for some time before the suspicion began to arise that maybe *Hipper*'s Arado pilot had been reporting Marschall's own ships. The search was called off just before 2pm on the 8th, Marschall signalling to Group West at 1.47pm.: 'Hauling to the north to operational area Tromso-Harstad'.

By then Marschall was convinced that the British Admiralty *must* know of his ships' presence. *Hipper* and the destroyers were not likely to have another chance to refuel undisturbed, so Marschall detached them at 1.48 to Trondheim to refuel and then to operate in support of the German supply route from Trondheim to Bodo. This action weakened his force and eventually led to an earlier end of Operation JUNO. It was also directly opposite to the instructions signalled by Saalwaechter. *Hipper* and the destroyers were supposed to have gone after the convoys and were now on their way to Trondheim. The heavy ships were supposed to have gone to Trondheim and were now on their way to look for the convoys. But it is an old naval dictum that the man on the spot knows best, and Marschall was prepared to back his own judgement and, as he said later, 'to answer for my decision before a court-martial'. In any case, Raeder had given him verbal permission to attack 'worthwhile targets at sea'.

Thus Marschall turned north again in some haste. Much ground had been lost in the fruitless search to the south, which must now be made up. His B-Dienst intelligence section in *Gneisenau*, under Lieutenant-Commander Reichardt, had been reporting numerous transmissions from the north, from *Southampton*, from *Ark Royal* and from *Glorious*. That was where the best targets were now — to the north.

In fact the Admiralty did *not* know that *Scharnhorst* and *Gneisenau* were at sea, although they might have deduced it had they accepted some of the advice they were offered. As the Germans conquered more of Norway, the German naval signals system was further extended and better established in the country. The Naval Section at the Government Code and Cypher School at Bletchley Park had devised techniques for making inferences about the movements of German ships from the wireless traffic. Any increases or decreases in wireless traffic, any additions or alterations to call-signs, anything unusual, could give valuable clues as to which ships were operating and where.

The Naval Section had begun to report to the Operational Intelligence Centre in the Admiralty at least a fortnight before *Scharnhorst* and *Gneisenau* sailed that inferences made from the behaviour of German naval signal traffic suggested that German heavy units were getting ready to move from the Baltic northwards up the Norwegian coast. The Naval Section's warning's were so numerous and frequent that by 29 May they were included in the OIC Daily Reports, that 'from a study of German naval W/T traffic... there would appear to be a movement of certain enemy ships, class and type unknown, from the Baltic to the Skagerrak'. By 7 June the reports were specific enough to say that 'Wireless Telegraphy Intelligence indicates that German naval forces in Norwegian waters may in future be associated in any offensive action taken by German units in the North Sea'.

In some curious way *Scharnhorst* and *Gneisenau* seemed to have dropped out of the combined consciousness of staff and intelligence officers. They had not been seen or heard of for weeks and everybody seemed to have developed a mental blind spot over their very existence. OIC was not convinced by the Naval Section's urgings and refused to issue even a qualified warning to the Home Fleet. Coastal Command was not warned (although it was stated later in Parliament that the A-O-C-in-C Coastal Command was) and thus carried out no special reconnaissance flights over the routes which the homeward-bound convoys were to take. This was because the evacuation from Narvik was carried out in such secrecy that only the most senior officers in OIC knew of it; the duty officer in OIC knew nothing of naval movements from Norway. At that stage of the war the Naval Section at Bletchley Park was not informed of British naval movements in general, let alone such a closely guarded secret as the Narvik evacuation, or they might have pressed their warnings harder. Contacts between operational and intelligence staff in the Admiralty left room for improvement.

The only agencies to sight *Scharnhorst* and *Gneisenau* were the Norwegian coast-watchers. A message of their report of 'two battleships' was passed by telephone to Wing Commander Atcherley's operations room at Bardufoss, where it caused some hilarity. (Atcherley's parting remark as he left Bardufoss was, 'Look out for the bloody battleships!') In any case, it was felt, understandably, that battleships were the Navy's responsibility and the Navy must already know about them.

Thus it came about that the Royal Navy was caught totally unaware at 3.45pm on 8 June when Midshipman Siegfried Goss, on watch in the foretop of *Scharnhorst*, saw and reported a wisp of smoke far away on the eastern horizon, range more than twenty-eight miles.

CHAPTER 10: THE LOSS OF
GLORIOUS

IN HIS OLD cabin near the quarterdeck Bing Cross slept the sleep of the just — and of the utterly exhausted. He and his squadron were entitled to their rest. They had, as they thought, saved ten priceless Hurricanes for service at home ('I had saved some equipment from Norway and got it on the warship,' he told *The Scotsman* circumspectly) and in so doing had unknowingly performed a tremendous service for the Fleet Air Arm, by demonstrating that high-performance fighters could land on carriers. The only defects were three damaged tail-wheel struts, which were repaired that day. 'I am convinced that the Hurricane is a practical proposition as a fleet fighter,' Cross wrote to Heath, 'and I am going to put in a report to the Air Ministry to that effect.'

When Cross woke up late that forenoon and went on deck he was puzzled by the lack of activity. In contrast to his previous stay in the ship, when there had been anti-submarine patrols and CAPs flying almost round the clock, the flight deck was silent and deserted. There was no flying and there had been none since *Glorious* detached to proceed home independently. One Swordfish and a section of three Sea Gladiators were at ten minutes' notice, but they were not ranged on the flight deck.

It seemed that risk of attack by surface ships had been completely discounted, but there were still other dangers 'When I woke up I went up to the island,' said Cross; 'everybody not on watch was sitting in corners. I saw in the Plot the line [on the chart] from where we were, straight to

Scapa. "We're short of fuel," somebody told me. We were 200 miles off the Norwegian coast. Exactly right for the Luftwaffe! A nice convenient distance away. I said, "Have we got a search up?" And whoever it was said, "No, we're doing seventeen knots and that's too fast for any submarine to torpedo us."' With that explanation Cross had to be satisfied. (However, as he noted, his Hurricanes were stowed in the after part of the hangar, leaving the forward part of the hangar and the forward lift clear, so theories put forward later, that the RAF fighters on board in some way hindered the operation of the ship's own aircraft, were without foundation.)

The whole ship seemed gripped by a curious lassitude, as though everybody was out on his feet after the exertions of the past few days and the tensions of operating off an enemy coastline. There was almost a 'holiday' atmosphere on board. Dick Leggott, with the other Sea Gladiator pilots, had been flying or on stand-by until the early hours of the morning. 'We were to report at our aircraft in the hangar at 0900. Our C.O. and the C.O. of 823 appeared some twenty minutes later, having conferred with the Captain. One of our pilots noticed that warheads were being removed from torpedoes and other armaments that were normally in "ready-use" stowages when we were in the war zone were being struck down or stowed away. The Chief Torpedo Instructor, in reply to one of our squadron, said with a happy smile that they were getting a "lap ahead" to get ready for giving leave. This seemed very wrong to some of us.'

But the feeling of excitement at being on the way home, and of relief that dangers were past, were infectious. 'It was a nice warm day, not much wind blowing over the flight deck, and we pilots of the fighter squadron left the hangar, climbed the ladders to the flight deck, enjoyed the sunshine and watched the wake making a trail to the horizon astern of us in a fairly calm sea. We relaxed and laughed about this and that… Not a care in the world. Other people may have had their problems, but not us. These were the golden days of our lives. Courts-martial? Not us. Our fighter squadron was "fire-proof". Half the squadron at a time were stood down for forty-five minutes to go to lunch and similarly for tea. Otherwise we remained on the flight deck or in the aircrew ready room in the island.'

At least one man had some form of premonition. Petty Officer George Elliott was a seaman P.O., a member of the flight-deck party. He had been on board since commissioning in January, 1937. His action station was on the 20mm pom-pom director on the lower flying-off deck. On that lovely afternoon he was sitting with his back to the bulkhead in one of the boat bays on the gallery deck, with the sun streaming down: 'Warm as anything. But somewhere about three o'clock I thought there was something wrong. I could feel the engines vibrating. I felt a bit uneasy. We'd been up there before and we'd been bombed repeatedly. So I went down to the mess then for a cup of tea. It was teatime. Four o'clock. They were a bit uneasy down the mess. Knew something was happening but didn't know what.'

There seemed nothing to justify such unease. *Glorious* had reduced to 17 knots at 7am that morning, with twelve of her eighteen boilers connected, and was zig-zagging about a mean course of 250°. The ship's company were at cruising stations, in the fourth degree of readiness. *Glorious* had no radar, but there was no look-out in the crow's nest on that day of extreme visibility. The wind was light, northwesterly, force 2-3, with a north-westerly swell. The two escorting destroyers *Ardent* and *Acasta* were keeping station ahead of *Glorious*, one on each bow.

Almost everybody was having tea when the incredible happened. Leggott was in the aircrew mess, enjoying tea, toast with strawberry jam and a thick slice of Madeira cake (liquid and sustenance which very probably helped to save his life) when 'sharply and suddenly *Glorious* heeled over to port as she turned hard to starboard and through the glass of a closed porthole I saw SPLASH SPLASH SPLASH and heard the sharp crack of explosions. Over the Tannoy system came a "pipe" and the boatswain's mate's voice: "Range one Swordfish". It sounded mighty odd to me... when the pipe came again: "Range two Swordfish" and within seconds: "Range all Swordfish aircraft". I had finished my cup of tea, also my toast and the remnants of the Madeira cake, when the alarm [came]. My most beauteous and indulgent "Guardian Angel" had just laid a gently restraining hand on my shoulder. For then I heard the pipe: "All aircrew muster at their aircraft"!'

When the smoke on the horizon was sighted *Scharnhorst* and *Gneisenau* were steering 330° at 19 knots, on their way to keep a rendezvous with *Dithmarschen* (who had already signalled that day that she had sighted 'two large unknown steamers'). The smoke was just a momentary puff which disappeared and the Germans later admitted that, had it not been for that burst of smoke and the sharp-sighted Midshipman, they would have steamed onwards.

Both battle cruisers were fitted with Seetakt surface radar and it seems they had a radar contact at the time; 'The enemy warship was traced passing to starboard at full speed.' Certainly the target-bearing was moving rapidly right, but Marschall stood on to the north-west for some time 'until he had enough steam for high speed'. He then turned to the north-east and then at 4.21 to the south-east at 16 knots. If the enemy was one of the aircraft carriers reported, Marschall's ships were now to windward of her; in the language of the days of sail, they had the weather gauge.

When the Germans first saw what they described as the 'lattice mast' of the enemy, they thought it was a battleship. At 4.10 *Scharnhorst's* Gunnery Officer, Commander Wolf Lowisch, reported that he could see a large funnel, a mast with a turret and probably a flight deck. Three minutes later he identified the target as *Ark Royal* and, now that two smaller masts were visible, an escort of two destroyers.

Scharnhorst, now the leading ship, opened fire at 4.32 with her two forward 11" turrets, 'Anton' and 'Bruno', at a range of some 28,000 yards (fourteen nautical miles). Ranging by radar and by superb optical range-finders, the German shooting opened, as always, fast and accurate. Her first salvo was short, her second a straddle and her third at 4.38 a hit. Between the distant tiny columns of leaping water, on the blur of a grey hull, there was a momentary glow and an unmistakeable smudge of brown smoke which hung in the air. Soon after, *Scharnhorst* had a second hit, and a third, and, when *Gneisenau's* main armament opened at 4.46, the target was soon hidden behind shell-splashes, from which an ominous smoke pall was streaming downwind. Meanwhile the 'northernmost destroyer', actually *Ardent*, was approaching the battle cruisers, flashing a challenge, and soon afterwards opening with her 4.7" guns, which were well out of range. Neither battle cruiser answered the challenge: *Gneisenau* replied with her secondary 5.9" guns.

When two sizeable strange ships were sighted on the northwestern horizon, bearing Green 070, broad on the starboard bow, then D'Oyly-Hughes, his detractors might have said, should have realized that this was his opportunity. After all, he had always said that when the time came he would use *Glorious* as a capital ship. He had alarmed his ship's company with his expressed designs on *Graf Spee* in the Indian Ocean. He was, as the Fleet Air Arm saying had it, a 'kick the tyre, light the fire — and *smash off*' type himself. Now, surely, cynics might say, was his chance to win the Victoria Cross and advance towards the enemy, all guns firing.

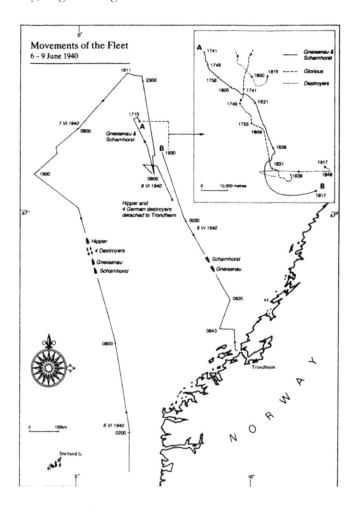

In fact the reality was somewhat different. Very prudently and sensibly D'Oyly-Hughes turned away, first to the south and then to the south-east (which was downwind). According to the recollections of two officers of 823 Squadron, Sub-Lieutenant (A) Ian MacLachlan, who was on the flight deck for most of the action, and Midshipman (A) Eric Baldwin, who was in the Plot, the two strange ships were sighted at about 4pm. They did not reply to a challenge from *Glorious*. The Gunner's Mate was sent aloft to identify them. By the time he had returned, saying they were cruisers, one 8" *Hipper* Class and one 6" class, the ships had opened fire on *Ardent* who had closed them to investigate. Neither MacLachlan nor Baldwin saw anything of *Ardent* again.

One Swordfish was piped to be ranged at about 4.05 and immediately afterwards all five Swordfish were piped, with torpedoes. But only three of the Swordfish were fitted with torpedo-carrying racks; the others had been removed for a bombing raid the previous day and had not been replaced. At this time D'Oyly-Hughes was heard to order a course of 1600 and a speed of 27 knots. Once again, and for the last time, the engine-room department exerted themselves to the utmost to flash up and connect boilers and warm through steam piping, processes which normally took some time but now had to be completed in a very short time indeed. Once again the engine-room accomplished it: Marschall was well aware that he had a speedy opponent and he must close the range quickly. At one stage in the action *Scharnhorst* and *Gneisenau* were going 29 knots and the *Scharnhorst*'s officers noted that the enemy was 'at great range' and apparently gaining on them. Marine Ronald Healiss, closed up at P.7 4.7", noted that *Glorious* was 'shuddering with speed'.

But the spectacle which engrossed everybody, friend and foe, was the intense activity on *Glorious'* flight deck and the frantic race to get the Swordfish armed and away. From the flag-bridge in *Gneisenau* Marschall himself watched through binoculars the aircraft being ranged and the figures swarming around them, before, in his own words, gunfire tore up large sections of the flight deck 'like the lid of a box'.

At least one member of 823 Squadron actually manned his Swordfish. He was Naval Airman and Air Gunner 3rd Class Bob McBride. He was nineteen years old, newly drafted to the squadron from the replacement pool. He had made only a couple of flights with his new crew 'Sub-Lieutenant King [sic: the name is not in the list of *Glorious'* aircrew] as pilot and Midshipman Baldwin as observer... I was flat on my back trying to decide what to get for tea from the NAAFI when "Stand by Aircraft" was piped to be ranged, and "Crews to the Ops Room". Two Swordfish, mine and another, were ranged and in the Ops Room I learned we were to carry out an "identification flight" to find out about two unknown ships, hull down, but closing. At this stage everything seemed normal. I manned the aircraft and carried out my checks but when I looked out of the office I saw water spouts from salvoes which had dropped short. At this time the ship broadcast an Alarm Report addressed to the Admiralty. I was wearing headphones... the noise nearly blew my head off! Since this was the first time I had ever heard such a message, it stuck in my memory and I recorded the entire message in my W/T log... It read: "Broadcast Alarm — Two battleships bearing 310 degrees distance eight miles", followed by a position.

'The flight deck was completely clear of personnel. I appeared to be entirely alone, with no signs of the pilot or observer, whom I presumed to be still in the Ops Room. I left the aircraft and headed for the Island to find out what was happening. I reached the starboard nets and heard shells coming, so I dropped into the nets. There was a loud explosion, and both aircraft were gone.'

That signal was probably transmitted at 4.15 and, although its signal strength was enough nearly to blow McBride's head off, it was not received by any other ship or shore station. It was not even received by Reichardt and the B-Dienst crews in *Gneisenau*, although they were listening out on what they called 'all the relevant enemy channels', waiting to jam any signal. Mr Edward Blackwell, *Glorious*' Warrant Telegraphist, was closely questioned when he returned from PoW camp after the war. He recalled that *Glorious* had shifted from Narvik to Home Station frequencies at 1pm on the 8th and an enemy report was made at 4.15 on 253 kilocycles. The cruisers were keeping radio watch on 230 k/cs and the carriers themselves on area wave 3,700 k/cs and 51.5 k/cs. *Ardent* and *Acasta* were probably keeping watch on 3,700 or 51.5 k/cs but no ship received any signal from them at any time. 'Blood' Scarlett, captured by the Italians at Taranto, shared a PoW camp with Blackwell for a period and recalls Blackwell saying that D'Oyly-Hughes gave him a signal saying, 'Here, send this: "Two pocket battleships etc…".' But Reichardt later said that he and his staff heard no station acknowledging *Glorious*' 4.15 signal and it seems it was somehow lost in the ether.

But there could be no possible doubt about that first 11" shell hit which demolished McBride's Swordfish, penetrated the flight deck and detonated inside the hanger. It seemed to Healiss to be almost above his head: 'The flightdeck above us was wreathed in smoke, then tongues of flame, then the staccato sounds of fire rose to a great roar and a red wall like a living furnace rose from the hanger-well.'

The blast wrecked the Hurricanes (somebody actually said to Cross, 'Bad luck your Hurricanes have copped it!') and started a major fire in which exploding .303 ammunition, ricocheting off aircraft and bulkheads, added to the confusion. The C.O. and some of the pilots of 802 were also in the hangar. Marmont had been to see D'Oyly-Hughes with a suggestion that a Sea Gladiator fly off to find *Ark Royal* and had just come back with the Captain's reply. According to Leggott, D'Oyly-Hughes 'had repudiated his (Marmont's) proposals in no uncertain terms, with a final statement to the effect that "Surely you don't wish your pilots to behave like rats leaving a sinking ship".'

802 had no more time to debate the justice of the reply. 'We had been so engrossed in our discussion that the first shock of exploding shells barely registered until, in my case, I saw that my fitter had been hit in the chest with a largish heavy fragment of black smoking shell. He fell flat on his back on the hanger deck. He exclaimed, "Oh my wife and children" and was dead before a move to assist him could be made.'

Supply Chief Petty Officer (Stores) Arthur Lidstone's action station was the Fleet Air Arm store rooms in the upper hangar. He had made his way there with his storeroom keys and an electric torch and an inflatable lifejacket. 'Almost as soon as I reached my station I heard the "scream" of the first salvo from the enemy passing over the ship, followed by the roar of the explosions just beyond us. The very next came inboard and although it is hard to remember very clearly what actually happened from now on, I know the hangar I was in was soon aflame and the aircraft stowed there were wrecked and afire. Everything was utter chaos and I felt the hangar was not the place for me so I returned to the port gallery deck for a short while.' This was a prudent retreat. Fed by streams of petrol from the shattered aircraft, the fire in the hangar was almost put of control. The hangar had to be evacuated, the fire curtains lowered and the hangar sprayed, which temporarily quenched the flames.

In the third or fourth salvo at about 5pm *Glorious* suffered another hit. 'Then it came again,' wrote Healiss, 'like distant thunder, culminating in a sudden wall of vicious sound, leaving the whole gun platform shuddering with the impact. Merciful God, they'd got their range right...

'I looked up the cliff face of the wall of steel forward of the bridge and saw the steel shattering. Plumes of smoke filled the air as I watched in horror. They'd hit the bridge. At the impact I threw myself on the platform instinctively.'

It seems that shell was a direct hit on the island and it killed almost everybody on the bridge and in the adjacent compartments. There were the wildest rumours that D'Oyly-Hughes recovered consciousness to find he had lost both legs and to ask for a cigarette, but it seems virtually certain he was killed outright, with Slessor and Newnham and Parkin and Wells and Guy Steel. Blast plays curious tricks and there were selective miracles of survival. At the wheel in the steering compartment directly below the bridge was the action helmsman, Able Seaman Bill Pascoe, a burly, jovial three-badge West-countryman, captain and centre-forward of the ship's water polo team and one of the ship's characters. He said later that when he had recovered from the effect of the blast and got to his feet again he found himself literally standing in the open air with nothing over his head and the body of Newnham the Navigating Officer, in two halves, on the deck either side of him. But the ship was still answering the helm and, as he had been given no instructions to leave the wheel, he carried on steering the last course he had been given.

Glorious did transmit at least one more signal before the island and bridge were destroyed, although it is possible that the signal was sent after the shell hit; the main W/T office, coding office and transmitting equipment were in compartments on the starboard side of the upper gallery deck (one deck below the flight deck) and just forward of the island. The main W/T aerial masts would have been lowered at action stations, but, even though damaged, they might still have been capable of transmitting a message at reduced power.

At 5.20 the cruiser *Devonshire* picked up a faint and puzzling message ('reception very doubtful' was her signals staff's description) on 3,700 k/cs. It read: 'R.A.A. from *Glorious*, followed by a word or words which were corrupt, (possibly the single word 'CONFIRM') MY 1615 2 P.B. TIME OF ORIGIN 1640.' R.A.A. was of course, Rear Admiral Aircraft Carriers, Vice-Admiral Wells, and '2 P.B.' has been taken to refer to 'Two Pocket Battleships'.

At 4pm on the 8th *Devonshire* bore 078° (eastward) of *Glorious*, eighty to a hundred miles away. *Ark Royal* and her escorting destroyers bore 063° (northeast) 190 miles. *Southampton* and *Coventry* bore 0750 (east) 200 miles and *Valiant* 2120 (south-west) 470 miles. None of these ships received *Glorious'* '2, P.B.' signal of 1615 and only *Devonshire* received the 1640 signal, faintly and in what seemed to be a corrupt form. No shore station received either signal. Neither *Acasta* nor *Ardent* appear to have made any signal.

Devonshire had King Haakon and his retinue embarked and Vice-Admiral John Cunningham did not feel justified in breaking radio silence to pass on this cryptic whisper, which was not addressed to him or his ship and which, on the face of it, had no discernible relevance or significance. The 1615 signal, like the 1640, would have been addressed to Vice-

Admiral Wells and it would be reasonable to conclude that it referred to carrier squadron business. In the circumstances Admiral Cunningham's decision was unquestionably correct.

Ironically, it was the enemy who had the best radio reception from *Glorious*. At 4.52 Reichardt's listeners picked up a signal to Scapa Flow on the Home Fleet's short 36.19-metre wavelength, timing the sighting of the enemy at 1615. But, according to a German account, 'The transmission oscillated badly and frequently went dead and the monitoring Germans were hard put to it to make sense of the broken fragments.' At 5.19 the Germans detected an attempt by *Glorious* to call 'the C-in-C Aircraft Carriers on the northern Norway band. But her operators got no further: the transmission was promptly jammed' by *Gneisenau* who transmitted at full power a previously prepared signal which purported to be from the Admiralty.

Although by 4.52pm *Glorious* had become 'a pillar of smoke and flame' she was still, according to the Germans, 'moving at full speed'. Provided she could maintain speed it was just remotely possible *Glorious* could escape. A message over the Tannoy had broadcast that Commander Lovell, from the Lower Conning Tower (which was deep down in the ship on the lower deck) had taken command. The Commander's action station was purposely chosen to be as far from the bridge as practicable, so that both Captain and Commander should not be killed in the same incident — a sensible precaution, as *Glorious* had just proved. With luck and speed Lovell might be able to take the ship to safety.

But it was not to be. A hit in the boiler uptakes, or possibly smoke from a fire being drawn down into the boiler-rooms caused a drop in steam pressure (the boiler-room crew might have evacuated). *Glorious*' speed faltered, allowing *Scharnhorst* and *Gneisenau* to close and station themselves one on each of *Glorious'* quarters, whence they could shell her at will.

Stoker James O'Neill was a member of a fire and repair party. His action station was in the heavy machine workshop on the main deck above the centre forward engine room. He had been ordered to go forward to the stokers' messdeck to fetch the Leading Stokers' anti-flash gear. 'On the way there I could see it was a losing fight because Jerry was hitting hard and heavy and we could not get close enough with 4.7ins to return fire. After getting to the mess deck I was wondering if I should ever make my way back again. It seemed hours getting back but it must only have been a matter of minutes. Orders came through for us to go and put a fire out on P.4 gun. When we got to it all about the place were dead bodies. Some played hoses on the flames, others had to throw ammunition overboard. The hoses were washing the remains of some of our shipmates off the bulkheads. Having managed the fire, we were ordered to go below again; some of the young lads were wondering when their turn would come. Then a fire started in the intake to "C" boiler room and the boilers had to be shut down.'

The order was passed to 'Abandon Ship' but cancelled. 'We scrambled up the hatches,' wrote James O'Neill, 'thankful for having a chance to save our own lives, but disappointment was at hand. The order was belayed, so we had to return. The time was about 17.10.'

By this time *Glorious* was being hit almost continuously, but there was one hit, in or around the centre engine room, which all the survivors subsequently remembered. The ship's hull seemed to shake for some moments, like a horse lashed by a whip. 'It was that instant another salvo hit,' wrote Healiss, 'and the whole side of the *Glorious* seemed to cave in, leaving a choking cloud of smoke and a thunderous roar that echoed away to the darkening sky. The sea, so calm before the action, was now churned up and flecked with ugly grey. God, I thought, we've nearly had our chips. Stupefied, we waited. And I wish we hadn't. For that's when I saw Ginger McColl. He was walking over from his post with P.5. Walking. Holding on the crazily twisted rails of the ship and laughing at me.

'Then I saw why he was walking oddly. His uniform was ragged, what was left of it. Just a torn shirt and part of his trousers. One leg was shot off and there was the splintered bone, dripping red and black blood, and white strings of sinews. My throat was full of spittle and I could vomit just to look at him.'

Another enormous fire was raging in the lower hangar and O'Neill's party was sent to try and deal with it. 'I was senior hand after the leading stoker so we had to go together. We looked in the hanger; it was a terrific fire by now. We had no need to go through the doors because the sides in places had been blown away. It was a hopeless job trying to seam the fire, all the planes were burning and water was useless against it. Shrapnel was flying all over the place; it was a miracle how I never got hit. I saw one chap with no legs, burning; he was lying on a fire. I picked him up and dropped him against the bulkhead. It was a sickly thud when his body hit and even now I hear it in my sleep. I put the flames out on his clothing but it was useless; the poor lad had died.'

Meanwhile, Healiss and his guns' crew were trying to open a door into the lower hangar on the other side of the ship. 'Another swing and we've done it, boys... With our combined weight we heaved and the door gave. It gave so suddenly we were all flung on our backsides and the flame gushed out like the very flames of hell. I thought the huge steel door of the hangar would never swing back. It was like the boiler end of an express train coming up at you.

'We scrambled up, cursing the fire, cursing the door, shouting to one another for help to get it shut again, as the giant inrush of air gave new zest to the furnace. As tongues of flame shot out I got to one side of the door... and as we began to heave it shut there was a sight on the deck such as I could never picture even in a nightmare.

'The wheel-lock of that door had huge star-fish spokes. The spokes of that wheel had pinned one of the crew, running right through his body with a clear X pattern like a bruised hot-cross bun. He must have died instantly, the way the imprint of the wheel was left right through his diaphragm. And there was a bit of his shirt, squelching blood, still hanging from the wheel-lock.'

In the noise and the confusion the minute-by-minute experience of some of the ship's company took on the disjointed surrealism of a nightmare. Stoker Cyril Hobbs' action station was the after lift. He and a colleague took the Swordfish up to the fighter deck. Hobbs normally stood on the quarterdeck while the other stoker was on the flight deck. 'Unfortunately my friend was blown over the side... Don't remember his name. Another stoker. It is very difficult to remember who you really saw. One chap, a stoker, I remember he was a diver, did deep diving, he said to me, "I'm sorry Cyril, I've got to go back and get my lifejacket. I haven't got it." He disappeared towards midships and that was the last I saw of him. This RAF chap, a sergeant, he wanted to go back and get his keys. For the petrol, fuel for the Hurricanes. But Hurricanes only had machine guns, what could they do? It was very noisy... Lot of flame and smoke... There was a terrific crash on the flight deck... All you could see was daylight up there... The RAF sergeant, as far as I know, was thrown overboard with the rest of the planes. The action was an hour and a half. Quite a long time to stick to it... Machine-gun bullets were flying about, left, right and centre... There were terrific fires going. We thought the torpedoes in the hangar were going to go up... We were told to lie down and stay where we were. Then somebody told us to abandon ship.'

It was very probably Lovell himself who countermanded the first order to abandon ship. After finding himself in command he would wish to assess the latest situation. Also there was an unexpected lull in the action when the German ships (according to German sources) had to cease fire for some twenty minutes because they could no longer see through the dense smokescreens laid by *Ardent* and *Acasta* and, involuntarily, because of her action damage, by *Glorious* herself.

Scharnhorst had a defect in one boiler room and her speed dropped to 28½ knots. Because of this the distance between her and *Gneisenau* opened to 4,000 metres, causing Marschall some concern; he required both ships to keep together to provide mutual protection against torpedo attack. He now felt particularly the need for the four destroyers which he had dispatched to Trondheim; indeed he signalled them and *Hipper* to turn back, but they had no chance of taking any part in the action.

The vulnerability even of capital ships to attack by one destroyer was dramatically illustrated by *Ardent* (Lieutenant-Commander J.F. Barker). Having sallied out to challenge the enemy, and having laid a protective smokescreen, *Ardent* continued to close *Scharnhorst* and *Gneisenau* at full speed, firing her two forward 4.7" guns, although they could only barely have been within range. *Scharnhorst* fought off the destroyer with her secondary armament and her anti-aircraft flak guns, expending a large amount of ammunition, with *Gneisenau* also firing from time to time.

Ardent continued to close, even though she was badly damaged. 'Very soon we knew they were German battleships,' wrote Able Seaman Roger Hooke, a member of *Ardent*'s 'X' gun's crew, 'and then the fun started. They opened fire on us and hit us in No 1 boiler room with the very first salvo, which naturally reduced our speed a little. We endeavoured to put them off by zigzagging but time after time we were hit and, considering the distance between us, it proved the accuracy of their guns and rangefinders. Our guns were really of no great hindrance to the German ships and we got into position for torpedo firing. We fired four torpedoes but the ships did not seem to make any alteration in course at all.'

Ardent was more effective than Hooke knew. It seems that she did obtain one 4.7" hit on *Scharnhorst* on the upper deck abreast 'B' Turret. Lieutenant Siegfried Flister, the officer of the quarters of 'A' turret, became a U-boat officer later in the war and when the U-boat he was serving in was sunk by the destroyer *Vanoc* in March, 1941, he told one of *Vanoc*'s midshipmen that he saw a flash from one of the destroyer's guns and 'the shell hit the middle gun of "B" turret and tore up the deck where he (Flister) had just been standing.'

Nobody admired *Ardent*'s last attack more than her opponents. 'She fought with outstanding resolution,' wrote Commander Schubert, *Scharnhorst*'s Executive Officer, 'in a situation that was hopeless for her. The destroyer received numerous hits and finally went down, her bow armament firing to the last and her engines apparently in order and driving her at high speed. The final range was about five miles.' *Ardent* appears to have capsized and sunk at about 5.28. Her last torpedo passed only a few yards in front of *Scharnhorst*'s bows.

Roger Hooke was one of *Ardent*'s survivors: 'All this time we were being hit time and again and many men were being injured so that it soon became a call of every man for himself. The ship was listing well to port and still doing about 15 knots and there seemed to be no way of stopping her, so that boats could not be lowered to pick up men who had already jumped for it. What with the smoke and steam escaping everywhere it was impossible to see or do anything. After half an hour of this ordeal the ship began to sink and I had helped to get a raft over the side on which I managed to scramble. Five men and myself eventually got on the raft but as we could not get the paddles from underneath the raft quickly enough we weren't able to give any help to more of our shipmates. From that raft I saw the end of a good ship, officers and men. The other two ships when I last saw them were steaming away to the south with the German ships in full cry after them.'

Cross's first reaction when he saw the enemy salvoes was one of professional curiosity. He was going to see a full-scale naval action and he must watch it closely. 'I was in the wardroom having a cup of tea when they sounded Action Stations. I thought it was a practice. I went to my cabin, put on my Irwin flying jacket and my Mae West. I had £110 of squadron funds on me, and I also put my logbook and a file of squadron records in my jacket. I went on to the quarterdeck, which was crowded. The first salvo arrived twenty yards on the starboard side. On the horizon were two little bits of smoke. I thought, this is *extraordinary*! I thought I'd go up to the bridge and see how they fought a naval action. The second salvo arrived as I stepped on the flight deck. It wrote off the ladder I had just come up! There was a damned great hole in the flight deck. I crossed the flight deck and went down the other side to the quarterdeck. "Abandon ship" was passed by word of mouth.'

When *Scharnhorst* and *Gneisenau* penetrated the smokescreen, *Glorious* was at 'great range' but both ships opened fire again and the range decreased rapidly. *Glorious* was now a pyre of flame and black smoke which rose in a towering cloud to the sky. She had developed a noticeable list to starboard which was increasing. Clearly the end could not be far off.

McBride was still on the flight deck, where 'men were lying around dead, resembling bundles of rubbish more than people. By this time I had reached the starboard forrard gun sponson and an officer called for a volunteer to go the bridge for information. Somebody in the crowd behind me yelled, "I'll go!" and shoved *me* up the ladder! Around this area chaos reigned. Various people whose Action Stations positions had been knocked out were wandering around looking for something useful to do. At this point I met the Senior Pilot, who told me that the hangar was an inferno. I turned to go forrard and Lieutenant-Commander Stephens, the C.O. of my squadron, told me that the order to "Abandon" had been given. His words were "Pass it on and jump". At this point men who appeared to be mostly stokers began to pop up from all sorts of places, through hatches and holes, escaping the searing heat below. I met Taney Lee who had been a boy seaman with me in the *Ganges* and he told me he had lost his life-jacket. I told him he could have mine (I was wearing a Mae West) if he wanted to get it from the Air Gunners' mess. He said O.K. and left but I never saw him again.'

The final order to 'Abandon ship' was passed at about 5.40. By then the ship's list to starboard was about 15-20° and still increasing. The ship had slowed from her headlong rush to the south but still had way on and was making a wide slow swing to port, as though seeking to turn up into the wind. The firing seemed to have stopped, but there was still the sound of fans running and the muted, ominous rustling and muttering of the gigantic fire burning in the centre of the ship. *Acasta*, who had been making protective smoke and keeping station so close astern that men thought they could almost have jumped from *Glorious* on to her upper deck, had now disappeared, having hauled off to the north-west towards the enemy.

The ship's company had exercised 'Abandon ship' as a drill, but this was real and there was no time for the shipwrights to construct rafts, or the stokers longest off watch to provide timber for the fo'c'sle stowage, and mess tables and stools from the Fleet Air Arm mess, or for the torpedo party to man the winches. This, as Ronald Healiss and everybody discovered, was no peacetime evolution: 'The Abandon Ship order came again soon after, not in the precise metallic way of the Tannoy but with one of the officers running along the battery shouting words which on the *Glorious* sounded brutally unreal: "*Abandon ship. All hands prepare to abandon ship.*"

'And off we went like sheep, a thin file of bewildered, scorched and oil-scarred men, joining throngs of others struggling against the sharply listing deck until we became a flood of humanity, pressing through the shell debris and the wreckage, running with the ugly current of a crowd towards our appointed stations for Abandon Ship.

'We knew where to go. Week after week, in peacetime and in war, we'd practised it. A lot of bull, just to conform to regulations. We'd never need to know.

'Week after week we went through the motions, but not through the actions.

'That's the part of the deck you'll stand on, but for Christ's sake don't stand on it now when I've just swabbed it down.

That's the guy-rope you'll hang on, but don't hang on the blamed thing now, because it's just been painted.

'Now the decks were deep in dust and debris and the new paint as scorched as we were ourselves, and we stood there in flocks, sheep-like, wondering what came next after Abandon Ship. We'd never been told what came next.'

There were several twenty-five-man Carley floats on each side of the ship, which could be released from the upper gallery deck. Most of these reached the water. Some ship's boats were also lowered, although the list was so pronounced that the falls on the port side were not long enough for the boat to be lowered to the water-line and the falls had to be cut. But the ship was abandoned in an orderly manner and several hundred men got away, although many were injured or burned. 'Jamie' Jameson of 46 Squadron much admired the composure of the ship's company: 'I shall always remember the calm, businesslike way in which the officers and men of the Royal Navy set about their task. The discipline was superb and there was never the slightest sign of panic. They could have been getting ready for a picnic or a boat race!'

'Then it was we saw how wonderful the officers could be,' wrote Healiss. 'There were the hordes of bruised and injured men waiting like an untidy crowd at the end of a seaside pier, and there was the Major of Marines and two other officers by the hatchway leading down from the centre of the quarterdeck.

'"Come on lads. Don't panic now. Get into line."

'It was nothing they said, really, but the way they stood there and said it. They could have buggered off and left us.

'Orders were what we wanted, so they gave us orders. "You and you and you. That's right, lads. The three of you. Check the cutter in the storage bay."'

Bing Cross was also on the quarterdeck. Understandably, abandoning a ship was for him an unfamiliar procedure. 'I said to Marmont, who was standing beside me, "What's the form on this?" We were still doing a fair speed. There was a stream of Carley floats going past. He said, "Wait until they drop one of those, and then go. Otherwise you'll have a long way to swim". So that's what I did.'

For every man there was the personal decision of whether, when and where to jump. For James O'Neill 'there was only one course for me to take and that was over the ship's side. I climbed down on the ship's bulge. There was a good crowd stood there. They were in two minds what to do. I stood there, blew up my lifebelt and got enough false courage to go in. I looked aside and saw the Master at Arms, so I wished him goodbye and told him it was the last time he would put me in the "rattle", then I jumped. The coldness of the water when my body hit it is something I will never be able to describe. I surfaced again and started swimming and got as far away as I could. There were a lot of sizzling noises and I thought it was shrapnel. There was a strong sea running and it took me by the ship. One poor lad got hit on the head with an oar thrown from the ship. A little further on I saw a motor-cutter full of men resting on the bulge; it would not lower further because the davits were at their limit. I swam further on but kept a safe distance away when I saw the gangway fall on a good number of men swimming under it at the time. I was past the ship now. I heard my name called and turned round to see a stoker just about all in. I swam back knowing I could not help him because there was nothing I could do. I asked him if I swam along with him would he stick it; he replied he would. I got a little in front of him and when I looked around he had gone without even a shout. I saw a lot in front of me but I had to swim around because most of them were drowning with the cold and it would have been suicide to help anyone because there was nothing to swim for and nothing to hold on to and my strength was about at the end. It was terrible to hear men cry out for their Mothers and for God to help them. (There was no singing here.) I turned and saw the ship but she was burning from stem to stern with volumes of smoke coming from the hangars.'

A great many men congregated on the quarterdeck and the lower flying-off deck and all along the high port side. Among them was Petty Officer Elliott: 'Somebody came along and said, "Abandon ship; make your own way off." But she still had way on her. She was going too fast through the water. Anyway, it started me thinking, was there anything I could use as a float. I knew we couldn't get the boats out. We had no power. A bloke said to me, "I'm going." I said, "Please yourself." They went. They all had their own ideas. I stayed there for a while, because there was still stuff flying around. I thought to myself, I'll wait a little while until it perhaps eases down a bit. Then there appeared to be a lull. Stopped firing for a while. There was no float; they'd all gone. So I thought to myself, now we'll go. I climbed down a rope on to the bulge. I stood there. They started firing again. I thought to myself, well I'm off. So I dived in.'

Some men had the only vaguest idea what was happening. Joiner 4th Class Joe Brown was a member of a fire and repair party amidships. 'We were told to abandon ship but before we got half-way up the ladder we were told to disregard the previous order. Apparently somebody else had taken over command. Down below, we had heard a few bumps. We could hear thumps but didn't know exactly what it was. We'd heard bombs, which missed us. We knew this was something different. But it was all conjecture. They didn't tell us the ships were there. When I got up to the lower flying-off deck, there was only one officer there. Most of the others had gone, into the sea, in boats and Carley floats. The officer said to me, "Go on, Chippie, jump in." So I hopped over and jumped. It was quite a big jump, like jumping off twice as high as the roof. I saw the nearest Carley float and I struck out for it.'

Healiss was one of those who jumped from the quarterdeck which 'was sloping at an angle of nearly forty-five degrees, and as each man prepared to jump, it meant a struggle to climb up for it. Little knots of men clawed each other round the waist as they clambered up to the rails, laughing and swearing as they stripped off their boots and trousers and prepared to jump. Then my turn came. I got to the top of the deck and stood there looking down. It must have been thirty feet. And down there I saw the ship's screw on the starboard side (sic) still churning beneath me.

'It was going to be one hell of a jump. I didn't want to hit that ruddy great green bronze screw, nor any of those oily black bobbing heads in the water.

'"Teach you to drown, young 'un." A voice was driving through my brain. It was my brother Bill. We were at New Brighton again when I was a kid and he was teaching me to swim. Swim? Well, he held me up by my chin, then yelled: "*Teach you to drown, young 'un.*" That laughing voice followed me as I jumped.'

The German ships first became aware of *Acasta*, the 'southernmost' destroyer, when she emerged from the right-hand edge of the smokescreen at full speed, firing her guns, and appeared to make a torpedo attack. *Acasta*'s part was recorded by Leading Seaman C.G. ('Nick') Carter, whose action station was in charge of the after torpedo tubes. Like almost everybody else, Carter had a cup of tea in his hand when the action began, as he stood on *Acasta*'s upper deck in the afternoon sunshine, preparing to go on watch for the First Dog at 4 o'clock.

Carter saw 'a great column of water shoot up astern' which he naturally thought was another air attack. He heard a rumble, which he thought was *Ardent* carrying out a depth-charge attack. Then the alarm rattlers went and Carter ran to the after tubes. He saw *Ardent* laying 'a very effective smokescreen' and *Glorious* with 'three Swordfish aircraft on her flight deck; there was a lot of movement, men running about.'

Acasta's final attack and last moments were recalled by Carter in a famous passage, worthy of Hakluyt: 'Whilst looking at *Glorious*, I heard a whistling noise pass over me, and it was a shell which hit *Glorious*, because I could see a lot of smoke coming from her starboard quarter. I then looked over towards *Ardent*, but I could not see enemy ships as the smokescreen *Ardent* put up was very good indeed. I noticed the *Ardent* was firing her guns, also that shots were falling near her; it became obvious that the enemy was concentrating on the *Ardent*', in a very short space of time I see a flash and a column of smoke rise in the air. The *Ardent* had been hit; she had appeared to stop dead, and very soon went to the bottom.

'We then started making a smokescreen, still being on the starboard quarter of the *Glorious*, also very, very close to her. I still had not seen the enemy. The fire on HMS *Glorious* was now, as it seemed to me, out of control, flames could be seen rising to a great height. The enemy then renewed their attack on *Glorious*, and believe me if ever a ship took a lot of punishment she did, she did not appear to slow down at all despite all her starboard side was heavily battered, she took a terrible list and going round in a circle finally settled, I never actually saw her sink.

'On board our ship, what a deathly calm, hardly a word spoken, the ship was now steaming full speed away from the enemy, then came a host of orders, prepare all smoke floats, set the inner torpedo tubes of both tubes to "W", hose pipes connected up, various other jobs were prepared, we were still steaming away from the enemy and making smoke, and all our smoke floats had been set going. The Captain (Commander Charles Glasfurd) had this message passed to all positions:

'"You may think we are running away from the enemy, we are not, our chummy ship (*Ardent*) has sunk, the *Glorious* is sinking, the least we can do is make a show, good luck to you all." We then altered course into our own smoke screen. I had the order stand by to fire tubes 6 and 7, we then came out of the smokescreen, altered course to starboard firing our torpedoes from port side, it was then I had my first glimpse of the enemy, to be honest it appeared to me to be a large one (ship) and a small one, and we were very close, I fired my two torpedoes from my tubes (aft) the foremost tubes fired theirs, we were all watching results. I'll never forget that cheer that went up, on the port bow of one of the ships a yellow flash and a great column of smoke and water shot up from her, we knew we had hit, personally I could not see how we could have missed so close as we were. The enemy never fired a shot at us, I feel they must have been very surprised. After we had fired our torpedoes we went back into our own smokescreen, altered course again to starboard, stand by to fire remaining torpedoes, and this time as soon as we poked our nose out of the smokescreen, the enemy let us have it, a shell hit the engine room, killed my tubes crew, I was blown to the after end of the tubes, I must have been knocked out for a while because when

I came to, my arm hurt me, the ship had stopped with a list to port, here is something believe it or not I climbed back into the control seat, I see those two ships, I fired the remaining torpedoes, no one told me to, I guess I was raving mad, God alone knows why I fired them but I did. The *Acasta*'s guns were firing the whole time, even firing with a list on the ship, the enemy then hit us several times, but one big explosion took place right aft, I have often wondered whether the enemy hit us with a torpedo, in any case it seemed to lift the ship out of the water, at last the Captain gave orders to abandon ship. I will always remember the Surgeon Lieutenant (H.J. Stammers RNVR) his first ship, his first action, before I jumped over the side, I saw him still attending to the wounded, a hopeless task and when I was in the water I saw the Captain leaning over the bridge, take a cigarette from a case and light it, we shouted to him to come on our raft, he waved "Goodbye and good luck", a ridiculous end to a gallant man.'

Acasta's first torpedo attack was carried out at a range of about 8,000 yards and none of the torpedoes hit. Carter and his shipmates were hoping for and expecting a torpedo hit, but it seems the yellow flash, smoke and water they saw and cheered might well have been a shell hit, forward on *Scharnhorst*. Naturally the Germans could not distinguish between *Ardent* and *Acasta*, either at the time or in their later reports, and one German account suggests that it was the second destroyer (i.e. *Acasta*) which obtained a hit on *Scharnhorst*'s 'B' turret.

But there could be no possible doubt about the hit from her last torpedo. It was fired at 13,000 yards, or more than six miles, a long range for a torpedo attack. It seems that *Scharnhorst*'s Captain saw, or guessed, the torpedo had been fired and steered to 'comb' its track. But the torpedo had been fired at such long range that Hoffman decided it must have passed his ship when, at 5.38, he altered course to port to resume the original course to pursue *Glorious*. As the ship turned to port, her stern swung out to starboard and the torpedo hit her on the starboard side aft, abreast 'C' [Caesar] 11" gun turret.

This was a very great surprise (for a long time the Germans thought the torpedo had been fired from a British submarine) and caused a great deal of damage. Two officers and forty-six ratings were killed. 'C' turret and the nearest 5.9" secondary armament turret were put out of action and their magazines flooded. Some 2,500 tons of water flooded into the after compartments and flooding eventually reached the centre and starboard engine rooms. *Scharnhorst*'s speed dropped to 20 knots.

Sitting in a Carley float, Stoker Cyril Hobbs actually saw *Acasta*'s last torpedo. 'From the raft to the destroyer, it was no more than three or four hundred feet at the most. I watched that torpedo go and heard the explosion. That's why I thought something would happen to us.' The Germans continued to shell the stationary *Acasta* and finally dispatched her at about 6.08pm. 'Bing' Cross, also in a carley float, saw her 'at a sort of drunken angle, and then she disappeared'.

Glorious herself sank shortly afterwards, at about 6.10, approximately in position 69°N., 5°E. Chief Petty Officer Lidstone, from his Carley float, watched her go. She 'was well over on her starboard side and not long after the last of her was seen in an enormous flurry of spray and foam with the final plunge. There were still survivors on her side as she heeled over, and I feel sure they must have perished in the enormous suction as the ship plunged. Meanwhile the enemy had passed the whole sordid scene and I feel certain in my own mind that small arms fire on the men in the water was used as they steamed past. I am sure I saw splashes between us and the enemy as they passed.'

Other *Glorious* survivors believed they were fired on and Hobbs was not alone in thinking that 'something would happen to us'. The German ships passed within a mile of the Carley floats, so close that Cross thought it prudent to throw his flying logbook and 46 Squadron files over the side, lest he be captured and the documents fall into enemy hands. Jameson, in the same float, followed his C.O.'s example. He had camera-gun film taken from his Hurricane when he attacked two German flying boats, clearly showing them blazing. Jameson thought it more tactful not to let the Germans see this and reluctantly disposed of it over the side. Cross and Jameson thought it probable the Germans were either going to pick them up or use them as target practise for their machine-gunners.

In fact the Germans did neither. *Gneisenau* fired 175 rounds of 11" during the action, *Scharnhorst* 212; together, the ships had fired 1,148 rounds of 5.9". Although both ships did come close to the Carley floats and although several *Glorious* survivors are convinced that they and the floats were fired on, it seems most improbable that any small arms fire was deliberately directed at survivors (especially as the German ships ceased fire on *Glorious* herself at 5.43 when it was seen that she was listing 40° with no way on, and was clearly no longer a fighting force). More probably, the fire was aimed at *Acasta* who, according to German accounts, floated for some time after *Glorious*, with a fire raging along two-thirds of her length. *Gneisenau* ceased fire on *Acasta* at 6.16 and *Acasta* sank shortly afterwards.

At 6.17 both German ships steered south-east for Trondheim and cleared the area at 19 knots, the best

Scharnhorst could make. Because of the damage to *Scharnhorst* (who had a hole twelve metres long by four metres wide in her hull below the waterline) and the danger that a British submarine was present, neither ship paused to recover survivors.

The damage to *Scharnhorst* had put a completely different aspect on the situation as far as Marschall was concerned. Throughout the war it was emphasized to German naval commanders that they must avoid damage which might affect their ships' speed or ability to evade pursuers. Time and again damage meant return to base. So it was in this case. Marschall abandoned the sortie against Harstad and the troop convoys although he was, in fact, very favourably placed to intercept the second group of troopships. *Scharnhorst* and *Gneisenau* arrived in Trondheim and anchored without further incident at 4pm on the 9th. (*Scharnhorst* had some 700 cubic metres, almost 700 tons, of water pumped out of her after compartments during the next few days.)

So a great silence descended upon the scene of battle. The last gunfire died away. The surface of the sea, torn and churned by exploding shells, subsided. The long north-westerly swell reasserted itself. All was quiet except for one strong, confident voice from one of the Carley floats. It was *Glorious'* Chaplain, the Reverend John Bernard King, leading his fellow survivors in song, as he had led so many congregations on board in the past.

The hymn-singing may well have been, as McBride said of the singing in his own Carley float, 'a futile effort by the most miserable choir I've heard', but the choice of hymn showed a nice sense of irony: 'Lead us Heavenly Father, lead us, O'er the world's tempestuous sea,' and the next words of the first verse, 'Guard us, guide us, keep us, feed us, for we have no help but

Thee' were, for *Glorious*' survivors, to have a terrible accuracy in the ordeal to come.

CHAPTER 11: THE ORDEAL OF THE SURVIVORS

AT HOME IN England it was summer, Battle of Britain summer, one of the finest, longest and warmest summers in living memory. 'It was the most beautiful June morning,' said one *Glorious* wife who, though she did not yet know it, was already a widow that morning. 'The sun was shining and all the birds were singing. I heard our garden gate click, rather earlier than usual. Our local Head Postmaster always delivered that sort of telegram himself. I could see him in his uniform, with his peak cap and his medal ribbons from the First World War. He came up the path, and I just *knew*.'

It was some time before the Admiralty knew of the loss and much longer before anybody was aware of the sheer scale of the catastrophe. A short time after *Glorious* was sunk a German ship (almost certainly *Gneisenau*) transmitted four signals, one of them classified 'Immediate', from a position which 'poor' D/F placed off the Norwegian coast. The Duty Officer in the OIC, who did not know of the evacuation from Narvik or of the naval movements in the area, attached no particular significance to these signals and took no action. But they were, in fact, signals reporting the action against *Glorious*. (A report was also flown to Trondheim in *Scharnhorst*'s Arado.)

Not until the morning of Sunday, 9 June did the truth begin to emerge, when the hospital ship *Atlantis* met *Valiant*, who was returning to the north to join Admiral Vivian's convoy of troopships, and gave an account of a battleship and two destroyers attacking a two-funnelled transport (*Oratna*) at 9am on the 8th. *Valiant* broadcast this information in a signal at

9.01 and pressed on at increased speed to meet the troopships which were then some 400 miles to the north and about one hundred miles from where *Atlantis* said she had seen the enemy.

When Admiral Cunningham in *Devonshire* received *Valiant*'s signal he at once realized the possible significance of that garbled message they had picked up the day before. At 1031 he signalled to the C-in-C: '*Valiant*'s 0901/9. Following was read reception very doubtful on 3700 k/cs at 1720/8. Begins — Vice-Admiral (A) from *Glorious*: my 1615, two P.B. Time of origin 1640 — ends. *Glorious*' 1615 not received'. *Glorious*' 1640/8 had been 'a barely readable signal' and for technical reasons had been considered 'probably corrupt and referred to some other matter' but now at last it was being seen as a desperate cry for help.

Until *Valiant* broadcast *Atlantis*' news, nobody had suspected the presence of a battleship anywhere in the Norwegian sea. At Scapa Forbes took steps to reinforce the troop convoys against what might now be an imminent danger. He ordered *Valiant* and her four destroyers to join Vivian at full speed (which they were already doing). *Repulse*, *Newcastle*, *Sussex* and three destroyers, at sea between Iceland and the Faeroes, were also told to join Vivian. At 10.33 Forbes signalled *Glorious* to join *Valiant*, if her fuel situation permitted. Forbes himself sailed, with *Rodney*, *Renown* and destroyers, just after midday on the 9th.

Admiral Wells in *Ark Royal* received *Valiant*'s signal at 10.14. 'This was,' as he said, 'the first intimation received that enemy surface forces were at sea.' *Ark* had closed the main convoy at about midnight and had been flying patrols to cover herself and the convoy since 10pm on the 8th. At 4am on the 9th four Swordfish had taken off to search, to a depth of eighty miles, in a broad sector from 130° round to 225°, which were considered the most probable directions of any possible enemy surface craft's approach to the convoy. (This was, of course, a sensible precaution, such as *Glorious* should have taken long before *Valiant*'s signal was received.) The storeship convoy was sighted and some stragglers from the main convoys leaving the Norwegian coast, but no enemy ships (*Scharnhorst* and *Gneisenau* were far to the southwards by that time).

At about 7am two Swordfish were flown off to search for the 13,000-ton armed boarding vessel *Van Dyck*, who was missing from the convoy. (She was a spare troopship, but instead of going back alone, like *Orama*, she had been ordered to cruise in a position 130 miles offshore, while the other ships loaded, and was then to join them. By mistake she went to one of the inner rendezvous and reported herself there by signal some time after the convoy had left. Neither *Ark Royal*'s Swordfish nor a destroyer sent to search could find her. But German aircraft did and sank her off Andenes on the 10th.)

Admiral Wells received Cunningham's signal of 1031 that morning, giving details of *Glorious*' last message, at 11.15. *Ark Royal* flew off three Swordfish to search to a depth of eighty miles between bearing 225°, and 275°, and at 1pm another six Swordfish and two Walrus to search for a hundred miles between 110° and 285°. Three Skuas patrolled twenty miles from the convoy between 310° and 085°. The 1pm search pattern was repeated at 3.45, but nothing was sighted on any bearing.

The first definite news was heard at 3pm on the 9th in a German broadcast: 'German naval units, including the two battleships *Gneisenau* and *Scharnhorst*, operated under Admiral Marschall to relieve the troops fighting round Narvik. On 8

June a fighting unit sank the British aircraft carrier *Glorious* (22,500 tons) and an enemy destroyer.

'A second fighting unit destroyed the 21,000-ton troop transport *Oranta*, the British tanker *Oil Pioneer* (910 tons), and a modern submarine chaser (refers to *Juniper*).

'Many prisoners were taken. Our own forces continued their operations.'

The statement about 'many prisoners', printed in the British newspapers, gave many a widow false hopes for many months. In fact all the prisoners were from *Oranta*, *Oil Pioneer* and *Juniper*, none from *Glorious* and indeed, by the time that statement was issued, there were very few survivors from *Glorious* still alive. *Ark Royal's* aircraft had seen nothing, but *Glorious'* survivors had seen them and had tried to attract attention. Now, with their hopes dashed and their numbers still dwindling, the survivors faced their second day in the Carley floats.

From the eventual survivors' estimates of the numbers initially on the floats, it seems that some 900 men abandoned the ship, but of those many succumbed almost at once to the shock, the cold and their wounds, and drowned before they could reach a float. The rest swam as best they could through the oil and debris, the cries and clutches of the drowning, the prayers and pleadings, to whatever boat or float or support they could find.

Healiss swam 'not only in self-preservation but in anger', using a 'cruel, crude, hard-hitting trudgeon stoke which slowly pulled me farther away from the other bobbing heads in the stinking circle of oily water. And the *Glorious*, still with way on her though her engines were crippled, was well away over there, no more than an ugly wreck on the skyline. Around me were probably nearly 1,500 others, yet I felt alone, terribly alone. The more I saw of the others, the more I realized the intensity of my loneliness. For some of them were dead already.

'Some were almost non-swimmers and the shock of the deep dive had been fatal. They knew they were jumping to their certain death, poor devils, but they jumped unflinchingly because they got the order Abandon Ship. Now the ship had abandoned them. And they were dead, gripped in their lifebelts, bobbing like a mute chorus of flotsam.

'"Christ," I said, "that's not going to be me. That's not the way I'm going. And I'm not going now. I'm not prepared for it."'

After spending some time with three other men in an 'air cushion' from a lifeboat, Healiss left it after seeing a boat not far off. He had been in the water an hour when he reached one of the ship's motorboats, which was half waterlogged, but held some twenty men, including the PMO, Surgeon Commander C.H. Egan, the ship's dentist, Surgeon Lieutenant (D) G.P. Pearse, a Marine corporal and a Marine sergeant called Tim Healy (*sic*: no such name appears in *Glorious'* casualty list, although there was a RAF Sergeant Heathly). They sang *Roll Out the Barrel, We're going to hang out the washing on the Siegfried Line* and *Bless' Em' All*.

McBride was also singing *Roll out the Barrel* on his Carley float, which had forty-four men in it. That song 'stays with me to this day, particularly since it was sung by a collection of men with white faces, red noses and bloodshot running eyes. We also shared some Wrigley's chewing gum between us which one of the men found in his pocket. I had one pellet which lasted me until the following Tuesday.'

The Carley float was essentially an oval-shaped roll of canvas, painted to make it watertight and stuffed with kapok or granulated cork. Inside the oval, a wooden lattice deck was laced with ropes, and another rope ran around the outside rim for men to cling to. The Carley float had no 'right' or 'wrong way up'. The wooden deck would settle in the water whichever way the float fell. But as the floats were all free-flooding the survivors' feet and legs were in sea-water. Most of the floats held twenty-five men, but some of the larger floats were designed for fifty. None of *Glorious*' Carley floats had any food or drinking water in them, and few of them even had a paddle. Some survivors retrieved oars from the sea.

James O'Neill swam towards a float which had so many men in it they were standing up, shoulder to shoulder. He hung on the rope for a while and then tried to get in. 'I was a good swimmer. I'd passed my life-saving test. But I daren't swim near to anybody. If they gripped you, you would die too. I saw this Carley float. "Full up," somebody said. "There's no room." I said, "This isn't a bus service, you know, I'm getting in," and so I did. The Padre was in this float. He had a water-tight watch and he said the time was 7.40. They were singing hymns. I said, "These are Protestant hymns, I'm a Catholic, these are no use to me!"'

Dick Leggott had noticed that the nearest Carley floats were already overburdened and decided to swim for two distant floats which were higher in the water. As he swam he passed 'lots of people who couldn't swim properly, screaming, "Help me!" One could only point them in the direction and say, "For Christ's sake *try*." One had an eye to the fact that one still had a long way to go. I carried on swimming and eventually got to the distant Carley. I'd just about had it. I hung on for a moment. Who should be in this float but my airframe rigger, who helped me over the side. I said, "Thank you very much. You've been looking after my aeroplane for all these months and now you've looked after me." We started out with about twelve or fourteen (in the float) and eventually finished sitting up to our waists in water, with about forty-five on board.'

The proper etiquette was preserved, even on the Carley floats. Jameson swam up to one float and saw Bing Cross, his C.O., sitting in it. 'Hallo, sir!' he called, 'Can I come on your raft?' Jameson dived in again to retrieve an oar and a 'little Marine whom I discovered later, was known as "Geordie", who had a bad head injury'. In Cross's float there were two RAF officers, a leading aircraftman RAF and twenty-six sailors and marines, to make a total of twenty-nine.

Arthur Lidstone was a good swimmer and 'started a very steady breast stroke' towards a float which had just been dropped and 'after what seemed an eternity', but was actually about twenty minutes, he grasped a rope on the side of the float and hung on for a while to gather his strength before hoisting himself out of the water. There were already some twenty-five men in the float and 'already some bodies in the water under or alongside our feet. The only one I knew was the Warrant Supply Officer (Victualling) and he was talking gibberish and before long he fell backward into the sea again. This happened to several others as time went by.'

The survivors were all surprised how quickly some of their shipmates 'gave up' and died. In Leggott's float the first man, a stoker, died in two hours. Some of the badly wounded had never had a chance but it was by no means always the weakest who died first. Often it was the strongest and fittest — in one float the ship's P.T. instructor, in another a Marine, six foot tall and strongly built, who had been devoted to personal fitness.

Joiner Joe Brown's float was almost awash, being designed for twenty-four and having forty on board. There was only one officer, the Warrant Telegraphist, Mr Blackwell, and men from several departments, seamen, stokers, wardroom stewards, and one other shipwright, Norman Pike. 'It didn't take long before they started passing out — *dying*. I really was surprised, especially as it was some of the youngsters who went pretty quick. I was a man of twenty-eight then, and I thought, if these boys are going, it'll be *my* turn soon!'

George Elliott's float was also full, with about forty men in it, most of them standing up. Elliott kept himself occupied (and alive) by doing exercises of his arms and upper body. 'I kept it up for days. I was seeing others die and telling them, "Come on, do the exercises." They'd start doing them and then they were falling asleep. I suppose it must have been the cold. I had no feeling whatsoever. I just watched them die. You'd think that you'd be horrified. To tell the truth I wasn't. They just seemed to be going naturally. They were simply falling asleep, gradually going down and down and down eventually they'd finish up in the bottom of the raft. There were so many we chucked over the side. Eventually we didn't have the strength to do it. Eventually we just rested our feet on them. Kept us a bit out of the water.' Elliott's float had mostly stokers, whom he did not know, and some seamen whose faces he knew, and Midshipman Franklin. 'Some of the engine room chaps started to sing hymns, well known ones. But they didn't do that for very long. The cold seemed to be getting at everybody. The Middy (Franklin) lasted pretty well really. He did the exercises for a time but he was gradually sinking down.'

Horrifyingly quickly, there was much more room on the floats. Of the twenty-nine on Cross's float only ten survived the first night, of Lidstone's sixty or seventy only six. The living continued to put the dead over the side while they had the strength. 'I actually sat on one leading stoker for almost a day and a half,' said Cyril Hobbs. 'But his face was floating in the water.' Hobbs's float started with fifty-seven, but was down to a handful after twenty-four hours, and to two, Hobbs and 'an Irishman', by the second evening.

On James O'Neill's float, 'it wasn't long before the first man died. I felt a terrible feeling come over me to watch a man die like that at first. The second man was my mate, Stoker Bartlett, one of the finest lads I knew. It was a sad end to such a man as him. The Padre said a few prayers and told the man nearest to put him over the side. After these two it was one man after the other going to their Maker. A few looked at me when they were on their last with a look in their eyes asking me to help them but they were past help and it was that cold I couldn't move if I could have helped them. It was a terrible thing the look they gave me at times it haunts me, I wish I could forget it.

'One chap died with his hand gripping my lifebelt and I had to ask a Marine to help me get his hand open, otherwise I should have been pulled into the water. We drifted on till we saw a raft with some more men in it; there were two Warrant Engineers and a Stoker P.O. I knew. I asked them did they think we had a chance of being picked up and I was told we should be picked up tomorrow forenoon. Then we drifted apart and lost sight of each other. It was around this time the Padre departed from this world. It reminded me of a nun to see his white face under his anti-flash gear.

'The second evening saw us with six left out of forty. A Mechanic who had been a pal of mine went. It was an awful sight to open your eyes and see them looking up at us with glassy eyes fixed on us. On this second night a Marine went mad; if he could have had enough strength I feel sure he would have killed someone, but he calmed down and the cold got him. At the end of that night three of us were left and we were wondering who the next would be.'

The lack of food and water and, worst of all, the lack of hope, began to affect some men's minds. On Elliott's float, 'I wouldn't say they were off their heads. They lost control of themselves really. Some seemed to lose hope so quickly. That surprised me. A matter of five or six hours. So quick. The cold got at them quickly. I said, "Something will turn up in a minute." But they were thrashing about, threatening to jump over the side. Some people were trying to stop them, but it was impossible really. Some people deliberately gave up. Jumped over the side and swam away. Despair, I suppose.'

On occasions despair took on the shape of a sinister and dangerous *dementia*. After some thirty-six hours everybody on the water-logged motorboat had died except Healiss. The boat happened to drift very close to Leggott's Carley float, in which 'there was a steady death rate for about thirty hours, by which time there were four left. The Signal Bosun, Mr Charles Rogers, an RAF type, and one other chap who doesn't register with me. Obviously just sitting there. And me. We drifted alongside this boat and there was this chap Healiss. I shouted over to him, "That thing's not much use to you". I take my hat off to him. He dived in and swam across.'

It was, of course, an appalling risk for Healiss to take but he succeeded in climbing into the float. He and Leggott decided to remove jerseys and jackets from the corpses to clothe themselves. But one other survivor went much further than they had ever intended: 'One of the chaps with a bit of strength left was scrambling round the float, heaving bodies over the side. But, in a sort of frenzy, he clawed at the pockets and belts first, stuffing notes, silver and photographs into his own belt... Then came a terrifying moment. The crazed fool scrounging the money off the bodies began to mumble and moan, blubbering wildly to himself. He took out a roll of notes from the belt and rubbed them in his hands, crying like a child. Then without warning he rose and faced the fore part of the Carley and ran with almost superhuman strength and speed, with a laugh that echoed as he leaped.

'He sank and drifted by us; the pound and ten shilling notes he had collected fluttered around. Then, pulped and soggy, they drifted and sank away, too.'

Both Healiss and Leggott saw a Walrus, and possibly a second, fly close to their float. They stood up like oily scarecrows, clasping each other for support, and waved and shouted and screeched through parched, cracked lips, but neither aircraft saw them. In his float McBride made 'eight different sightings of ships but only a smoke on the horizon and three or five aircraft, one of which came close enough for me to identify as a Walrus. We got quite excited about this.' But, as McBride himself was to find out, 'It is very very difficult indeed to spot a grey raft on a grey sea.'

From one of *Acasta*'s Carley floats Carter also saw 'a long line of ships', two of which he thought were escorting destroyers. From Carter's account about eighty of *Acasta*'s people (though only one officer, the Gunner) got away, mainly in three floats. But many died from shock, exposure and wounds. Carter and Able Seaman Barnes put many corpses over the side, 'sometimes, in a final eruption of maddened energy, they flailed about, shouting, cursing, kicking, blaspheming, while Barney and I fought to quieten them on the dangerously rocking float.'

By the following morning there were only Carter, Barnes and Able Seaman Smith alive on their raft, a signalman and a telegraphist on another, and a gunner with a leading seaman on the third. In an act of what can only be called madness, Carter had thrown his float's barricoe of fresh water and tin of corned beef and biscuits over the side because he was sure they would soon be picked up. By the second day the trio had been reduced by the cold, hunger and thirst to a state where they spent hours without speaking or moving, except for Smith who suffered from coughing fits.

The Walrus and Swordfish which the survivors saw were certainly from *Ark Royal*, and one of the ships they saw was *Coventry*, Admiral Vivian's flagship. On the 9th the returning troop convoy crossed the track of the German ships the day before. *Ark Royal*'s aircraft sighted wreckage and watchers on the bridge of the cruiser *Southampton* actually saw bodies in the water. Had *Acasta*'s torpedo not hit *Scharnhorst* and made Marschall break off and steam to Trondheim, *Scharnhorst* and *Gneisenau* would surely have come across the troop convoy later that evening or early on the 9th and would have wreaked terrible havoc amongst the troopships.

The Admiralty had had no more news of *Glorious* after the German statement of 3 pm on the 9th except a derisive propaganda broadcast by Lord Haw Haw that evening that all the ships had 'been sunk with all hands'. On the 10th the Admiralty issued a communique that 'as, up to the present, it has not been found possible to establish communication with certain ships, the Secretary of the Admiralty regrets that it must now be presumed that the following vessels have been lost: HMS *Glorious*, Transport SS *Orama*, Tanker SS *Oil Pioneer*. The following two destroyers must also be presumed to have been sunk: HMS *Acasta*, HMS *Ardent*. These ships were in company with the *Glorious* and are probably the vessels referred to in the German communique as a destroyer and a submarine chaser. No news has so far been received from either of these vessels.

The German communique states that there are several hundred survivors from our ships. Next of kin are being informed as quickly as possible.'

Meanwhile the search for *Glorious* went on and there was the possibility that powerful German ships might be at sea. The main burden fell upon *Ark Royal* in three days of intensive flying virtually around the clock — a truly magnificent demonstration of the carrier art — to provide air cover and anti-submarine patrols for the convoy, launch Swordfish and Walrus to search for survivors and for enemy ships; and to fly off Skuas to drive off the shadowers which had located *Valiant*, *Ark Royal* herself and the convoy (and to shoot one of them down).

The Swordfish and Walrus and some of the ships the survivors saw were real enough. But, as time passed, some survivors became light-headed and delirious, and began to have hallucinations. On the second day the sea was calm and the sun shone. For Elliott, who was still continuing with his exercises, 'It was quite pleasant, sitting on the side of the float, the sun warming you, at times it was like being on the beach.' But Elliott said that 'after twenty-four hours I thought I saw a naval battle. There seemed to be about three or four ships there and I saw tons of smoke. We thought we saw land a couple of times, but I knew it wasn't as I'd heard of these things before.'

Another Petty Officer, who may have been on the same float as Elliott, also saw a naval battle on the horizon after about two days, with 'flashes and smoke and, soon after, the outlines of ships'. It all lasted about half an hour. Marine Wootton, on another float, also saw what he thought were smoke and ships, and he also thought he saw a small fishing fleet of trawlers. But he put it all down to imagination 'or clouds'. Another survivor, one of only three on another float, saw 'a big hulk' which he took to be a battleship or a cruiser, at a distance of about two miles. He was quite positive about the identification and said it stayed in sight for hours.

A dockyard was a favourite mirage. Carter saw a dockyard, a crane and a ship. Arthur Lidstone, towards the end of the second day, 'had an impression of seeing a distinct outline of what I imagined to be a dockyard. I could see many poplar trees. I can remember it now vividly, a rising road which appeared like a wall and a ship similar to an aircraft carrier alongside the wharf in outline… On another occasion I imagined I saw a group of ships with aircraft flying over them, having a mimic battle.' One of six remaining survivors in Lidstone's float, twenty-year-old Supply Assistant Kenneth Cleave, said, 'Later in the evening the sun seemed to be going down. We thought we saw a dockyard with cranes and ships, and at the same time green fields and trees.' Stoker Petty Officer Phillips, in the same float as Wootton, said, 'It was just like as if you was looking down where the dockyard wall was. You could see slipways and cranes.'

Many of the survivors influenced each other (Phillips said that the four left on his float 'used to talk about the mirages in the desert') and persuaded each other that they all saw the same thing. Naturally, survivors imagined they saw what they most longed to see, ships and aircraft coming to rescue them. One hallucination was clearly governed by thirst. Able Seaman John Russell, one of four survivors from forty, said, 'Most of the time I thought I was in a ship. I kept going hazy. Then sometimes I'd see orange trees, then sometimes I'd be in a bar' which 'seemed to be on the edge of the float. I would rub my eyes and then see nothing, only sea. Then it would come again.' He saw lots of ships about and aeroplanes, but the most vivid impression was of the orange trees which he and the others badly wanted. 'The oranges were yellow and colourful and plain and the leaves were on the trees. A couple of fellows seemed to be going for it and I was going to follow them and they walked over the side' (and were drowned in the heavy sea running).

By the evening of Monday, 10 June, two days after the sinking, Carley floats with dead and dying men were spread over a wide area. On many floats everybody was dead, but here and there a spark of life survived, although, by that time, most of the survivors were only barely alive. Their feet and legs long since ceased to have any feeling. Their hands had been frozen into swollen, crooked claws. Their eyes were red-rimmed and bloodshot, their hair and eyebrows shaggy with salt rime.

Most had stopped feeling hungry, but had that constant raging thirst. One or two drank their own urine. A few experimented in desperation with sea water, with generally disastrous results. In one float they tried to knock down a seagull and drink its blood although nobody quite knew how to achieve such an object. McBride had discarded his chewing gum, which had at last 'gone woolly', and sucked instead a pebble picked up as a souvenir from Bardufoss airfield, where he had flown in one of the Swordfish sent to guide 46 Squadron to the ship. They had seen the army demolition trucks and equipment and even the cooks shooting .303 bullet holes into pots and pans, to prevent the enemy using them. Somebody gave McBride a half-gallon Thermos flask, which had gone down in *Glorious*. He thought of it wistfully many times on the Carley float. But the survivors dared not talk of food or drink, even had their swollen throats permitted conversation, because it would have made their mental agonies even worse.

But, amazingly, miraculously, rescue was at hand — not by aircraft or by warship, but by the 350-ton motor vessel *Borgund*, registered in Aalesund and owned by the Statens Kjoleunlegg, who came upon the first Carley floats and circled them, her single diesel puffing black smoke into the clear Arctic air, late in the evening of the 10th. For a time some survivors thought she was going to leave them and frantically waved oars, shirts, Mae Wests and, in Lidstone's float, an inordinately long blue woollen scarf knitted for McBride by 'my girlfriend, my mother, her mother, my next-door neighbour and a number of other ladies who lived nearby'.

Borgund's Master, Captain Fjortoft, later told his story succinctly and unemotionally. He 'says he left Tromso on Saturday, 8 June, at 2300 bound for the Faeroes. He was ordered to do so by Director of Shipping. No convoy available. Steering out through Hammer Fjord and then on approx. W.S.W. (True) Course.

'When in Lt. 68 degrees 15 minutes North, Long. 4 degrees 20 mins East on Monday, 10 June at 2245, picked up raft with two living. At 2315 one raft was found. Five living were taken aboard. Up till midnight more dead were passed.

'On Tuesday, 11 June at 0045 several rafts with dead were passed. At 0455 stopped, then circled slow for 1½ hours during which 32 more men were picked up. Number of rafts passed, approximately 21.

'Nothing further was sighted. At 0530 proceeded to Faeroes from Lat. 67 degrees 59 minutes North, Long. 3 degrees 42 minutes East.

'A German trawler was seen to pass steering opposite course 3 hours before first position was reached.'

No precise tally of which survivors were in which Carley floats can now be made but by piecing together survivors' stories (some of which were told forty years after the events described) and from matching some of them up to each other, a picture at least of the scale of the loss emerges. It seems that Lidstone's float had six survivors from an original sixty or seventy: himself, Cleave, McBride, Engine Room Artificer Fern and two others. Lidstone was the senior, by rate and by age (he was thirty-nine) and although Cleave said 'the Chief was the weakest', Lidstone seems to have organized his float very well: their single oar was laid across the float and one man at a time lay with his legs over the oar and his body on the side of the float, to get some rest. The next man hooked his forearm around the body of the first, to maintain his balance, and the third around the second, and so on, leaving the sixth man, in a watchkeeping rota, to keep watch.

Another float had five survivors, including Lieutenant-Commander Rupert Hill, the only ship's officer to survive. Hill was a retired officer, in his forties, who had rejoined for the war and joined *Glorious* (after being a tea planter) in Ceylon in December, 1939. With him were MacLachlan, of 823 Squadron, and three ratings, all that were left of the original fifty.

Most of the floats had only four survivors or less. Marine Paddy Donnan and one other were all that remained of thirty-three; Healiss and Leggott of forty-five; Elliott, Pascoe the action helmsman, and a third, of forty; Hobbs and 'an Irishman' of fifty-seven; Ordinary Seaman Niccols and another sailor, of twenty-seven; O'Neill and Able Seaman Fred Thornton, of forty; one Petty Officer, 'aged twenty-eight' (all that is known of him) and three others of around eighty; Stoker Petty Officer Phillips, Marine Wootton and two others, of fifty-eight; and Leading Seaman Carter and Able Seaman

Smith were the only survivors of *Acasta*, Barnes having died when *Borgund* was actually in sight.

In the float led by Bing Cross, seven were still alive of the original twenty-nine: Cross himself, Jameson, Chief Ordnance Artificer Potter, Sergeant Jagger, Royal Marines, Corporal Etheridge, Royal Marines, L.A.C. Spencer and (probably) one Able Seamen. This high proportion of survivors, the highest of any float, was largely the result of Cross's leadership. Cross himself knew the value of morale and *esprit de corps*. 'If we could have got all 46 Squadron on one float,' he said, 'we would *all* have survived.' The mood in the float seems to have been optimistic. Etheridge said he was 'full of hope' and 'all on the raft remained good friends; comparative strangers talked to each other as if they had known one another all their lives'.

Cross kept his 'ship's company' busy. Jameson said, 'Bing came up with the brilliant idea of cutting the ropes which held the wooden trellis bottom to the oval-shaped outer tube, lifting it out and putting it sideways across the top, giving us a platform which enabled us to get some sleep and get our legs out of the water. It was no mean task, cutting about 100 ropes of ¾ inch diameter with my little, rather blunt pocket knife, and it took several hours. However, it gave us something to do, took our minds off our plight and made us more comfortable.' Cross also knew when to temper compassion with discretion. Said Jameson, 'That night one of the young seamen who was sitting on the platform must have dozed off. He fell back into the water, panicked as he couldn't swim and thrashed about with his arms, so forcing himself farther and farther from the raft. I wanted to go in after him but Bing forbade me as he felt that I would be too weak to get back on board. It was terrible to hear his last despairing cries for help. I realized later that Bing was right. This was confirmed when another member of the crew fell overboard. Fortunately I managed to grab him before he got too far way. He panicked and seemed to think that we didn't want him back. It was quite obvious that we couldn't get him back on board without his cooperation. I talked to him and eventually gave him a flat-handed swipe across the face which quietened him down somewhat enabling me to convince him that he had to help. Eventually, thankfully, we retrieved him.'

Borgund lowered a Jacob's ladder but most of the survivors were too weak to climb unaided. The Norwegians climbed down into the floats to put lines around the worst cases and to help those who could get up to the deck. Healiss, hearing them speak Norwegian, thought they were German and was greatly alarmed, but most of the survivors were in no state to worry who their rescuers were. Captain Fjortoft and his crew did their best for their guests, within their very limited facilities on board. Their only error, and that was well meant, was to put some survivors' feet into buckets of hot water — precisely the opposite to the right treatment. But otherwise, as one (unnamed) survivor said, soon after the event, 'No one could have been kinder to us than those Norwegians — their kindness was beyond praise! They gave up their bunks for the worst cases — there were thirty-six (sic) survivors in all. They gave us cigarettes, shared out their only half-bottle of whisky among us and made tea and coffee for us. Then they pointed out the best and warmest places in which to sleep, while they slept on deck or anywhere else they could find.'

Borgund had no radio, so the outside world still had no news of *Glorious'* survivors. At 9pm on the 11th everybody on board *Borgund* held their breath whilst a Heinkel He.115 circled the ship suspiciously for some time before flying off. At 6pm on the next day Sergeant Jagger died and it was clear that some of the others, particularly Potter and Smith of *Acasta*, were sinking fast.

Borgund arrived at Thorshavn in the Faeroes at 6.30pm on the 13th. There she was joined unexpectedly by another Norwegian ship, the 1136-ton SS *Marita* of Drammen. Her Master, Captain P. Tedemann Anderson, said, 'On 7 June I sailed from Tromso on the orders of the Norwegian Naval Authorities. I was ordered to get away from my berth. I proceeded to the Faeroes on my own initiative, hoping to get in touch with the Norwegian shipping authority in London. On 10 June at 1500 in position 68 degrees 39 minutes North 4 degrees 5 minutes East a German plane circled and fired gun then a bomb to attract attention. We kept look-out and sighted raft with two dead, a second raft with two dead, and a third with one. They were all dead. We saw several other rafts with no one on board. Heavy oil surrounded the ship. No sign of life. After two hours we proceeded to the Faeroes with the five dead which we had picked up.'

The five dead included one man unidentified, who had wounds on his body and limbs, a tourniquet applied to his left arm and had an eagle tattooed on his right forearm. The other four were definitely from *Glorious*: Able Seaman W.F. Blake, who had died of exposure; Ordinary Seaman Albert C. Cox, who was scalded and burned on his arms and legs, and had died of his injuries and exposure; Stoker W. Newland, who had died of exposure: and Able Seaman H. Starke(y) who had died of wounds, severe burns and exposure.

Shortly after, a third vessel arrived, the Faeroese motor fishing vessel *Rokur*, who had on board one dead man, Stoker J. Wedgewood of *Ardent*. There was a fourth vessel with survivors, the Norwegian *Svalbard* ZZ, who had also been on her way to the Faeroes until she was unfortunately sighted by a

German aircraft and forced to return to Norway. On board her were Mr Blackwell, Joiner Joe Brown, Shipwright Norman Pike, and Stoker P.O.W. Tabb, with a fifth unnamed man who died. Those four were all that survived from the original forty on that float.

Borgund's crew had given freely of their own clothing and the people of Thorshavn were just as generous, providing thick woollen jerseys and stockings for every man. Meanwhile, it was the duty of the Naval Officer in Charge, Faeroes, Captain W.R.D. Crowther, with his small staff of three officers and 'four pensioner ratings', and with great help in medical staff, stores and transport from the army, to signal the news to the Admiralty, make nominal lists of the living and the dead, take details of next-of-kin, get an account of what had happened on 8 June from Jameson, MacLachlan, and Midshipman Eric Baldwin, the only three officers fit enough to be cross-questioned, arrange for death certificates and burials, take statements from the masters of *Borgund* and *Marita*, take on charge sums of money found in dead men's belts and burn the survivors' torn and salt-stained clothing.

There were messages and mementoes from the living on behalf of the dead. Ordinary Seaman Niccols handed in a wrist watch given him by 'Engineer Lieutenant-Commander Smith' (actually Smeeton, *Glorious*' Senior Engineer) which he had been asked to send home. There was the Padre's Zenith wristwatch, which a rating had handed to the military chaplain at Thorshavn when he arrived at the hospital. He stated that the Padre 'was on a raft for about twenty hours during which he did much to encourage the others on the raft by getting them to sing with him. He died peacefully and without pain.'

The dead mens' belongings made a melancholy catalogue. There was a leather wallet containing £1, belonging to Sub-

Lieutenant Thomas Jeffrey Earle (whose body was not recovered), an identity card from HMS *King Alfred*, and some private papers with the address 'Marestead House, Nr Winchester, Hampshire'. From Sergeant Jagger's body they took £11 4s. 7½d in cash, a gold wrist watch, a blue Royal Marine Jacket, a dungaree jacket, a signet ring and a letter from his mother addressed from '5 Lower Luton Road, Cold Harbour, Harpenden, Herts'.

Borgund had picked up thirty-eight men, and landed thirty-seven alive. But of those Chief O.A. Potter died in Thorshavn Hospital on the morning of 15 June and A.B. Smith of *Acasta* died twenty-four hours later. The five men from *Marita*, with Stoker Wedgewood, Sergeant Jagger, and Chief O.A. Potter were all buried in Thorshavn Cemetery on 15 June with full military honours, escorts and bearers from the Lovat Scouts and funeral services conducted by army chaplains. Able Seaman Smith was buried on the 17th.

Thus, there were only thirty-nine true survivors from *Glorious* and *Acasta*: thirty-five from *Borgund*, and four in *Svalbard II*, who were taken to hospital in Norway and then to PoW camps in Germany. Of *Borgund*'s thirty-five, Rupert Hill was the only ship's officer, MacLachlan and Baldwin of 823 the only FAA officers. Cross, Jameson and LAC Spencer were the only three from the RAF. The rest of *Glorious*' survivors were from several departments, seamen, stokers, marines, with one cook, John Millington, one air artificer, E.W. Stephens, and two air mechanics, J.A. Duffy and V.H. Day. Leading Seaman Carter was the sole survivor from *Acasta*.

Naturally, in after years, survivors came to wonder why they survived when so many did not. Age was no criterion. Hill was forty, Stoker PO Phillips was thirty-nine, like Lidstone, and Marine Wootton was thirty-five, while McBride was nineteen and Hobbs and Cleave were twenty. Healiss, whose nickname was 'Tubby', thanked his body weight. Hobbs said 'the Good Lord looked after me'. Rupert Hill said simply, 'It was a miracle.' O'Neill said, 'I wouldn't give in, although many times I felt like it.' He also had in his belt, along with his Post Office Bank savings book, a baby's caul, bought by his mother from a sea captain in the Isle of Man and given to her son to keep him safe at sea. (The superstition that the possession of the amniotic membrane from a child's head at birth will preserve the holder from death by drowning goes back to ancient times.) Leggott put his survival down to a country upbringing and country food, his own powerful physique and physical fitness, the extra slice of cake and cup of tea and an attitude of mind, of determination and fatalism: 'I survived the last day by getting my head down and just letting the wind blow where it wanted. I said to myself, hang on for four hours, and then, hang on for another hour. I was so incensed by the bloody Germans. It was an exercise in being bloody stubborn.' Elliott had no idea why he lasted out, except that he kept his exercises going (and he happened to be *born* with a caul over his head).

The loss of *Glorious* came as a very great shock to the Navy, and especially to Fleet Air Arm officers who had watched their colleagues' and friends' progress off Norway with admiration, tinged with apprehension. They had been delighted by their arm's successes, but knew that they were outclassed by the Luftwaffe. 'I watch with eagerness every move of the *Glorious*,' Guy Willoughby wrote from the Admiralty to Heath, 'and as far as I am able every move of every aircraft in the *Glorious*. The chaps are putting up an amazingly good show... I was most excited to hear of 802 knocking down that He.111 last evening.' But of the night the news arrived, Commander Rotherham wrote: 'I had often heard critical remarks in the

Operations Division including some by our Directors, but that night the conversation could only be called RED MUTINY. The Division had a small bar for the comfort of the Duty Office in peacetime, as this office was always manned. It had not been closed for the war but naturally was little used. However, that night it was in full use. We mourned our friends and we damned the crass stupidity which had caused the loss of this fine old ship. Such errors showed what little influence the few professional aviators of the day had upon current operations.'

But from initial shock and mourning, the mood quickly changed to a desire for some form of retribution — in a word, vengeance. Thus *Glorious*, by her loss, became directly responsible for yet another sad episode in Fleet Air Arm history: the Skua dive-bombing attacks on *Scharnhorst* and *Gneisenau* in Trondheim.

Admiral Marschall had scored an important success by sinking *Glorious*, but Raeder and Saalwaechter and the Naval Staff were unimpressed, indeed they were highly critical of Marschall's handling of JUNO. In their opinion his decision to attack the troop convoys instead of going on to Harstad was 'operationally false'. It had risked revealing his force's position before the main operation against Harstad could be carried out, and it did nothing to help the troops around Narvik (although, in fact, Marschall would have found the Harstad anchorages empty had he gone there). They were critical of the handling of *Scharnhorst* when she was hit by a torpedo and they did not agree with Marschall's decision to head for Trondheim. As for the sinking of *Glorious*, that was 'an extraordinary stroke of luck'.

Accordingly, the Naval Staff ordered Marschall to resume operations against the convoy. *Gneisenau* and *Hipper* sailed on the 10th, but were sighted and reported as 'a *Scheer* and a *Hipper* steering 300' at 2pm that day by the submarine *Clyde*. But it was clear to Marschall by that time that the troop convoys had escaped and *Gneisenau* and *Hipper* were recalled to Trondheim that evening of the 10th.

Clyde's report was one more indication to the Admiralty and to the C-in-C Home Fleet of where the best targets, in fact the ideal targets, for retribution now probably lay. Coastal Command aircraft had flown reconnaissances over Trondheim on the 9th, reporting first 'four enemy cruisers' (*Hipper* and four destroyers had arrived there on the morning of the 9th) and subsequently 'a battle cruiser, two cruisers and about seven destroyers' (*Scharnhorst* and *Gneisenau* arrived in the evening).

Sir Charles Forbes sailed from Scapa Flow at 12.50pm on the 9th and the flag he flew from *Rodney*'s mainmast was a Union Jack. He had been promoted Admiral of the Fleet on 8 May and this (as HM King George VI pointed out to Forbes) was the first time in history that an Admiral of the Fleet had flown the Union flag at the main as a Commander in Chief of a fleet in time of war. *Rodney*, with *Renown* and a destroyer screen, steered north to cover the troop convoy.

By the 10th the idea of an attack on the ships in Trondheim had taken shape. The Admiralty asked the C-in-C to arrange a torpedo attack by aircraft if the RAF reconnaissance found the enemy in port. So, when Forbes received the reports of the 9th, he ordered *Ark Royal* to leave the troop convoy and close him. But when the Admiralty received *Clyde*'s report they cancelled the Trondheim attack and ordered Forbes to search for the ships *Clyde* had seen. Forbes then took his ships east and then south-east to intercept. But nothing had been seen by midnight and Forbes turned back to the north-west again to cover the troop convoy. He had also asked Wells if *Ark Royal* could send an air striking force 'as the only hope of getting the ships'. But this too was put in abeyance for the time being.

On the 11th twelve RAF Hudsons raided Trondheim and reported a capital ship and two cruisers. They claimed a hit with a 250lb bomb on each of the cruisers. In fact, none of the German ships suffered any damage, but the attack confirmed that here at Trondheim were the culprits of the attack on *Glorious*. During the afternoon of the 11th the Admiralty signalled Forbes suggesting that Skuas be used to 'finish off the enemy ships'.

The proposal was that *Ark Royal*'s two Skua squadrons should fly into Trondheim and bomb the German ships. When Partridge, C.O. of 800 Squadron, was asked by Wells for his reaction he wanted to say, 'Whoever thought this one up must be absolutely bonkers. I'm not going and neither are any of my squadron!' But of course Partridge said no such thing. He did suspect that what everybody had in mind was a repeat of the great *coup* at Bergen against the *Königsberg*. Partridge pointed out that this time there was perpetual daylight and no night cover, clear skies and good weather and thus no cloud cover, and that the distance from the offshore islands to Trondheim was eighty miles and the Skuas were bound to be reported as they crossed the coastline. There were Me.109 and Me.110 fighter squadrons at Vaernes airfield, near Trondheim.

The plan was for the Skuas to fly off at midnight on the 12th and attack at 0200, to coincide with a diversionary attack on Vaernes by four Bristol Beauforts of 18 Group. Six Blenheims of 18 Group were to give Skuas cover as they flew in and out again. The attack was to be made by fifteen Skuas (nine from 803 Squadron, six from 800) because fifteen was the maximum number which could be flown off at full load in one range (and also because it was the maximum number of pilots on board who had Skua dive-bombing experience). The strike leader was Lieutenant-Commander John Casson, C.O. of 803 Squadron.

There were some thoughtful faces in *Ark Royal*'s wardroom and ready room that afternoon and evening. On the face of it this was an enterprise even more rash and ill-conceived than anything D'Oyly-Hughes had ever proposed, especially as German aircraft discovered the fleet soon after lunch and shadowed until the evening. Even Forbes signalled Wells, 'It does not look too hopeful for tomorrow; his reconnaissance is too efficient.' However *Ark Royal* continued to steer towards the flying-off position, passing the last store convoy from Tromso on the way and sighting many other merchantmen and trawlers, mostly Norwegian, 'all over the ocean'. The last Skua cleared the flight deck two minutes after midnight on the 13th. The fifteen Skuas formed up, climbed to 11,000 feet and set course for the mainland.

In the event, what happened over Trondheim exceeded everybody's worst fears. The weather was clear except for mist low down over the sea and the Skuas must have been sighted long before they reached Trondheim fjord. Over the town they encountered the fiercest flak barrage from ship and shore any of the crews had ever seen. The Beauforts appeared to have stirred up Vaernes rather than subdued it. The Skuas were engaged by Me.109s and 110s as they tried to deploy to attack their targets.

In short, each squadron lost four Skuas. Casson was shot down west of Trondheim; he and his observer Lieutenant P.E. Fanshawe became PoWs, as did Lieutenant C.H. Filmer and his observer, Midshipman (A) T.A. McKee. Sub-Lieutenant J.A. Harris was shot down; he and his crew, Naval Airman S.R. Stevenson both died of their injuries. Sub-Lieutenant R.E. Bartlett was also shot down. Of 800, Partridge had to bale out and, though badly burned, became a PoW, but his Observer, Lieutenant R.S. Bostock, was killed. Lieutenant G.E.D. Finch-Noyes was shot down and killed, but his crewman, Pilot Officer H.G. Cunningham survived. Midshipman (A) L.M. Gallagher and his crew, Petty Officer W. Crawford, both died when their Skua crashed in the forest near Trondheim. The Blenheims were seen as the Skuas retreated over the coastline, but it was a very subdued remnant of seven Skuas which landed on *Ark Royal* at 3.45 that morning. One 500lb bomb hit *Scharnhorst* port side aft, between No 4 5.9" turret and the ship's side. It rolled under the turret but did not explode.

Ark Royal and her escorting destroyers arrived at Scapa on 14 June, *Rodney*, *Renown* and their screen at 5pm on the 15th. The last convoys arrived without any further incident. As far as the Allies were concerned, the Norwegian campaign was over.

At Trondheim Admiral Marschall went sick — sick very probably with disgust rather than any clinical ailment. On 18 June he was relieved as C-in-C Afloat by Vice-Admiral Lutjens, who flew his flag in *Gneisenau* on 20 June when she, *Hipper* and a destroyer made a sortie westward towards Iceland. Possibly this was a diversion to cover the escape of *Scharnhorst* who sailed from Trondheim the same day on two shafts which gave her 24 knots, escorted by two destroyers and two torpedo boats. If so, it was a short-lived diversion, because *Gneisenau* was torpedoed by *Clyde* late on the 23rd. A large hole was blown in her hull forward and she had to return to Trondheim.

Scharnhorst was sighted by reconnaissance aircraft as she crept down the coast of Norway on the 21st and striking forces were improvised, of six torpedo-carrying Swordfish from Hatston and nine Hudsons with bombs, who carried out what the Germans called 'continuous air attacks' from 4pm onwards. *Scharnhorst* beat off her attackers with a prodigious expenditure of ammunition, shooting down two Swordfish, but retired into Stavanger fjord. She sailed from there next day and arrived in Kiel on the 23rd. *Gneisenau* was repaired sufficiently to be able to steam back to Germany and arrived, in company with the cruiser *Nürnberg*, on 28 July. For the German Navy the Norwegian campaign was over.

The fourth Skua of 800 shot down in the Trondheim raid was piloted by Midshipman Derek Martin, who was attacked by two German fighters which, approaching from the black mass of the mountain, were virtually invisible. 'I did not see the two which dealt with me until they were turned in on my tail; neither did my air gunner (Leading Airman W.J. Tremeer), though he did say, down the Gosport tubing, "Just a minute, sir". Perhaps he had seen them and this was his cool way of saying so, but I do not know. I turned into one fighter and his incendiaries, which I do remember seeing very clearly, missed. However the second fighter of which I was unaware was more successful. His bullets came through the back of the aircraft — and, I now believe, my air gunner, alas — under my seat and between my legs. They shot away all my control columns and the aircraft started to go into a dive which I had no means of stopping. I yelled "jump" several times.'

As Martin had feared, Tremeer had been killed, but he himself descended safely by parachute into a fjord, where a German seaplane landed close by and taxied towards him. 'I was very conscious of the machine-gun in the nose of the aircraft as it approached and waited — no doubt nervously; but nothing happened until a German airman climbed down on to the port float, called out in clear English, "Wait a minute," and threw me a rope. I climbed into the aircraft, under the pilot. I cannot remember what my feelings were, but they may have been influenced by my surprise at finding two seamen already on board. They were in a simply *dreadful* state. One of them said they were from *Ardent*.'

The speaker (the only one of the pair capable of speech) was Able Seaman Roger Hooke who had got away from *Ardent* on a raft with five other men. They had no food or water and the first man to die was a stoker after about twenty-four hours. A second, an Able Seaman, died later the same day. On the next day, a third man, an Engine-Room Artificer died. In the early hours of the following morning Hooke saw 'away to the north-west quite a lot of smoke on the horizon. As it increased we could see quite a large number of ships and of course hoped for the best. Well, on came the ships which turned out to be a big convoy of our soldiers withdrawing from Norway. With our two paddles we tried to get toward them but although the ships appeared quite plainly to us no one aboard was able to spot us.'

Hooke and his companions had the worst of luck. Later they saw a flying boat trying to attract a trawler's attention (clearly *Marita*). 'Three times she circled the trawler and then headed towards us but soon turned back again to the ship.' But evidently the trawlers' crew were watching the aircraft and passed on without spotting Hooke's raft. At last, towards midnight on 11 June, when a fourth man, a Leading Seaman, had died, and Hooke and the remaining survivor, Ordinary Seaman Robert Jones, had been on their raft without food or water for more than four days, the seaplane landed beside them, picked them up and flew them to Trondheim. Jones died after a fortnight in hospital, leaving Hooke, like Carter, the only survivor of his ship.

Thus, in *Glorious*, thirty-three officers were killed and another forty-two were missing. There were seventy-two R.N. ratings killed or died of wounds, with another 865 missing. Nineteen

Royal Marines were killed and eighty missing. One Maltese rating was killed and another thirty missing. There were six NAAFI staff missing. Of the RAF personnel on board five were killed and thirty-six were missing. Finally, eighteen RAF pilots of 46 and 263 Squadron were killed or missing. The total number killed or missing in *Glorious* was 1,207.

Of the two destroyers, *Acasta* had two officers killed and six missing, twelve ratings killed or died of wounds, and 139 ratings missing; also one NAAFI staff missing, for a total killed or missing of 160. In *Ardent* ten officers were missing presumed killed, two ratings were killed or died of wounds and 139 ratings missing; also one NAAFI staff missing, for a total of 152 killed or missing.

The total casualty list for all three ships was therefore 1,519 killed or missing.

The thirty-four survivors in Thorshavn (Able Seaman W. Smith of *Glorious* was not fit to leave hospital) embarked, or were carried, on board the destroyer *Veteran* on 16 June and sailed the same day. *Veteran* had been one of two destroyers ordered to join *Glorious* on 8 June, before it was known she had been sunk (and her Captain, Commander J.E. Broome, had incidentally stood best man at Charles Glasfurd's wedding).

The weather was bright and sunny and Broome made arrangements for *Glorious'* survivors to come up on deck and take the air. 'But no,' Broome discovered, 'they had had enough unrelieved daylight in the latitudes of the midnight sun. They had had fifty-six hours in the water, uncertain whether the enemy would return and find them. All they wanted now was food, warmth, some light music from the BBC and — darkness'. By torchlight Broome interviewed such survivors as were fit enough, wrote the first report of the sinking and, when *Veteran* passed through the Pentland Skerries on her way south, the report was fired across by rocket gunline to another destroyer which came alongside. While the report went to the C-in-C at Scapa, *Veteran* went on to Rosyth where *Glorious'* survivors were landed. (British Movietone News was there to film them going ashore but unfortunately this historic film deteriorated after the war and was 'junked'.)

The officers were taken to the Gleneagles Hotel, now a hospital, the ratings to Queensferry and then Kingseat, a former hospital for mental patients outside Aberdeen, to recover from their ordeal. At Gleneagles Hill and Cross both received letters from J.B. Heath. Heath was still at Scapa, still awaiting court-martial. In all the violent events since *Glorious* had left Scapa Flow J.B. Heath had been completely forgotten. His predicament was now more serious than ever. His accuser was dead, but so too were all his defenders.

EPILOGUE

'WHAT IS TO be done now about J.B. Heath?' That question appeared more awkward and embarrassing the more anybody in authority considered it. Heath had not been formally charged with anything. Nevertheless, the most serious and damaging accusations had been made against his professional conduct and his honour in what Heath called a 'most derogatory letter' which D'Oyly-Hughes had written about him and sent to Admiral Wells. The Admiral's Secretary, Commander Jasper Parrott, showed it to Heath. Heath was not the man to try then (or ever) to bring the Navy into disrepute by 'washing dirty linen in public' but he was determined to try to restore his good name and reputation, and he was perfectly entitled to do so.

Heath found an unexpected ally in 'this very splendid old gentleman', Captain R.T. Down DSO, the Captain of *Dunluce Castle*. 'He saw me with a face about sixteen feet long and he said, "Look lad, you've got something hanging round your neck. Are you prepared to tell me?"' Down was as downy an old bird as his name suggested. He knew his world and his Navy. He advised Heath to write an official letter to Wells, asking for a court-martial, and putting his own case. He helped Heath compose the letter.

At this point the news arrived that *Glorious* had been sunk. Heath realized that his accuser, and all his defenders, were now dead or at best, prisoners-of-war, and the only remaining evidence was the account written by Slessor and himself, which Heath had brought ashore with him. With this knowledge Heath wrote to Wells on 11 June: 'Sir, I have the honour to bring to your notice the very serious and painful position in which I find myself as a result of my suspension from duty in HMS *Glorious* on her arrival at Scapa on 30 May, a position, moreover, which has now been rendered infinitely more anxious and uncertain by the loss of that ship which has taken place through enemy action.'

Heath went on to say that he understood he was being detained in *Dunluce Castle* pending the Commander-in-Chief's decision, because of an adverse report made on him by his Captain but that he 'was still wholly unaware, officially, if this is the case or of the specific nature of any charges which may have been preferred against me'. Heath asked for 'the opportunity through trial by Court-Martial, or other means, of presenting my case for impartial judgment, with a view to clearing my honour and vindicating my professional reputation, both of which I have grave reason to believe have been directly or indirectly impugned.'

Heath enclosed with his letter a statement of events, based on the account he and Slessor had written; a copy of the contentious Air Operation Orders for 27 May, 1940, 'for five TSRs to bomb any suitable objective'; and 'Orders for Fighter Patrol over Squadron' in D'Oyly-Hughes' handwriting, with notes by Heath himself.

These documents, when they arrived in *Ark Royal*, understandably gave Wells food for thought. He forwarded them to the Commander-in-Chief, who in turn sent then to the Admiralty. Meanwhile, Parrott wrote to Heath on 15 June to say, 'I shall be only too pleased to help you in any way I can. The situation at the moment is that until last night V. A. A. had only received your Captain's story of what occurred. He now has yours as well and will consider it most carefully, as no doubt the C. in C. will consult him on his return to harbour.

For the present I don't think you can do any more. You have written down exactly what occurred and your account seemed to me (although it is not my place to offer an opinion on it) to put the matter in an entirely different light. This was not unexpected as certain difficulties you had were well known. At the moment, then, the only thing to do is to wait. When any line of action is decided upon by the Powers that Be I will come over and see you. I can be of no use until then.' Parrott went on to express his 'personal sympathy' and to hope that Heath would be 'able to clear himself completely of any allegations that have been made'.

Heath went on leave, while the Powers that Be pondered the problem. He could not be court-martialled. There were no charges and nobody to bring any. Even if he were court-martialled, Parrott (who had legal training and became a Barrister-at-Law) was in no doubt he would be acquitted. This would reflect upon officers senior to Heath, not least Wells himself. He had known of the state of affairs in *Glorious*, the 'certain difficulties' Parrott referred to in his letter. Further, he should never, for any reason, and certainly not merely for a court-martial, have allowed *Glorious* to proceed independently.

The Admiralty solved the problem, for the time being, by adopting what Stephen Roskill called 'the immemorial custom of successive Boards of rusticating officers with intractable problems to a remote station'. Heath was appointed Executive Officer of the seaplane carrier *Vindictive*, under Captain Halfhide, based at Freetown, Sierra Leone.

But even this appointment had had ramifications. Guy Willoughby, then in the Naval Air Division of the Admiralty, was one of those particularly indignant over Heath's treatment. 'I felt so keenly about it [the situation in *Glorious*] that I went to my Director, Captain Clement Moody, and told him of the

Captain's instability, and that if the ship was lost, only the Captain was to blame.' Willoughby was sent for by the Second Sea Lord (Admiral Sir Charles Little) 'to discuss what Heath's future should be, as he could not now demand a Court-Martial to clear his name, and his future must be adjusted so that this happening should not jeopardize his career.' Heath, like many senior FA A officers, was short of what Pound called 'sea time' for promotion; hence the appointment to *Vindictive*.

But Captain Down also took a hand. He had continued to encourage Heath, writing to him on z July: 'I feel sure all *must* be well and the more I think of it the more I feel you have an overwhelming case. But I expect you agree that you must try and make certain that you are "cleared" altogether.'

All was certainly *not* well, as Down discovered when he himself went on leave and called on the Second Sea Lord and the Fifth Sea Lord (Ramsay), who were both old friends, to talk about Heath and his case. 'For reasons I dare not commit to paper,' he wrote to Heath on 19 July, 'I am exceedingly glad I did, for, though I do not wish to seem boastful, your present job is in fact the happy result.

'I dare not say more here than that, to my intense surprise, things were not quite so well for you as I had confidently anticipated. But I was lucky, as, far from resenting my interference, my intervention was welcomed and extremely well received and I was able to convince them as I wanted and to smash the opposition with the view I so strongly hold about the whole case. That there was opposition from an extremely powerful quarter I shall never be able to understand or reconcile with my sense of elementary justice. But it was so. Remember, won't you, my little friendly caution to you, given in my cabin.' Down said no more. But the 'extremely powerful

353

quarter' hostile to Heath could, it seems, only have been either Pound or Winston Churchill.

When Halfhide died, Heath was given rank of Acting Captain in October, 1940, and confirmed in command of *Vindictive*. This (accepting command of *Vindictive*) Guy Willoughby considered a mistake on Heath's part, 'as we wanted very much indeed to get him back into the flying world which was getting very short of experienced senior officers.' But soon Heath went ever farther afield, to Singapore to advise on the possibilities of constructing airfields there, and then to Java as British Naval Liaison Officer on the staff of the Dutch Admiral Helfrich.

Cross and Hill both wrote from Gleneagles to assure Heath that they would do whatever they could. 'I am of course completely at your disposal,' Cross said on 2 July, 'and I remember very clearly the passage you mention on the bridge. I was astounded at the time. Also no one could have taken more trouble than yourself with the stowage, plans for ranging, ranging and taking off, and I am prepared to state that to anybody.' Hill, writing on 28 June, had, he said, only just regained the use of his fingers and could only scrawl with a pencil. Hill said that Heath was 'certainly well out of 8 June, as you would have copped it for a certainty on the bridge, as everyone there was killed by a salvo early on.' As for Heath's trouble, 'Vaguely I thought that the sinking of *Glorious* would wash the whole show out. Certainly, if I can do anything to help, I will do my utmost, but unfortunately I was never actually present when he did one of his turns at your expense. He slanged me a number of times before all and sundry on the bridge, but was mostly justified, I suppose, due to my lack of experience of keeping station with a squadron!'

The Admiralty held a Board of Inquiry into the circumstances of the loss of *Glorious* under the chairmanship of the Assistant Chief of Naval Staff, Rear-Admiral Arthur John Power (the same man who had been Captain of *Ark Royal* for two years before his promotion). The Board began by interrogating survivors while they were still at Queensferry and trying to come to terms with their disabilities. The experience in the floats had marked them: 'As I climbed out of the engine room of *Borgund*,' wrote McBride, 'I saw a mirror hanging on the door. I looked into it and my father stared back at me — a man of middle age.'

But the aftermath was as bad as, or worse than, the ordeal on the floats. 'We couldn't bear blankets on our feet so they stuck out at the end of the bed,' said O'Neill. 'The Sister used to come round and say, "Look at these *Glorious* feet!" The pain when they were starting to thaw was terrible. It is an experience you can never forget. There was nothing much they could do for you.' Jameson's feet resisted all attempts at treatment until, as he said, 'a dear old lady who owned some stables nearby brought along a bottle of stuff called "Mermaid Oil". It said on the bottle: "For use in stables, kennels, and piggeries". But I didn't care. The oil certainly did my feet good.' Some survivors retained a certain macabre sense of humour about their damaged feet. Marine Donnan carefully worked the dead skin off one foot until it came away in a shape like a deflated balloon made of wet blotting paper. He held it up and said to one nurse, 'Look, Nurse, I think my foot's just come off!' whereupon the poor young VAD fainted dead away. All the survivors found one totally unexpected reaction: their skins were so impregnated with salt they could never work up a lather with soap in the shower.

Of the Board, Hobbs recalls: 'We were all taken into a big room on our stretchers and placed in a semi-circle around a table. There was a Captain, a Commander and a shorthand typist and there were Marine sentries at the door. They asked us what happened, when did we go to action stations, did we hear that the Captain had been killed and so on.' According to Hobbs' recollection, the Board concluded with a farewell which might have been better put: 'Thank you gentlemen, and we hope you'll survive.'

The Board restricted themselves to the evidence of survivors and thus did not (as one would have imagined they would) interview Heath. Nor, curiously, did they interview Cross. Later he wrote his own report for the Air Ministry which was markedly restrained; Cross did not wish to criticise a sister service or a dead man, but he did note his surprise when he landed on board and found no patrols being flown. (It was not until months later, when Cross went out to the Mediterranean, that he was interrogated by the Navy. He was closely cross-questioned by Admiral Cunningham, the C-in-C, who eventually concluded from Cross's 'evidence' what he wanted to know, 'that *Scharnhorst* and *Gneisenau* must have been firing by radar'.)

The full report of the Board, which has not yet been published, was critical of *Glorious* and made clear that her state at the time of her loss left a great deal to be desired. But, after commenting that *Glorious* had no aircraft in the air for twelve hours prior to or during the action, that provisions and water were not provided in the Carley floats, that there was no lookout in the crow's nest in conditions of extreme visibility and other comments on the lengths of boats' falls (not long enough), shells and fuses supplied to the guns (of the wrong sort), the report concluded that 'the consequences of the action could not have been avoided in the situation in which the ships found themselves which arose from circumstances outside the scope of this enquiry, which has been confined to taking the evidence of survivors'. However, the Board also reported that all officers and men behaved with the utmost devotion to duty both during the action and afterwards, in accordance with the traditions of the Service.

That was well said, and needed saying. Nevertheless, the Vice-Chief of Naval Staff, Rear-Admiral Tom Phillips, in the notes made on 20 June in his handwriting on Commander Broome's account, pressed home some deadly points. 'It is hard to believe that the times are accurate. If so it appears *Glorious* was in a very bad state.' 'Why did she part company with *Ark Royal*? Having done so it would have been only prudent to have one aircraft in the air and remainder armed.' 'Wind N.W. and enemy came from windward. *Glorious* could not fly off without closing the range. I know her catapults were no good."1600: Enemy sighted. AIRCRAFT AT 10 MINS Notice. 1620: No aircraft in air and ship intact. 1640: No aircraft in air, but five TSRs ranged and UN-MANNED & UN-ARMED." I estimate *Ark Royal* must have been within aircraft striking distance when all this happened.'

Just as the Board was reporting its findings, tributes to D'Oyly-Hughes began to appear in *The Times*. His old submarine captain of the First War, Martin Dunbar-Nasmith, concluded his tribute on 1 July: 'He was held in great affection and always admired by his many friends. It was stimulating to meet him, always abounding in original ideas which he expounded with a sort of magnetic force. Often one disagreed with him, but always his ideas left their mark and gave one food for thought. Always one loved him. He is gone but his spirit lives as an example to all who follow him and in his death, like Cradock, he had fitted himself to have carved on his memorial:

"If our time be come,
Let us die manfully
For our brethren
And let us not stain our honour.'"

On 4 July, 'a correspondent' wrote: 'We who knew him just as a friend know we have lost one of the most loyal, honest and most gallant of men, who carried in him a peaceful heart, and we feel proud to have counted him our friend.' A 'Fellow Student' wrote of D'Oyly-Hughes' early days on 6 July, and Admiral Drax concluded on the 10th: 'Beyond all this he was an officer and a gentleman in the best sense of the word, and a lovable personality whose friendship was for all who knew him a very treasured possession.' It is Guy D'Oyly-Hughes' best defence, if indeed he needs any such defence, that he prompted such tributes (of which the quotations are only short extracts) from those who knew him.

The sinking of *Glorious*, *Ardent* and *Acasta*, with the loss of over 1,500 lives, was an immense tragedy in human terms, but it was overshadowed by larger events at the time. The battle in France was ending. The Battle of Britain was about to begin. Italy had just entered the war on the side of the Axis — on 10 June when the *Glorious* survivors were still in their floats. The losses had been suffered during an evacuation, and evacuations by their very nature, normally being carried out under pressure from the enemy, cannot be strictly planned or controlled. There was a further technical difficulty in command. The ships had sailed under the orders of Lord Cork and were to remain under his command until they passed south of Latitude 60° North. *Glorious* was still under Lord Cork's command when she was sunk, but the C-in-C resumed command of all warships when signalled to do so by the Admiralty on the afternoon of the 9th and of all operations in the north when Lord Cork hauled down his flag at midnight on 9/10 June. Commander Charles Hughes Hallett was Staff Officer Plans on Forbes' staff throughout the Norwegian campaign and according to him 'the sailing of *Glorious* with her two destroyers was by order of Flag Officer Narvik [Cork] and indeed I am not sure C-in-C Home Fleet knew anything about it until she was at sea. I am not suggesting that Forbes would have done anything different, but he had some heavy ships under his orders which Flag Officer Narvik had *not*, and could have provided cover. Admiral Forbes, I suppose out of a feeling of loyalty, did not make this point after she was sunk.'

Nevertheless, there had been a failure in intelligence (which steps were taken at once to remedy). There had, to put it more bluntly, been a failure to brief Coastal Command adequately. *Glorious* should never have been allowed to proceed by herself for any reason. Above all, it had been demonstrated that the price of security in war was eternal vigilance and for an aircraft carrier that vigilance meant flying her aircraft. The Admiralty are not normally great respecters of personal reputations and could have expected to emphasize this vital principle, not just throughout the Fleet Air Arm but throughout the whole Navy, no matter whose reputation suffered. Instead, the Admiralty seems to have taken the view that *Glorious* had been a disaster on all accounts and there was nothing to be gained by crying over spilt blood. There is also, even today, the faintest suspicion that some powerful influence, maybe even the 'extremely powerful quarter' at which Captain Down had hinted, wanted the matter of *Glorious* laid to rest.

If that was so, if it was hoped that the matter of *Glorious* would be interred along with the bones of those who died in her, then the Admiralty were soon to be disappointed. There were more than a thousand bereaved families. Some of them soon began to write to their Members of Parliament. On 31 July, 1940, Mr Ammon, Member for Camberwell North, got up in the House to ask the First Lord of the Admiralty, Mr A.V. Alexander, whether the established custom of holding naval courts-martial following the loss of ships was still being adhered to, whether such courts-martial had been held as to the sinking of *Glorious* and what the findings of those courts were. He also asked whether there had been any inquiry into the conduct of naval operations after the evacuation of Narvik, which led to the loss of *Glorious*, *Orama* and two destroyers and, if so, whether the findings would be promulgated.

The First Lord replied that courts-martial were not always held. The loss of *Glorious* had been investigated by a Board of Inquiry, 'but it was decided that there was no advantage to be gained by holding a court-martial in addition'. The Board's findings were confidential and the First Lord regretted that he could not add anything further.

Mr Ammon then asked whether his Rt Hon Friend was aware that 'there is considerable perturbation in the Navy among the officers concerned?'. The First Lord said he did not know where there was evidence of perturbation and if anybody was so perturbed they should get in touch with him. Commander Sir Archibald Southby said that courts-martial were old-established customs and naval officers welcomed them because they made the circumstances of the loss of a ship public. The First Lord replied if a court-martial wars held, 'All the evidence is in public, and in the present circumstances I am not prepared to publish it.'

The mood of the House was good-humoured. (On a subsequent question, about the number of enemy submarines sunk or captured, another MP asked the First Lord, 'Is it true that British seamen when out on the water call out "Waiter" and Italian submarines come to the top?') But the matter did not end there. The next question on the subject was put by Richard Stokes, Labour Member for Ipswich, who was to be the Government's most dangerous and persistent questioner on the loss of *Glorious*.

Dick Stokes, a very popular MP, was an unusual figure for the Labour benches. He went to Downside and Trinity, Cambridge, was a member of White's Club and managing director of his family business of engineers, Ransome & Rapier. He seems to have made Churchill his principal political target and bombarded him with questions on such subjects as the supply of tanks to the Army — and *Glorious*.

Stokes was briefed by Wing Commander Edgar Kingston-McCloughry, a serving RAF officer; he had won a DSO and DFC with the Royal Flying Corps in the First War and wrote and published pre-war on matters to do with the air. McCloughry wrote on 1 August to suggest to Stokes a parliamentary question, on the basis that the A.O.C.-in-C Coastal Command, Air Chief Marshal Sir Frederick Bowhill, although responsible for air reconnaissance in the North Sea, had known nothing of the Narvik evacuation until he heard of *Glorious*' sinking. But details of the evacuation were known in the Air Ministry several days beforehand. Bowhill now claimed, according to McCloughry, that, if he had known of the evacuation, *Glorious* would almost certainly have been given air cover and Coastal Command would also have located and reported the ships which attacked her. Bowhill was reported to be furious and to have complained bitterly to the Chief of Air Staff.

Stokes also claimed other sources, among them Admiral Sir Max Horton, who had told him that after the loss of *Courageous* the Admiralty had decided that henceforth carriers would be given a permanent escort of one cruiser and four destroyers, but that, against the wishes of the Admiralty, Churchill had ordered *Glorious'* cruiser and two of the destroyers to bring home King Haakon of Norway instead. Later, Churchill went over the Admiralty's heads, so the story ran, and sent a direct order to *Glorious* to return home. Neither the Flag Officer Submarines, the A.O.C.-in-C Coastal Command nor the C-in-C Home Fleet was informed. (Stokes, incidentally, said he had discussed this incident with Pound just before Pound's death and Pound had agreed that much of it was true. As an example of how Churchill could sway Admiralty decisions, Pound told Stokes that *Prince of Wales* and *Repulse*, sunk by Japanese aircraft in the South China Sea in December, 1941, were sent out improperly escorted as a result of an all-night sitting with Churchill who 'argued and argued and argued and eventually about 6 o'clock in the morning Pound gave in and agreed to the ships going, but against his better judgement'.)

Whatever his sources, Stokes (who had been in correspondence with the Secretary of State for Air, Sir Archibald Sinclair, already on the subject) asked Sinclair in the House on 21 August whether the A.O.C.-in-C Coastal Command had been informed of the evacuation from Narvik prior to the sinking of *Glorious*. Sinclair replied that for reasons of security the decision to evacuate Narvik, 'which was of the highest secrecy', was not recorded in the log books of the staff officer Coastal Command, nor in that of the naval liaison officer Coastal Command, but that the A.O.C.-in-C had been informed of the decision.

Stokes was not satisfied with this and on 24 October he returned to the charge with another question to the First Lord, to ask whether he was aware that for forty-eight hours after the sinking of *Glorious* a considerable number of survivors had remained afloat on rafts and to ask why no adequate steps were taken to rescue them. The Parliamentary Secretary to the Admiralty, Sir Victor Warrender, took the question on his chief's behalf and replied that it was a fact that a considerable number of survivors remained afloat on rafts for some time and unfortunately, although ships and aircraft passed close, they did not sight them. Stokes then asked, was it not fact that many hundreds of survivors were not saved, was it not true that the A.O.C.-in-C Coastal Command had not been informed of the movements of *Glorious* and, if that was so, why not?

Warrender evidently bridled at this and replied that he hoped the Honourable Gentleman was not going to suggest that there was neglect to rescue these men. It was inconceivable to anyone who knew anything about the Royal Navy that the Admiralty would not take every step to rescue survivors. In this case, for some 'completely inexplicable cause', no signals from *Glorious* were intercepted. Mr Ammon here intervened to ask Warrender if he was aware that nearly 1,000 men were lost, at which there were cries from Hon Members of 'No'. He asked for a court-martial. Stokes asked why no instructions were passed to the operational staff of the Admiralty concerning *Glorious*' movements. Warrender retorted that that was an entirely different question. Southby asked if it were not time that the name of the officer responsible for the disaster was made public. Stokes said that, 'owing to the unsatisfactory nature of the reply', he was going to raise the matter again.

Warrender had been given a somewhat bumpy ride, but there was worse to come for the First Lord himself in an adjournment debate on the loss of *Glorious* on 7 November, 1940. Opening the debate, Stokes said he was not using it as a stick to beat Ministers or naval officers but he regarded it as his duty to the House and particularly to many relatives of the people who lost their lives 'in that accident' and survivors, some of whom had provided him with facts and information.

He said that it was idle to deny that public opinion had been disturbed by the loss of *Glorious*. There had been, he said, a feeling in the Lobby that it was unfair to take the matter up because the Captain had died. He said he did not know whether the Captain was to blame or not. He took it that the First Lord would tell them. It was fair that the Captain's name should be cleared once and for all if it was not his fault that the *Glorious* went down. If it was his fault, there was no disgrace attached to him. If the Captain's death was claimed as an excuse for not giving publicity and investigation to the matter, then Stokes's excuse was that 1,200 gallant men went down at the same time and their relatives have a right to know what happened. Some people might say that the bereaved would be distressed by this debate. Stokes said that was not his experience, from the numerous letters he had received. What *was* upsetting people was the thought that facts had been burked and hidden in order to protect people in high places.

Stokes said he would try to say nothing that would help the enemy. He knew *Glorious* had been engaged in the relief of Narvik, a delicate and difficult operation when secrecy was essential. But there were certain questions he was going to ask the First Lord. First, whether the First Lord was entirely satisfied that the proper instructions, the best that could be devised, were issued to the ship. Second, the ships which sank

Glorious must have been absent from their bases for some time beforehand; did the Admiralty know the movements of these ships, or was intelligence once again at fault? Third, the Grand Fleet (sic) under Forbes was within 800 miles of the sinking; did Forbes know generally of *Glorious*' movements and were his ships disposed so that, if he did not know, he could still give aid if *Glorious* met disaster? Fourth, when and at what hour did *Glorious* sink, were any signals received by Forbes or other high naval officers, and, if so, what action was taken? Fifth, did the Board of Inquiry, who must have known of the fate of *Courageous*, consider that an escort of two destroyers was enough for *Glorious* at such a time, and, if two destroyers were not enough, why were extra precautions not taken to protect *Glorious*?

At this point another Member jumped up to ask Stokes to think twice before he pressed for answers to most of his questions. Unabashed, Stokes replied that he would put the questions and leave the First Lord to decide whether he would answer them. Were the Operations Division and other appropriate divisions of the Admiralty informed fully by the Chief of Naval Staff of *Glorious*' movements? Was the A.O.C.-in-C Coastal Command told? Was the Vice-Admiral in charge of submarines? Stokes said he had been told not. Was the Admiral commanding aircraft carriers told? Stokes assumed the Board must have gone into these points. Another point might reflect on the gallant Captain. It was said that *Glorious* had not got her own reconnaissance flight up. Were her decks cluttered with extra aircraft?

Finally, Stokes said, he came to the most tragic part. From the three sunk ships there were only thirty-nine survivors. Is it true as was stated in the Press — Stokes had cuttings of interviews with survivors — that 1,000 or more men were on rafts for three days and two nights? Stokes complained of what he called the 'Gestapo methods' of Ministers. He said he had learned the names of one or two survivors and had got in touch with one of the officers and had been astonished when that officer sent him a telegram — here Stokes produced the telegram and read it — REGRET UNABLE TO SEE YOU. ADMIRALTY INSTRUCTIONS.

Although Stokes said he was 'not in the least unmindful' of the 'good things' the Navy had done — the River Plate, operations in the Mediterranean, submarine patrols, mine-sweeping, convoys, what he called 'the guts of the business' — he identified a sense of public unease about the Naval Staff's responsibility for the losses of *Courageous* and *Royal Oak*, the 'inconclusive action at Oran', the Dakar 'fiasco' and the passage of French cruisers through the Straits of Gibraltar. But he returned to the 1,200 dead men and their suffering relatives, said he was acting in good faith and hoped the First Lord would answer him, 'even if I am also to get a stiff naval wigging'.

Stokes must have known that he could not, in wartime, expect an answer to most, or even any, of his questions. Nevertheless, the House sensed that Stokes was speaking of a very real unease in the country over the loss of *Glorious* and a widespread suspicion that the Admiralty had slipped up. (In fact, many naval officers would themselves have dearly liked to have had the answers to Stokes' questions.) The repeated references to the dead men and their relatives, the mental picture skilfully created of *Glorious* herself, sunk far from any help and without proper escort, with nobody in authority having any real idea of where she was and what she was doing, all amounted to a most damaging political attack on the Navy.

The attack was maintained by the next speaker, Commander Bower, a serving naval officer and Member for Cleveland. He had just come back from three months at sea on convoy work, but before that he had been naval liaison officer to Coastal Command and in almost daily touch, he said, with the Operations Division of the Admiralty. He said that there had been no co-operation between the Admiralty, Coastal Command, Flag Officer Submarines and other high officers during the Narvik evacuation. 'I was myself on duty at Coastal Command at the time,' he said. 'We knew nothing about it.' Nor, he said, had the Director of Operations been fully informed about what was happening in the evacuation from Narvik.

At this point, Bower was in a position to complete the discomfiture of the Government and the Naval Staff. But he pressed too hard, wandered off the point into personal complaints about the way he had been treated; about a letter he had written, in his capacity as an MP, to the First Lord; about what he said was the way he had been victimized by being given a sea command, a corvette, unworthy of his rank and capabilities. Bower criticized Pound and cast doubts on his physical fitness for the duties of First Sea Lord. He continued for some time in the same aggrieved and resentful vein, generating more heat than light.

Mr Alexander replied flatly that he was not going to give the sort of operational information he had been asked for that day. He would, he said, with some sarcasm, have been very glad for the Board of Admiralty to have had a chance of attending an inquest held in public in Germany upon the sinking of *Graf Spee* in the River Plate. As for Pound, 'All I can say is that, day after day and night after night, working usually for about eighteen hours out of the twenty-four, and sometimes longer, he has shown a youthfulness and a capacity which some junior officers might well desire to emulate.' (The First Lord seemed unaware that not everybody would have been reassured by the news that the First Sea Lord, however youthful and capable, worked eighteen hours a day or more, day after day.)

The First Lord, in fact, answered none of Stokes's points. Bower had saved the day for him. Subscribers to the 'conspiracy theory' of public life might well suspect that Bower had been specially prepared as a decoy to divert fire from the Admiralty. But Bower's sense of grievance, and his sole concern for slights, real or fancied, are clear even from Hansard and it is quite evident that he was blissfully unaware that he had just performed a much greater service for the Admiralty than he could ever have done in all the years of his naval career. The First Lord must have been a very relieved man when, it being the hour appointed, Mr Speaker adjourned the House without the Question being put.

The loss of *Glorious* was never debated again. Stokes asked four more questions on 11 November, but the heat had gone from the topic. There was even a feeling that the only result of the debate had been the blackguarding of D'Oyly-Hughes' reputation. Admiral Sir Roger Keyes, then Member for North Portsmouth, in a generally disgruntled letter to Admiral Sir Herbert Richmond on 21 November, wrote: 'I must confess I was surprised to find the C-in-C and the Naval Staff still in office and apparently not at all discredited — all ready to do something *Glorious* (sic). What infuriates me is that they have tried to make D'Oyly-Hughes, a splendid fellow, the scapegoat for the frightful miscarriage.'

Many of the bereaved families Richard Stokes had referred to were not sure for a very long time whether, in fact, they were bereaved or not. The first telegrams were sent on 10 June and were followed on 1 July by a printed letter from Commodore V.A.C. Crutchley VC, Commodore of the Naval Barracks, Devonport, stating that thirty-five survivors from *Glorious* and *Acasta* had been rescued but as 'your brother/father/husband/son is not included in the list of survivors or in the list of those known to have been killed, My Lords must continue to regard him as "Missing" though They regret to have to state that in Their opinion the possibility of his being still alive is extremely remote.' In the same letter, next of kin were warned that 'it is not in the public interest that some of the information given should be generally published, and I am to ask that for the time being you will not communicate the contents of this letter to any but your immediate relatives.'

On 2 January, 1941, Crutchley wrote again, reporting further efforts to trace prisoners-of-war through the International Red Cross. Finally, on 20 October, 1941, Crutchley wrote formally, 'I am commanded by My Lords Commissioners of the Admiralty to inform you, with very deep regret, that They have now been obliged to presume the death of all the Officers and men who have been regarded as missing from H.M. Ships *Glorious*, *Ardent* and *Acasta*.' Only then could the administrative loose ends, the proving of wills, the widows' pensions, the life insurance policies, be tied up.

Answering a parliamentary question from Mr Lipson, Member for Cheltenham, on 12 November, 1940, the First Lord had refused to give details of survivors, saying he did not think any useful purpose would be served by publishing their names. Nevertheless, some names were reported in the papers and the whereabouts of some survivors became known. They were besieged with letters and visits from next of kin, desperate for information.

The survivors did their best and at least one, Ordinary Seaman Andrew Niccols, called on the widow of Lieutenant-Commander Smeeton to deliver her husband's watch. He was able to reassure her that her husband's end was peaceful; in fact towards the end Niccols had almost wished he could go the same way. The end seemed so quiet and easy. They appeared to go to sleep and passed away very soon.

But for many widows like Mrs Smeeton wartime life, with young children, seemed to stretch out like a dreary endless desert, with no joyful homecoming to hope for, not even the thrill of a letter to look forward to. One widow, Hope Slessor, went back to her native Australia with her young son to try and made a new life for herself. She got a job with the Naval Intelligence Department in the Navy Office in Melbourne, where, one day in March, 1942, she had an unexpected visitor — J.B. Heath.

Heath had managed to escape from Java after the Japanese invasion and by what he called some 'incredible strokes of luck' had made his way to Australia. He still had with him the precious document which he and Slessor had written on the incident in *Glorious* with D'Oyly-Hughes. Hope Slessor persuaded Heath to have the paper copied and the second copy left in Australia for safekeeping until the war was over, lest something happened to Heath on his way back to the United Kingdom. Hope Slessor was determined that some time, in some way, the true story of her husband and those who served with him in *Glorious* would be told.

Heath returned to England in July, 1942, 'dodging people building empires who hadn't got a chap with wings on' along the way, and went into the Admiralty as Assistant Director of Air Material, still with the acting rank of Captain. He still had not been court-martialled and now realized that he never would be. But he also had never had any reply to his letter of 11 June, with its enclosures, setting out his side of the case. Heath was quite confident of the rightness of his cause. The last letter from Jasper Parrott, in July, 1940, said, 'I thought your statement was a complete answer to any charges that might have been made and my personal opinion is that a Court-Martial would have vindicated you. I had intended offering my services to you in the preparation of your defence because I felt strongly that you were being wrongly accused. I only hope for your sake that justice will still be done in spite of the circumstances which have deprived you of trial by court-martial.' But justice had still not been done. Heath appealed to Admiral Sir Frederick Dreyer.

The appointment of Dreyer, in July, 1942, as Chief of Naval Air Staff, without a seat on the Board of Admiralty, must be one of the strangest aberrations of the whole war. At a time when naval air power was becoming ever more important, a retired Admiral was put in charge, of whom the kindest remark was that he 'was a dugout from the Boer War'. (He was, in fact, Jellicoe's flag captain at Jutland.) Certainly he had no great knowledge of naval air affairs.

Heath first went to see Dreyer and then wrote to him, enclosing the relevant papers, on 31 October, 1942, pointing out that, 'I am still without any definite information whether my honour and professional reputation are considered to have been affected by the events to which these papers refer.' Dreyer duly passed tire letter and papers on and up. Thus it came about that, two and a half years after he had been dismissed from *Glorious*, J.B. Heath received a letter dated 21 December, 1942: 'Their Lordships have had under review the circumstances which led to your leaving H.M.S. *Glorious* in May, 1940, and I am to inform you that in the official view of the Admiralty no charges involving your honour or professional reputation stand against you.

'The notation of the reason for your removal from the *Glorious* has been erased from your record. BY COMMAND OF THEIR LORDSHIPS, signed by the Secretary of the Admiralty.'

Later Heath commanded HMS *Nightjar*, the Royal Naval Air Station at Inskip in Lancashire, which was an anti-submarine Operational Training Unit, and was later still Captain in command of HMS *Heron* at Yeovilton. He was never known to mention his time in *Glorious* but it was common knowledge in the wardroom, 'the general feeling being that he had been treated very badly by Their Lordships, even though his personal honour and professional reputation had been cleared.' Heath tried very hard to persuade one of his officers at Inskip, Lieutenant-Commander Gerard Woods RNVR, to take a permanent commission but ironically, as Woods said, 'It was his [Heath's] personal history which persuaded me against such a step. One can do everything correctly as both man and officer, yet still get the dirty end of the stick.'

Many of the *Glorious*' survivors went back to active service, although a proportion were invalided. Cross and Jameson, that seemingly indestructible pair, returned to operational flying. Indeed Jameson, obviously under the healing influence of the miraculous 'Mermaid Oil', left hospital after only six weeks and after six weeks' leave took over command of No 266 Spitfire Squadron at Wittering, near Stamford.

Of the Fleet Air Arm survivors, Eric Baldwin was discharged from the Navy as medically unfit on 31 December, 1940. MacLachlan, who had also been a survivor of *Courageous*, went to 773 Squadron, the Fleet Requirement Unit at HMS *Malabar* in Bermuda, an excellent appointment for a man still suffering from frost-bitten feet, and later in December, 1943, to the escort carrier *Campania* (on Arctic convoy duties, a much less suitable berth). Leggott, after overcoming some initial reluctance, accepted a commission and by March, 1946, he was a Lieutenant-Commander and MBE commanding 1831 Squadron Corsairs in the light fleet carriers *Glory* and *Vengeance* in the Far East. McBride survived another ditching, in the Straits of Gibraltar in May, 1942, and narrowly escaped a third; then, serving in *Eagle*, he flew ashore with the rest of 813 Squadron to North Front, Gibraltar, shortly before the ship sailed for the PEDESTAL convoy to Malta, on which she was sunk, in August, 1942. He too was commissioned but never completely threw off the effects of his ordeal in the Arctic and was finally discharged as medically unfit in 1949, with the rank of Lieutenant-Commander.

Rupert Hill also had a busy war. He left Gleneagles early in August, 1940, and after leave joined HMS *Orlando*, the naval base at Greenock, in December. Later he was in *Furious* in 1942, as an acting Commander commanded the landing ship *Empire Arquebus* in 1944, and in 1945 went to HMS *Spartiate*, the naval base in Glasgow. He retired again after the war and died, at what must have been a fair age, on the thirtieth anniversary of D-Day in June, 1974.

Of the sailors and Marines, Donnan took nine months to recover from his frostbite, and then went to light duties in the Globe Cinema, R.M. Barracks, Stonehouse, Plymouth (where he met the Women's Royal Marine cinema projector operator who became his wife) and then to Burnham-on-Crouch, in Essex, as an instructor on landing craft. Elliott went to sea again, 'probably too early' in his later opinion, as a Petty Officer Gunner in *Ulster Queen*, and then went to the cruiser *Bermuda* in the Far East. Hobbs went to the destroyer *Westcott* on Arctic convoys and then the depot ship *Adamant* in the Far East. Cook Millington also went out to the Far East to join the cruiser *Exeter* and became a survivor for the second time when she was sunk in action with Japanese ships in the Java Sea on 1 March, 1942; he was a PoW of the Japanese for three and a half years and could be said to have had a hard war.

Of those who were PoWs in Europe, Roger Hooke, the sole survivor of *Ardent*, never recovered his health. He had one toe amputated and lost the use of the rest so that he had to wear surgical boots. His hair was black in 1940 but it was snow white when he was repatriated in 1943. He contracted pulmonary tuberculosis and remained an invalid, nursed by his wife Lilian until his death in November, 1978.

Of the other PoWs, Stoker Petty Officer Tabb never came home. He died on a prison working party in Silesia. But Joiner Joe Brown, Norman Pike and Mr Blackwell were flown back to England on 11 April, 1945, and were all interrogated about *Glorious'* fate. Mr Blackwell, as the ship's Warrant Telegraphist, was particularly closely questioned about the ship's last signals.

When the war was over it might have been expected that the story of *Glorious* could be told, but the official silence continued. Richard Stokes had never ceased to prod at the subject, hammering away with parliamentary questions on the subject of a proper inquiry or court-martial, the failure to inform Coastal Command and the question of the removal of *Glorious'* escort (on which Stokes had definitely been misled: no aircraft carrier was allocated a specific number or type of ship as 'her escort'). On 6 June, 1945, Stokes asked again for the publication of the *Glorious'* Board of Inquiry's report and was again told that such reports were confidential and never published.

At last, in response to yet another question from Stokes on 8 May, 1946, Mr John Dugdale, the Parliamentary and Financial Secretary to the Admiralty, released the official account of the loss of *Glorious*, *Ardent* and *Acasta*. The account did not explain why *Glorious* was not flying reconnaissance patrols for her own defence, nor why the survivors were not found for more than two days and then only by accident, nor why naval intelligence had been unaware that *Scharnhorst* and *Gneisenau* were at sea. But it did explain why *Glorious* was detached to proceed home independently: 'The aircraft carriers *Ark Royal* and *Glorious* had been dispatched from Scapa to Narvik on 31 May — the *Ark Royal* to provide fighter protection during the embarkation — the *Glorious* to evacuate Gladiator and Hurricane planes of the RAF from Bardufoss in the north of Norway. For some months prior to this date, aircraft carriers and other heavy ships had, in the absence of any threat from the German Navy, been proceeding independently across the North Sea without incident. Had the *Glorious* had sufficient fuel, she would have accompanied the second large group of ships as did her sister aircraft carrier, the *Ark Royal*. The *Glorious*, however, was unfortunately an old ship, whose endurance was limited, and it was consequently necessary that she should proceed immediately the fighters were flown on without waiting for the forming-up of the big group, as otherwise it was calculated that she would have insufficient fuel to reach British territory.'

Even in that one paragraph the official account contained inaccuracies. *Glorious* did not *sail* with the intention of recovering the Hurricanes; they flew back on board at Cross's suggestion, and after a gamble taken by him and his pilots. Also, *Ark Royal* was not *Glorious'* sister ship. However, the report was inaccurate in one much more important aspect. It appeared to confuse *Ardent* and *Acasta*, stating that *Acasta* was sunk first at about 5.28, and that it was *Ardent*'s torpedo which hit *Scharnhorst*, after which *Ardent* was sunk at 6.08.

Leading Seaman Nick Carter, *Acasta*'s sole survivor, went to the cruiser *Manchester* after his survivor's leave and was in her when she was hit by an aerial torpedo in the Mediterranean in July, 1941. Carter went in her to the United States for repairs and later served in the battleship *Howe* in the British Pacific Fleet. He had been cross-examined several times over his account of *Acasta*'s last moments and had even been threatened with punishment under King's Regulations and Admiralty Instructions if he had not told the truth. But he told his interrogators, and everybody else, of *Acasta*'s final torpedo attack. When he left the Navy in December, 1945, knowing that he was the last survivor, he saw himself as the guardian of his dead shipmates' reputations.

The official report now called Carter, officially, a liar. People stopped him in the street in his native Portsmouth to tell him he was a liar. Men he had served with said to him, 'You told us a good one about *Acasta*, didn't you?' He received abusive letters from next of kin accusing him of lying and of trying to be a hero at their dead relatives' expense. One letter simply said, 'Why, Mr Carter, why?'

Carter now began a one-man campaign to put the official record right. He enlisted the help of Stokes, who wrote to the Admiralty and obtained an admission of error from Dugdale. As a result of yet another question from Stokes, on 19 March, 1947, Dugdale published the correction, blaming an 'important source' (the German account of 1940) for the error, and now transposing the two names of *Ardent* and *Acasta* in the official account. As Carter told the Daily Express, 'I can hold my head up again'.

The German account Dugdale referred to was almost certainly the German News Agency item broadcast on 16 June, 1940, relayed by the Press Association and printed in British newspapers on the 17th. In fact, the Germans neither named nor distinguished between either of the destroyers: 'A glow of fire was to be seen in the *Glorious*. Slowly the giant began to turn on to her side. Pouring out flames and smoke, she drifted with the wind. A moment later she sank. But the (second) destroyer does not give up. Our guns silence her forward guns, but the aft guns continue firing. More salvoes from our guns and the enemy is at length silenced. The destroyer is in flames and slowly begins to sink. Steam arises, probably through the boilers bursting. Then the waves close over these brave opponents too.'

The Germans were unanimous in their praise of the destroyers. Kontre-Admiral Schubert, writing an account of the action in July, 1945, at the instigation of Rear-Admiral H.T. Baillie-Grohman, concluded, 'Not only the tactical handling but also the offensive spirit and pluck of the two destroyers was excellent. Every officer who went through this battle was of the same opinion. The destroyers did their job absolutely thoroughly, although it was a foregone conclusion that success could not be vouchsafed them in their hopeless situation.'

Despite the bravery and devotion to duty of both destroyers' officers and ships' companies, there were no awards for gallantry and only one posthumous mention in dispatches, for Commander Charles Glasfurd. Similarly, there was one award for *Glorious*' officers, ironically an OBE for J.B. Heath. Arthur Lidstone, promoted to Commissioned Stores Officer in 1942, was awarded a BEM.

With or without medals, the survivors went back to their peacetime lives. Carter got a job with the Water Board in

Portsmouth. Healiss joined the Corps of Commissionaires and worked for a ball-bearing manufacturers in Luton. James O'Neill, with a disability pension, went home to the Isle of Man where, believing that 'Our Lady had spared me for a purpose', he organized and raised funds for the King George's Fund for Sailors. Leggott went into agricultural administration in Zambia. Lidstone was Secretary of his local Kingsbridge (Devon) Branch of the British Legion. Donnan, though suffering from a bad back and recurrent frostbite every winter (as did Lidstone) went to sea again — in the 51-foot fishing boat *Bonnie Ann* and in the Sail Training Association's *Winston Churchill*.

Cross and Jameson resumed their RAF careers, Cross eventually retiring as Air Chief Marshal Sir Kenneth Cross, KCB, CBE, DSO, DFC and Jameson returned to his native New Zealand as Air Commodore Patrick Jameson, CB, DSO, DFC and Bar. By contrast, MacLachlan continued in the Fleet Air Arm but met his end in a most bizarre accident. In 1950 MacLachlan was a Lieutenant-Commander, commanding 800 Squadron flying Seafire FR.47S from the light fleet carrier *Triumph* in the Far East. On 29 August, off the Korean coast, a Firefly, landing on, tipped onto its nose. The propeller shattered and a large fragment smashed through a scuttle in the island and struck MacLachlan, inflicting head wounds from which he died. (MacLachlan had also, incidentally, been a survivor from *Courageous* as well as *Glorious*.)

If the Admiralty had ever expected that the official account would finally lay the last doubts about *Glorious*' fate to rest, once again they were disappointed. Winston Churchill, when writing *The Second World War*, examined the Norwegian campaign in general and *Glorious* in particular. He asked if he could quote a long extract from the account Carter wrote of

Acasta's last action for Stokes (whereat there was much balm in Gilead for Carter, after all the insults he had suffered).

Churchill did not think much of the 'shortage of fuel' theory. He recounted how *Glorious* had been detached early on 8 June to proceed home independently owing to shortage of fuel and when she was attacked was nearly 200 miles ahead of the main troop convoy. 'This explanation is not convincing,' Churchill wrote, in Volume I of his history, published in 1949. 'The *Glorious* presumably had enough fuel to steam at the speed of the convoy. All should have kept together.'

The explanation may not have been convincing, but it was given by the writers of the official naval staff account of naval operations in the campaign in Norway, prepared in 1946; by Dr T.K. Derry, the official historian of the Norwegian campaign, in his account published in 1952; and by Captain Stephen Roskill, the official historian of the war at sea, in his account published in 1954. All these probably, and Roskill certainly, had access to all ships' reports of proceedings, signals and the report of the Board of Inquiry presided over by Rear-Admiral Power.

Of *Glorious* Roskill wrote: 'It is reasonable to suppose that such an unusual operation (i.e. landing on the RAF Gladiators and Hurricanes) may have disorganized the normal arrangements in the aircraft carrier, but she had on board sufficient Swordfish aircraft wherewith to maintain reconnaissance flights and to form a small striking force should the need arise. While the truth regarding her condition is unlikely ever to be known, it seems strange that no patrols were flown at this time for her own protection, nor a striking force kept prepared. What is certain is that she was caught not only unawares but virtually defenceless when, at 4pm, the German battle cruisers sighted her smoke.'

J.B. Heath, living in retirement at his home in Somerset with his memories and his OBE, made no public comment on the official history. He still had all his papers and could give a clear account of all that had happened, but he had never done so, except to a very few, very close friends. He had no bitterness over his own treatment, and never regretted the action he and Paul Slessor took. But his one terrible regret was that their action 'did not avert a disastrous end, the loss of so many friends and a most valuable ship'.

But if Roskill got no response from Heath, he had a great deal more than he expected from the D'Oyly-Hughes family. He had a resentful letter from Mrs D'Oyly-Hughes and later a 'savagely angry' letter from Colonel Richard D'Oyly-Hughes, Guy D'Oyly-Hughes' brother. Roskill himself felt that he had made only a 'mild criticism' of the state of *Glorious* and the circumstances leading to her sinking. But, as his history was about to be reprinted, he consulted Cross (who agreed with his criticism) and went over the evidence again, including the report of the Board of Inquiry. From these Roskill concluded that he had been too charitable the first time and that, if anything, he should strengthen his criticism of D'Oyly-Hughes rather than relax or eliminate it. He decided to let the original version stand, largely because D'Oyly-Hughes was, of course, unable to speak in his own defence. He could not send Colonel D'Oyly-Hughes the complete riposte, which would have been the Board of Inquiry's findings, because it was (and still is) jealously guarded by the Admiralty and he would have been contravening the Official Secrets Act. However, luckily Cross had known Richard D'Oyly-Hughes when he was serving in a Gurkha regiment and Cross wrote him a tactful and calming letter.

Roskill himself took no further action and must have thought that the *Glorious* story was now finally settled, but in July, 1963, he happened to meet Mrs Hope Slessor in London. Roskill and Paul Slessor had served together in *Eagle* on the China Station in 1933-35 and Roskill had also known the Slessors in Malta shortly before the war. It was natural that they should talk over old times, and especially *Glorious*. Hope Slessor stunned Roskill by telling him that his official history was wrong, so far as it related to *Glorious*. Furthermore she had documentary proof.

When Roskill had read the papers Hope Slessor produced for him, he at once began to exercise his formidable talent for collecting and weighing historical evidence. He wrote, among others, to Heath — a letter which arrived in Somerset like a bolt from the blue. Heath had kept his story bottled up inside him for nearly thirty years. It was now a very great relief and pleasure to tell it all to such a sympathetic — and prestigious — audience. From the papers and interviews that J.B. Heath, Hope Slessor and others provided, Roskill had no doubt that Guy D'Oyly-Hughes' behaviour and his conduct of his ship's operations were much greater factors in bringing about the ship's loss than he had realized.

Clearly the record should be put straight. Neither Roskill nor Hope Slessor wanted anything published while D'Oyly-Hughes' widow was still alive. But in his book *Churchill and the Admirals*, published in 1977, Roskill wrote: 'The story of fuel shortage is false. Not only had she replenished at Scapa before sailing for the last time, but the Captain of the destroyer *Diana* took in a long visual signal made by the *Glorious* to the *Ark Royal* asking permission to proceed to Scapa "in order to expedite Courts-Martial".' Roskill also wrote that he 'would be publishing elsewhere a full account of the circumstances attending the loss of *Glorious*.'

'Elsewhere' was, in the end, an article in *The Sunday Times* which appeared on 15 June, 1980, under the headline 'The Cantankerous Captain of HMS *Glorious*'. It relates the story of the loss of the ship, but this time in the light of the situation on board as told by Heath and Slessor, and D'Oyly-Hughes' intention of court-martialling Heath (and almost certainly Slessor — the memories of Le Geyt in *Diana*, and others who heard wardroom gossip of the time, insist that it was 'courts-martial, plural'), with additional information from officers such as Ben Bolt, who had previously served in *Glorious*, and letters such as that from Blakeney, provided by Heath.

True to the D'Oyly-Hughes family tradition, there was a reply the next week, in the form of a letter to the Editor, this time from the next generation, D'Oyly-Hughes' elder daughter Bridget, now Mrs Michael Riviere. To Mrs Riviere, Roskill's article had (understandably) appeared 'to be an unpleasant personal attack in the guise of naval history'. She made several good points: that her father was an enthusiastic student and exponent of naval aviation and had learned to fly; that he had made a particular study of the vulnerability of capital ships to air attack; that he was rightly concerned that his sailors were overdue for leave and his ship desperately in need of a long refit; and that her father would attack the enemy whenever he might be found, no matter how unorthodox professional aviators might think his methods. Mrs Riviere also made one uncontrovertible point: the decision to detach *Glorious* and her escort was made by Admiral Wells, not her father, and the Admiral must have had what seemed to him a good reason. As for the fuel, Mrs Riviere made another valid point: nobody should assume, as the article did, that *Ark Royal* and *Glorious* consumed fuel at exactly the same rate and began with the same quantity of fuel in their tanks.

The letter was altogether a brave and very competent defence by a daughter of her late father. Certainly it enraged Roskill who wrote another letter, a reply to the reply, but it was not printed. It also enraged others, especially some who read that 'Lord Mountbatten wrote to my mother and said that so highly did he value my father that even the loss of a capital ship was probably of less consequence to England than the loss of her captain'. This, as the family later explained, was a private letter of condolence to a widow, and the 'capital ship' was not intended to mean *Glorious*.

Mrs Riviere's comments, in her letter and quoted in Roskill's article, on the quality of the officers her father found in *Glorious* (e.g. that he 'had the feeling of endlessly kicking a ball which proved to be half-full of argumentative soggy cotton wool') provoked Ben Bolt into carrying out some research, through the Second Sea Lord's department, on the subsequent careers of those officers. He established that between them they won five DSOs and twenty-eight DSCs and two Bars, in actions from Taranto to Matapan to the *Bismarck* chase, the Arctic convoys and the attacks on *Tirpitz*.

On 11 July, 1978, one of several modern stained glass windows by Jane Gray, was dedicated to St Nicholas, patron saint of sailors, in the church of St Peter's, Martindale, Cumbria. The design shows the full length of an aircraft carrier in plan view, with her bows cleaving the waters and the stars of heaven above to guide. The round leading edge of her flight deck, the island on the right-hand starboard side, the horizontal bars of arrestor wires and the shapes of gun sponsons can all be seen. On the flight deck are depicted a phoenix, rising perpetually from the flames, the rose and sunburst of HMS *Glorious'* ship's badge, surmounted by a naval crown, an anchor and the arms of St Nicholas — three sacks of gold, upon an open Book of the Gospels, with the Latin words telling of God who in the beginning made all things.

The window is inscribed to Parkin, friend of Heath and Slessor. He was a parishioner of St Peter's and his family have lived in the area for generations. The inscription reads: 'In memory of Commander William Hugh Parkin Fleet Air Arm RN and the Officers and men killed in action H.M.S. *Glorious* sunk in Norwegian waters 8 June 1940'.

A few Fleet Air Arm Officers' Association members have adopted this church as a F.A.A. shrine and, in September, 1984, held Sunday Divisions there. In that tiny church, hidden away in the folds of remote hills beside Ullswater, the story of *Glorious* and the men who served and died in her comes to an end.

APPENDIX I: EXTRACT FROM THE LOG OF THE *GNEISENAU* FOR 8.6.40.

(N.B. German time was one hour ahead of British time.)

1640: *Gneisenau* and *Scharnhorst* in position 69°N 3°10'W Course 330° Speed 19 knots. On their way to warn the 'Dithmarschen' of the imminent danger of the 'Southampton' Group and to order her to move her position line further to the North. After this they intended to attack the *Ark Royal* and *Glorious*, who had been picked up by the 'B — Dienst' (= Y Service).

1646: 'Dithmarschen' not yet reached. Midshipman in the *Scharnhorst* sights a small cloud of smoke on the starboard quarter on a true bearing of 060°. *Gneisenau* immediately informed.

1657: *Gneisenau* reports: 'Heavy unit, 20° on the port bow'. (This was inaccurate as *Glorious*' actual position was on the starboard bow.)

1700: 'Action Stations'. Alter course to 030°. Heavy unit identified as an aircraft carrier. Speed increased to 24 knots. (At this point she still only had steam for cruising speed, although she had started to raise steam in all boilers at 1647 on being informed of the vicinity of the *Glorious*.)

1709: Carrier 50° on the starboard bow, range 36,130 yds. Altered 40° to starboard on the Course 070°.

1713: Carrier bearing Green 30°, 10 miles. Two small masts sighted to port of the *Glorious* thought to be destroyers. There was considerable doubt throughout the action as to the identity of the three British ships, and they are referred to during the action as the 'Aircraft Carrier' and the 'North' and 'South' destroyer.

1718: Orders for C-in-C to turn to starboard and proceed on Course 200°. This was a poor position strategically for the guns, but had to be made the best of.

1719: One destroyer reported to be turning towards the *Gneisenau*, A/A Gunnery Officer warned of the danger of dive bombers. No aircraft took off from the *Glorious*, however, at any time.

1722: *Scharnhorst* bore 0550 from *Gneisenau*. Range of enemy 21,540yd.

1726: Proceeding at 26 knots. Secondary Armament opened fire on British destroyer.

1727: C-in-C ordered increase to 29 knots.

1728: Torpedo warning issued from Foretop. Engine room informed that port side was open to attack.

1729: Carrier identified as the *Glorious*. Range 16,400 yds.

1733: A/C to 170°.

1735: *Glorious* enveloped in smoke screen laid by the destroyers. Conditions for the guns very difficult.

1736: Reduced to 20 knots as *Scharnhorst* was dropping astern, and the *Gneisenau* was consequently coming up on her engaged side. Orders from C-in-C to proceed on 180° at 30 knots.

1740: Speed 29 knots. The destroyer *Ardent* also enveloped in a smoke screen, now became visible again, and opened fire at a range of 16,400 yds. C-in-C requested: 'May *Gneisenau* proceed ahead of *Scharnhorst*?'

1742: Orders from C-in-C to proceed at full speed. *Gneisenau* turned hard to starboard to avoid a torpedo track, but it proved a false alarm and she resumed her previous course.

1743: The *Gneisenau* passed the *Scharnhorst*, at the same time receiving orders from the C-in-C to alter to 170°.

1745: *Gneisenau* proceeding at 30 knots opened fire on the *Glorious*. The Captain decided not to fly off the seaplane as it had been damaged by the *Gneisenau*'s own salvoes. The battle with the *Ardent* was being taken over more and more by the *Scharnhorst*. The Captain of the *Gneisenau*, Netzband, is reported to have said, 'the conduct of the *Ardent* was particularly spirited and clever. She outmanoeuvred the fall of shot very capably, laid smoke and used it with great skill, and varied her speed from 10 to 35 knots. In this way she made the task of our guns very difficult.' The observing of definite hits on the enemy was made difficult by the thick smoke and white vapour. At about 1742 however, a hit was observed at a range of about 15,730 yds. on the *Acasta*, who then proceeded at about 10 knots with a heavy list. From then on she was left to the *Scharnhorst*.

1747: Speed 30 knots. *Glorious* bearing 90°. Range 27,340 yds.

1750: *Glorious* again concealed by smoke. The *Ardent*, who had originally been to starboard of the carrier, now moved over to her port side. Course now 150°. Second Gunnery Officer warned to beware of the destroyer when she emerged from the smoke screen. This warning was passed on to the entire crew.

1755: *Glorious* visible. Opened fire.

1756: Hit observed on afterdeck superstructure of carrier.

1757: *Glorious* once again enveloped in thick smoke screen. Lookouts warned to keep special watch for torpedo tracks.

1758: The *Ardent* sighted to port of the carrier. *Gneisenau* opened fire on her with her secondary armament, and the destroyer altered towards. Distance between two ships estimated at 18,370 yds. At this stage of the action orders were received from C-in-C not to make unnecessary expenditure of ammunition. The *Gneisenau* ceased fire.

1803: Lookout reports 'Destroyer has fired three Torpedoes.'

1804: De-Te Apparatus (Type of Radar) trained on the smoke screen covering the carrier, but no useful result was obtained. The distance between the smoke screen and the *Gneisenau* was decreasing rapidly, and orders were passed to the Second Gunnery Officer to open fire without delay with Main Armament on any British Warship emerging from the smoke.

1805: Speed 31 knots.

1808: Proceeding on Course 140°.

1809: A/C to 130°. Main Armament gun crews warned of a destroyer in the smoke ahead.

1812: *Glorious* came in sight again. Opened fire, range 26,460 yds.

1815: Ceased firing due to poor visibility. *Glorious* observed to alter to 090° and at 1820 was once again enveloped in a thick smoke screen.

1823: *Ardent* observed to capsize.

1825: The distance between the *Gneisenau* and *Glorious* was decreasing steadily (at that time approx. 21,870 yds.) and the carrier was lying abreast our port bow. The *Acasta* also was faintly visible.

1829: *Gneisenau* opened fire again. The *Acasta* observed to fire another salvo of torpedoes, at which *Gneisenau* turned to port and the destroyer swinging to starboard after making her attack, came in position right ahead and was fired on with the Secondary Armament.

1835: Course 115°; range of carrier 9,840 yds.

1836: Report 'torpedo track approaching, bearing 270°.'

1837: A/C 180°.

1838: *Glorious* observed to list heavily and burn fiercely.

1840: Carrier in position right ahead at a distance of 5,060 yds directly in *Gneisenau*'s line of advance.

1841: *Gneisenau* ceased fire on orders from C-in-C, but at 1845 opened fire again on the *Acasta*. Range 14,220 yds. Course 200° altering to 170° in order to close range.

1852: Orders from C-in-C: 'Proceed on new course 155° at 24 knots, Range 12,250 yds.'

1855: 'Engage Destroyer ahead.'

1906: *Gneisenau* turning to course 080°, range decreasing.

1907: Range 11,490 yds. Hit and heavy explosion observed aboard the *Acasta* followed by further hits.

1908: Last salvo fired at a range of 10,940 yds silenced the destroyer. The carrier had already sunk.

1909: Permission granted to open fire on the *Acasta* once again with the Anti-Aircraft Guns as she was now within range of these.

1913: 'Cease fire all guns' as the destroyer was obviously sinking as a result of hits received from the secondary armament. The entire engagement lasted 1 hour 8 minutes, and 1 hour 30 minutes after the firing of the first salvo, the *Glorious* sank.

APPENDIX II: EXTRACT FROM THE LOG OF THE *SCHARNHORST* FOR 8.6.1940

1730: Secondary armament opened fire on the *Ardent*. Bearing 120°. Range 16,000 yds.

1732: Orders received from C-in-C to open fire on the *Glorious* with main armament, Range 28,600 yds. For the first 15 minutes of the engagement the *Glorious* bore approx. Green 40°, proceeding at 28/30 knots. After this she drew aft on an average bearing of 90° with a decrease in speed to 25 knots, and at ranges varying between 24,200-25,900 yds. After 1826 the range diminished rapidly due to *Glorious*'s decreased speed, and at 1840 when *Scharnhorst* fired her last salvo, the range was 8,700 yds. The *Scharnhorst* arc of fire lay between 327° and 028°.

1733: Secondary armament ceased firing due to interference with Main armament.

1735: 'P' turn executed on to Course 170°. *Ardent* lays smoke.

1736: Speed 29 knots.

1738: Increased to 30 knots. Hit observed on *Glorious* and *Ardent* opened fire.

1740: Secondary armament opened fire on *Ardent* who turned towards, and made firing very difficult by skilful smoke screening. *Acasta* also laid smoke to conceal the carrier.

1743: Order received from C-in-C that operational orders were to be issued to the *Scharnhorst*'s seaplane at the discretion of the Captain. The Captain decided to wait for a suitable opportunity which, however, never arose.

1744: Signal from C-in-C: '*Gneisenau* is taking up station ahead of *Scharnhorst*.'

1745: Torpedo track approaching on bearing of 330°. Turned hard to port, and minute later resumed her original course.

1747: *Ardent* fired torpedoes and retired into smoke screen. Immediately after the hydrophone listening watch reported a Torpedo passing close on the port side.

1750: *Ardent*'s salvoes fell short.

1753: Signal from C-in-C: 'Proceed on Action Course 130°'. This course brought the *Glorious* and *Ardent* right ahead.

1755: Hydrophone Watch reported Torpedo approaching on a bearing of 110°. *Glorious* hidden by smoke screen.

1801: *Ardent* engaged with secondary armament on appearing out of smoke. Range decreasing rapidly and adding to the danger of torpedo attack. Foretop instructed to keep a careful watch.

1802: Proceeding at 27 knots on middle engine; one boiler out of action due to suspected tube fraction.

1804: *Ardent* proceeding rather slowly with a heavy list, received a direct hit. Signal received from C-in-C: '*Ardent* has fired three Torpedoes.'

1807: Hydrophone Contact reports Torpedo approaching on a bearing of 330°. *Scharnhorst* turned 20° to port.

1808: Signal addressed Gruppe West (Group Command West) from C-in-C: 'Enemy Aircraft Carrier in position 60°36'N 0°05'W, proceeding at full speed on a south easterly course.'

1809: Resumed original course. A further hydrophone contact reported a Torpedo approaching on a bearing of 320°.

1811: Further hit observed on *Ardent*, and the Captain opened fire on her with the anti-aircraft Guns, using fuze-settings.

1813: *Glorious* visible once more. Foretop reported Torpedo track to port. Immediate alteration 20° to port and Torpedo crossed the bows. Resumed original course.

1817: *Glorious* observed burning fiercely aft, and a minute later the main armament opened fire on her again. The *Ardent* listing more heavily.

1819: Signal to C-in-C: 'Unable to maintain speed owing to defect in Engine Room. Able to proceed at 28.5 knots.'

1825: *Ardent*'s mast broke off, and, listing even more heavily, she finally capsized. Secondary armament ceased fire.

1823: Hydrophone contact reported Torpedo approaching on bearing 010°, and a minute later was reported to have passed ahead. *Scharnhorst* engaged *Acasta* with her secondary armament. *Glorious* burning more fiercely.

1826: Secondary armament opened fire on *Acasta* without permission. As the latter was outside the effective range, they were ordered to cease fire. Further signal received from C-in-C requesting every possible economy in the use of ammunition.

1831: *Acasta* still laying smoke opened fire. Salvoes fell 55 yds short of *Scharnhorst*'s bows.

1832: *Acasta* appeared to be altering towards. Course 170° with the intention of engaging *Acasta* 20° to starboard.

1833: Foretop reported that *Acasta* had fired three torpedoes from a bearing of 10° to starboard, and was now laying smoke and zigzagging past the bows of the carrier, making accurate firing of our secondary armament which now engaged her, very difficult.

1834: Course 150° altering to 170°. VH/F apparatus reported out of order.

1835: Violent shudder astern. Suspected torpedo hit. This was confirmed later when pieces of the casing were found by the crew. There was considerable doubt as to whether the torpedo had been fired by the *Acasta* or a British submarine. The C-in-C, Admiral Marschall, was of the opinion that it had been fired by a submarine, as the damage was on the starboard side, and the *Acasta* had been to port. The Captain of the *Scharnhorst*, Hoffmann, however, considered it more likely to have been the *Acasta* on account of the intricate turns she had been executing at this time, and it was thought quite possible that she may have been to starboard at this time. The C-in-C, Admiral Marschall, delayed attempts to rescue survivors on account of the suspected presence of a British submarine.

1839: The De-Te (Type of Radar) Apparatus was reported defective. A further reduction in speed was also necessary. Altered course to 090° in order to close the *Gneisenau*.

1842: *Acasta* engaged by the Secondary Armament.

1843: A/C to 190°. The gun's crew was forced to abandon one of the turrets, which was later flooded. The Ammunition Chamber was reported to be flooded. Starboard Engine failure. Speed maintained at 26 knots.

1846: Course 260°. List increasing to starboard with flooding in various compartments.

1851: A/C to 180°.

1852: Pumping in progress. The *Acasta* was now outside potential torpedo range, but still in sight and was engaged by the secondary armament. Signal received from C-in-C: 'Take up station astern of the *Gneisenau*.' The Engineer Officer reported that no damage had been sustained affecting the ship's seaworthiness.

1859: C-in-C requested confirmation that *Scharnhorst* was able to maintain speed at 28 knots.

1900: Reply made: 'Able to proceed at maximum speed of 27.5 knots'. One turbine reported defective.

1905: The middle engine slowed down and a minute later stopped completely. A second turbine was flooding, and one propeller limping badly.

1908: The *Acasta* was observed burning fiercely aft, and the secondary armament was ordered to cease fire in order to conserve ammunition. The *Glorious* was no longer visible.

1909: Speed further reduced to 25 knots, and the limp in the propeller became more marked.

1910: *Acasta* was continuing to fire. The secondary armament engaged her again. The *Scharnhorst* received another shell in one of her turrets.

1912: Orders received from C-in-C to cease fire. The damage in the Engine Room was considerable. The middle engine was flooded and out of action. Revolutions on the starboard engine had to be reduced due to heavy knocking and shaft vibration.

1915: All positions were informed of a pause in the action.

1917: Orders received by VH/F to proceed on Course 070°, speed 24 knots. The Engineer Officer reported that the starboard propeller was limping, and that the after 'tween deck was flooded. Pumping was in progress, and fuel was pumped out to even the list.

1922: Speed reduced to 21.5 knots and Action Stations secured. The *Acasta* was then in a position astern, burning fiercely and out of control. The *Scharnhorst* was under no difficulties with her steering and the damage was under control.

1932: Speed maintained at 24 knots.

2000: In position 68° 30'N 5° 50'W. Course 160°, 24 knots.

APPENDIX III: REPORT BY THE CAPTAIN OF THE *SCHARNHORST*, HOFFMANN, ON THE GUNNERY ACTION.

Ammunition Expenditure Main Armament
69 Salvoes — Total 212 Rounds: 160 Armour Piercing Shells; 45 Base Fuze Shells; 7 H.E. Nose Fuze.

Secondary Armament
Total 842 Rounds: 489 H.E. Nose Fuze; 353 H.E. Base Fuze; 136 H.E. Time Fuze Shells.

Heavy anti-aircraft armament

Main Armament
Fire was opened at 1732, Range 28,600 yds.
1732-1747: *Glorious* proceeding at 28-30 knots on an average bearing of 40°. Range later decreased rapidly.
1747: *Glorious* proceeding at 25 knots. On an average bearing of 90°, Ranges 24,200-25,900 yds.
1836: Range again reduced rapidly dud to the carrier's decrease in speed.
1840: Fired last salvo, Range 9,460 yds. The arc of fire during this action lay between 3270 and 028°.

Secondary Armament
Two separate actions took place; one against the *Ardent* and one against the *Acasta*.

1729-1810: *Ardent* engaged. There was a pause in the firing between 1744-1740 on account of the Main Armament, and at other times owing to the very effective smoke-screening. Firing was made very difficult by the skilful manoeuvring of the *Ardent*, which was finally sunk at 1820. The heavy *Ardent* anti-aircraft guns were fired from 1819 onwards at range from 10,500-10,800 yds.

The Gunnery Engagement against the *Acasta* falls into four parts:

1823-1828: *Acasta* engaged.

1832-1849

1852-1908: Several direct hits were observed from the *Scharnhorst*.

1911-1913

This action took place entirely to port of the *Scharnhorst* and firing was again made difficult by the extremely skilful manoeuvring of the *Acasta*. The pauses were due to the *Acasta* being out of range and at times enveloped in smoke.

At 1913 the *Acasta* was left burning fiercely and out of control.

BIBLIOGRAPHY

Printed Sources

ACWORTH, Captain Bernard, DSO RN (Retired), *The Navies of Today and Tomorrow*, (Eyre & Spottiswoode, London, 1930), Ch. XIV: The Future of the Naval Air Arm

AIR MONTHLY, February, 1978, 'H.M.S. *Glorious*' (Short history; lists of operational aircraft and units embarked; and places visited, with dates of arriving and sailing)

A NAVAL WIFE, *My Deeds and Misdeeds*, (William Blackwood & Sons Ltd., 1932), Chs. IV, XIII and XIV on life in Malta

ANDERSON, Surgeon Lt. Cdr. E.W., RNVR, *Abnormal Mental States in Survivors, with Special Reference to Collective Hallucinations*, Journal of the Royal Naval Medical Service, Vol.XXVIII, 1942. (John Bale & Staples Ltd., London), pp.361-377, (Interviews with eleven survivors from *Glorious*, 8-12 months after the sinking)

ASH, Bernard, *Norway 1940*, (Cassell, London, 1964)

ASSMANN, Vice-Admiral Kurt, *The Invasion of Norway*, U.S. Naval Institute Proceedings, April 1952, pp.400-413

ASSMANN, Vice-Admiral Kurt, *The German Campaign in Norway*, German Naval History Series B.R. 1840(1) (Tactical and Staff Duties Division, Foreign Documents Section, Naval Staff Admiralty, N.I.D. 2613/48, 1948)

AUCHINLECK, Lieutenant-General C.J.E., CB, CSI, DSO, OBE, *Report on Operations in Northern Norway, 13th May to 8th June, 1940*, Appendix "B" to Admiral of the Fleet The Earl of Cork and Orrery's Report, Supplement to the *London Gazette*, 8th July, 1947, pp.3181-3196

AUSTIN, John, *The Man Who Hit the Scharnhorst: The Ordeal of Leading Seaman Nick Carter*, John Austin with Nick Carter, (Seeley Service & Co., London, 1973)

BACON, Admiral Sir R.H., KCB, KCVO, DSO, *The life of Lord Fisher of Kilverstone*, (Hodder & Stoughton, 1929), Vol. Two, Ch. XVII: Lord Fisher's Return to the Admiralty, and Ch. XVIII: The Baltic Project

BAEDEKER, Karl, *Norway, Sweden* and *Denmark* (Karl Baedeker, Leipzig, Tenth Edition, 1912)

BARKER, A J., *The Civilising Mission: the Italo-Ethiopian War of 1935-6*, (Collins, London, 1968)

BARRAND, Rev. C.N., *A Short Guide to Martindale*, Third Edition (Reed's Ltd., Penrith, Cumbria, 1978)

BEKKER, Cajus, *Hitler's Naval War* (Macdonalds, London, 1974) Ch.2: Norwegian Gamble

BOLT, Rear-Admiral A.S., CB, DSO, DSC, *Taranto: How the tactics for the raid were developed*, Air Pictorial, October 1967

BROOME, Captain Jack, DSC, *Convoy Is To Scatter*, (William Kimber, London, 1972), Part One *Make A Signal!* (Putnam, London, 1955) pp.96-100, Sinking of *Glorious* 8th June, BROWN, D.K., *A Century of Naval Construction: The History of the Royal Corps of Naval Constructors*, (Conway Maritime Press, London, 1983). *The Design of Aircraft Carriers Prior to World War II*, Interdisciplinary Science Reviews, Vol.8, No. 4,1983, pp.358-369

BUCKLEY, Christopher, *Norway: The Commandos: Dieppe*, (H.M.S.O., London, 1952)

BUSCH, Corvette-Captain Fritz-Otto, *The Drama of the Scharnhorst* (Robert Hale Ltd., London, 1957) Ch. 1: Biography of a Battleship

CAMPBELL, N.J.M., *Warship Special 1.Battle cruisers. The design and development of British and German Battle cruisers of the First World War era*, pp.65-7, *COURAGEOUS* Class

CARTON DE WIART, Lieutenant-General Sir Adrian, VC, KBE, CB, CMG, DSO, *Happy Odyssey* (Jonathan Cape, London, 1950), Ch. XIII: The Unhappy Norwegian Campaign

CATHCART-JONES, Owen, *Aviation Memories* (Hutchinson, London, 1931)

CHALMERS, Rear-Admiral W.S., CBE, DSC, *Max Horton and the Western Approaches* (Hodder & Stoughton, London, 1954), Ch. III, 1935-37 Mare Nostrum

CHAPMAN, J.H.B., CB, RCNC, *The Development of the Aircraft Carrier*, Transactions of the Royal Institution of Naval Architects, Vol. 102, No. 4, October, 1960 pp.495-533, and particularly the written contribution to the later discussion by Mr W.A.D. Forbes RNCN, p.528-9

CHATFIELD, Admiral of the Fleet Lord, PC, GCB, OM, *The Navy and Defence* (Heinemann, London, 1942) Ch. XXIII: Commander in Chief, 1929-32. *It Might Happen Again*, (Heinemann, London, 1947), Ch. XII: The Abyssinian Crisis, Ch. XIII: The Spanish Civil War, Ch. XV: The Fleet Air Arm

CHURCHILL, The Rt. Hon. Winston S., CH, MP, *Great Contemporaries* (Thornton Butterworth, London, 1937) Lord Fisher and his Biographer. *The Second World War*, Volume I The Gathering Storm (Cassell & Co., London, 1948), Ch. X: Sanctions Against Italy, 1935, Ch. XXXIV: Narvik, Ch. XXXV: Trondheim, Ch. XXXVI: Frustration in Norway, Ch. XXXVII: Norway: The Final Phase. *The World Crisis 1911-1914* (Thornton Butterworth, London, 1923) Ch. XIX: With Fisher at the Admiralty

CORK AND ORRERY, Admiral of the Fleet The Earl of, GCB, GCVO, *My Naval Life 1886-1941* (Hutchinson, London, 1942)

Ch. LXXI. *Norway Campaign 1940*, Report in Supplement to the *London Gazette*, 8 July, 1947, pp.3167-3179

CUNNINGHAM OF HYNDHOPE, Admiral of the Fleet Viscount, KT, GCB, OM, DSO, *A Sailor's Odyssey* (Hutchinson, London, 1951). Chs. XIV-XVIII

Daily Mail, 17th August, 1932, 'Their Royal Highnesses' Air experience'

DAVIES, Vice-Admiral Richard Bell, VC, CB, DSO, AFC, *Sailor in the Air* (Peter Davies, London, 1967)

DENHAM, Captain Henry, CMG, *Inside the Nazi Ring* (John Murray, London, 1984) Ch. 1: Arrested by the Gestapo

DERRY, T.K., *The Campaign in Norway* (H.M.S.O., London, 1952)

DIXON, Jim, *H.M.S. Glorious in the First World War, H.M.S. Glorious in the Second World War*, Ship's Monthly, Volume 11, Nos 1 (January, 1976) to 4 (April, 1976)

DOMVILLE-FIFE, Charles W. (Ed.) *Evolution of Sea Power* (Rich and Cowan Ltd., London, 1939)

DONOVAN, Don, *The Day We Met the Devil-Wind* (Hal Far Cyclone), TAGS: The Journal of the Telegraphist Air Gunners Association, March 1984

Evening Standard, 2nd April, 1931, *Liner Crash: 26 Passengers Dead or Missing*

FISHER OF KILVERSTONE, Admiral of the Fleet Lord, *Memories* (Hodder and Stoughton, London 1919) Ch. V: The Dardanelles

FRENCH, Captain Godfrey, CBE, *Admiral Sir Charles Kennedy-Purvis, GBE, KCB, The Naval Review*, Volume 64, No.2, April, 1976, pp.101-105. *Some Operations of H.M.S. Furious and Her Aircraft 1939-1940 The Naval Review*, Volume 50, No. 1, January, 1962, pp.42-54

GARDINER, Leslie, *The Royal Oak Courts-Martial* (William Blackwood & Sons, Edinburgh and London, 1965)

GARRETT, Richard, *Scharnhorst and Gneisenau: The elusive sisters*, (David & Charles, Newton Abbot, 1978) Ch.4: Death of an Aircraft Carrier

GRAHAM, R.R., *A Day with the Torpedo Planes, The Naval Review*, Volume 17, No. 4, November, 1928, pp.750-754

GRETTON, Vice-Admiral Sir Peter, KCB, DSO, OBE, DSC, *The Royal Navy in the Spanish Civil War of 1936-39, The Naval Review*, Volume 62, No. 1 January, 1974 pp.8-17, No.2 April, 1974 pp.96-103, No.3 July, 1974, pp.203-213

HALLIFAX, Rear-Admiral R.H.C., *The First and Second Battles of Narvik*, Supplement to the *London Gazette*, 1st July 1947, pp.3047-3051

Hansard, The House of Commons, Oral Answers: 31 July, 21 August, 24 October, 1940; Adjournment debate, 7 November, 1940; Statement on the loss of the *Glorious, Acasta*, and *Ardent*, 8 May, 1946; Oral Answers, 19 March, 1947

HEALISS, Ronald, *Arctic Rescue*, from *70 True Stories of the Second World War* (Odhams, London, n.d., c.1954) pp.24-29. *Adventure Glorious* (Frederick Muller, London, 1955)

HEZLET, Vice-Admiral Sir Arthur, KBE, CB, DSO, DSC, *The Electron and Sea Power* (Peter Davies, London, 1975) Ch. VIII: The Second World War, 1939-41

HINSLEY, F.H., *British Intelligence in the Second World War*, (HMSO, London, 1979), Volume 1, Ch.4: From the Invasion of Norway to the Fall of France

HOUGH, Richard, *First Sea Lord*: An Authorized Biography of Admiral Lord Fisher (Unwin Bros., London, 1969), Part Three, Ch.2: 'The Real Focus': War and Return to Power

HUBATSCH, Walter, *Weserubung* (Gottingen, 1960), trans. J.L. Moulton and Colin McFadyean. *Problems of the Norwegian*

Campaign, Journal of the Royal United Services Institution, 1958

HUMBLE, Richard, *Fraser of North Cape*: The Life of Admiral of the Fleet Lord Fraser (1888-1981) (Routledge & Kegan Paul, London, 1983) Part Two, Ch. 12: Carrier *Glorious*

JAMES, Admiral Sir William, GCB, *Admiral Sir William Fisher* (Macmillan, London, 1943) Ch. X: 1932-1937. *The Sky Was Always Blue* (Methuen & Co., London, 1951) Ch. XIII: Naval Assistant First Sea Lord; Chief of Staff, Home and Mediterranean Fleets, 1928-1931

JAMESON, Rear-Admiral William, KBE, CB, *Ark Royal* 1939-1941 (Rupert Hart-Davis, London, 1957), Ch. IV: Norway and Denmark Invaded, Ch. V: Trondheim and Narvik, Ch.VI: Narvik Captured: Norway Evacuated

JELLICOE, Admiral of the Fleet Earl, *The Jellicoe Papers*, Ed. A. Temple Patterson M.A., (Navy Records Society, Volume III 1986), Volume II: 1916-1935, pp.230-238, Documents relating to the Operation in Heligoland Bight, 17th November 1917)

JENKINS, Cdr. C.A. OBE, *Days of a Dogsbody*, (Harrap, London, 1946), Ch. XVII: War Profile Warship 23 and 24, HMS *Furious*/Aircraft Carrier 1917-1948, Part 1: The First Eight Years, Part II: 1925-1948 (Profile Publications, Windsor, 1972)

JOHNS, Sir Arthur W., RCNC, *Aircraft carriers*, Transactions of Institution of Naval Architects, JOHNSON, Brian, *Fly Navy*: The History of Maritime Aviation, (David & Charles, Newton Abbot, 1981) Ch.3: The Years of Peace

KEYES, Admiral of the Fleet Baron, of Zeebrugge, *The Keyes Papers*, Ed. Paul G. Halpern, (Navy Records Society, Volumes 121 and 122, 1980 and 1981) Volume II, 1919-1938, pp.345-350, Letters from Lt. F.M. Crichton, of 21st December, 1935 and 25th February 1936; Volume III, 1939-1945, p. 115, letter to Admiral Sir Herbert Richmond, 21 November, 1940

KILROY, Cdr. Robin A., DSC, *Boleh* (Hodder & Stoughton, London, 1951)

KIMMINS, Anthony, *Half-Time* (Heinemann, London, 1947)

KINGSTON MCGLOUGHRY, Sq. Ldr. E.J., DSO, DFC, *Winged Warfare* (Jonathan Cape, London, 1937) Ch.3: The Mediterranean Today

LLOYD'S LIST LAW REPORTS, Volume 43, August 4,1932 pp.450-465, 'Admiralty Division, July 12-18, 1932, H.M.S. *"Glorious"*; Volume 44, January 12.1933, pp.323-330, 'Court of Appeal', December 6-13, 1932, H.M.S. *"Glorious"*

LOMBARD-HOBSON, Captain S.R. Le. H., CVO, OBE, *A Sailor's War* (Orbis, London, 1983)

MABEY, John, *HMS Campania 1914-1918*, "Warship" Volume 7, No. 3, July 1983

MACINTYRE, Donald, *Narvik*, (Evans Bros, London, 1959)

MACKAY, Ruddock F., *Fisher of Kilverstone* (Clarendon Press, Oxford, 1973) Ch.9: Fisher and Churchill (1910-1915)

MACKESY, Major-General P.J., CB, DSO, MC, *Report on Operations in Northern Norway*, Supplement to *London Gazette*, 10 July 1947, pp.3179-3181

MACLURE, Victor A., *With the Gladiators in Norway*, Blackwoods Magazine, Volume 249, February and March 1941

"MANOEL", *Alexandria 1935-36*, *The Naval Review* Volume 63, No.3, July 1975, PP.Z69-274, No. 4, October 1975, pp.344-349

MARDER, Arthur J., *Fear God and Dread Nought*: The Correspondence of Admiral of the Fleet Lord Fisher of Kilverstone, Volume III (Jonathan Cape, London, 1959) letters to Churchill of 21 December 1914, p.104; to Jellicoe of 23rd December, 1914, p.107; to Beatty, of 8th February 1915, p.155. *From the Dardanelles to Oran* (Oxford University Press, 1974) Ch. III: The Royal Navy and the Ethiopian Crisis of 1935-1936

MARDER, Arther J., *From the Dreadnought to Scapa Flow*, Volume IV: 1917: Year of Crisis, (Oxford University Press, 1969), Ch. XI: Home Waters: A Tale of Woe (October 1917-December 1917)

MARSH, Major A.E., *Flying Marines* (Royal Marine Museum, Portsmouth, 1980)

MASON, F.K., *The Gloster Gladiator*, (Macdonald, London, 1964)

MASSY, Lieutenant-General H.R.S., DSO, MC, *Operations in Central Norway*, Supplement to *London Gazette*, 29 May 1946, pp. 2597-2610

MASTERS, David, *"So Few"*: The Immortal Record of the Royal Air Force (Eyre & Spottiswoode London, 1941) Ch.4: The Loss of the *Glorious*

MILLER, M.O.W., *Dawn Flight*, Blackwoods Magazine, November 1938

MINISTRY OF INFORMATION, *Fleet Air Arm* (H.M.S.O., London, 1943) Ch.8: The Triumph at Taranto

MORAN, Lord, *The Anatomy of Courage*, (Constable, London, 1945) Ch. VIII: Exposure

MOULTON, Major General J.L., CB, DSO, OBE, RM, *The Norwegian Campaign of 1940* (Eyre & Spottiswoode, 1966)

MOUNTEVANS, Admiral Lord, KCB, DSO, LLD, *Adventurous life*, (Hutchinson, London, n.d.), Ch. XXVIII; Invasion of Norway

Naval Review, Anonymous, Pseudonymous or initialled articles on 'Air Power and its Effect on Naval Operations', Volume 19, No.3, August, 1931; 'The Fleet Air Arm', Volume 19, No. 4, November, 1931; 'The Fleet Air Arm Today', Volume 20, No. 1, February, 1932; 'The Faireys Fly Over the Ocean', Volume 20, No. 4, November, 1932; 'Dual Control', Volume 20, No. 4, November, 1932; 'An Aircraft Carrier Visits Egypt', Volume 21, No. 1, February, 1933; 'The Combined Fleet Exercises,

1934', Volume 22, No.2, May, 1934; 'The Evacuation of Refugees from Bilbao by H.M.S. *Esk* on Thursday, 17th September, 1936'. Volume 25, No. 1, February, 1937; 'The Coronation Naval Review', Volume 25, No.3, August, 1937; 'The Battle of Bilbao Bay: St George's Day, 1937', Volume 25, No.3, August, 1937; 'Combined Navy and Air Force Exercises of 1937' Volume 25, No. 4, November, 1937; 'H.M.S. *Hunter*, 13th May, 1937' Volume 25, No. 4, November, 1937; Admiral of the Fleet Sir Dudley Pound, volume 31, No. 4, November, 1943

NAVAL STAFF, Tactical and Staff Duties Division, *Naval Operations in the Campaign in Norway*, B. R.1 736(46), (Admiralty, London, 1946)

NEWBOLT, Henry, *History of the Great War: Naval Operations*, Volume V (Longmans Green & Co London, 1931), Ch. IV: The Campaign in Home Waters, October and November 1917

NEWTON, Don, and HAMPSHIRE, A. Cecil, *Taranto* (William Kimber, London, 1959)

OXSPRING, Group Capt. Bobby, *Spitfire Command*, (William Kimber, London, 1984), pp.43-46

PARKES, Oscar, OBE, AssINA, *British Battleships: Warrior* i860 to *Vanguard* 1950 (Seeley Service & Co., London, 1957), Ch. 108: *Courageous, Glorious* and *Furious*

PARTRIDGE, Major R.T., DSO, RM, *Operation Skua* (Fleet Air Arm Museum, Yeovilton, 1983)

POPHAM, Hugh, *Into Wind*: A History of British Naval Flying, (Hamish Hamilton, London, 1969)

RAWLINGS, John D.R., *Fighter Squadrons of the RAF and their Aircraft* (Macdonald & Jane's, London, 1969, new revised edition 1976), pp. 126-129 No. 46 Squadron, pp.374-378 No. 263 Squadron

REXFORD-WELCH, Sq. Ldr. S.C., *R.A.F. Medical Services*, Volume III: Campaigns (H.M.S.O., London, 1958), Ch.2: Norway, 1940

RICHARDS, Denis, *The Royal Air Force 1939-1945*, Volume I: The Fight At Odds (H.M.S.O., London, 1953)

RIVIERE, Bridget, Letter to *The Sunday Times*, June 22, 1980 'Lord Louis prized the captain of the *Glorious*'

ROSKILL, Captain Stephen, DSC, *Churchill and the Admirals* (Collins, London, 1977), Ch.8: Return to Power and the Norwegian Campaign: 1939-1940. H.M.S. *Warspite* (Collins, London, 1957) Ch.VI: Between the Wars, 1919-1939; Ch. VII: From Alexandria to Narvik and Back Again, September 1939-July, 1940. *Naval Policy Between the Wars*, Volume II: The Period of Reluctant Rearmament 1930-1939, (Collins, London, 1976). 'The Cantankerous Captain of HMS *Glorious*', *The Sunday Times*, June 15, 1980. *The War At Sea 1939-1945*, Volume I: The Defensive, (H.M.S.O., London, 1954), Ch. X: The Norwegian Campaign 8th April-15th June, 1940

Royal United Services Institution, Journal, 'Navy Notes', various issues 1930-1939

RUSSELL, D.A. Editor, *Aircraft of the Fighting Powers*, Volume I, compiled by H.J. Cooper and O.G. Thetford, (Harborough Publishing Co., Leicester, 1941)

SCHMALENBACH, Fregatten Kapitan Paul, Profile warship 3 3: German Battle cruisers *Scharnhorst* and *Gneisenau* (Profile publications, Windsor, 1974)

STRABOLGI, Lord, *Narvik and After. A study of the Scandinavian Campaign* (Hutchinson, London, 1941)

STURTIVANT, Ray, *The Squadrons of the Fleet Air Arm*, (Air-Britain (Historians) Ltd., Tonbridge, 1984)

TENNYSON-D'EYNCOURT, Sir Eustace, B. RCNC, 'Naval Construction during the War', *Engineering*, 11th April, *The Times*,

Obituaries and Tributes: Kennedy-Purvis, 27th May, 1946; Lumley Lyster, 5th August, 1957; Guy Royle, 6th, 28th January, 1954; Clive Rawlings, 31st December, 1965; Richard Stokes, 5th, 6th, 14th August, 1957; D'Oyly-Hughes, 29th June, 1st, 4th, 7th July, 1940; obituary notices for some of *Glorious'* officers, including Pringle-Nicholson, Marett, Marmont, Ogilvy, Wells, Newnham, Parkin, Franklin, Egan, in various issues early July, 1940

THETFORD, Owen, *British Naval Aircraft Since 1912*, (Putnam, London, 1962)

THOMAS, Hugh, *The Spanish Civil War*, (Penguin Books, London, 1965)

THOMPSON, Wing Cdr. H.L., *New Zealanders with the RAF*, Volume I: European Theatre, Sep. 1939-Dec. 1942, Ch.2: Meeting the German Attack

TILL, Geoffrey, *Air Power and the Royal Navy 1914-1945*, (Jane's, London, 1979)

TROUP, Captain J. A.G., *On The Bridge*, (Rich & Cowan, London, 1934) Ch. XII: Malta *United Services Review*, 'Royal Navy and Royal Dockyards', (weekly summaries of service and social news and gossip), various issues, 1937-39

VULLIEZ, Albert, and MORDAL, Jacques, *Battleship Scharnhorst*, (Hutchinson, London, 1958) Ch.5: Back into the Norwegian Sea.

WAAGE, Johan, *The Narvik Campaign*, trans, from the Norwegian by Ewan Butler, (George G. Harrap, London, 1964)

WATERMAN, Lt. Cdr. J., RD RNR, *The Fleet Air Arm History*, (Old Bond Street Publishing, London, 1975)

WHITWORTH, Vice-Admiral W.J., CB, DSO, Report of Attack at Narvik, 13th April, 1940, Supplement to London Gazette, 3rd July, 1947, pp.3051-3056

WILLOUGHBY, Rear-Admiral Guy, CB, My Service Career, *News & Journal*, Stroud (Glos), 30th October, 1976

WINDSOR, HRH The Duke of, KG, *A King's Story* (Cassell, London, 1951) Ch. XIII (visit to Mediterranean Fleet.)

WYKEHAM, Peter, *Fighter Command: A Study of Air Defence 1914-1960* (Putnam, London, 1960), Ch.3: The Pause

Sources In Public Record Office

ADM 1/8691-237/25. Pilot training (1925)

ADM 1/8702-151/26. Plan to convert *Glorious* and *Courageous* to aircraft carriers.

ADM 1/11065. Report of Proceedings HMS *Vanoc*, April, 1941 (Sinking of U.100). Appendix: Report by Midshipman Rowe on conversation with Korv. Kapitan Siegfried Flister re. sinking of *Glorious*

ADM 1/19910. NID translations of German documents relating to the sinking of HMS *Glorious*

ADM 53/108961-108927. Log HMS *Glorious* January-December, 1939

ADM 53/112337-9. Log HMS *Glorious* January-March, 1940

ADM 116/3677-89. The Royal Navy in the Spanish Civil War

ADM 116/3008. Fleet Air Arm Committee Report. 12/4/35 (Deficiencies of System)

ADM 137/584. Action in Heligoland Bight, November, 1917

ADM 137/625, and /1947. The *'Mary Rose'* Convoy.

ADM 186/149-185/159. Operations and Exercises 1931-1938.

ADM 187/7. 'Pink List' (Movements of warships) April-May, 1940

ADM 199/393. Dispatch of C-in-C Home Fleet, 1st March-15th June, 1940

ADM 199/478. Reports on *Glorious'* survivors.

ADM 199/479. Air operations in Norway. Operation DX

ADM 199/480. Air operations in Norway. Operation ALPHABET and attack on Trondheim.

ADM 199/486. Narvik.

ADM 205/49. Report by Kontre Admiral Schubert on sinking of *Glorious* AIR 27/460. 46 Sq. Operational Record Book.

AIR 27/1547. 263 Sq. Operational Record Book.

AIR 36/16. 46 Sq. *Glorious* to Skaanland.

AIR 36/17 263 Sq. *Furious* to Bardufoss.

AIR 36/14 Air patrols Narvik AIR 36/12 Air patrols Bardufoss

AIR 36/20 Fighter sorties 23 May-4 June

AIR 36/24 Enemy aircraft brought down in Narvik area 22-28 May

AIR 36/33 Operations in Norway May-June

AIR 36/34 Auchinleck's report on operations in Norway to 8 June

AIR 41. Air Historical Branch narratives.

Unprinted Sources

ANON. Roll of Honour of 263 Squadron. (RAF Museum)

BIRCH, Ron. Letters of 29 February and 20 March, 1984; life in *Glorious* 1938-40

BLAIR-OLIPHANT, Air-Vice Marshal Nigel, CB, OBE. "HMS *Glorious* 1938-1939 Some Recollections", 12 March 1985

BLAKENEY, Lt. Cdr. W.G.D. Letter to J.B. Heath of May 30, 1940

BOLT, Rear-Admiral A.S., CB, DSO, DSC. interview of 16.11.83; 'Notes on the organization of H.M.S. *Glorious* 1938-1939', 5 January, 1984; Summary of promotions and decorations of *Glorious'* air group

BROWN, Joe. Interview of 19 May, 1984 on experiences as a survivor of *Glorious*

BUCHANAN-DUNLOP, Captain David, DSC. Letters of 17 November, 1983 and 12 December, 1983 on some *Glorious* personalities; flying log, HMS *Glorious* and Hal Far July, 1937-July, 1939

CARPENTER, Alf. Letters of 21 February, 9 March, 6 June, 1984: Ill-spent youth in *Glorious*

CARTER, Ldg Seaman C. G. Letter to Richard Stokes MP of 20 June, 1946, headed 'June 8th, 1940' (Stokes' Papers, Bodleian, Oxford)

CASSON, Lt. Cdr. John. OBE. Interview of 14.8.84 on *Glorious* and *Ark Royal*, August, 1935-June, 1940

CLOGSTOUN-WILLMOTT, Captain Nigel, DSO, DSC. Letter of 9 August, 1984 on 'Brownrigg's Light Horse'

COLLIER, Bill. Letter of 7 March, 1984. Flight deck party HMS *Glorious* 1934-36.

COX, Trevor. Photograph album of Midshipman Franklin. Notes on *Courageous* Class.

CRACROFT, Air-Vice Marshal Peter, CB, AFC. Interview 4.10.83 on *Glorious* 1930-31

CROSS, Air Chief Marshal Sir Kenneth, KCB, CBE, DSO, DFC. Letter of 26.6.40 to Marchant; letters to J.B. Heath of 20.6.40 and 2.7.40; and interview of 14.3.85 on experience in Norway and as survivor of *Glorious*, May/June, 1940

DONALDSON, Rear-Admiral V.D'A. Interview of 31.1.84 on *Glorious* December, 1937-January, 1940

DONNAN, Mrs Patricia. Letter of 5 July, 1984 on experiences of Marine Donnan as survivor of *Glorious*

DOWN, Captain R.T., DSO. Letters to J.B. Heath of 2 and 19 July, 1940,13 September and 23 October, 1940

DRUCKER, Graham Roy. Letter of 24 March, 1985, on Sub. Lt. (A) Roy Baker Falkner in *Glorious* 1938-39

DUNCAN, Lt. Cdr George. OBE. Interview of 3.12.83 on *Glorious* 1931-32

DUNHILL, Trevor. Letter of 30 November, 1984 on HMS *Devonshire* June 1940; 'Nationwide' BBC-TV, 30 March, 1983

ELLIOTT, Petty Officer George. Interview of 6 June, 1984 on *Glorious* 1937-40 and experience as a survivor

ELLISON, David. Photograph album of Petty Officer Telegraphist Albert Neilly

ELLYATT, Lt. Cdr. John, DSC, VRD. Letter of 8 July, 1984 on 'Rastus' Carnduff in *Glorious*

EVELEIGH, Air Vice Marshal Geoffrey CB, OBE. 'Recollections of life in HMS *Glorious* 1935-1938', 14 April, 1984

FAGAN, Air Commodore T.P.P.F., CBE. Interview of 14 August, 1984 on *Glorious* 1931-34

FANCOURT, Captain H.L.St.J., DSO. Interview of 19 March, 1984 on Fleet Air Arm personalities in 1930s and D'Oyly-Hughes in *Courageous* 1931.

FORBES, Admiral of the Fleet Sir Charles. Letter to Roskill of 1 December, 1949 on sinking of the *Glorious*, *Orama* etc. (Churchill College, Cambridge)

FRASER, Captain Bruce OBE, Report of conversation with First Lord on 'Dual Control', on board *Glorious*, Malta, 30 August, 1936. Chatfield Papers CHT 4/10 (Nat. Maritime Museum)

FRENCH, Captain Godfrey, CBE. Papers on *Glorious* GDFR1/4,1/5 (Churchill College, Cambridge). Interview of 8 December, 1983 on *Glorious* 1931-1933

GODFREY, Admiral John Henry. Memoirs (esp. 2 vols on Spanish Civil War) Churchill College, Cambridge) GDFY.

GOING, Cdr. G.R.M., DSO, OBE. Interview of 7 December, 1983 on *Glorious* 1938-39

GOODMAN, Mrs Betty. Interview of 20 November, 1983

GOWER, Captain J.R., DSC. Midshipman's Journal of 1931

GOWLLAND, Captain The Rev. Geoffrey. Letters of 21 February, 14 and 23 March, 1984, on *Glorious* 1931-32, and 1936-38

GRINTER, Roy. Letter of 2 May, 1984 on Chief Mechanician Grinter

GROVE, Eric J., MA. Letter of 12 January, 1984, on Admiral Chatfield

HAGGARD, Cdr. Hugh DSO DSC. Interview of 3 June, 1984 on 1st Submarine Flotilla, Med., 1934-35

HALE, Cdr. J.W., DSO. Letter of 18 June, 1984 on *Glorious* 1938-39

HARLAND, Peter. Log of the *Glorious*, March-June, 1940 from various sources indicated

HAY, Cdr. R.C., DSO, DSC. 'Experiences in *Ark Royal* off Norway, 1940' of 18 May, 1978

HEATH, Captain J.B., OBE. Heath Papers: Documents and letters, most importantly Enclosure No.1, headed 'Statement by Commander J.B. Heath RN' to Heath's letter dated 11th June, 1940 to Vice-Admiral Aircraft Carriers; interviews of 9 March and 4 October, 1983 on *Glorious* 1930-32, and January to June, 1940

HILL, Lt. Cdr Rupert. Letters to J.B. Heath of 28 June, 1940 and to Mollie Steel of 18 July and 30 July, 1940

HINTON, Roy. Interview of 18 May, 1984 on *Glorious* 1939-40

HOBBS, Cyril. Interview of 22 June, 1984 on experiences as survivor of *Glorious*

HODGSON, Charles. 'A Personal Impression of *Glorious* 1938-1940', 20 September, 1984, 'Some Further Impressions, 1938-1939'. 5 October, 1984

HOOKE, Roger. Typescripts of 'My service in H.M.S. *Ardent*' and 'My story continues'

HUGHES-HALLETT, Admiral Sir Charles, KCB, CBE. Letter of 6 February, 1984 on HMS *Glorious*

IMPERIAL WAR MUSEUM. Film ADM 1144-1, Part P1/16/A "Seesh lacht Im Nordmeer" (Battle in North Sea); ADM 1144-3 Part P1/16/A, "*Gneisenau* Und *Scharnhorst* Gegen Den Feind" (*Gneisenau* and *Scharnhorst* against the enemy). German 1940 Newsreels.

Imperial War Museum Tape 1034/D/A (recorded 11 May, 1943, broadcast in 'Calling New Zealand', Pacific Service); 'No. 46 Hurricane Fighter Squadron, In and Out of Norway per HMS *Glorious*, Aircraft Carrier', of 3 December, 1984

JAMESON, Air Commodore P.G., CB, DSO, DFC, 'Flying Hurricanes in the Norway Campaign'

JENKINS, Trevor. Letter to *Daily Telegraph*, 15 September, 1972, 'King Haakon's flight from Norway'; letter to Martin Dawes of Sheffield *Star*, 23 February, 1983

JOLLIFF, David. Letter of 15 May 1984, on *Glorious* June, 1937-April, 1940

KEIGHLEY-PEACH, Captain C.L., DSO. Interview of 4 December, 1983 on Fleet Air Arm in the 1930s

KENNEDY, Ludovic. 'The Life and Death of the *Scharnhorst*', Tuesday Documentary, BBC-1 26th December, 1971

LAYARD, Cdr. A.F.C., DSO, DSC. Letter of 4 February, 1984 on *Wakeful*, *Glorious*' attendant destroyer, 1931

LEA, Cdr. W. Sitwell, OBE. Interview of 7 June, 1984, on *Glorious* 1931

LE BRETON, Lt. H.W. Letters of 30 March, 17 and 23 April, 1984, on *Glorious* in 1935

LE GEYT, Captain E.G., DSC. Conversation of 10 August, 1984 re exchange of signals *Ark Royal*/*Glorious*, am 8 June, 1940

LEGGOTT, Lt. Cdr. R.L., MBE. Interview of 13 January, 1984 and typescripts of 16 February and 14 March, 1984 on experiences as survivor of *Glorious*

LEVIS, Air Commodore L., OBE. Interview of 13 January, 1984 on *Glorious* 1935-36

LIDSTONE, Cmm. Stores Officer Arthur. 'The sinking of HMS *Glorious*, *Ardent* and *Acasta*, 8 June, 1940, "My personal experience"'

LITCHFIELD, Captain J.S.S., OBE. Letter of 7 January, 1985

MADDEN, Cdr. H.P. Typescript of 'Night Flying and the Fairey 111F'

MARSH, Major A.E., RM. Letter of 15 May, 1984 on *Glorious*

MARTIN, Lt. Cdr. Derek. Letter of July, 1984 on experiences as Skua pilot in *Ark Royal* and attack on Trondheim June, 1940

McBRIDE, Lt. Cdr. Robert. Typescript of 'Final Action' in *Glorious* and experience as survivor, 16 January, 1985, and letter of 19 February, 1985

McFADYEAN, Colin. Translation of Hubatsch's *Weserubung*

MOULTON, Major General J.L., CB, DSO. Translation of Hubatsch's *Weserubung*

O'NEILL, James. Interview of 4 April, 1984 on experience as survivor of *Glorious*; letter of 1940 to Sir John Hammerton of *War Illustrated* on *Glorious*' sinking

PARROTT, Captain Jasper, CBE. Letters to J.B. Heath of 15 June and 22nd July, 1940

PICKERING, James, AFC, AE, FGS, FSA. Letter of 14 December, 1984 and enclosures on Fleet Air Arm and RAF in late 1930s

POWER, Captain A.J. Diary 14 April-18 April, 1940, in British Library Add. MSS. 56096

POUND, Admiral of the Fleet Sir Dudley, Correspondence with Cunningham, Aug. 1939-1943, in British Library Add. MS. 52561 (Cunningham Papers)

RIVIERE, Mrs Bridget. Interview of 2 June, 1984

RODGER, Cdr. R.H.S. OBE. Interview of 7 December, 1983 on *Glorious* 1932-1933

ROSKILL, Captain Stephen, DSC. Typescripts of 'The Sinking of the *Glorious* (Captain G. D'Oyly-Hughes) by the *Scharnhorst* and *Gneisenau*, 8 June, 1940'; 'The Loss of the *Glorious*'; and 'A Naval Disaster Explained at last'; and letters to and from various correspondents concerning *Sunday Times* article (files 4/75, 4/76, 4/77 and 4/77A in Roskill papers, Churchill College, Cambridge)

ROTHERHAM, Captain G.A., DSO, OBE. Letter of 24 January, 1984 on *Glorious* in the 1930s

RUSHER, Wing Cdr. Peter, DSO. Interview of 7 June, 1984 on *Glorious* 1938-1939

SCARLETT-STREATFEILD, Cdr. Norman, DSC. Interview of 21 November, 1983 on *Glorious* January 1938-January 1940

SEYMOUR-PRICE, Air Commodore G.P., CBE, AFC. Interview of 20 March, 1984 on *Glorious* September 1936-January 1938

SHEPHERD, Group Captain John. Interview of 16 November, 1983, and letter of 6 February, 1984 on *Glorious* 1936

SHIPS' COVERS for *Furious*, *Courageous* and *Glorious*, formerly ADM 138/453, 454, National Maritime Museum

SLESSOR, Lt. Cdr. A.H.P. Letters to his wife, various dates, 1939-1940

SLESSOR, Hope, 'A Quaint Present', Memoirs, privately printed by T. Slessor, 1986

STOKES, Richard, MP. Family and political papers. Bodleian Library, Oxford

SUTTON, Captain A.W.F., CBE, DSC. Interview of 20 March, 1984 on *Glorious* in 1939 and letters of 25 and 27 March, 1984

TORLESSE, Rear-Admiral A.D., CB. DSO. Journal for 1932 and 1933; 'Notes on the Fleet Air Arm, with special reference to HMS *Glorious*, 1930-1934' in typescript, 27 January, 1984; Interview of 19 March, 1984 on *Glorious* 1932 and 1933; typescript from History of Naval Observers, 'The loss of the *Glorious* and the subsequent attack by *Ark Royal*'s Skuas on the *Scharnhorst* at Trondheim'

WARD, Lt. N.E. Letter to J.B. Heath of 30 May, 1940

WELLS, Captain T.A. Letter of 28 April, 1984 and 'Miscellaneous Notes from Memory on L.V. Wells'

WHITWORTH, Vice-Admiral W.J., CB, DSO. Letter to T.K. Derry of 5 June, 1950 on Norwegian Campaign (Roskill Papers, Churchill College, Cambridge)

WILLOUGHBY, Rear-Admiral Guy, CB. Interview of 20 November 1938 on *Glorious* 1938-1939; Letter to Roskill of 16 January, 1970 on *Glorious* and D'Oyly-Hughes; Letter to J.B. Heath of 29 May, 1940

WOODCOCK, Master at Arms Fred. Letters to his wife, various times, 1939-1940

A NOTE TO THE READER

If you have enjoyed this book enough to leave a review on **Amazon** and **Goodreads**, then we would be truly grateful.

The Estate of John Winton

Sapere Books is an exciting new publisher of brilliant fiction and popular history.

To find out more about our latest releases and our monthly bargain books visit our website:
saperebooks.com

Printed in Great Britain
by Amazon

45513976R00235